# WANNABE
## HOW THE SPICE GIRLS REINVENTED POP FAME

# WANNABE
## HOW THE SPICE GIRLS REINVENTED POP FAME

David Sinclair

**OMNIBUS PRESS**
London · New York · Paris · Sydney · Copenhagen · Berlin · Madrid · Tokyo

Copyright © 2004 David Sinclair
This edition copyright © 2004 Omnibus Press
(A Division of Music Sales Limited)

Cover designed by Chloë Alexander

ISBN: 0.7119.8643.6
Order No: OP 48224

The Author hereby asserts his right to be identified as the author of this work in accordance with Sections 77 to 78 of the Copyright, Designs and Patents Act 1988.

All rights reserved. No part of this book may be reproduced in any form or by any electronic or mechanical means, including information storage or retrieval systems, without permission in writing from the publisher, except by a reviewer who may quote brief passages.

**Exclusive Distributors:**
Music Sales Limited,
8/9 Frith Street,
London W1D 3JB, UK.

Music Sales Corporation,
257 Park Avenue South,
New York, NY 10010, USA.

Macmillan Distribution Services,
53 Park West Drive,
Derrimut, Vic 3030,
Australia.

**To the Music Trade only:**
Music Sales Limited,
8/9 Frith Street,
London W1D 3JB, UK.

Every effort has been made to trace the copyright holders of the photographs in this book but one or two were unreachable. We would be grateful if the photographers concerned would contact us.

'So You Want To Be A Rock'n'Roll Star'
Words & Music by James McGuinn & Chris Hillman
© Copyright Tickson Music Company. Tro Essex Music Limited.
All Rights Reserved. International Copyright Secured.

'If Six Was Nine'
Words & Music by Jimi Hendrix
© Copyright 1967 Experience Hendrix L.L.C. (ASCAP) All Rights Reserved. International Copyright Secured.

'2 Become 1'
Words & Music by Matt Rowe, Richard Stannard, Melanie Brown, Victoria Adams, Geri Halliwell, Emma Bunton & Melanie Chisholm
© Copyright 1996 Universal Music Publishing Limited (50%)/EMI Music Publishing (WP) Limited (50%). All Rights Reserved. International Copyright Secured.

'Wannabe'
Words & Music by Matt Rowe, Richard Stannard, Melanie Brown, Victoria Adams, Geri Halliwell, Emma Bunton & Melanie Chisholm
© Copyright 1996 Universal Music Publishing Limited (50%)/EMI Music Publishing (WP) Limited (50%). All Rights Reserved. International Copyright Secured.

'Look At Me'
Words & Music by Geri Halliwell, Andy Watkins & Paul Wilson
© Copyright 1999 19 Music Limited/BMG Music Publishing Limited (66.66%)/EMI Music Publishing (WP) Limited (33.34%). All Rights Reserved. International Copyright Secured.

Typeset by Galleon Typesetting, Ipswich
Printed and bound in Great Britain by Creative Print & Design, Ebbw Vale, Wales

A catalogue record for this book is available from the British Library.

www.omnibuspress.com

*To Faith & Jack*

**By the same author**

*Tres Hombres: The Story of ZZ Top*
(Virgin, 1986)

*Rock On CD – The Essential Guide*
(Kyle Cathie, 1992, updated 1993)

# Contents

**Introduction** ix

| | | |
|---|---|---|
| 1 | So You Want To Be A . . . Popstar | 1 |
| 2 | The House Of Fun | 19 |
| 3 | You Hum It, We'll Play It | 40 |
| 4 | Girl Power | 59 |
| 5 | Children Of The Revolution | 79 |
| 6 | Automatic For The People | 102 |
| 7 | Queens Of The Spice Age | 123 |
| 8 | Help! | 141 |
| 9 | Ginger Snaps | 163 |
| 10 | Back In 15 Mins | 179 |
| 11 | That Difficult Solo/Third Album | 204 |
| 12 | Gone West | 225 |
| 13 | Fuller Himself | 246 |
| 14 | The Million Dollar Woman | 265 |
| 15 | Never Ends | 283 |

**Discography** 297
**Acknowledgements** 307
**Source Notes & References** 309
**Index** 316

# Introduction

I remember exactly when I decided to write a book about the Spice Girls. I was in a shop called Helter Skelter in the West End of London in the summer of 2000, and I thought I would see if there was a book about the Spice Girls I could buy for my then 11-year-old daughter, Faith. Helter Skelter was *the* rock'n'roll bookshop; perhaps the only shop in London dedicated entirely to selling books about popular music. If you wanted to find a book about a pop group, this was surely the place to go. Except I couldn't find one about the Spice Girls. Nothing. So I asked the guy on the counter.

"We don't do books like that," he said, sniffily. "It's not that kind of shop."

Next to the counter, hot off the presses, was a pile of copies of Clinton Heylin's newly updated biography *Dylan – Behind The Shades (Take Two)*. I looked across at a shelf already groaning under the weight of publications dedicated to the life and music of Bob Dylan and I thought, How on earth is this guy going to fit any more books on there? And who is going to buy, let alone actually *read*, yet another massive tome about Bob Almighty Dylan?

I looked around for something a bit more modern, a book that might appeal to an intelligent teenager, or perhaps address a subject that hadn't been chewed over dozens of times already. But surprisingly few of the items on offer fitted this description. I did, however, find about six books promising to tell the inside story of Oasis in amongst the retrospectives and reappraisals of Jimi Hendrix and The Doors and the entire sections devoted to The Beatles and the Stones.

So, no one had written a book about the Spice Girls – or at least no one had written a book about the Spice Girls that would find shelf space in "that kind of shop". What was going on? The Spice Girls were the biggest British popular music act of the Nineties and probably the biggest selling pop act in the world during the latter half of that decade. Not only that, their influence extended way beyond the selling of vast quantities of records. Ginger, Posh, Baby, Sporty and Scary were the most widely recognised group of individuals since John, Paul, George and Ringo. They were a social phenomenon that changed the course of popular music and popular culture. And yet their achievements had gone unrecognised and unchronicled by the army of self-appointed biographers and historians which has attached itself like a barnacle to the pop industry over the years. Shouldn't someone have been keeping an eye on this stuff?

It occurred to me that for Faith and her friends, Helter Skelter would have seemed more like a museum than a bookshop. If this place couldn't find a Spice Girls book that they could bear to stock, perhaps I'd better write one for them, before the world – and a new generation of readers – had completely passed them by. After all, how hard could it be?

I quickly discovered that one reason why no one had written a sensible book about the Spice Girls was because very few people believed such a book could be written or was worth writing. The songwriter Biff Stannard, who co-wrote 'Wannabe' and many other hits with the Spice Girls, told me that when he went to a dinner party, or met people socially, he would try his best to avoid the subject of what he did for a living – not because he was ashamed in any way, but for exactly the opposite reason.

"Whenever you get on to the Spice Girls thing," he said, "you end up getting into a two-hour discussion, and I get quite heated about it."

I soon found out what he meant. To announce that you were writing a book about the Spice Girls was to be forced, ipso facto, to defend both the group's honour and, pretty quickly, your own. Why write a book about the Spice Girls? I was asked time and again, although curiously, never once, anywhere in the world, did I have to explain to anyone who the Spice Girls actually were. Such was the level of prejudice that had taken root against them, it was simply assumed that unless I was going to reveal some salacious details about their sex lives or pen a worthy polemic condemning them and everything they stood for, then I must be slightly bonkers.

I didn't want to do either. I just thought it was about time somebody attempted to tell the Spice Girls story in a way that made common sense and gave them the benefit of the doubt. I had had some dealings with the group, and I knew some of the people who worked closely with them in a professional capacity. And I had observed at first hand the effect that they had on my children and their friends. The caricatures which I read about in newspapers and magazines bore so little resemblance to the people I had met and heard about from my friends in the business that I had become intrigued.

Here were five girls who, we were assured, couldn't sing, couldn't dance, couldn't write music, couldn't act, couldn't manage their business affairs or even tie up their shoelaces without someone to tell them how to do it. Yet they had somehow managed to notch up – both collectively and individually – seventeen number one hit singles, five million-selling albums, a stadium tour of Europe and North America and one of the highest-grossing British movies of the decade, all in the space of just five years. In so doing, they had avoided being ripped off in the way that has traditionally been the case with even the most clued-up young pop stars, and become five of the richest entertainers that have ever scaled the peaks of planet pop. How did this all happen, I wondered, and what did it mean?

I have tried to answer those questions in this book without resorting to the lurid innuendo and negative spin which has become so much the norm when reporting on the Spice Girls that I don't think most people even notice it any more. I spoke to the people who had worked with them to achieve such an extraordinary result: all three of their managers, all the key songwriters and producers, the executives at Virgin Records, their press and promotions officers. I read the books the Girls had written, I sifted through a mountain of press cuttings and, yes, I listened with pleasure to their records. I did not talk to any chauffeurs or former boyfriends or disgruntled catering staff.

The Spice Girls' press officer, Alan Edwards, spoke for a lot of the people who worked with them when he told me that: "Doing the Spice Girls was not like doing a normal PR job. For me it became something very intense and very personally felt. It was just one of those things where you go way beyond the normal parameters of work. By the time they finished, it was in my blood." By the time I had written this book, I knew what he meant.

Sadly, Helter Skelter closed down in May 2004, one month before I finished writing this book. So I will have to forego the satisfaction of seeing the book about the Spice Girls, which I really, really wanted to buy for Faith, finding its way at last onto their hallowed shelves.

However, Helter Skelter still runs an Internet mail order service, so I checked out their website the other day just to see what was fresh and happening. Blow me down if right at the top of the news page they were trumpeting the arrival of . . . a new Bob Dylan anthology assembled by Isis, the team behind "the best-selling, longest-lasting most highly acclaimed Dylan fanzine."

Meanwhile . . .

*David Sinclair*
*London, July, 2004*

# 1
# So You Want To Be A . . . *Popstar*

Madonna is the woman most closely associated with the rise of the pop wannabe. Her fans in the mid-Eighties copied her street urchin style; they wore dozens of plastic bracelets, crosses and fingerless lace gloves and cultivated a disconcerting habit of wearing their underwear as outer-wear. Most of them wanted to look, and maybe even be a bit like Madonna. But that is not quite the same thing as wanting to be a famous pop star.

That desire was identified by an American group, The Byrds, who as long ago as 1967, enjoyed a US hit with their song 'So You Want To Be A Rock'n'Roll Star'. Its lyric was a virtual manual for the hordes of hippy hopefuls setting out on the path to fame and fortune in the Sixties:

> *Just get an electric guitar*
> *And take some time and learn how to play.*
> *And when your hair's combed right and your pants fit tight*
> *It's gonna be all right . . .*

Back then, of course, it all seemed so easy, so natural, so straightforward, and so effortlessly alternative. Getting into a group was not especially about being famous – although that was certainly part of the deal. It was more to do with having fun, being creative, having girls swoon in your presence, making a fortune (and then blowing it), discreetly taking drugs, avoiding the humdrum routine of nine-to-five living, travelling the world, and all the while retaining the blithe innocence of youth thanks to the careful attention which the true artist is prepared to lavish at all times on the inner child. Above all, there was to be no kow-towing to The Man. The breadheads and the straights and the people who wanted to push you and mould you into something that could be marketed like a tin of baked beans – those people were banished from the wacky world of rock'n'roll, or at the very least confined, tactfully, to the sidelines.

Well, that was the Sixties for you, an era of utopian idealism shored up, it is true, by a hefty dose of self-deception. Was it ever really like that? Probably not. There were some horrendous rip-offs, and in most (but not all) cases it was the musicians who got shafted. But whatever deals went down behind closed doors, there was nevertheless a perception that rock stars were supposed to operate according to their own agendas, not those of their record company and management taskmasters. Jimi Hendrix summed up the great "us and them" divide in his 1968 song 'If Six Was Nine', a celebration of the non-conformist ethos which now seems strangely poignant:

> *White-collared conservative, flashing down the street,*
> *Pointing their plastic finger at me.*
> *They're hoping soon my kind will drop and die*
> *But I'm gonna wave my freak flag high, high!*

Unfortunately, a little less than three years later, Hendrix did indeed drop and die. The suits, on the other hand, have rarely missed a beat since.

★ ★ ★

In the advertising world, when an agency is given a new product to promote, the creative directors will often start by building what is called a "mood board". On to an initially blank canvas will go pictures, words, fragments of ideas, anything which they might have come across in the media or elsewhere that relates to the image they are hoping to put across or the market they are trying to reach with their product. Days, possibly even weeks, will be spent pondering and discussing the resulting collage of images in a vibing-up process which points the creatives in a direction that will determine the ultimate shape of their ad.

The Spice Girls began life as an idea on a mood board, not in an advertising agency but in the offices of the father and son management team of Bob and Chris Herbert in Lightwater, Surrey.

Bob Herbert, born in 1942, was an accountant specialising in musicians' finances, who drifted into management in 1986 when he was introduced to a band featuring one of Chris's schoolfriends on drums. The friend's name was Luke Goss and he had a twin brother, Matt, who was the singer. Their band was called Gloss. Bob Herbert suggested they changed the name to Bros.

## So You Want To Be A . . . Popstar

To begin with Bob let the brothers use his summer house to rehearse in. But it wasn't long before he was investing a lot more than time and friendly encouragement in Bros.

"I paid for studio sessions to get their songs recorded. I did a video, styled them, paid for everything. It must have come to £40,000 to £50,000," he subsequently recalled. For a while, he even moved the boys into a house he had bought in Camberley while they were getting together the songs (and wardrobe) that would eventually make them famous – for a while.

What Bob Herbert didn't do, however, was to sign the boys (who were both under 18) or their parents to a formal contract. So when, as is the nature of things in the pop world, they were snapped up by a more experienced manager – Tom Watkins of Pet Shop Boys fame – who quickly proceeded to steer them to the top of the charts, Herbert found himself in a peculiarly vulnerable situation.

According to Erwin Keiles, a guitarist and songwriter who was a close associate of the Herberts at that time and for many years afterwards, Bob Herbert actually "did OK" out of the Bros affair.

"His daughter, Nicola, was going out with one of the brothers," Keiles said, "and the group's relationship with him continued after Tom Watkins became their manager. So they took care of him."

Even so, few people in the music business willingly display such philanthropic tendencies, and none of them are managers. So you would think that Bob would have taken great care to avoid getting himself into a similar position again. But the Bros venture was not the last occasion on which he was to find himself unable to capitalise on his investment in a pop group. Even worse – compared to the jackpot he was going to miss out on next time, the Bros prize was roughly on a par with a funfair goldfish brought home in a plastic bag of water.

The years passed and Bob was joined in his management activities by Chris. They worked on a succession of humdrum pop acts including the aptly named Optimistic and the unconvincing Worlds Apart, until, in 1994, they set their minds to the task of creating something different. Which is where the mood board came in.

Why was it, they wondered, that apart from Bananarama in the Eighties, and to a lesser extent Eternal in the Nineties, there had never been a massive-selling, all-female British group? They suspected that it was because female groups, unlike the boy bands that were such an established feature of the pop landscape, tended to be of limited interest to girls. The Herberts' starting point, therefore, and the one unarguable stroke of genius in their vision, was to come up with the idea of a female version of Take That which would aim to appeal primarily to young girls.

"The whole teen-band scene at the time was saturated by boy bands," Chris Herbert later recalled. "It was all clones of New Kids On The Block and Take That. That was all a bit of a yawn for me, and only appealed to female audiences. I felt that if you could appeal to the boys as well, you'd be laughing. If you could put together a girl band which was both sassy, for the girls, and with obvious sex appeal, to attract the boys, you'd double your audience and double everything else that went with it."

From there the details quickly fell into place. They reasoned that like Take That there would have to be five in the group, because a gang of four will invariably split up into two separate camps, increasing the likelihood of feuds and potentially damaging disputes (the wisdom of this was demonstrated years later when All Saints – the quartet who were touted as the successors to the Spice Girls – ended up, divided into pairs, at each other's throats). A five-piece, the Herberts decided, would feel like a proper group and be a good, democratically balanced number.

So what would they look like? The mood board brightened up as the Herberts started going through magazines, tearing out pictures of girls – models, actresses, singers, whoever – who looked like the ones they would want to see in their band.

"Here's some expenses. Find some girls," Bob told Chris, which must rank as one of the more agreeable tasks a 23-year-old man might expect to be saddled with by his father. Chris rose to the challenge with predictable enthusiasm, but rather than searching for singers per se, let alone musicians, he began his quest by looking in clubs and pubs for girls with the "right" image. This may have looked suspiciously like an excuse to go out on the pull – and perhaps it was – but such a method was not without precedent. In 1980, Phil Oakey famously invited Joanne Catherall and Suzanne Sulley, a pair of cocktail waitresses whom he had met in a Sheffield nightclub, to join the Human League before he had heard any evidence of their ability to sing. The group's ensuing hit 'Don't You Want Me?' – whose lyric celebrated this unusual method of recruitment – was the biggest-selling British single of 1981 and a US number one the following year.

*So You Want To Be A . . .* Popstar

The Herberts, however, were more systematic than Oakey in their approach, sifting through photographs from stage schools and dance academies throughout the country. Meanwhile Chris extended his activities in the field, so to speak, and as well as trawling the local nightspots, took to hanging out at stage doors, handing out flyers whenever West End shows held auditions for singers or dancers.

Whether to protect Chris from the increasingly likely risk of getting his collar felt by the vice squad, or simply to speed up the whole process, they eventually placed an advertisement in showbiz trade paper *The Stage*: "R.U. 18-23 with the ability to sing/dance? R.U. streetwise, outgoing, ambitious and dedicated?" Those who thought they fitted this somewhat exhausting description were invited to turn up at the Dance Works studio off Oxford Street in central London on March 4, 1994 to an open audition for "a choreographed, singing/dancing all female pop act . . . please bring sheet music or backing cassette." In a process which continued over two more sessions at Nomis Studios in Shepherds Bush, and which seven years later would provide the template for the *Popstars* TV programme, the Herberts proceeded to whittle down more than 400 applicants to a shortlist of 10 from which were picked the five lucky survivors: Geri Estelle Halliwell, 21, from Watford; Victoria Adams, 19, from Goff's Oak, Hertfordshire; Melanie Jayne Chisholm, 20, from Liverpool; Melanie Janine Brown, 18, from Leeds; and Michelle Stephenson, 19, from Abingdon, Hertfordshire.

Looking back on his first impressions of the girls at the auditions, Chris Herbert remembered Mel B as being the most immediately suitable candidate.

"Mel B put her head round the door and she was immediately right for the project. It was obvious why we went for her. She was confident. She'd got a real presence. She was the obvious star to me. Mel C – she'd got a very good range, very strong vocals, quite diva-ish. Victoria was a very good-looking girl. She represented a more sophisticated look, whereas the others were a lot more pop. She probably stuck out a little bit until you put them all into the melting pot and the whole thing started gelling."

Geri wasn't at Dance Works on the original day, having suffered sunburn after a skiing trip to the Pyrenees ("My face had swelled until I looked like the Elephant Man"). But she barged into Nomis when they were down to the last 12 candidates, and demanded to be given a chance to prove herself, demonstrating not for the last time what could be achieved given a sufficient degree of self-belief and determination. Even by then she had turned the knack of "blagging it" into an art form, and it was the barefaced cheek of her approach as much as anything she did as a performer that won the approval of the Herberts.

"The main thing was to get really good, sassy, bubbly characters," Chris Herbert recalled. Attitude was the watchword. And in the case of Geri, they got more than they had bargained for.

"She completely disrupted the whole session. She was as bold as brass," Chris Herbert said. "I remember asking her how old she was and she said, 'I can be as young or as old as you want me to be. I can be a 15-year-old with big boobs if you like.' I just thought, 'You've got some real cheek. You're perfect.'"

"Geri was the worst dancer I've seen in my entire life," Melanie B later recalled. "I think my mum could have danced better than Geri could – she had no rhythm at all. She's come a long way since then, though."

It's often been said that the Spice Girls were a "manufactured" group. And in all material respects, that's exactly what they were. But the criticism which is implied by that description obscures the unbelievably harsh nature of the audition experience. As TV viewers saw for themselves on the *Popstars* programme – albeit in a way that was artificially hyped-up to make an even more sadistic spectacle for the cameras – it is a selection process which applies the maxim of "survival of the fittest" with a brutal rigour. The open audition is like a particularly messy gladiatorial contest, in which any weaknesses – whether technical or psychological – are ruthlessly exposed, and the lesser combatants tossed to the lions as a matter of course.

To this day, Melanie C is in no doubt that the Spice Girls were the original *Popstars*, although this is not a thought from which she derives any pleasure.

"I think it's such an exploitation of those poor kids," she said of the programme that produced the groups which became known as Hear'say and Liberty X. "To be honest, I think the ones that haven't got through are the lucky ones. A lot of it is just a very public ritual humiliation. But I'm sure if I hadn't been in the Spice Girls I would have been up there going for it myself. Thank God I didn't have to. I was with Mel B the other day and we were talking about it and I said, 'Mel, how awful is it?' and she said, 'Yeah, it makes you realise how lucky we were.'"

## So You Want To Be A . . . Popstar

It is easy – and indeed not unreasonable – to deride those who participate in such procedures, and to scorn the process as an "unnatural" or "artificial" way to put together a group. Musically and aesthetically it is the showbiz antithesis of the kid who just gets an electric guitar and takes some time, learns how to play and becomes a Byrds-type rock'n'roll star. But perhaps it is worth bearing in mind that few members of "real" groups, who tend to get together by a sequence of chance meetings and happy accidents, ever have to endure an induction procedure that is so specifically designed to test the reserves of resilience, determination and raw ambition of the participants. In surviving such an ordeal, the Spice Girls had cleared an immense hurdle even before they had sung or written a note together.

What an organically grown "traditional" group does have, as a matter of course, is a mutual background and shared sense of values from which to draw strength and inspiration, both creatively and in terms of its long-term goals. These may involve anything from a vaguely defined desire to give up the day job, to the Napoleonic ambitions displayed from day one by bands such as Oasis and The Verve. Usually, the manufactured (pop) group lacks this common bond which gives the real (rock) group its musical identity and unique sense of camaraderie. From Milli Vanilli to Westlife to Hear'say themselves, the image of the manager/producer-driven, bolted-together pop act with a musical agenda designed to appeal to the lowest common denominator, has become an easily recognised cliché for very good reasons.

Even if such mediocrity is avoided, it is rare indeed for a collection of individuals assembled by an outside agency to come up with an original musical format or shared artistic vision of any depth since they are effectively marching to someone else's beat. It's a bit like session musicians – those singers and instrumentalists who possess such a highly developed level of technical expertise that they can adapt their performance to suit the needs of whoever the client happens to be. These nerveless individuals can go into any studio, pick up the dots (sheet music) and just do it – whatever "it" may be – while the clock ticks away, forbiddingly, on the studio wall. But they rarely become stars in their own right, because their expertise is more of a transferable skill than a true expression of their personality.

A manufactured pop group does not ordinarily possess the skill of session musicians, but they are required to look exactly right for the job and to be just as malleable. However, rather like computer dating, the artificial route can occasionally lead to a marriage of minds and personalities that defies such predictable expectations. And if ever a group transcended the sum of its collective origins it was the Spice Girls. For while they undoubtedly possessed the steely determination and resilience of the android-like troopers that have staffed so many instantly forgettable manufactured bands over the years, they also had highly distinctive personalities of their own. Moreover, they took the time to forge a group identity and philosophy that was more than skin deep. By the time they were ready to face the world there was a sensational chemistry at work between the five Spice Girls, founded on a genuine bond, that was to prove a match for any of the "real" groups with whom they were so often unfavourably compared.

Much of this was, once again, down to the foresight and organisational benevolence of the Herberts and their financial backer, a Surrey businessman called Chic Murphy. A shadowy figure, Murphy was the third key part of the team, known as Heart Management, that gave the Spice Girls their unusually well-starred start in life. A tall, grey-haired cockney with a small cross tattooed in one ear, he was described by Geri as "an endearing old rogue, the sort of character who I imagined would have known all the East End haunts in the days of Reggie and Ronnie Kray." Geri may have known more than she was letting on. For although Murphy was, and still is, a multi-millionaire, no one is prepared to say how he came by his conspicuous wealth. Some of it, eventually, was earned from the music business, when he set up a management company with the American vocal group The Three Degrees, although this was certainly not how he made his fortune.

Along with the Herberts' mood board, The Three Degrees can also claim, albeit unwittingly, to have played a key part in the conception of the Spice Girls. The group was convened in Philadelphia in 1963 where they were quickly discovered by Richard Barrett, a producer and songwriter who had been a key force behind Fifties vocal-pop acts including The Chantels, Little Anthony & The Imperials, Frankie Lymon & The Teenagers, and his own group The Valentines. After various line-up changes and minor successes, The Three Degrees finally achieved international success in 1974 with 'When Will I See You Again', which has since become an easy-listening soul standard and remains their signature song to this day.

Although the group's career subsequently faltered in America, they enjoyed a string of Top 10 hits in the UK during the late Seventies, including 'The Runner', 'My Simple Heart', 'Giving Up Giving In' and 'Woman In Love'. By the time Murphy hooked up with them, their best days were behind them, but they were still a big draw on the concert circuit, where their slick presentation and mellifluous arrangements increasingly led them into the arms of the upmarket cabaret crowd. They were favourites of Prince Charles who, long before he got smothered in red lipstick and had his bottom pinched by the Spice Girls, invited The Three Degrees to perform at Buckingham Palace on his 30th birthday. Several years later, the group were guests at his wedding to Diana, Princess of Wales.

Although little mention is made of Murphy's connection with The Three Degrees in official biographies, he was so closely involved with them that, for a while, he became known to insiders as "the Fourth Degree". As he watched them performing night after night for anything up to 40 weeks a year, Murphy would often get to wondering how much more successful a younger, fashionable girl group might become if they could apply themselves with a similar degree of professionalism to cracking the modern pop market. The Three Degrees' Musical Director, Erwin Keiles, remembered Murphy trying to sell the idea to the group itself.

"For ages he'd be saying to the girls: 'You guys, you shouldn't be working now. You should be using all your knowledge and stagecraft and business acumen to be managing a young girl group.' That's definitely where the idea for a girl group started. He kept on saying to them: 'Take some of your money, let's put it into a management company and let's put a girl group together. You guys could be earning much more than you can now by using your knowledge and skills to find and audition the right girls and then to teach them the whole stage act – singing and dancing.' They couldn't see it of course, because they aren't business people."

The Three Degrees are still performing at events such as the closing ceremony of the Gay Games in Amsterdam in August 1998. It's hardly cutting edge, and God knows who is in the line-up nowadays. But for better or worse, they hold the title of the Longest Running Female Vocal Trio in the *Guinness Book Of Records*. Keiles still does "bits and pieces" with them when they come over to Britain. But Murphy is no longer involved. According to some reports the group dumped him – a turn of events which was already becoming a recurring theme in this story before the Spice Girls had even properly met! But however the split occurred, The Fourth Degree now had bigger fish to fry.

Putting together a young, all-girl group was clearly an idea whose time had come, and it wasn't long before Murphy got together with Bob Herbert, who was Keiles's accountant at the time and part of the same circle of Surrey-based music business entrepreneurs. Despite his experience with The Three Degrees, Murphy felt out of his depth as a potential manager of such a group and out of touch with current trends, so it was agreed that while Bob supplied the management expertise, and Chris Herbert took care of the hands-on organisation and development of the group, Murphy's role would be to provide financial backing, which he duly did.

Murphy owned a house in Boyne Hill Road, Maidenhead, where it was decided that the girls should be installed for the spring and summer of 1994, a period when they would learn the skills necessary to be in a modern pop group, but also, and even more importantly, experience the sort of bonding process that would turn them into a "proper" group. Bands from The Byrds era would certainly have recognised the procedure. Indeed, towards the end of the Sixties the old hippy notion of groups "getting it together in the country" became something of a joke, as ever longer periods of time spent smoking dope and otherwise not doing very much were chalked up to record company A&R budgets as an essential part of the rock'n'roll nurturing and development process.

But in the real world of the struggling new band, the intense period of rehearsing and living in each other's pockets, while surviving on a shoestring budget, confers a collective identity on a group of individuals which no amount of consciously contrived "image building" can possibly reproduce. In the case of the Spice Girls, getting it together in the country meant rent-free lodging in Maidenhead, where there were no lost months spent idling around in rooms full of cushions and smouldering joss sticks. Indeed very little time was wasted, full stop. Even before they moved into the house together, they began a programme of coaching and rehearsals at Trinity Studios in Woking. This dilapidated dance, rehearsal and recording studio with paint peeling from the walls and, as Geri described it, "radiators that rattled but remained permanently cold", was run by Ian Lee.

"They were originally based here for a week to see if they were going to make it, to see what sort of a mess they made of some songs," Lee said. "When they first arrived they were like five schoolgirls – a bit giggly, a bit insecure. When they came back on a full-time basis, they started to gel together. That's when Geri and Mel B began to emerge as the dominant ones. You wouldn't say they were all singers by any stretch. And as for dancing, Geri couldn't dance either! The only thing she had was big tits."

A crude analysis (and there would be plenty more of those) but it was clear that the girls needed training. Keiles, who had been hired to organise the auditions and to provide some original material for the girls to cut their teeth on, knew of a singing teacher called Pepe Lemer who was duly charged with the task of knocking the girls into shape.

Lemer was an old school performer somewhat in the Barbra Streisand mould, whose bid for stardom in the Sixties had been crowded out by stars of a more homely and waif-like inclination such as Lulu, Marianne Faithfull, Cilla Black and Sandie Shaw. Since then she had worked as a backing singer with innumerable bands and solo artists while giving singing lessons to a growing but surprisingly secretive roster of clients, of which more later.

Her first step with the girls was to establish the scale of the job. To begin with she sat down with each of them in turn and listened to them sing 'Take Me Away', one of several numbers composed for them by Kieles and his songwriting partner John Thirkell. The performances were conducted while looking at themselves in a mirror.

"Each one had an individuality about them," Lemer recalled. "Mel C was very lithe and lean, very much a dancer's body. And when she sang and looked in the mirror it was as if she was looking in the camera, which is how it should be when you perform; very professional, I thought. Victoria had a pretty little voice. With her ponytail and pretty face, there was a sweetness about her. Melanie B was very fiery. There was a time when her tuning was bad and she burst into tears with me. She had this good, solid, soulful singing sound – she knew how to project – but there were times when, because she was a very strong character, she would challenge the training and get upset with the intensity of it all. What you see now is exactly what she was then, but without the fame and the money. There were altercations with Mel B.

"Geri had an amazing personality, but she didn't quite know what to do with her voice. She had the hardest job. Her co-ordination had to be worked on for the dancing. And when she sang she had to learn how to soften all that strength in her voice. The others had all sung before, but Geri hadn't. She had the potential – she just had to work the hardest. And by God, she did work the hardest. I watched her, on her own, in the corner practising her breathing, practising that dance step. She was not obviously a physical performer, but she persevered."

Lemer took the girls for lessons for two hours a day, two days a week, during which they had to do "scale after scale after scale, learn how to project, and learn how far they could take their voices." She taught them how to sing individually, then she made them sing in groups of two, then three and four and so on. They learnt how to breathe together, how to sing in unison, then split their voices and go straight into harmonies. She taught them how to apply diaphragm breathing techniques, how to open their mouths properly, and how to sing and dance simultaneously without getting out of breath. The training was intense, the attention to detail absolute.

Which makes it all the more difficult to comprehend why, of all the myths that have grown up about the Spice Girls, the idea that they "can't sing" has become so widely and unquestioningly taken on board. It is true that none of the Spice Girls are singers in the way that Celine Dion, Whitney Houston or Mariah Carey are singers. But then, very few singers in the pop or rock tradition aspire to that state of super-heated excellence. Nor do the Spice Girls hail from the gospel tradition that informs the work of various highly skilled American vocal groups such as Boyz II Men. But, both individually and collectively, Geri, Emma, Victoria, and the two Mels are all singers of a standard that is perfectly acceptable in the broad run of the pop world. And indeed, when you start to think about it in any detail, what is the mark of a "good" singer in pop anyway?

I remember being invited to speak in a radio discussion on the current state of planet pop or some such. One of the other participants was Rick "Rock" McMurray, the then mohican-haired drummer with Irish indie-rockers Ash, who vouchsafed the opinion that Westlife were absolute rubbish. Hardly a controversial position to take but nevertheless, in order to convey his group's depth of feeling about this important matter (and not in any way as a stunt to publicise their own new single), Ash had earlier in the day purchased 200 or so copies of Westlife's record and publicly torched the lot. Among his various criticisms of Westlife, which basically amounted to the fact that their dull, bland, formulaic, hand-me-down crap made them a disgrace to the Irish nation – certainly a difficult argument to refute – McMurray insisted that "they can't sing".

Now as it happened, a few days prior to this, Ash had played their own single, 'Shining Light', live on *Top Of The Pops*, during which their singer Tim Wheeler had turned in a performance of such startling ineptitude it was a wonder the producer hadn't prefaced it with a warning to viewers who might be disturbed by scenes of random violence being inflicted on an innocent tune. Out of breath and out of key, the Ash frontman's thin, reedy croak bobbed fitfully among the waves of overdriven guitars like a piece of cork adrift in a high sea. And here was his chum, a party to the crime no less, airily telling the world that Westlife "can't sing".

Now I think Ash are an infinitely more exciting, characterful and musically involving group than Westlife. Ash write their own songs, they have tremendous punch, they are the real deal. 'Goldfinger' and 'Girl From Mars' are classics of the Britpop era. Westlife, on the other hand, are a group of manicured dullards without a spark of wit or originality in their bones. But actually, any one member of Westlife could sing the pants off the whole of Ash, any day of the week. And, I'm sorry to say, the same holds true, in a technical sense, for the late Joe Strummer, Shane MacGowan, Ian Brown and any number of punk-rock-indie renegades and their self-righteous camp followers who habitually look down their noses at their less-than-hip mainstream pop cousins and castigate them for not being able to sing.

Indeed, I get a definite sense of déjà vu whenever I hear the accusation that particular pop performers "can't sing" since it wasn't that long ago that a certain sort of saloon bar bore would happily tell anyone within earshot that Johnny Rotten and Joey Ramone couldn't sing either. The irony then was that you could bet a pound to a penny the person making this lofty pronouncement would take it for granted that Bob Dylan was one of the quintessential voices in rock'n'roll. Now Dylan may be many things: spokesman for a generation, a lyricist on a par with the best, an icon, a legend, a man whose work has helped define the cultural landscape in which all discussion of modern music exists. And a great many people like the sound of his voice. But can he "really" sing? And while we're on the subject, how is it possible for a person to play harmonica for a living for 40 years and still not get any better at it than he has?

The fact is that for all the flak they've taken over the years about their supposed lack of ability as singers (and the flak which they continued to take as they racked up number one hit after number one hit as solo artists) the Spice Girls put every bit as much effort into learning their craft as did the hippy wannabe in The Byrds song who was told to "take some time and learn how to play".

One of their most distinctive and successful strategies for wooing the movers and shakers in the music business (before they had released any records) was simply to go into offices and TV and radio stations and anywhere else that they could get a foot in the door and sing. Robert Sandall, who later became the group's press officer at Virgin Records, was chief pop critic of *The Sunday Times* in 1995, when he met them for the first time at a corporate junket at Kempton racecourse.

"They took me into the gents' toilets and sang to me," he said. "I can't remember what the song was, but I remember thinking they could certainly sing. There was a clear five-part vocal arrangement going on. It was an unusually bold thing for a group in their position to do. And they did seem keen on selling themselves as a serious singing proposition. They wanted to let people know they could actually do it."

Nicki Chapman, who later became famous as one of the *Pop Idol* judges, was working as head of TV promotion at RCA in July 1995, in charge of acts including M People, Kylie Minogue, Take That and Robson & Jerome, when the group, then known only as Spice, came into the office to see the Managing Director, Hugh Goldsmith.

"I was asked to sit in on the meeting," Chapman said. "So I took my place and next thing I know five mad young girls came flying through the office on roller blades and jumped up on the table and started strutting their stuff. And they just blew me away."

It was especially odd that the myth that the Spice Girls couldn't sing should gain such widespread currency when in fact for the first six months or so after they had signed to Virgin (later in 1995) they did little else. They would sing at the drop of a hat, virtually anywhere, anytime, as when Chapman, who subsequently left RCA to start her own PR company Brilliant!, took the girls to meet the production team of *The Big Breakfast* at the Planet 24 production company. "There they were," she said, "with their little bashed-up tape recorder, and they put the cassette in and did an impromptu performance in the middle of this huge open-plan office in front of about 60 people. And it worked. It really worked."

However, there is no smoke without fire, and it seems to me that the bizarre accusation that the Spice Girls can't "really" sing reflects a more widespread suspicion about the performing abilities of pop artists in general and the technical wherewithal of producers and record companies to pull the wool over their audience's eyes (or perhaps that should be ears) with increasingly sophisticated studio effects. For whereas in the pop eras of the Fifties, Sixties and Seventies the quality of singing that you heard on a record was, for better or worse, a pretty fair representation of a performer's ability in the flesh, you now have equipment in recording studios which can make a voice that isn't in tune sound as if it is. Just as every professional recording studio has, as a matter of course, microphones and a mixing board with devices for compressing and equalising the sound frequencies, so they now also have a device called an Autotune for getting a vocal part in tune and another called a Vocaline for "lining-up" different vocal parts (i.e. getting them synchronised with each other). In other words, it is now perfectly possible to take a person who can't sing and, provided they've got a reasonable tone of voice, make them sound as if they can sing, or to record a group of non-singers, all performing out of time with each other, and make them sound like the slickest of barbershop quartets.

The upshot of this is what we might call Human League Syndrome run riot – a sense in which if you're an A&R person or management mogul on the look-out nowadays for a performer with "star potential" in the music business, then the ability to sing exceptionally well, or even at all, is relegated to a fairly low position in the order of priorities. Thus it undoubtedly was with the original selection of the Spice Girls. The Herberts weren't looking for great singers, they were looking for a certain type of girl ("streetwise, outgoing, ambitious, dedicated, 18-23), albeit with "the ability to sing/dance". Chris Herbert wasn't put off in the slightest by Geri's almost complete lack of singing experience. It was her "cheek" (among other assets) which made her perfect for the job.

"What you had here was five girls who looked a certain way that was extremely marketable," said Erwin Keiles, the producer and songwriter who was present at the original auditions to choose the girls. "You had the sporty girl, the pretty girl, the sophisticated girl, the black girl . . . it's almost as if they went out and did a survey to decide how they were going to design a new model of car. It was a great concept. But none of them could sing any better than the girl who lives down the street who sings in the local youth club or is a keen amateur. They can sing much better now than they could on Day One. But they're still not singers."

As something of a connoisseur of singing voices who has worked at the production coalface for many years, Keiles observed a sea change in the approach to the making and marketing of pop during the Eighties and Nineties.

"The point is that once this equipment had become widely available and installed, suddenly you didn't need to have singers any more," he said. "I was in the studio when Take That were being auditioned. I was involved with Bros and several other boy bands, and I've seen the same thing over and over again. The record company doesn't have to deal any more with some fantastic singer who is also a great songwriter and has got an opinion about what they want. Instead, they can take people who are completely mouldable and who are grateful to be given the opportunity of a lifetime.

"We produced a boy band for a management company. Five guys came in to the studio. They looked fantastic. They could all dance brilliantly. But not one of them could sing. We had to spend hours and hours of studio time fixing and time-stretching their voices – doing what a good singer could have done in no time at all. I think we spent 19 hours 'tuning' the vocals on one song alone. The finished product sounded fantastic, but believe me, none of those guys could sing."

According to Keiles, the equipment that tunes voices is now so well developed that the trick can actually be done in real time. In other words, it can be used "live". "It works on stage. I'll say no more," he concluded darkly, before adding: "I know the Spice Girls used it."

There have been many startling changes in what is now felt to constitute a "live" performance in recent years. Most people – but not all – accept sampling and sequencing as perfectly legitimate techniques. But the staging of various multi-artist events, such as the Party In The Park concerts in Hyde Park, where the majority of acts simply mime to their records, is just one of the more obvious cases in which the "fake" performing aesthetic of *Top Of The Pops* has been imported into the "live" arena (although, curiously, in recent times it has become increasingly fashionable for artists to perform live on *Top Of The Pops* itself – once the bastion of the mimed performance). The antics of vocal groups such as All Saints, who have habitually mimed during parts of their concert performances, and Steps, who have done likewise and indeed don't even bother to take musicians on tour with them when backing tapes will evidently suffice, have further eroded the idea of what constitutes an authentic concert experience.

However, the proposition that because some manufactured pop bands cannot or do not sing, therefore all such groups cannot sing, is based on obviously flawed logic. The Backstreet Boys are clearly tremendous singers, all blessed with beautiful voices and fully aware of the various nuances of phrasing and pitching. Conversely, some great or "credible" pop artists are not especially accomplished singers. Madonna is not much of a singer, and was even less so when she was going through her 'Material Girl' phase, but that's not to say she hasn't proved herself, time and again, to be a fantastic talent. After all, there's hundreds of singers who can walk into a studio and sing brilliantly, but who haven't got the larger-than-life personality or the ambition or the looks or whatever it takes to be a star.

As with so many other aspects of their story, the Spice Girls came through the doorway to pop stardom at a time when both the media and the masses were just wising up to the new rules of engagement. Not only did Posh, Sporty, Ginger, Baby and Scary seem to embody the ethos of the no-brains, no-talent, "put-together" group, but they swiftly became the most successful representatives of the "genre" in the entire history of pop. And, of course, they were pretty girls. Small wonder then that they became a conduit for all the suspicion and antipathy towards stars of that kind, a kind of giant lightning conductor for every "can't sing" horror story flashing across the pop skyline.

"I get so angry when I hear people say that the Spice Girls can't sing," Pepi Lemer said. "I cannot bear that put-down, because I know differently. It's totally unjustified. If they can't sing, how come they've lasted so long, putting out single after single, each one different from the last one, and many of them difficult songs to sing? 'Wannabe', 'Say You'll Be There', 'Mama', when you listen to those songs you hear each individual voice – the depth of Geri's voice, the lightness of Emma's voice, the soulful sound of the two Mels – you can always identify their sound. Of course they can sing."

There is also a curious prejudice that has grown up in the pop world when it comes to the matter of voice training that runs counter to the received wisdom in just about every other line of endeavour that you can think of. Lemer has trained many well-known performers – including Keith Duffy of Boyzone, the comedian Jennifer Saunders and boy band Five – but rather than boast about it, most of her famous clients have made her sign secrecy clauses in her contract with them which forbid her from revealing to the world that they have availed themselves of her services. It is something which Lemer has got used to.

"They don't want anyone to know that they've been vocally trained, because they want to be known as 'natural' talents," she explained. "It's as if people will feel that if they had to be trained, then they couldn't have been that talented in the first place."

One only has to apply the same logic to, say, an athlete or a tennis player or even an opera singer to realise what nonsense this is. But there is, nevertheless, a deep-rooted suspicion among certain people (especially critics and other tastemakers) of pop stars, particularly singers, who have undertaken any sort of training or advanced coaching in their art. Here again the Spice Girls were peculiarly vulnerable to the criticism that theirs was an "artificially" created talent, as opposed to the raw, God-given brilliance of a group such as Prodigy (with their classically trained keyboard player Liam Howlett) or Primal Scream. Well the Spice Girls were certainly more a product of the *Fame* school way of doing things than the old-fashioned rock'n'roll method of simply opening your mouth and expressing yourself – but that is hardly sufficient grounds for arguing that the Spice Girls can't "really sing" and that Keith Flint and Bobby Gillespie can.

# 2
# The House Of Fun

With the benefit of hindsight, Chris Herbert could look back on the days when the five girls were living and working together in Chic Murphy's house in Maidenhead with a degree of rueful admiration.

"They never spoke about 'if' we make it. It was always 'when' we make it and, 'How big are we going to make it?'" he subsequently recalled.

But at the time, the youthful management svengali quickly found himself out of his depth.

"Geri was probably a bit frustrated as to how long the actual process was going to take," Herbert said. "We always had it in our minds that it was going to take twelve to eighteen months to develop them before we could get the group signed or get any kind of record released."

The girls, it transpired, had their own ideas. And despite all the time, energy and money which was being invested in them, no one had thought to make them sign a contract. Chris Herbert's explanation for this catastrophic oversight was that "one of the other guys involved [i.e Murphy] was adamant that he didn't want to put them under contract. I suppose it's that old school management thing where he wanted that insecurity to play a part in it, so that they were always on their toes, always hungry for it and always had something to prove. Because if any one of them had played up, he'd have shipped one out and shipped the next one in."

Poor old Murphy. Here was a man who had come up in a world where it was the manager, with his business experience and financial clout, who called the shots. The artists were expected to live and work like indentured slaves, never aware of the bigger picture, always fearful that they might be the next to feel the swish of the axe about to fall on their heads.

"What I would do is work 'em," Murphy said of his plans for the girls at the time.

And in an earlier era, or with a different group of people, maybe that's the way it would have been. But not this time. And most certainly not with this lot. Murphy and the Herberts had started out by inventing the perfect girl group. But like the scientist in a sci-fi movie who grows a culture in a Petri dish that ends up threatening to take over the world, they were about to discover that the organism they had created was completely beyond their ability to control or even contain. They were only five inexperienced girls. But in truth, Heart Management had no idea what they had got hold of.

★ ★ ★

## VICTORIA CAROLINE ADAMS

Standing 5′ 6″ tall, with a nose like a ski jump and ever-so-slightly inward-facing teeth like a baby shark's, Victoria was the most poised and sophisticated of the girls, but also the most introverted. She was born on April 17, 1974 and brought up with a younger sister, Louise, and a younger brother, Christian. Her mother Jacqueline Adams (née Cannon) trained as a hairdresser and worked as an insurance clerk. Her father, Tony Adams, is a self-made man, who enjoyed a spell as a singer in covers bands such as The Soniks and The Calettos during the Sixties, and then worked as a sales representative in North London before he and Jackie set up their own electrical wholesale business. Thanks to a combination of hard work and business acumen, it became a flourishing concern, which enabled the family to enjoy a comfortable lifestyle in a large house in Goff's Oak, Hertfordshire with regular sorties to the holiday playgrounds of the nouveau riche in places such as the Canary Islands and Spain. Encouraged by her parents, Victoria showed an early enthusiasm for music and drama, and enrolled at the tender age of eight for after-school classes at the Jason Theatre School in Broxbourne.

She started secondary school at St Mary's High in Cheshunt in 1985, where she was given a rough ride by fellow pupils who were envious of her family's wealth – her father would drop her off at the school gates in a Rolls-Royce – and teased her because she suffered from acne.

"I was one of the most unpopular kids there," she said. "I was a complete wreck. I would wake up worrying who I was going to sit next to in class. It was sheer hell.

"The reason I was hated is because I wasn't doing what you do when you're at school – bunking off and going with loads of boys. I never had any boyfriends at school. And when everybody else was going down the chip shop, I was going to ballet lessons . . . and that wasn't the cool thing to do."

She left St Mary's in the summer of 1990 with a handful of O levels, and won a place at the Laine Theatre Arts School in Epsom, where she completed her higher education. On leaving there in 1993 she landed a part as a dancer in a musical called *Bertie* in Birmingham, after which she joined a two-man, three-woman group called Persuasion. She was still performing with them, when she went for the audition for an all-girl group advertised in *The Stage*.

## MELANIE JANINE BROWN

Even before she had a stud rammed through her tongue, and her birth sign, Gemini, tattooed on her bum, Melanie B was the loudest and lewdest of the girls, with a laugh dirtier than a gang of sailors on shore leave. She is 5′ 5″ tall, wears glasses and smokes Marlborough Lights. Her younger sister, Danielle, is an actress, who has appeared in *Emmerdale*.

"I'm one of those people that's nice in small doses," Melanie would say in a voice that is more Yorkshire than pudding. But she was not so scary when she was born in Leeds on May 29, 1975. In fact her features were so perfect that one of the nurses declared her to be "the bonniest baby that's been born here all week."

Her mother, Andrea Dixon, and father, Martin Brown, were married three months after Melanie was born. Martin, who was born on the island of Nevis in the West Indies, was an engineer's assistant at Yorkshire Imperial Metals, where he has worked shifts for more than 25 years. Andrea, Yorkshire born and bred, has worked in a variety of unskilled occupations in offices, factories, shops and elsewhere, often holding down two or three jobs simultaneously while the daughters were growing up. After 27 years of marriage, the couple separated in 2002 and subsequently divorced.

The family lived in Burley, a suburb of Leeds, for most of Melanie's childhood. Holidays were spent, without fail, at a campsite in Abersoch on the Welsh coast in the company of her extended family (mostly from her mother's side), an experience which Melanie adored. As a child she was hyperactive.

"Literally I could not sit still. It's one of the reasons my mum sent me to dancing classes. I didn't want to miss out on anything. I was a whirlwind."

From her very first lesson at the Jean Pearce School of Dance – a cold, basement studio with no heating – she was hooked. "I began a blissful journey into tap, ballet, jazz and modern." While still at school she took a handful of acting lessons and taught herself how to play the drums. At the age of 15, she left school and home to take up a job as a dancer during the summer season in Blackpool. Returning to Leeds at the end of the season, she took up a place at The Northern School of Contemporary Dance in Chapeltown, which she subsidised by teaching aerobics classes at a local leisure centre. In 1992, she won the Miss *Leeds Weekly News* beauty pageant. After dropping out of college she sold advertising space for a car magazine, and worked as an extra on the set of *A Touch Of Frost* and *Coronation Street*.

"I don't count myself as black or white – I'm mixed race," she says. "I'm proud of that. I don't see colour as a problem, it's to be enjoyed. You should never deny one side of your colour – some people get it wrong and stick to either the white side or the black side. But if you're mixed race it's proving a point that things are changing . . . it's getting better."

## EMMA LEE BUNTON

Blue-eyed, blonde-haired and a petite 5′ 2″ tall, Emma was the youngest, the smallest, the sweetest and the last of the five girls. No wonder the others all took her so immediately under their collective wing. She was also the only one to have a blue belt in karate. She would later have "Baby" tattooed on her hip and a Chinese symbol tattooed at the base of her spine.

Emma was born on January 21, 1976 in Barnet, North London and grew up in nearby East Finchley. Her father, Trevor Bunton was a milkman, and when she was old enough, Emma would sometimes go out and help on his rounds. But long before that, when she was still only two, her mother, Pauline Bunton (née Davitt), began taking the little, moon-faced toddler on photographic shoots for Mothercare and other clients of the child modelling agency Norrie Carr. She won a beauty contest and started ballet classes when she was three and had enrolled in disco and tap classes at the Kay School of Dance in Finchley by the age of five. It was here that she made her first solo stage appearances, as a moonbeam dressed in a peach tutu, and then as a tap-dancing bear cub. She advanced to a role as the Milky Bar Kid's girlfriend in a TV advertisement for the white chocolate, before winning a place at the Sylvia Young Theatre School in Islington, where her contemporaries included Denise Van Outen, Samantha Janus and three future members of All Saints: Melanie Blatt and Nicole and Natalie Appleton.

Soon after Emma had started there her parents were divorced.

"I don't remember being upset by the break-up at all," Emma recalls. "The only thing I remember saying about it was, 'Does this mean I'll get two lots of pocket money?'"

If anything the reverse was the case. Despite supplementing his milk rounds with stints at window-cleaning and mini-cabbing, her father could no longer afford to pay the fees at Sylvia Young's. Fortunately the school offered her a scholarship and Emma was able to continue her theatrical training. Her mother, meanwhile, embarked on a new life as a karate instructor, and now holds a black belt. The indomitable Pauline has since moved to Hertfordshire, where she lives with her second husband, Steve, whom she married on February 14, 2001, and Emma's younger brother, Paul James (aka PJ).

"My mum taught me that whoever you are, and whatever age, you can achieve what you want," Emma says.

Although her childhood dream was to be a dancer, after suffering a back injury at the age of 14, Emma switched her attention to acting. She left school at 16 to begin a two-year drama course at Barnet Technical College. Meanwhile other assignments included appearing in a photo-story in a teen magazine called *Top Chat* as a karate student who had a crush on her teacher, and being the featured face of an anti-smoking poster. Having played the part of a teenage tearaway in the TV soap *EastEnders*, it seemed as if she was on the verge of greater things.

But no one could have predicted just how great a leap she was about to make when Pepe Lemer, her former singing teacher from Sylvia Young's, invited her to go and meet up with a group of girls she was coaching at a studio in Woking.

## MELANIE JAYNE CHISHOLM

Melanie C ended up with a nose stud, a gold incisor and at least ten tattoos, probably more, including the word "angel" written across her belly and a huge turquoise phoenix with its wings spread across the rippling musculature of her shoulders. When she met the other girls, she was a trim, and rather less-illustrated woman, 5′ 6″ tall, who regarded herself as fearless in most situations, except where spiders are involved. Obsessively fit and strong, even then, she was also short-sighted and continues to wear glasses for reading and driving.

Melanie was born on January 12, 1974 in Rainhill, a suburb of Liverpool, known locally for its mental asylum. Brought up on council estates in the suburbs of Runcorn and Widnes, she attended Brookvale Junior School and Fairfield Junior School, where she displayed an early aptitude for sports: netball, hockey, rounders, athletics, gymnastics, you name it. She also gravitated towards dance, taking classes and appearing in amateur revues and pantomimes. But music was her true calling. Her mother, Joan O'Neill, who worked as a secretary/PA, has been singing in bands since she was 14, and currently performs in River Deep, a Tina Turner tribute group, in which her husband (Melanie's stepfather), Dennis O'Neill plays bass.

"I always wanted to be a pop star," Melanie says. "It was my mum's job and I wanted it to be mine too. I used to go to gigs and watch her. I'd sit there at the front, miming every word she sang."

Melanie has a complicated Christmas card list. She is the only child of Alan and Joan Chisholm, who were married on July 24, 1971 and who separated in 1978. Alan, who at that time worked as a fitter at Otis Elevators, sired a daughter Emma Williams (Melanie's half-sister) after he and Joan had divorced – a fact which Melanie only became aware of when she and Emma first met many years later in 1998. Melanie's mother married Dennis O'Neill who had two sons, Jarrod and Stuart, from his first marriage, who then became Melanie's stepbrothers. Dennis O'Neill and Joan had a boy, Paul, who is Melanie's half-brother. Meanwhile, Alan Chisholm had moved into the travel industry, and married again. His new wife Carole had two boys, Liam and Declan, giving Melanie a grand tally of one half-sister, two stepbrothers and three half-brothers. For most of the time, when she was growing up, Melanie lived with her mother, her stepfather, Jarrod, Stuart and Paul.

Melanie's parents separated when she was four-and-a-half, and although she now declares herself "lucky" to have two mums and two dads, she admits to feelings of insecurity as a child. "I felt like I was in the way and I had to make my own life and be independent."

After leaving Fairfield County High School, Melanie attended the Doreen Bird College of Performing Arts in Kent, where she trained in theatre studies and singing. Following graduation in 1993, she auditioned for work in London. Unemployed and hungry, she had resorted to stealing food from grocery stores when she saw a flyer inviting applicants to audition for an all-girl pop group. "This is it. This is definitely it," she thought.

## GERALDINE ESTELLE HALLIWELL

A bundle of nervous, flirtatious energy, Geri was the oldest and most experienced of the five girls. But she was also the one with the most to prove. Everything about her was subject to constant change: her weight, her hair colour, her look, her lifestyle. Even her height and age were subject to discreet adjustments, depending on the circumstances.

According to her birth certificate however, she was born on August 6, 1972 and eventually grew to a height of no more than 5′ 2″, no matter what it said on her modelling "zeb" card. She has a brother, Max and a sister, Natalie, both older than her, as well as a half-brother, Paul, and half-sister, Karen, from her father, Laurence Halliwell's previous marriage. Geri was extremely fond of her father, describing him as a "car dealer, entrepreneur, womaniser and chancer" who was old enough to be mistaken for her grandfather when she was growing up. One wonders what she might have said about him if she *hadn't* liked him.

Geri's mother, Ana Maria Hidalgo, was born and brought up in rural Spain. She emigrated to England when she was 21, and spent her working life cleaning offices and libraries. She became a Jehovah's Witness for a while and would take the young Geri doorstepping with her, until she lost interest in it.

Geri was born and brought up in Watford, where she attended the Walter de Merton Junior School. She won a place at Watford Girls' Grammar School where she joined the drama club. She already knew that she wanted to be famous.

"I didn't know exactly how I was going to achieve it," she later recalled. "Probably by being a TV presenter, or a pop star or an actress, I thought. The precise details weren't particularly relevant to a teenager; it was simply going to happen."

Her parents separated when Geri was ten years old, after which she was brought up by her mother, while maintaining a close, if erratic, relationship with her father until his death in 1993 at the age of 71.

She left school with eight O levels and went to Casio College to study travel, tourism and finance. But this was 1989 – during the so-called second "summer of love" – and she was cheerfully sucked into the 24-hour party people lifestyle, a nocturnal existence organised around the huge weekend raves which took place on farmland and in warehouse properties adjacent to London's orbital motorway, the M25.

Her studies lapsed. She moved into a squat in South Oxhey and got a job as a go-go dancer at the Crazy Club at the London Astoria. This led in turn to a job as a dancer in a nightclub in Majorca from whence she entered the shadowy world of glamour modelling.

The pressures of modelling and auditioning (nearly always unsuccessfully) aggravated deep-rooted feelings of insecurity, and Geri was suffering a full-blown case of bulimia by the time she was 19. Such problems did not prevent her from being selected to host a game show called *Let's Make A Deal* on a new Turkish TV channel. But becoming a minor celebrity in a country where she could neither speak nor understand the language was not nearly good enough for Geri.

"It didn't feel like fame to me," she said. "I wanted to be able to say, 'Hey, look at me,' to my family and friends." She later vowed to streak at Wimbledon if she hadn't become properly famous by her 22nd birthday.

Back in England she took up various odd jobs to make ends meet, becoming an aerobics instructor (Miss Motivator) and a make-up/makeover artist. A chance comment by a theatre casting director about her lack of reading experience, prompted her to enrol for an A level course in English Literature at Watford College at the age of 21.

As well as pursuing her studies – more conscientiously this time – she worked in a hairdresser's, a restaurant and as a domestic cleaner, while continuing to spend weekends hosting the TV game show in Istanbul. Finding herself at a very low ebb – "My weight had fallen to six stone and I barely had the energy to get out of bed" – she nearly didn't go to the audition at Nomis Studios in Shepherds Bush in May 1994.

Chris Herbert had agreed to see her, despite her failure to attend the first audition. "It's down to the last twelve girls," a friend pointed out. "Five get chosen. They're great odds."

And then there was Michelle Stephenson, the girl from Abingdon, Hertfordshire, who saw her opportunity to acquire fame and riches beyond belief trickle through her fingers like sand. As with Pete Best, the drummer who was booted out of The Beatles to make way for Ringo Starr just weeks before the group released their first record, Stephenson's brief tenure in the group was a one-way ticket to pop's all-time losers' club. What must it feel like to be an also-ran on such a mind-boggling scale? To have held one of life's winning lottery tickets in your hand, only to have it fed into the shredding machine before you could cash it in?

"Of course I regret I'm not a multi-millionaire like them," Stephenson said many years later in one of the great understatements of pop. "But at the time I left the group I knew I was doing the right thing. And I still think it was the right thing. It wasn't my kind of music and they were not living the lifestyle I wanted."

Stephenson came from a secure, tightly knit family. Her father, George, worked for the Chubb lock company and her brother Simon was an art director. Together with her mum, Penny, they supported and encouraged her efforts to work on the stage, a dream which began at the age of five when she was picked to play the part of a sunflower in a village hall production. She was in her first year of studying Theatre and English at London's Goldsmith's University when she saw the Herberts' advertisement in *The Stage*. By then she had already been a member of both the Young Vic and the National Youth Theatre and had performed at the Edinburgh Festival.

She was actually the first of the girls to be chosen from the final 20 who made it to the second audition, at which they were split into groups and instructed to sing the Stevie Wonder song 'Signed, Sealed, Delivered, I'm Yours'. After the auditions were completed and the other four – Melanie B, Melanie C, Victoria and Geri – had been selected, the girls were moved into a bed and breakfast near Windsor for a week to get to know each other, before moving "full time" into the house in Maidenhead.

There was one tiny single room which Geri appropriated, apparently on the grounds that she was the oldest and the least able to "share her space". Then there was a room with two single beds which Stephenson shared with Victoria. The two Melanies shared a double bed in the third room. There was always a queue for the bathroom, in which every available horizontal surface, apart from the floor, was piled up with soaps, shampoos, make-up and sundry cosmetics. There was a single bath and a shower attachment that could be fitted on to the taps. It was all a very far cry from the luxurious accommodation that would be laid on years later for the young hopefuls in *Popstars*.

"We did subsidise them a bit," Chris Herbert said. "And we gave them a weekly wage as well towards food and keep and all that sort of stuff. The girls were signing on and probably getting housing benefit at the time as well."

According to Geri, the girls each had £60 a week to live on. Every morning they would squeeze into her Fiat Uno and drive the thirty miles to Trinity Studios in Woking, where they worked on their voice coaching and dance lessons and began the task of building up a repertoire of songs.

The Herberts had decided that the group would be called Touch; something to do with the word having five letters, one for each of the five girls. The number "five" seems to have had some mystical significance for Chris Herbert. Five was the name he chose for the boy band which several years later finally did bring home the bacon for Heart Management. And there were also five letters in Spice, which became the interim name that the group devised before they became the Spice Girls.

In the early days of Touch, Herbert Jr remained nominally in charge, although as the months went by an increasingly open power struggle between him and Geri over who was in charge of the group began to develop.

"Geri was very much the engine behind the band," Herbert said. "She was the rocket that kept the whole thing moving. She kept everyone focused and motivated. She knew her vision. Very, very, very streetwise. She knew exactly what she wanted and how it was all going to look, probably even more so than I did at the time."

Fortunately, Herbert was not the kind of manager who would regard this as a threat to his authority.

"Geri wasn't an awful lot younger than me and she had a lot of strong ideas. I'm not knocking them. In fact, I've got most respect for Geri this side of things because I've never worked with someone who was so driven and ambitious and has got such a good grasp on the mechanics of how things work for someone who was a novice at it."

Herbert nevertheless attempted to maintain a hands-on approach to the matter of how the girls ought to look and what songs they would perform. Stephenson described it as "very, very young pop" and recalls the lyrics to one song which went: "Where do you come from?/ Falling from the sky/ You're someone very special/ I'm flying, I feel so high." Another song which they practised incessantly at this stage was called 'We're Gonna Make It Happen', a pop-soul number with a gratingly bright singalong chorus that embraced the positive thinking that was such an important part of the group's motivational ethos. However, this was still early days and none of the songs they worked on or demoed at this stage were eventually used by the Spice Girls.

The girls would regularly work from early morning until late in the evening. While Geri's domain was the formulation of ideas, planning and overall group strategy, Melanie B quickly assumed the role of choreographer and chief taskmaster, bossing everyone about (especially Geri) in rehearsals, and generally making sure that everyone was keeping up to the mark.

"Their work ethic was really good," Chris Herbert recalled. "They were very hungry for it. They all had varying degrees of natural ability to sing and dance, and they all had strengths and weaknesses. Most of them hadn't even considered music as their career. They kind of stumbled across it. The process was to try and bring them all up to speed so that they were all at a similar level. That's really what that period was all about."

While most aspects were going according to plan, differences between Stephenson and the other four were quick to surface. While the others threw themselves into the project with a no-holds-barred approach, Stephenson kept her option of returning to university open. She maintained her Saturday job at Harrods. On a more fundamental level, she simply wasn't as hungry for success as the rest of them.

"I don't think Michelle had ever struggled for anything in her life," Melanie B said.

"She lacked the same intensity or enthusiasm to learn and at times it bordered on laziness," said Geri, who remembered working through her lunch break to master a particular dance step while Stephenson, who was no great shakes as a dancer either, went and lay outside in the sun. Indeed her fondness for sunbathing seemed to act as a focus for the negative reactions of all the other girls who nicknamed her the sun-worshipper.

And while Stephenson *was* a good singer, she had a more formal style – what Victoria called "cruise-ship operatic" – which grated against rather than complemented the voices of the other four.

This was no mere detail. Surprisingly little attention has been paid to the vocal style of the Spice Girls, but they evolved a way of arranging songs for five voices that was highly distinctive. Instead of writing a lead line for one of the voices and arranging the others in a supporting role as pop vocal groups have done since time immemorial, they maintained a strictly equal five-way split in the workload (and the glory). They didn't want any one person to emerge as the lead singer – not even in one song – so they would divide songs up into a line or two each, before blending the voices together for the chorus. To this day it can be hard to recall who was singing which precise bit of a Spice Girls song – a feature which was used as a stick to beat them with by many critics – but which was actually a clever device to ensure that they gained the maximum impact and mileage from their all-in-it-together girl-gang image. Even at this early stage, it was imperative that the sound of the five voices should be as intertwined as the fortunes of the girls themselves.

Melanie B gave Stephenson a pep talk, after which she began to make more of an effort. But it was too late. The other girls discussed the situation with Bob and Chris Herbert and they agreed that she wasn't right for the group.

"She just wasn't fitting in," Bob Herbert said. "She would never have gelled with it and we had to tell her to go."

At this point, the management's decision *not* to give the girls contracts or to offer them security of any sort would appear to have been vindicated. Herbert could send Stephenson on her way without any compensation, secure in the knowledge that she had no comeback, legally or in any other way. Stephenson has since maintained that she took the decision to leave of her own accord, because she felt it wasn't the right situation for her, and because she wanted to be close to her family at a time when her mother had just been diagnosed with cancer.

"It wasn't my kind of music and I had different plans for the future," she said.

After leaving the group, Stephenson travelled in Europe and then returned to Goldsmith's to complete her degree. She still harbours ambitions to be a singer and has talked of working on an album of her own. She has recorded backing vocals for singers such as Ricky Martin and Julio Iglesias. She has also been a reporter for Carlton TV's *Wired* series and a presenter on the LWT series *Wild Weekends*.

"I'm very happy with what I'm doing and don't regret a thing," she said much later. "People often ask me about the Spice Girls. I don't get fed up with it, but it was only six months of my life. There aren't any bad feelings. I never look back on things, you have to look forward."

However, she was less conciliatory after reading Victoria's version of events in her autobiography, *Learning To Fly*, published in 2001, in which she claimed that her former room-mate was sacked because she had "less rhythm than a cement mixer" and "just couldn't be arsed" to do the work needed to improve.

"Right from the start [Victoria] was very much the high and mighty one, sticking her nose in the air," Stephenson responded. "I can't pretend that I wasn't very hurt by the things she said about my singing and dancing. But to say that I was turfed out of the group, when I left because I wanted to be with my sick mother . . . well, what kind of person does that? She knows my mother had breast cancer."

Inevitably, you end up wondering if Stephenson would have worked harder both on a personal and a professional level to make things work if she had known what was at stake. Many years later, in 2002, Chris Herbert bumped into her in a restaurant in Richmond. Stephenson was working there as a waitress.

"She served me a drink and we started chatting," Herbert said. "She was fine. She said she'd got her own band together and wanted to come and see me to talk about managing them. That's the last time I spoke to her."

With Stephenson gone, the search for a replacement started with Pepe Lemer's recommendation of a singer she'd come across some years before called Abigail Kas. She auditioned for the Herberts and Murphy, but there were reservations on both sides. She became an aerobics teacher. Then Lemer remembered one of her former pupils from the Sylvia Young Theatre School – Emma Bunton. Chris Herbert went to audition her and had no hesitation in offering her a place in the group, subject to her getting on with the other girls. Emma arrived with her mother, Pauline, at Maidenhead station, in July 1994, where she was met by the four girls.

"Straight away I knew she was the one," Geri recalled. And so it turned out to be. Emma fitted into Stephenson's shoes perfectly in all departments, and clicked immediately on a more fundamental personal level. Geri thought of her as the younger sister she had never had while Melanie B became her soul sister, a friend with whom she could have long heart-to-heart talks deep into the night.

Work continued apace at Trinity Studios, and with everyone now pulling in the same direction, the momentum picked up dramatically. But despite constant badgering from the girls to quicken the pace of their promotional activities, the management seemed to be in no great hurry to bring the project to fruition. On many occasions the girls badgered Bob and Chris Herbert to give them a proper contract, but were always brushed off. This made the girls feel insecure, as it was supposed to do, but an unintended consequence was that it also made them more determined than ever to succeed on their own terms with or without Heart Management.

"We reassured each other a lot and constantly reaffirmed that we were 'in this for us' and nobody else was going to take control," Melanie B recalled.

As the weeks went by, the girls formed an emotional and spiritual bond that became far stronger than the pact of convenience that you might have expected from a manufactured group. Ric Blaxill who, as the producer of *Top Of The Pops*, was a man who had a lot of experience of working with "manufactured" groups, picked up on the difference between the girls and other groups straight away.

"You cannot manufacture what those girls had," Blaxill said. "I know there was a plot behind it, and I know someone had an ambition for creating this group. But they chose the right people."

Reading the constant stream of autobiographies by members of the Spice Girls – there have been four in recent years – you get a constant sense of déjà vu, not just because of the parallel accounts of the Spice years, which you would expect, but also from the extraordinary similarities in their backgrounds.

These go well beyond obvious factors such as their age and social class. They all endured difficult childhoods for one reason or another. Four out of the five come from broken homes, but all – apart from Geri perhaps – have enjoyed very strong, nurturing relationships with their mothers. All of them were bitten by the *Fame* bug at a very young age, and all – apart from Geri – managed to pester their parents into letting them take dance classes from an equally early age. Once on the road to the temple of the performing arts, these born exhibitionists all discovered an obsessive streak in their natures which fed on a burning sense of ambition. The constant craving for attention and the yearning to "get even" with the kids and grown-ups who had rejected them is a theme that runs through all their accounts.

"When I visualised fame," Geri wrote, "I wanted people to recognise my face and know my name. I wanted them to like me. Even more importantly, it was the best form of revenge, the ultimate way of saying, 'I told you so,' to all the boyfriends who'd dumped me, the bosses who wouldn't employ me, the directors who hadn't cast me and the agencies who didn't sign me."

While the girls all liked music and dancing, they saw the business of making music as simply one means of achieving their goal of being loved and recognised and being able to give the finger to anyone who had ever put them down.

But they weren't afraid of working hard to get it. And with Emma on board the girls started to become rather good at what they did. Once again, the management was lagging behind the beat and it was the girls who made the running. Fed up with the meagre material with which they had been supplied so far, and rather taken aback at the lack of positive, or indeed any, outside feedback, they lobbied Chris and Bob Herbert to organise a showcase for them. The principal object of the exercise was to attract songwriters who might provide the group with better material.

"We haven't really got any decent songs," Mel B said at the time. "We haven't really got anything to work on."

Additionally, they wanted to set out their stall for the music business in general, so that they could gauge the reaction of publishers, record company people and so forth.

"I was confident that we would be able to get a team together of writers and producers," Chris Herbert said.

A showcase day was fixed in December 1994 in Nomis Studios, Shepherds Bush, scene of the original auditions to get the group together. The girls performed their "set" several times during the day to an audience of producers, writers and record company A&R men. The response was overwhelmingly positive, so much so that the Herberts were somewhat taken aback. Within days, the girls had the management contracts they had been agitating to get for so long. But they also had a gathering sense of their own worth.

Among the guests who had been invited to the showcase was Richard "Biff" Stannard who, along with his songwriting partner Matt Rowe had been a co-writer of hits by East 17. On the strength of what Stannard saw there, the team agreed to start working with the girls on new material. Over the course of the next couple of months, they began working with Stannard and Rowe at their London studio, The Strong Room, in Curtain Road. It was during one of these sessions that they wrote a song called 'Wannabe'.

"It was all looking good," Herbert recalled. The sound was coming together, the songs were coming together, and in the background, the business was going on where Bob and the girls were talking about the contracts.

Ah yes, those pesky contracts. The girls' earlier enthusiasm for getting their relationship with Heart Management on to a legally binding footing had been replaced by a mysterious hesitance to sign on the dotted line. They took the contracts to their parents to look at. "Forget it," was Tony Adams's advice, presumably drawing on his experience of management deals from when he was singing in bands in the Sixties. Then they sought independent legal advice and spent several weeks with various lawyers, tinkering with one clause after another. But the truth was that since the day of the showcase, the balance of power had shifted irrevocably, a fact which it took the management team with all its years of shared experience and financial clout longer to realise than five girls who less than a year before were just hopeful faces at a crowded audition.

"All sorts of yarns were being spun," Chris Herbert said, "and we kind of went along with that. I think Bob was more acute to it than I was."

Finally in March 1995, the crunch came. By then, the girls had taken the decision to part company with Heart Management. But rather than precipitate a face-to-face showdown, they pulled off a daring and carefully orchestrated bunk. Geri and the two Mels went to the management offices and, by means that remain unclear to this day, managed to retrieve the master recordings of their songs – another lapse on the part of the management, who thus relinquished the only potential bargaining chip they had. Victoria and Emma, meanwhile, went to Trinity Studios to collect various odds and ends belonging to the group. They met up at a roundabout outside Maidenhead and took off.

Their departure came like a bolt out of the blue to Chris Herbert.

"In hindsight, I can probably spot some of the signs. But it was a huge surprise to me when it happened. You couldn't really feel a rising tension before it happened. It was quite odd really."

In hindsight a lot of things look clearer than they did at the time.

But the relaxed attitude of the Herberts and Murphy – who clearly regarded the girls' reliance on their money and management expertise as a given – only serves to underline what a breathtakingly bold and ballsy step they had taken. Who would have predicted, under the circumstances, that these five novices would have had the first idea of how to find and negotiate a better management deal than the one to which they owed their very existence as a group?

It was surely bad enough that they had given up their rent-free house, their access to free rehearsal space and their weekly wage. But they had no way of knowing what leverage the Herberts might have been able to exert if they had so chosen. What if Bob and Chris put pressure on the outside songwriters, such as Stannard and Rowe, not to carry on working with the girls? It was a courageous step to take.

It was also incredibly self-serving and underhand. The Herberts and Murphy had subsidised their existence, paid for voice coaching and provided accommodation for nine months. And on a personal level, Chris Herbert had devoted a substantial chunk of his life for more than nine months, during which he had become intimately entwined in the development of the group. But notions of trust and loyalty, let alone deference, simply didn't come into the equation. This wasn't so much a case of biting the hand that fed them as a full-scale amputation.

"At the time you mourn," Herbert said. "Because you're left with a void. And then seeing them go on to have success . . . at the time, yes, you feel a bit raw about it. It was very underhand. And that's the bit that's hurtful really. Because day in, day out we all spent so much time together. We were of similar ages and I think it could have been dealt with better. But we were all young . . ."

Herbert is older and wiser now, and can see where he went wrong. He has also maintained a remarkably philosophical view of the way events unfolded.

"We had put in a lot of effort and I can walk away feeling proud that I was involved in it and that I came up with an idea that worked so incredibly well," he said many years later.

"I couldn't honestly, hand on my heart, say that I could have taken them to the success that they had with Simon Fuller, not at that age. It was a big stepping stone in my career. I was a first-time manager. I think I had some great ideas and since then I've learnt how to follow those through and make the successes of them that they deserve. It was definitely a business lesson for me."

History has obviously vindicated the group's decision, and if the Spice Girls ever felt even the slightest twinge of a guilty conscience over grabbing everything that was on offer and then scarpering, they have managed to conceal it.

"Any time I feel sorry for Chris and Bob and Chic having missed out on the pop phenomenon of the Nineties," Victoria said, "I have to remind myself that if they'd had their way we'd all be dressed the same, and one of us would have been the lead singer. The Spice Girls were so huge precisely because we didn't do any of that."

"I didn't feel guilty about leaving Bob and Chris. We were just going in different directions," was the sum total of Melanie B's public musings on the matter.

Later, after the Girls had signed with Simon Fuller, they came to a settlement with the Herberts and Murphy, paying them a lump sum which included all the money that had been spent on them plus a substantial amount on top. As a ballpark figure, Bob Herbert had estimated that by the day of the showcase in December 1994, the project had cost Heart Management somewhere in the region of £20,000, and he was expecting to fork out roughly the same amount again to get them to the stage of signing a recording contract. But even if the Girls paid them five times that amount, it would still have been peanuts compared to the payday the Herberts and Murphy could have looked forward to if they had retained their management stake in the group. They may not have been left out of pocket, but it was nevertheless a salutary experience for the three men at the heart of Heart Management.

Murphy has since retired from management and now lives "abroad". Chris Herbert, who still speaks to him from time to time, laughs off the suggestion that the experience with the Spice Girls had anything to do with his decision to quit. "He has various other lines of business, I'm sure. His world didn't fall apart after the Spice Girls," Herbert said. "I think he was probably playing at it a bit with the Spice Girls."

Bob Herbert died in a car crash on August 9, 1999. The obituarists, not surprisingly, characterised him as "the unluckiest man in pop", the manager who "moulded and guided the two biggest pop bands of the Eighties and Nineties – Bros and the Spice Girls," only to see both groups leave him just as they were about to achieve stardom.

Chris Herbert went on to achieve significant success managing the boy band Five, which he auditioned and assembled during 1997 in exactly the same way as he did the Spice Girls – with one crucial difference. They were issued with formally binding contracts at a very early stage of their development.

Conceived as a harder-edged, British version of The Backstreet Boys, Five enjoyed a string of hit singles including 'When The Lights Go Out', 'Keep On Movin'' and a revival of the old stadium anthem, 'We Will Rock You', which they performed with the surviving members of Queen (who wrote it). By the time they split up at the end of 2001 they had sold seven million albums, including one million in America. A substantial success by most standards, but still small beer compared to the achievements of the Spice Girls.

In a somewhat fitting completion of the circle, Herbert's other managerial success in later years, albeit a brief one, was with Hear'say, the group which emerged from the TV talent show *Popstars*. Here again, it turned out that Herbert's idea of making and marketing the "perfect" group had provided an eerily accurate signpost for the future direction of pop. For as well as everything else, he had also set about documenting the process of putting the Spice Girls together on film, thereby producing, in effect, a forerunner of the reality TV shows which would later become such a ubiquitous and highly profitable phenomenon.

"The idea was to capture the whole process [of auditioning and developing the group] from start to finish, which hadn't been done before," Herbert said.

Unfortunately, because the girls flew the coop, the story was never completed in quite the way he had hoped. But a documentary, *Raw Spice*, featuring extensive footage shot by the late Matthew Bowers and Neil Davies in and around the house in Maidenhead and during rehearsals at Trinity Studios, did eventually surface. It was first screened on Granada TV on March 21, 2001 and became available on VHS soon afterwards, with some additional performance footage. With its grainy visuals and duff sound, it was nothing like as slick or well-organised as subsequent shows such as *Popstars: The Rivals*. But all the key elements were there – right down to the early "voting out" of Michelle Stephenson – providing a fascinating and at times voyeuristic insight into the making of a pop group.

Not bad going then for a 23-year-old kid with hardly any management experience, and if it was possible to patent an idea, Herbert would be an even richer man than he already is. Indeed there was a supreme irony in the fact that when he was managing Hear'say, the group was required to pay a percentage of their royalties to Screentime, the

Australian company which owned the *Popstars* TV format. Thus Herbert was in effect paying somebody else for the use of an idea which he had thought up himself all those years before with the Spice Girls.

So it was Chris Herbert, perhaps more than any other individual in the Nineties, who was responsible for opening the Pandora's box from which emerged the subsequent swarm of manufactured pop groups and reality TV shows which both sparked and fed off the mass-marketed cult of celebrity worship. A clever and successful man, if not a notably deep thinker, Herbert was mildly baffled when I asked him if he thought the changes that he had been in large part responsible for introducing had been good for the industry in the long run.

"Uhmmmmmmmmm... Yes. No. I think, uh, yeah... I do. I think it was very, very healthy for pop music for a period of time. All trends go in cycles and we've moved away from that trend in pop music. But for a period it sustained... a period, sort of thing."

If Herbert's experience with Hear'say was anything to go by, one effect of the boom in manufactured groups was to accelerate the life cycle of a pop act in the 21st century to the point where it resembled the fleeting existence of a butterfly. The members of Hear'say, who had been hand-picked in front of the cameras from a starting total of 3,000 applicants, became instant national celebrities as a huge TV audience shared the agony and ecstasy of the audition process over a period of months. Thus, when the group's debut single, 'Pure And Simple', was released in March 2001, it became the fastest-selling record in Britain of all time. Their album, *Popstars*, released the following month, outsold The Beatles compilation *1* – for a while. In a clear echo of the merchandising initiatives of the Spice Girls before them, a range of Hear'say dolls were put on the market.

And then as fast as it began, it was over. A second album, *Everybody*, released in December the same year, climbed no higher than number 24 in the chart. By October 2002, the band had formally split up. Without the TV series what other reason was there for them to continue? Their appeal certainly had nothing to do with music. Even a year later it was beyond most people's ability to remember with any great clarity who Hear'say even were.

Herbert pressed on, in his unshakeably upbeat way, managing the solo careers of Abs (Richard Breen) from Five and Kym Marsh from Hear'say, while knocking together another numerically named boy band called Triple Eight. According to their record company, they were going to "break the mould with their raw, edgy, energised, tough, punchy pop" when they released their debut single, 'Knockout', in April 2003.

"If you look back in history," Herbert said, "there have always been boy bands and girl bands, and there always will be. They take various forms, but whether it's The Supremes or The Monkees, it doesn't matter. Provided it's different enough or it shakes things up enough then it's worth doing."

He might also have mentioned that to really make it worth doing, you've also got to get hold of some memorable songs.

# 3

# You Hum It, We'll Play It

The received wisdom that the Spice Girls never *really* wrote any of their songs is almost as firmly ingrained in the popular imagination as the idea that they can't sing. They always took a co-writing credit on their songs but that is widely presumed to be part of the deal that would have been brokered with professional songwriters as a quid pro quo for getting their work on to a potential hit album. In other words, if the performer or the manager or both have sufficient clout, then the real songwriters will be prepared to hand over a proportion of their royalties to the artist in order to get *their* song, as opposed to somebody else's, included on the artist's album. This is certainly a practice which has been known to happen with increasing frequency in recent times. But the truth about the Spice Girls is rather different.

The credits on the first two Spice Girls albums, *Spice* and *Spiceworld*, reveal three key players in the writing and production department: Elliot Kennedy, a songwriter from Sheffield who had co-written 'Everything Changes' a number one hit for Take That in 1994; the novice writing and production duo Paul Wilson and Andy Watkins, better known as Absolute; and Richard "Biff" Stannard and Matt Rowe, a songwriting and production partnership best known at the time for their collaborations with East 17.

The first of these to cross paths with the girls, and the most important in shaping their sound were Stannard and Rowe. Stannard found himself in Nomis Studios on the day of the Spice showcase in December 1994, although he was actually there to meet faded Eighties pop star Jason Donovan, not to see Bob and Chris Herbert's new group. As he emerged from the room with Donovan, he saw Melanie B, and more to the point *heard* her, as she went charging across the corridor and into another room.

"I thought, 'Oh my God! She's mad. I want to find out about her,'"

Stannard recalled. And so it was that he found himself in the Spice showcase.

"More than anything they just made me laugh," he said. "I couldn't believe I'd walked into this situation. You didn't care if they were in time with the dance steps or whether one was overweight or one wasn't as good as the others. It was something more. It just made you feel happy. Like great pop records."

Stannard hung around until long after everyone else had left the showcase, chatting with the girls about "this, that and everything".

"I fell in love with them on the spot, like everybody did," he said.

Stannard reported back to his songwriting partner Rowe, that he had found the pop group of their dreams. As it happened, Stannard and Rowe were working at the time with another of the Herberts' acts, a singer called Maria Rowe, for whom they had produced a record called 'Sexual'. So they had already been aware from earlier conversations with Chris Herbert that he was developing a girl group. A date was duly slotted into their diary – via Herbert – and in January 1995 the girls arrived for their first "professional" songwriting session at The Strongroom in Curtain Road, East London.

Rowe remembered feeling much the same as Stannard the first time he met them.

"I loved them. Immediately. The studio was pretty small, and they all sat on one chair on each other's laps in a line. I don't know how they managed it. And they all fired off questions, asking how we worked and telling us what they wanted. They were like no one I'd met before, really."

Stannard and Rowe were, on the face of it, something of an odd partnership. Stannard, who was originally from East London, left school young, and became a dancer and stylist working mostly in videos. Although he had written songs continuously from the age of 12, his professional enthusiasm stemmed from the visual and fashion elements of pop as much as it did from the musical side of the creative process. His cartoon alias, Biff, became the semi-detached "fourth member" of a put-together boy trio called 2wo Third3, who were managed by Tom Watkins (the man who took Bros off the Herberts' hands).

Rowe, who was born Matthew Rowebottom in Middlesex, attended the Chester Cathedral Choir School, where he was formally trained and encouraged to sing and play piano and clarinet. When he was

18 he moved to London where he blagged a job making tea in a recording studio. Having worked on dance projects in the early Nineties, he started collaborating with Stannard on the 2wo Third3 operation.

Stannard and Rowe's initial break as a partnership came when they co-wrote and produced several songs with East 17 on their 1994 album, *Steam*, including the title track which was a number seven hit, 'Around The World' (a number three hit) and 'Hold My Body Tight', which reached number 12 in January 1995, the month they began writing with the Spice Girls.

The first song the girls wrote with Stannard and Rowe was called 'Feed Your Love', a slow, sensual, soulful number which was eventually recorded and mastered for the *Spice* album, but not used because it was considered "too rude" for their target audience. Having completed that one, the girls were in the mood to write something a bit more raucous and uptempo.

Rowe set up a drum loop on his MPC 3000 drum machine, which was quite fast but also had something of a strutting quality about it. For Stannard, the rhythm brought to mind the spirit of John Travolta and Olivia Newton-John performing 'You're The One That I Want' in *Grease*.

"Whenever I try and write songs for bands that have never had hit records before, I always try and imagine them walking in the video. As if they're walking and there's an arrogance. 'Here we are. We've arrived!' And I was thinking of John Travolta and that kind of rhythm and the way he used his body."

Next thing, the girls were all throwing their own contributions into the mix.

"They made all these different bits up," Rowe said. "Not thinking in terms of verse, chorus, bridge or what was going to go where, just coming up with all these sections of chanting and rapping and singing, which we recorded all higgledy-piggledy. And then we just sewed it together. It was rather like the way we'd been working on the dance remixes we'd been doing before. Kind of a cut-and-paste method."

'Wannabe' was completed – in more or less the shape that it appears on the record – by the second or third day of writing with Stannard and Rowe. Now on something of a roll they next wrote '2 Become 1', a song inspired by the "special" relationship which was developing between Geri and Rowe. This was a development which Melanie B hinted at in her autobiography.

"When Matt and Geri started making eyes at each other I knew what was going on, even though they denied it. I knew them both too well for it to be a secret from me."

Stannard also remembered the fondness that existed between the two. Asked if they had been lovers, he insisted that it was not his position to say.

"I don't want to get into that side of things. They were close. They clicked. And I think the lyrics in '2 Become 1' came from that, especially the first verse, which they wrote together."

A romantic ballad, which was destined to become the Spice Girls' third number one single, '2 Become 1' was a more melodically adept, mainstream number that added another string to their songwriting bow. As well as the obvious sexual connotations there was an aspirational undercurrent to the lyric and, as with so many of their subsequent songs, desire was explicitly linked to ambition: "Free your mind of doubt and danger/ Be for real don't be a stranger/ We can achieve it/ We can achieve it."

But in essence, '2 Become 1' was a makeout song. "Come a little bit closer baby/ [Get it on, Get it on]/ 'Cause tonight is the night when two become one."

Rowe himself remains coy about his relationship with Geri.

"We kind of flirted a little bit," he said.

Nothing more than that?

"No. We were all very close. That was the thing that I think was a big part of the music being so successful. It was done with a lot of love. We really loved them. I think they loved us as well. It wasn't really a financial exercise. It was a labour of love."

It remains a matter of speculation to what degree their songwriting sessions with Stannard and Rowe contributed to the girls' decision to split with the Herberts. Obviously the fact that the girls were now working with songwriters with a proven track record who had enabled them to come up with songs of this calibre, gave them a fantastic injection of confidence. But there was a social dimension to the relationship as well. Stannard, Rowe and Stannard's partner Sean Doyle, quickly got to know the girls really well.

"Right from Day One we would go out every night, back to Matt's flat or our flat and just hang out and get pissed," Stannard said. "We'd eat and write songs and play music for a long time during that period."

Stannard and Rowe were represented at that time by a manager called Ian Clifford, with whom they had been unhappy for a while (and indeed they split from him soon after 'Wannabe' was released). And before that Stannard had been managed by Tom Watkins. So the duo knew a lot more about the business side of the pop world than did the girls, who increasingly sought their advice in such matters.

"If they had a lack of knowledge about something they'd absolutely suck everyone they knew and loved dry to find out about it," Stannard said. "Geri was unbelievable at that, picking your brains, but in a charming, amazing way. In a way that made you think: 'God, you're just so keen and hungry for it that I'll tell you whatever you want to know.'"

Although Stannard and Rowe no longer work together as a partnership, they both continue to enjoy good working relationships with Chris Herbert, which is why neither of them would be drawn on the precise advice they gave to the girls on the matter of the management contracts that the Herberts had offered them. But it seems safe to assume that, at the very least, they supported, if not actively encouraged, the girls' decision to fly the coop.

"I remember them ringing me and Matt and saying, 'Are we making the right decision?'" said Stannard. His answer? "Yeah!"

It was a Friday towards the end of March 1995, when the girls fled the house in Maidenhead. On the following Monday they were due to be in Sheffield for their first songwriting session with Elliot Kennedy which had been arranged some weeks before by Chris Herbert. But without access to Herbert's address book, they knew nothing of Kennedy's whereabouts other than that he lived in Sheffield. Calling on the spectacular sense of mission and abandon that now seemed to inform their every move, Melanie B and Geri simply drove up to Sheffield and looked in the first phone book they came across. Elliot was the third Kennedy that they called. The other three travelled to Sheffield by train the next day.

"They didn't have anywhere to stay so I had to put them up," Kennedy said. "So I was 100 per cent immersed in Spiceworld straight away really. It was full on."

The first awkward situation which Kennedy had to negotiate was a phone call at eight o'clock on Monday morning from Bob Herbert.

"We've got a problem," Herbert told Kennedy. "Four out of the five girls have come down with flu and I don't think they're going to make the session today."

"Do you know what, Bob? They're here," Kennedy replied. "And I may as well work with them."

Kennedy was born in Sheffield, spent his childhood in Australia, and returned to Sheffield at secondary school age. He worked as a guitarist and singer in Spain for a while, then returned and began working as a studio engineer. His first success as a producer was on a comeback single by Lulu called 'Independence', which charted at number 11 in 1993. The record attracted the attention of Nigel Martin Smith, manager of Take That, who put Kennedy together with Gary Barlow. 'Everything Changes', which Kennedy wrote with Barlow was a number one hit for Take That in April 1994.

Like Stannard and Rowe, Kennedy had been in discussions with Chris Herbert about co-writing with Maria Rowe (whose Stannard and Rowe-produced single, 'Sexual', eventually peaked at number 67 in May 1995). But Kennedy was keener to work with the all-girl group which Herbert had also told him about, called Spice. So when Bob Herbert solemnly informed him during that "awkward" Monday morning telephone conversation that if he worked with the girls he couldn't work with Maria Rowe, it did not constitute much in the way of leverage.

"Are you threatening me?" Kennedy asked him. Herbert told Kennedy that if he worked with the girls under these circumstances he would be compromising the Herberts' ability as management. But not only had Herbert underestimated the girls' drive and ambition, he had also reckoned without their powers of persuasion.

"They had actually gone out and drawn all the cash that they could to pay for the studio," Kennedy recalled. "They were so dedicated and wanting me to work with them. I was so touched by it. They knew all about me, the records I'd had out. They were so into the idea."

Kennedy told Herbert that he was going to work with the girls and that if he had a problem with that to take it up with his (Kennedy's) management.

That first day they wrote 'Love Thing' which ended up on the *Spice* album. Kennedy remembered the process as being remarkably quick and fresh.

"None of them played instruments, so I was left to do the music and get that vibe together. What I said to them was, 'Look, I've got a chorus – check this out.' And I'd sing them the chorus and the melody – no lyrics or anything – and straight away five pads and pencils came out and they were throwing lines at us. Ten minutes later, the song was written. Then you go through and refine it. Then later, as you were recording it you might change a few things here and there. But pretty much it was a real quick process. They were confident in what they were doing, throwing it out there."

If there was ever a moment when the future of the girls looked uncertain this was surely it. With no management, no money and no track record they were out on their own winging it, and yet were still able to win over Kennedy.

"There was no reason why I should do it," Kennedy said. "If anything, there was every reason why I shouldn't do it. It was complicated. Were they going to be in some kind of legal situation? The chances of it coming out were pretty slim. They'd got nowhere to live."

The girls stayed with Kennedy, at his house, for the best part of a week, establishing a pattern for subsequent visits and laying the foundation of a working relationship which quickly became part of a deeper social and emotional bonding process. Once again, it was Geri who made the strongest impression.

"We actually ended up becoming quite close friends, Geri and I," Kennedy said. "When they were staying, all the girls would go to bed at quite a reasonable time, and Geri was a bit like me – a bit nocturnal. So I would either be finishing off on the demo or whatever we'd been doing that day, or sitting and watching TV, and Geri would be sitting there and we'd end up having quite a deep conversation. She's quite a philosophical person, Geri, when you get to it, and we got to know each other on quite a cool level really."

The following month, May 1995, the Girls were introduced to Paul Wilson and Andy Watkins, the songwriting and production duo otherwise known as Absolute, and the final part of the creative jigsaw fell into place. Watkins was brought up in the Forest of Dean where he joined a garage band in his teens and thrashed about on guitar playing covers of Sex Pistols and Clash songs. Wilson, meanwhile, was growing up in Bognor Regis from where he was sent to be a classically trained musician at the Royal Academy of Music. While honing his knowledge of musical theory he also played drums in a heavy metal band.

Watkins and Wilson met when they found themselves living together in the halls of residence at Bristol Polytechnic. They both went on to study for degrees in Food Science and Biology at Oxford Polytechnic. Having discovered a shared passion for black music and culture, they joined the Oxford Poly Afro-Caribbean Society, a curious affiliation for two otherwise very ordinary white kids of English suburban stock. Moving to Bath, they successfully applied for a government Enterprise Allowance Scheme which enabled them to start their own studio. The set-up was basically a Portastudio in a bedroom from where, calling themselves the Bristol Bass Line, they started putting out their own records and doing dance remixes.

Through their remixing work they acquired a manager, Pete Evans, who signed them to his company Native Management. As his business increased, Evans formed an association with one Simon Fuller, and Native became affiliated to Fuller's 19 Management company, an arrangement which remains in effect to the present.

Thus it was that, long before he had heard of the Spice Girls, Fuller met up with Watkins and Wilson, now known as Absolute. Having listened to their demos, Fuller declared that in his opinion they should give up the remixing and concentrate on songwriting. To this end, Fuller gave them an advance and brokered a publishing deal for them with BMG, where they met Mark Fox.

Fox, who used to play percussion and was latterly the singer in Eighties new wave pop combo Haircut 100, had since moved into publishing, and was another of the industry movers and shakers who had been present at the Spice showcase at Nomis. Since then he had been unofficially helping the girls to make contacts in the business, and obviously thought he could kill two birds with one stone by pairing them up with his own publishing company's latest signing. Fox phoned Watkins and Wilson.

"What do you want to do?" he asked them. "What do you want to write?"

"We're heavily into black music," Wilson told him. "We'd really like to develop a black act like SWV [Sisters With Voices] or something similar."

"You won't believe it," Fox told him, "but I've got your act. They've just walked in the door. They're beautiful, everything you've been looking for. I'll bring them down straight away."

At this time Absolute's studio was based on Taggs Island on the Thames situated next to the waterworks in Hampton near Chertsey. The building, which was basically "a shed with some equipment in it", according to Wilson, could only be accessed via a footbridge. So Watkins and Wilson were sitting in their studio mixing a cool soul track by Omar or Mica Paris and looking out over the bridge when the new act Fox had promised to bring over arrived.

"I saw Mark Fox," Watkins recalled. "And then I saw these little girls skipping and running around. And they looked about thirteen. This can't be them. No way!"

A knock on the door and they all piled in.

"We were expecting five black, Amazonian beauties and we got the cast of Grange Hill," Wilson said.

Nevertheless, the girls managed to impress Wilson and Watkins. Once again they'd done their homework and although Absolute had yet to have any significant success as a production/songwriting team the girls knew enough about them to indicate their respect and that they meant business.

"They knew their music," Wilson said. "Mel B was totally into rap and R&B. Geri was more into clubbing."

"They played us a few tracks [of their own] which we didn't particularly like," Watkins said. "But they played us a lot of other stuff that was actually rather dark and cool, particularly a track called 'Feed Your Love'.* So we thought, 'This is OK. We can work with this.'"

A songwriting session was booked within the next few days. But to begin with the musical association just didn't seem to gel.

Wilson: "When they started to sing it was never quite right from our point of view. It was always very poptastic. We'd play them tracks we thought they'd like – like [American soul diva] Adina Howard – and we'd say, 'Shall we do something like this?' And they'd say, 'Yes. We really want to do this.' But it just would not come out."

Watkins: "After two sessions we phoned up our managers and said, 'This just ain't happening.'"

It was at this point that Watkins and Wilson heard 'Wannabe' for the first time, which only served to confirm their misgivings.

"We listened to it," said Wilson, "and we didn't get it at all. It was so different to what we were doing. We thought, 'How's this gonna work? We're not the right people to be doing this band.'"

At the next session it was make or break.

---

* The song written with Stannard and Rowe that was eventually considered "too rude" to be included on *Spice*.

"Every previous time we'd met up with the girls we had prepared a backing track," said Wilson. "This time we had nothing. They came in. We had a completely empty computer. Empty screen."

Watkins: "They said they wanted to do something up and a bit of fun, so we just off the top of our heads started to come up with a full-on disco backing track which became 'Who Do You Think You Are'."

Wilson: "The thing is when they wrote they were also writing the dance routine, constructing the video, all at the same time as writing the song. And that's when the penny dropped."

Watkins: "They did what they did. They knew what they wanted to write about, right from Day One. You couldn't force your musical ideas upon them. If they didn't want to say it or sing it they wouldn't. We had no control over what they did, or what they wanted to say. We just hemmed it in and tried to make songs out of it, that's what we did."

Wilson: "They say that the mother of invention is copying somebody and getting it wrong. Their sound was actually not getting R&B quite right."

The girls went on to write 'Something Kinda Funny', 'Last Time Lover' and 'Naked' with Watkins and Wilson, none of them singles, but all of them tracks which lent a touch of classy, R&B bottom to the *Spice* album. Absolute also produced all of these as well as the two tracks penned with Elliot Kennedy – 'Say You'll Be There' and 'Love Thing' – giving the duo a guiding hand in seven of the ten tracks that eventually ended up on *Spice*.

Over the course of making the album, Watkins and Wilson developed a keen awareness of the girls' abilities as writers and musicians.

"They would know how to construct a harmony," Wilson said. "Mel C would usually do it. But they'd fall into the usual trap of just singing the main melody above it. But they would sort that out quickly."

Watkins: "None of them are musicians. I'd say none of them are God-given singers either. But the thing about all of them at that point was that they worked so incredibly hard at it. They knew their shortcomings. And the drive – it was unreal. When you look back, comparing it to what we've seen subsequently from other bands, there's nobody who we've worked with who's come close to that amount of hunger for it."

The tracks that Absolute produced were recorded for the most part at Olympic Studios in Barnes. At this time in 1995, the Autotune facility had yet to come on the market and most of the vocals were recorded with few adjustments made afterwards.

Wilson: "Because of the fact we were not using computers, we had to work them very hard. They were in that recording booth for hours because we just had to get the right take. There was no autotuning, so we worked them like dogs."

Watkins: "And with five different characters you had to take a different approach to getting the best vocal out of each of them. Someone like Mel C, who was just desperate to do it, you could really push her. But Geri who was more insecure, you had to carry her through it."

The way in which songs are written, and the conventions by which authorship of a song is credited has changed out of all recognition from the days when modern pop began. In the Fifties singing and songwriting were two clearly separated activities. Elvis Presley, still the biggest star in the history of planet pop, received a co-writing credit on less than a dozen of the many hundreds of songs he recorded. In those days, with some notable exceptions such as Buddy Holly, the performer was rarely involved in the creative process beforehand. Instead, songwriting was a task carried out by professional individuals, or teams such as those who worked in New York's famed Brill Building or the Motown stalwarts Holland/Dozier/Holland, whose job it was to keep the stars of the day supplied with a steady stream of tailor-made, completed songs.

The Beatles changed all that, just as they changed everything else in pop. John Lennon and Paul McCartney had always nurtured ambitions to be songwriters and after recording a couple of albums comprised mainly of other people's songs, they took to recording their own material almost exclusively. Mick Jagger and Keith Richards quickly followed suit on behalf of The Rolling Stones and a new template was devised whereby artists who wanted to be taken seriously were henceforth expected to write the great majority of their songs themselves.

It is hard to identify the point at which pop artists began to collaborate with professional songwriters and producers in a more integrated way. George Martin was often referred to as the fifth Beatle in recognition of his long-term contribution to the group's sound through his work as a producer and song arranger. And the notion of certain individuals combining songwriting and production skills stretches back to the days when Phil Spector and Burt Bacharach created the role of the star producer/writer.

However, Paul Wilson regards Absolute as operating in a tradition that goes back to Terry Britten who worked with Tina Turner on her 1984 album, *Private Dancer*. Britten wrote, played on and produced several of the tracks on that album which enabled Turner to reinvent herself at a particularly crucial point in her career, and he carried on working with her on subsequent recordings as an ongoing part of her creative team.

"Before *Private Dancer* it was unusual for a producer to write the song he was going to produce, and indeed it was unusual for a songwriter to produce his own song," Wilson said. "Terry Britten changed this whole scenario."

Even so, Turner did not contribute to the actual songwriting herself. Nor did pop acts such as Kylie Minogue, Jason Donovan and Rick Astley who enjoyed a succession of hits in the Eighties under the guidance of the Stock, Aitken & Waterman team of producer/writers.

The situation changed somewhat in the Nineties with the emergence of Take That and East 17, both of whom had members – Gary Barlow and Tony Mortimer respectively – who were talented songwriters but who nevertheless collaborated with outside writers on an ad hoc basis. Mortimer, who wrote many of East 17's hits single-handed, worked with Stannard and Rowe among others on the album *Steam*, while Barlow imported outside assistance on several occasions, notably for Take That's 1995 number one hit 'Everything Changes' which he co-wrote with Elliot Kennedy, Cary Baylis and Mike Ward.

But it was the Spice Girls who introduced two key innovations that have had a lasting impact on the way in which modern pop acts go about their creative business. Firstly, they introduced the idea of the group songwriting identity. This was a familiar enough concept at the rock end of the spectrum, where bands ranging from Queen to The Sex Pistols had adopted a policy of splitting the songwriting credits four ways in recognition of the members' equal contribution to the creative process as a whole. But not in the world of "manufactured" pop, where the credits for songwriting would be parcelled out strictly in accordance with whoever had written a given song, a list which rarely included the names of the artist or artists themselves.

What the Spice Girls recognised was that their solidarity as a group depended on maintaining parity in all departments, including that of songwriting credits and the resulting royalties. The deal between themselves was a strict five-way split on their share of the songwriting royalties *on all songs* irrespective of what any one member of the group had (or had not) contributed to any particular song. Apart from ease of administration, this was also a symbolic expression of the unity which was so much part and parcel of the Spice philosophy.

As Paul Wilson put it: "On the first album not all the girls contributed to all the songs on an equal level. It was usually down to illness or something like that. And on the second album, when things got a lot more hectic, one of the girls might not even be present for the writing of a song. But they would still get an equal split of the songwriting royalties. If they'd sat down and gone, 'Oooh no, I wrote three words in the second verse and your words were crap and anyway we changed them later, blah blah, blah,' it would have destroyed them."

Matt Rowe believed that the five-way split was a fair reflection of the effort that the girls put in.

"I can attribute great moments on all those records to each one of them. I remember Mel B coming up with the 'Mama' concept. And I remember Geri coming up with the lyrics for 'Viva Forever'. She was very good with lyrics."

The second thing the Spice Girls established from the outset was a straight 50-50 split between them and their various songwriting collaborators. And here they undoubtedly anticipated one of the key developments in the pop industry since the Nineties, namely the increasing importance of publishing royalties (i.e. copyright payments made for writing and owning the song) as opposed to royalty payments made for the performance of the song on the record (a percentage of the money accrued from each record sold).

This was an issue that had assumed critical importance from around 2003 onwards, when revenue from sales of CDs was in steep decline, thanks to file-sharing and illegal duplicating among other reasons, and yet the performance of music (which contributes to publishing revenues) was increasing thanks to all the different broadcasting and other outlets that were becoming available. But even when the Spice Girls were getting started, it was plain to see that the pop acts of the past who had been cut out of the songwriting process, for whatever reason, had earned significantly less – and earned it over a much shorter period of time – than those who had received a steady flow of publishing royalties.

The Spice Girls in early 1996, just before they unleashed themselves on the world with 'Wannabe'. Top row, left to right, Melanie B, Emma, Melanie C; below: Geri, Victoria. *(Guy Aroch/Retna)*

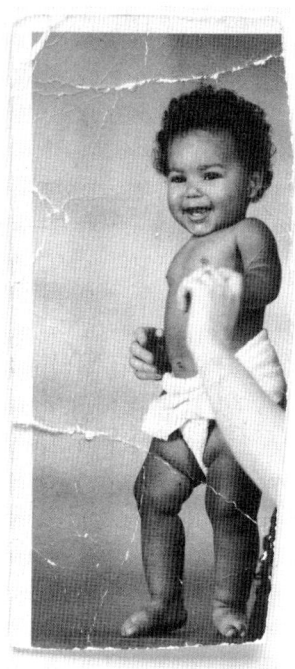

Melanie Janine Brown, the first photo.
*(Courtesy of 45 Management)*

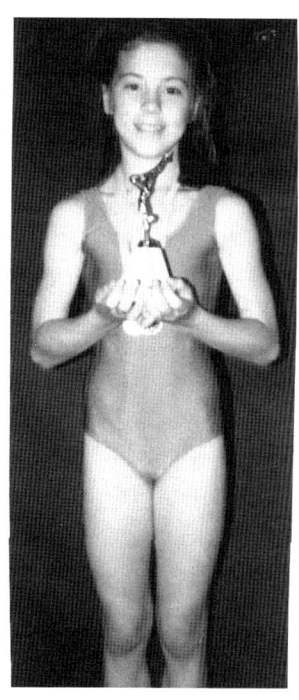

Melanie Jayne Chisholm, sports crazy from an early age, seen here with a swimming award.
*(Courtesy of 45 Management)*

Victoria Caroline Adams, aged around 18 months, evidently delighted at having her photograph taken.
*(Retna Ltd)*

Geraldine Estelle Halliwell, at nursery school. Born and brought up in Watford, she attended the Walter de Merton Junior school followed by Watford Girls' Grammar School where she joined the drama club. By then she already knew she wanted to be famous.
*(Retna Ltd)*

Emma Lee Bunton, aged about five, models a giant straw hat. She won a beauty contest and started ballet classes when she was three and had enrolled in disco and tap classes at the Kay School of Dance in Finchley by the age of five.
*(Retna Ltd)*

Melanie B, aged about three. As a child she was hyperactive. "Literally I could not sit still. It's one of the reasons my Mum sent me to dancing classes. I didn't want to miss out on anything. I was a whirlwind."
*(Courtesy of 45 Management)*

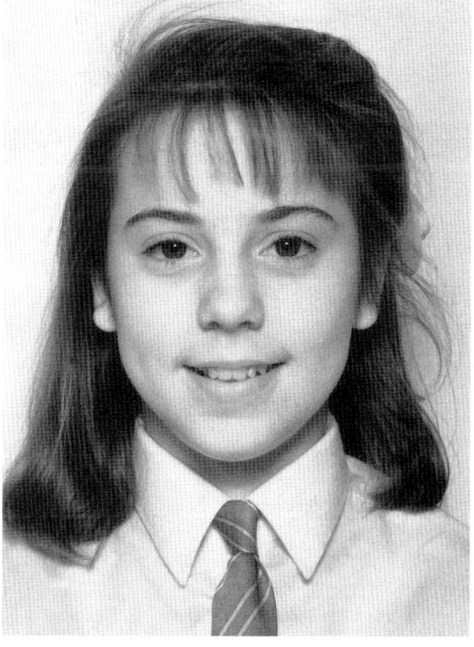

Melanie C at Brookvale Junior School. Later, at Fairfield Junior School, she displayed an early aptitude for sports: netball, hockey, rounders, athletics, gymnastics, you name it.
*(Courtesy of 45 Management)*

Victoria, aged 7, dressed up for a party at the family home in Goff's Oak, Hertfordshire. Encouraged by her parents, she showed an early enthusiasm for music and drama, and enrolled at the age of eight for after-school classes at the Jason Theatre School in Broxbourne. *(Retna Ltd)*

Geri as a glamour model. Everything about her was subject to constant change: her weight, her hair colour, her look, her lifestyle. Even her height and age were subject to discreet adjustments, depending on the circumstances. *(Chris House/Rex Features)*

Geri in Spain in 1991. "She was as bold as brass," said Chris Herbert. "I remember asking her how old she was and she said 'I can be as young or as old as you want me to be. I can be a 15-year-old with big boobs if you like.'"
*(left: Trevor Watson/Rex Features, right: Chris House/Rex Features)*

Victoria was the most poised and sophisticated of the Girls, but also the most introverted. This shot is one of the series of glamour poses she did in 1992, aged 16, in the hope of attracting interest from modelling agencies.
*(Geoff Marchant/Camera Press)*

Teenage Emma in karate gear. She appeared in a photo-story in teen magazine *Top Chat* as a karate student who had a crush on her teacher, and was also the featured face of an anti-smoking poster. *(IPC Magazines/Rex Features)*

Bob (left) and Chris Herbert, the father and son team who became the Spice Girls' first managers. They assembled the group in the spring of 1994 after auditions at Dance Works off Oxford Street in central London and Nomis Studios in Shepherd's Bush, but their wavering over signing them to a contract cost them millions.
*(left: Cassidy & Leigh, right: INS Newsgroup)*

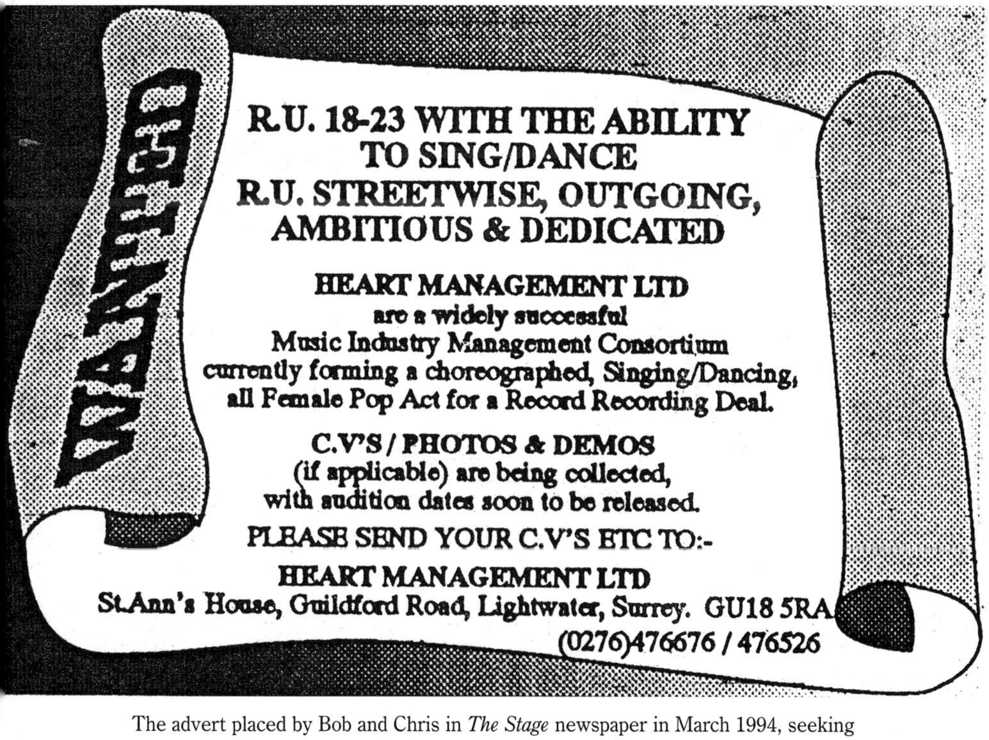

**WANTED**

**R.U. 18-23 WITH THE ABILITY TO SING/DANCE
R.U. STREETWISE, OUTGOING, AMBITIOUS & DEDICATED**

**HEART MANAGEMENT LTD**
are a widely successful
Music Industry Management Consortium
currently forming a choreographed, Singing/Dancing,
all Female Pop Act for a Record Recording Deal.

**C.V'S / PHOTOS & DEMOS**
(if applicable) are being collected,
with audition dates soon to be released.

PLEASE SEND YOUR C.V'S ETC TO:-

**HEART MANAGEMENT LTD**
St.Ann's House, Guildford Road, Lightwater, Surrey. GU18 5RA
(0276)476676 / 476526

The advert placed by Bob and Chris in *The Stage* newspaper in March 1994, seeking "streetwise, outgoing, ambitious and dedicated" females.

No sooner were the five girls chosen than they began rehearsals at Trinity Studios in Woking. It was a dilapidated studio with paint peeling from the walls and, as Geri described it, "radiators that rattled but remained permanently cold". Top left: Melanie C; top right: the girls rehearse a dance routine; bottom left: Melanie B; bottom right: Michelle Stephenson, who was replaced by Emma. "She lacked the same intensity or enthusiasm to learn," said Geri.
*(below left, top left and right:Rex Features, below right: INS Newsgroup)*

Unlike royalties from CD sales which are used to offset the vast sums of money that are spent establishing and promoting a group before any of it reaches the performers themselves, publishing royalties are collected and paid directly to the songwriter, who is likely to have incurred very few overheads in simply writing the song. In groups where one particular person has written all the songs – Pete Townshend in The Who, Sting in The Police, Noel Gallagher in Oasis – this creates a vast imbalance in the personal wealth of the songwriter concerned vis-à-vis the other members of the group. In the case of "manufactured" groups where the songwriting is done by someone other than the artist, it dramatically reduces the act's earning capacity, especially in the long term, a situation which the Spice Girls turned on its head.

Wilson: "A lot of very famous artists now take publishing off tracks. Some of them say, 'If I'm going to perform this song, I'm going to sell this song for you, then I want a piece of the publishing.' It's happened to us. We were told before we'd even written the song – 'This guy will want to take some of the publishing.' So we accepted that. So we actually wrote the song and this person didn't contribute anything and still took some of the publishing. It was a small amount. At the end of the day it went on to be a big hit. We were happy with it."

But according to Wilson this was never the case with the Spice Girls, who were fully involved in the writing of all their songs.

"The publishing with the girls was agreed beforehand, irrespective of what you write, because it will always change," Wilson said. "From our point of view, they wrote everything that we wrote with them. We'd maybe write a backing track that they'd put words to."

Watkins: "I wasn't an 18-year-old girl. They always had this weird ability to come up with phrases that you'd never heard of."

Elliot Kennedy remembered that they were very quick to learn what they were good at and very focused in achieving their songwriting goals.

"They were able to turn it on instantly. You could have very quick and short writing sessions with them and come up with something that was a Spice Girls record. I've never written with that many people like that before. It's usually a bit more one on one, or two guys that you're working with. With the girls it was all firing from the hip. 'Does that work?' 'No.' 'That?' 'No.' 'That?' 'No.' And eventually one out of five times they'd get a cracking line. And then you refine it. I was the guy who would sit there and gauge it all and write down the best of the lines that were being thrown at me. There was a collective energy about them. It was all of them in tune with each other. 'Right, we're writing about this.' Bang! It was that kind of energy that kept it going."

For Stannard and Rowe it was a process of bringing out of the girls what they had to offer.

Rowe: "Pop music used to be a lot more to do with telling people what to sing. If artists did have their own ideas they were sort of twisted around until it didn't sound like it any more. But that was a particular thing that we wanted to explore. Finding someone who wouldn't necessarily have been thought of as a great songwriter and bringing out what they wanted to say. And that's what we did with East 17 and the Spice Girls."

Presumably this is a process which works better with some artists than others.

"Well, you try it that way first. But if they don't get it then you go: 'Well, I've got this song here. Here's the lyrics.'"

Has Rowe ever found himself supposedly collaborating with someone where he ends up doing all the work himself?

"Yeah. It can get like that. Which can be a bit depressing. But you tend to avoid those scenarios where possible."

Their songwriting buddies stick up for them, to a man, but there is no doubt that the Spice Girls did significantly alter the ground rules for what constitutes a legitimate songwriting credit. Obviously they could sing a tune, and their brainstorming sessions produced some sparkling lyrics. "Yo I'll tell you what I want, what I really really want/ So tell me what you want, what you really really want," is now listed in *The Oxford Dictionary of 20th Century Quotations* (although it is credited, bizarrely, to Matthew Rowbottom [*sic*], Richard Stannard and the Spice Girls). Geri in particular was clearly a fund of ideas for songs, arriving at sessions with her book of jottings, notes and miscellaneous scribblings which often produced the starting point of a lyric or a song title or just an agenda for the day's work.

"They'd sing melodies," Watkins said. "Geri would come up with the concept for a song. Typically, she'd sing one line and the girls would pick up on it or we'd pick up on it and construct around it. And then Mel C and Emma would be very active. They'd really like to sit and sing melodies and go off and come up with little sections."

But as far as writing music was concerned, the girls were heavily dependent on their professional collaborators, to put it mildly. For one thing, the sum total of their mastery of any musical instrument was Melanie B's claim to be able to play the drums. They "conceptualised" and sang their bits of melody and wrote the lyrics. But in musical terms it was not a partnership of equals.

"We had to kind of steer it," Rowe said. "It was different for different tracks really. Some of them were when we were all jamming in a room. We'd just put up some drum sounds and start making things up. And other tracks me and Biff would prepare something beforehand and play it to them. We'd have some lyrics and make them write the second verse."

Later, when the girls were recording their second album, *Spiceworld*, during the height of Spicemania and making a movie at the same time, their contributions became even more erratic and piecemeal.

"I remember when they came in to record 'Spice Up Your Life'," Rowe said. "It was in the middle of the chaos. It had been booked in, that they were coming in to record their next single, and write it, with us. It was at Whitfield Street Studios and there was going to be an MTV crew there filming them as they did this, which there was. Well, how on earth can you possibly do this? You can't write and record a song in half-an-hour with a film crew watching. People in offices all round Whitfield Street were bombarding them – throwing things through the window, getting into the building, phoning up all the time. There was big crowds in the street outside.

"Eventually we got rid of the film crew and the song was done in one afternoon. All the writing and the recording of their vocals as well. But we did a lot of work on it afterwards."

The Absolute team fared no better.

Watkins: "We knew we were in trouble when they said, 'Right. You've got to write a song, but we're making a movie at the same time.'"

The idea was that they would set up a mobile studio on a lorry and follow the girls round between film sets.

"We'd sit there literally all day long and quite often we wouldn't even get them at all," Watkins said. "Mind you we were quite lucky. We had quite nice locations. We had Losely Park and Battersea Park. I know Matt and Biff sat all day at the side of a motorway once."

Wilson: "Because we were so desperate to write with them, we were literally holding on to *any* kind of input that they were giving us. Geri would literally run into the studio and she'd say: 'I just had this idea: Stop right there! Thank you very much – Right, gotta go.' And that's all she did. And then we would construct the entire backing track for the song that went on to become 'Stop'.

"It was the same with 'Too Much'. Geri came in and sang: 'Too much of something/ Da-da-da-da-da . . . Right. OK. You got that?' We started working on it and we wanted to do some sort of doo-wop vocal thing. So we constructed this backing track and then more of the girls started to come in – this was quite a good day – and gradually they started to add on their little bits."

This particular session was taking place on location in Docklands and the film set was besieged by fans. While mounted police struggled to control the baying mob, Watkins and Wilson doggedly worked on the track with whichever of the girls could be spared from the set at any given point. What later became one of their most chilled out hits was thus written, and the vocals recorded, in a caravan in the middle of a virtual riot. Again a considerable amount of production work was called for afterwards in order to knock the track into its final shape.

Perhaps the most extreme example of just how thinly the creative inspiration ended up being spread at this point, was the "writing" and recording of a track called 'Spice Invaders' which became the B-side of 'Spice Up Your Life'.

Wilson: "The single was all ready to go. But nothing existed to be a B-side. There was nothing recorded, because everyone's tracks had been used up on the first album. And they had to have something straight away. So they said, 'Right, just get the girls to do anything. Anything you like.' So we told them to talk. Just talk about anything. We set up four microphones and recorded them all talking to each other and then we put some hideous bubblegum backing track down behind their voices and just somehow pieced it all together."

After the girls had gone, the mixing of this bizarre track went on well into the night, during which, at some point, Watkins's wife gave birth to a baby boy. Watkins rushed off to the hospital, but then had to come straight back to the studio to finish off the track which the mix engineer, not surprisingly, couldn't make head nor tail of.

Elliot Kennedy who, largely thanks to his part in the success of the *Spice* album, was now working with Celine Dion and Bryan Adams, took one look at how things were shaping up with the second album and promptly dropped out of the picture.

"I did a couple of backing tracks [for *Spiceworld*]. But when I heard from Absolute and Matt and Biff how it was going and what a nightmare it was turning into I thought, 'I don't want to get involved. This is not what I'm into.'"

In the post-Spice world it is widely taken for granted that pop artists will take a writing credit for the songs they record, and in some cases pretty much irrespective of their actual contribution to the creative process. Sometimes they will not even have met the other songwriters or musicians involved. Take a look at the credits on a Sugababes record and it reads like the cast of a small movie. Their 2000 hit, 'Overload', was written by Lipsey, McVey, Howard, Simm, Donaghy, Buena & Buchanan, the last three being the girls in the group, the others being a committee of producers, mixers, musicians and professional writers all with their own managers who will have negotiated a split of the publishing proceeds.

As a measure of the changes that have come about since the Spice Girls took their first tentative steps as songwriters with Stannard and Rowe in 1995, consider too the shifting fortunes of Kylie Minogue in this regard. With hardly a songwriting credit to her name during the Eighties, and certainly never on one of her many hits in that decade, she has gone on to be nominated twice at the 2003 Ivor Novello Awards in the category of Most Performed Work. The songs that earned her this accolade were 'Love At First Sight' (written by Kylie Minogue, Richard Stannard, Julian Gallagher, Ashley Howes and Martin Harrington) and 'In Your Eyes' (written by Kylie Minogue, Richard Stannard, Julian Gallagher and Ashley Howes).

According to Stannard – who, since his stint with the Spice Girls, has worked with Gabrielle, Will Young, Paul Young, Victoria Beckham, Emma Bunton and, of course, Kylie Minogue – this is just the way things are now done, and he is all in favour of it.

"It's different from the days when a songwriting team would just hand the song over to an artist. I couldn't do that. This way you can actually get involved with the whole thing. You can create the lifestyle within the song and the lyrics and the whole imagery of it. I like getting involved with that especially with Kylie because she's a mad dancer. If I'm doing an album with an artist like Will [Young], we'll have a board in the studio and we'll cut out pictures of clothes and fashions and colours that we like."

In fact, Stannard has *never* had a hit that he hasn't co-written with the artist concerned and produced as well. And as for Kylie reaping the benefits of their songwriting collaboration, Stannard couldn't be more delighted.

"I'm thrilled for her," he said before the Novello Awards. "She hasn't written much before, just the odd album track. But for some reason when I work with people, we often end up doing singles."

Not all collaborations between production/writing teams and artists have ended so amicably, however, and the issue of who should receive due credit for creative input came under scrutiny in 2002 when a spectacular row flared up between the Canadian teen rock star Avril Lavigne and a songwriting/production team from Los Angeles called The Matrix. At issue was the precise contributions that had been made by each of the two parties to the writing of five songs on Lavigne's multi-million-selling album, *Let Go*.

Because Lavigne had been positioned in the market as a singer-songwriter, the issue of who had actually written a song such as her biggest hit 'Complicated' assumed a much greater significance than if she was being presented as a pure pop act. While the credits were split evenly between Lavigne and The Matrix, Lavigne claimed she had written the song virtually on her own in the space of a couple of hours. But according to Lauren Christy of The Matrix, it was they who had "conceived the ideas on guitar and piano" leaving Lavigne to "come in and sing a few melodies and maybe change a word here or there."

Curiously perhaps, Stannard instinctively sides with the artist in this situation.

"She's obviously a talented girl. Maybe she only did write a bit on that track, but she's selling millions of albums on the strength of people thinking that she did it all. So why should The Matrix complain? I don't get the ego side of that. I think the publishing and royalties more than suffice."

Clearly the Spice Girls did not write their own songs in the way that Elvis Costello or Paul Weller wrote theirs. But as with so many aspects of their phenomenal career, the five of them nevertheless took a firm grip on the songwriting reins from a very early stage and simply reshaped the process to suit their own abilities and ends. In many respects, the rest of the pop world has only just caught up with their methods.

# 4
# Girl Power

As spring turned into the summer of 1995, the girls began looking in earnest for new management. They were now based in London: Emma and Victoria living at home and the Mels and Geri in a rented flat in Cyprus Road, Finchley. With the help of Mark Fox, a music publishing agent who had been present at the Nomis showcase, they drew up a list of potential managers and other industry contacts who might be able to assist their cause. Once an appointment had been secured they would go to the office or wherever their target was to be found and perform a "Spice blitz".

Elliot Kennedy's manager, Martyn Barter, was one of the people who they went to see, albeit more for advice than with a view to securing him as their manager.

"They came through reception downstairs and it was like a whirlwind," Barter recalled. "Messengers, receptionists and all the people coming and going – everyone was stunned. 'What the hell was that?'

"Then they came into my office and this whole routine unfolded in front of me. They put the track on that they'd done with Elliot on the cassette player and they sang along to it karaoke style, with this dance routine going on. The whole thing was completely choreographed to turn me on. I remember Emma Bunton had a short skirt and a blouse on, the school uniform-looking thing with her hair in bunches and she pulled up a chair opposite me and sat down so I could see up her skirt. And the others were all cavorting and that sort of stuff and I said, 'Right. This is *really* impressive. Can we switch it off? *Please* switch it off. I'm an extremely happily married man, and I know exactly what you're doing. This is absolutely brilliant. Please switch it off.' And they all went and sat on the settee and said, 'Right. Let's get down to business then.'"

Much has been said and written about the idea of "girl power". The slogan first surfaced in public as the title of an album by the female duo Shampoo, and by a curious coincidence, their song 'Girl Power' was released as a single one week before 'Wannabe' in July 1996. While nothing more has ever been heard of Shampoo, the same can hardly be said about girl power.

Geri was the author of the concept, and always its most vocal proponent, although once they got the ball rolling the girls all took it up as a catch-all article of faith. A "Power Oath" duly evolved: "I, being of sound mind and new Wonderbra do solemnly promise to cheer and dance and zigazig-ah. Ariba! Girl Power!" It may not have been the most profound expression of sisterly solidarity, but the girl power philosophy was not as empty as people often supposed.

The idea, in essence, was that girls should stand up for themselves as individuals, stick up for each other collectively and, having identified what they want out of life, go out and grab it with both hands. Far from denying differences in gender – as the old school feminists had sought to do – girl power encouraged the use of sexual charm as a weapon to be deployed along with any other available skills that would help to get a result. Boys were OK in their place, but they shouldn't be allowed to distract a girl from her life goals or, even worse, distance her from her friends. Follow this advice and, so the theory goes, nothing will stop a girl from achieving her ambitions for long.

Apart from reclaiming the word "girl" from the clutches of the politically correct tendency – who for a decade or more had stigmatised it as a sexist put-down when referring to anyone of the female persuasion aged about 13 or over – girl power proved a remarkably inspirational slogan, a vague but persuasive notion, whose influence eventually extended well beyond the confines of the pop world.

"To be a feminist in the Nineties," Melanie C said, "means having something to say for yourself. You can wear mascara and high heels and look like a babe and make as much of a point as if you shaved your head and burnt your bra. There's no way I'm ever burning my Wonderbra. I couldn't. I'm nothing without it."

To make the formula work in the context of the music business required wit, charm and a ruthless sense of rational self-interest, qualities with which all five of the girls were unusually well endowed. In using their sexuality to get what they wanted out of a male-dominated industry, the Spice Girls turned the concept of the casting couch on its head. When they went into an office to meet a potential manager or agent, they were putting on a display of a sexually charged nature. But they were the ones who did the vetting.

Geri was the most outrageous.

"She was all very *Carry On*," Andy Watkins of Absolute remembered. "She would go into a record company office and if the A&R guy was late for a meeting or wouldn't give them an appointment, she would march over and put her tits on the photocopier and run off a copy. Then she would leave the picture on the guy's desk with a note saying, 'This is what you missed.' In a way they used it as a weapon to get attention or sometimes to humiliate certain record executives."

Recalling the first time that he and Paul Wilson met the girls at their studio on Taggs Island in the Thames, Watkins described a scene of memorable hilarity.

"They came in and just sexually harassed us for the first hour or so," he said. "It doesn't happen that you meet a group like them that often, it really doesn't. The amount of people who have come in since and said, 'You and me, we're gonna make this group into the next Spice Girls.' And then the girls and boys or whoever they are come in and they're sitting on the settee, not saying a word. If that was the Spice Girls, mate, it would be chaos in here. There was just something that they had that you couldn't argue with."

Wilson: "We had a band come in here the other day who had a little taste of it. But I've never seen it to the extent the Spice Girls had it. Most of them nowadays come in [adopting timid voice]: 'Oh we really like R&B, we really like pop music, we want to be the next Spice Girls' . . ."

Watkins: "Or the manager speaks for them. 'Well we're gonna do this and we're gonna be in your face.' Listen, mate. It's no good *telling* me you're gonna be in my face. You're either in my face or you're not in my face. I've had Geri's tits in my face, and that's the difference!"

Wilson: "The first thing Geri would do on meeting you was to squeeze your arse and go, 'Nice arse!' And that was the introduction. They did it to disarm people. Geri and Mel B between the two of them – terrifying!"

Watkins: "And Emma."

Wilson: "Victoria and Mel C did sort of stand back a bit. It was a three-pronged attack wasn't it? Geri, Mel B – and then Emma would sit there with her legs apart . . ."

Watkins (eyes misting over): "And the pigtails. She looked about 16."

Wilson: "They were all like little Lolitas weren't they?"

Watkins: "They definitely bewitched you. It was a case of by all means necessary to win you over. But they did it in a natural way. You were allowed to join in their gang for a small amount of time. You were allowed to see what it would be like to be in the Top Shop changing rooms."

"The effect they had – from the car park attendant to the executive boardroom – was certainly something to behold," recalled Paul Conroy, at that time President of Virgin Records. "They were pretty frightening in their level of confidence. It was as though they had gone to EST or had some sort of training. In their own sort of pop way, there was something quite anarchic, quite punk, in the way they physically assaulted an office. They'd turn over your desk. It reminded me of when I used to work at Stiff Records and The Damned would come into the office and just cause chaos. It was like they were everywhere."

Martyn Barter saw the whole operation as a touch of genius, orchestrated primarily by Geri.

"I realised that if they did this to blokes in the music business they would be drooling over them, because they wouldn't see it as an act. They'd just think, you know, they'd go for it. The girls had sussed out the susceptibility of A&R guys and senior executives to the sexy female. They'd worked out that this was definitely a male-orientated, chauvinist, sexist business and Geri absorbed that and played to it to get to where they wanted to be. And it was funny, 'cause Geri had worked all that out. She told the others what to do, how to behave and what their different roles were. It was so apparent to me. I know other executives felt the same thing, although I'm not sure they understood how brilliant it was. I'd say to them, 'Did you get the show?' And they said, 'Oh yes. The whole thing just happened.' When you talk about girl power that was it. Because they'd take anybody on."

It was a strategy that the Spice Girls employed, albeit in a somewhat toned-down way, throughout their career, often with extraordinary results. When they met Prince Charles in the Manchester Opera House at the start of a Royal Gala on behalf of his Prince's Trust, in May 1997, Geri planted a kiss on his cheek, leaving it smothered in lipstick, patted his bottom and told him, "You know I think you are very sexy. We could spice up your life." To this day, royal protocol requires that women should give a half-curtsey when meeting the heir to the throne, "placing the right foot behind the left heel, knees slightly bent while keeping the head erect". But far from earning a reprimand for their brazen and highly public breach of etiquette, the Spice Girls and Geri in particular won a lasting place in Charles's affections. Indeed when Geri left the Spice Girls in 1998, Charles sent a personal letter expressing his sadness at the news. "The group will not be the same without you," he wrote. "What will I do without your wonderfully friendly greeting?" The letter written on Royal notepaper was signed off "with lots of love".

Whether meeting heads of state or the lowliest of journalists, the Spice Girls could – and sometimes literally did – flirt for England. The actor Richard E. Grant, who played the part of their road manager in *Spiceworld – The Movie*, kept a diary of his time on the set with the Girls. He recalled the "sheer combined-energy force-field" that he encountered upon entering the communal make-up room for the first time.

"'Gi' us a feel of yer bum,' [Melanie B] commands, and lets rip a throttling laugh that provokes everyone into instant party mode. Despite having just cracked 40, offering up my cheeks for Mel B's delectation at 9am momentarily blinds me to the fact that I am old enough to be her father. Her verdict – 'You'll do . . .' – is the kind of approbation that, if bottled, would cure any impending male mid-life crisis."

When I interviewed the Girls at a venue called The Point in Dublin where they were rehearsing for their European tour of 1998, I was no less enchanted by their mixture of natural charm, calculated flattery and unaffected enthusiasm for what they were doing. Geri, in particular, had a manner that was quite unlike most pop stars – very direct, friendly and bold but not at all threatening or intimidating in the way that a lot of celebrities, men and women, try to be when confronted by a representative of the Fourth Estate. My arse remained unmolested, but if I had been wearing a tie I believe she would have straightened it for me. "Ooh, you're very nice," she said at one point. "We like you," she announced at the end of the interview, as if they'd taken a vote on it and this was the official result. In more than twenty years of meeting and interviewing famous people I can't remember being paid such a simple, well-calculated compliment.

But they had an edge to them as well. Melanie B made some friendly comment to which I responded, "That's very sweet of you."

"I'm not sweet," she said, giving me a severe warning look.

They were all young enough to be my daughters – indeed, I am older than all of their fathers, except Geri's – and there was nothing untoward in their behaviour. But it was seductive, just the same. And besides they were amazingly good fun to be around. Just being alone in a room with five girls like that was a hoot in itself. For most of the time they were physically interconnected: Geri lay sideways on a couch with her legs sprawled across the knees of Victoria, whose thighs in turn were hitched half across the lap of Mel B. Emma and Mel C were seated on separate chairs completing a semi-circle around me.

Paul McCartney once described the image of The Beatles as being "four parts of the same person", but if The Beatles – or indeed any male band – had been as tactile in their public relations with each other as the Spice Girls were, there would have been some very strange rumours circulating before too long. The Girls all talked, but were quick to give way to one another. In conversation, as in their life together, they formed a mutual support system. So if one of them strayed off message then the others would be quick to rescue her and steer the conversation back to safer territory.

"Together it was easy," Melanie B later recalled. "When one of us couldn't be arsed to answer a question, another person could. Where one person just wanted to go home, there would be another who was well up for staying. The energy vroomed around the group and you'd always catch it from someone else if you were feeling tired or bored . . . While one person was falling off the wheel another one would be pulling them back on again."

After my interview with them, instead of disappearing to their dressing rooms or banishing me to a different area – which would have been the more usual thing to do – they let me hang around with them for a while. It was the birthday of one of the musicians in their band, bass player Steve Lewinson (who used to play with Simply Red). The Girls descended on him en masse and presented him with a birthday cake, a gesture which clearly surprised and delighted him in equal measure.

The entertainment columnists Dominic Mohan and Victoria Newton from *The Sun* were also there. The girls had played the tabloid press like an orchestra, but by this point they were well past the honeymoon stage, and were reluctant to have their photograph taken with Mohan and Newton. But Mohan was adamant. As far as he was concerned without the money shot of him and Newton chumming up with the girls, the visit would have been a waste of time. Reluctantly the girls agreed to do the picture. Then Geri shouted over to me. "If he's having his done with us, you'd better come and have yours taken as well. That's only fair." And she dragged me into the middle of the girls and put my arms round her shoulders. They all huddled around me. Victoria put her hand on my right shoulder and Emma gently pushed her breast into my left arm. Here then was my own little glimpse of what it is like to be welcomed into the Top Shop changing rooms. When you strip it all away, I think that moment could be the reason I ended up writing this book.

Back in 1995, all that cheeky confidence and guile was channelled into the search for a manager; but not just any old manager. They'd already extricated themselves from the Herberts and Heart Management because they didn't consider them to be up to the job. So potential candidates were carefully sized up beforehand by Geri, who had a checklist of requirements before they would even consider approaching a particular person. Is he known to be comfortable working with women? Has he launched any successful female acts? Has he a well-established presence in America? Does he have an operation that can devote one person exclusively to the group?

Once a suitable candidate was identified, the girls swung into action. Among the various executives they approached were Oliver Smallman and Denis Ingoldsby – whose First Avenue management and record label had enjoyed success with Eternal and Dina Carroll – and Tony Gordon, formerly the manager of Culture Club. Rob Dickens, at that time Chairman of Warner Music UK, was Spiced up in a restaurant. Word soon spread around the business about these fearless five girls, and once they had gained access, they experienced little difficulty in impressing their targets. The problem was finding someone that impressed *them* sufficiently to be entrusted with the management of their career.

"It was strange having so much power," Geri said. "We had no record contract or performing background, yet we were turning heavyweight managers down."

Some of these heavy hitters did not respond gracefully to being passed over by the girls and Geri was told on more than one occasion of the big mistake they were making when she phoned to decline the services of certain management moguls.

However, one candidate stood out from the rest. Simon Fuller had been known to the girls from an early stage because of his connection with the Absolute boys through their manager Pete Evans (whose company, Native, was part of the 19 Management group). Fuller met the requirements on Geri's checklist. He had managed the solo career of Annie Lennox, whom he had steered to multi-platinum success in America and around the world. And he had launched the career of the Norwich-born singer Cathy Dennis, who had also enjoyed success in America with a string of hits in the early Nineties, including 'Touch Me (All Night Long)', which reached number two in the *Billboard* Hot 100 in 1991.

Although Fuller was one of the last candidates they got to meet, he was in many ways one jump ahead of the competition. For one thing, *he* contacted them. Thanks to his relationship with Andy Watkins and Paul Wilson, he had already listened to a tape of 'Something Kinda Funny', and immediately spotted the potential. He was also forewarned of what to expect when he met the girls, and when they did eventually convene in his management offices at Ransome's Dock Business Centre in Battersea near Chelsea Bridge, Fuller had taken discreet steps to subtly alter the balance of power in his favour

When the girls arrived at the bright, clean, open-plan offices, Fuller was not there. Instead of accosting him at his desk and zapping him with "the act", the girls were politely asked to wait until he arrived. He soon appeared. With his jet-black hair, nicely manicured fingers and a deep, all-year tan, Fuller cut a neat, slightly camp figure. His speaking voice, quiet and understated, was that of a cultured, well-bred Englishman – rather like Nigel Pargetter in *The Archers*.

The girls and he had an introductory chat before they hit him with the karaoke performance of 'Wannabe'. Fuller betrayed no immediate enthusiasm, but listened carefully and calmly to what they wanted from him and what they expected him to do for them. He spoke without any patronising bluster about what he felt he could offer, emphasising his belief in the importance of viewing the project from an international perspective right from the offset. Not for the first time in his career, Fuller had got the measure of the situation and was fully alert to its commercial potential before the competition had even properly got out of bed.

Born in Cyprus, Fuller grew up in Ghana for five years, and then Hastings on the south coast of England, where his father, a former RAF pilot, was headmaster of a primary school. Fuller's mother was also a teacher for a time, as was his eldest brother Kim. Another older brother Mark, later worked in a school with asthmatic children.

Simon, however, was not minded to join the teaching profession. Instead, to his father's initial dismay, he began promoting pop gigs on Hastings pier and managing local bands while still in the sixth form of his state secondary school. Kim remembered his brother as being both entrepreneurial and fearless in his outlook from an early age.

"He always knew what he wanted to do, from when he was a teenager," Kim said. "He wanted to be involved in music management in some way. He enjoyed putting the bands on and he usually made some money out of it. But not always. When he lost money, he took it as a little knock on the way. He never gives up. Some people might be daunted at the prospect of entering a world like that, but he had no qualms."

After leaving school Fuller travelled, spending two years in Germany and a year in Canada, experiences which he believes contributed to his global view. "I've always been very worldly in my perspective," he said.

He worked in the mid-Eighties as an A&R man (talent scout) for the Chrysalis label which is when he discovered Paul Hardcastle, a keyboard player and producer from London. Fuller became his manager, and in 1985 Hardcastle had a number one hit with 'Nineteen', a song about the Vietnam War.* Strangely, given the totemic significance which Fuller has since invested in 19 – the name he still uses for his management company – he was never able to steer Hardcastle towards anything like the same success again.

When he met the Spice Girls, Fuller was fully occupied with his long-standing clients, but was nevertheless in need of a new project to get his teeth into. Annie Lennox had just released her second album, *Medusa*, which topped the UK chart in April 1995, while Cathy Dennis, although still releasing successful singles, had peaked as an artist (though not as a songwriter; she later enjoyed success as the composer of Kylie Minogue's 2001 hit, 'Can't Get You Out Of My Head' and subsequently became one of the most in-demand songwriters in pop, thanks in no small part to Fuller's continuing loyalty to her cause). And

---

* Apparently 19 was the average age of the soldiers serving in that brutal theatre of conflict.

it was around this time that Fuller started managing Gary Barlow's solo career, an association that did not last long and was to yield disappointingly patchy results.

"I think you're fabulous," Fuller finally told the girls. "With or without me, you girls are going to make it. But if you tell me where you want to go, I will try to take you there. You tell me to stop and I'll stop."

Fuller got the job as the second Spice Girls manager in May 1995.

It is worth pausing for a moment at this point to consider another of the most pervasive myths about the Spice Girls – namely that the group was "invented" by Simon Fuller. Here is a typical version of events as described by an anonymous profiler in *The Sunday Times* as recently as July 2003.

"In the mid-Nineties [Fuller] came across a struggling group called Spice that had spent 18 months dismally chasing success. Looking at Emma, Geri, Mel B, Mel C and Victoria, Fuller saw something that had eluded others. 'I thought, shit, I know I can get them good songwriters and good songs,' he reflected . . . the Spice Girls had to be different, so that girls identified with them. He cottoned onto a sociological trend that he marketed as 'girl power'."

Now, there is no doubt that without Fuller's managerial chutzpah, marketing genius and uncanny ability to strategise on a number of fronts simultaneously all over the globe, the Spice Girls would not have been the phenomenal success that they were soon to become. Even Chris Herbert – who really *did* invent the group – will agree with that.

But they were already well established by the time Fuller came on the scene. They had been together for a year. They had their name – well, almost – and they had their look and "girl gang" identity. Most tellingly of all, they had already written a good part of their first album, including three future number one hits ('Wannabe', '2 Become 1' and 'Who Do You Think You Are'). It wasn't Fuller who put the girls in touch with Stannard and Rowe, Absolute and Elliot Kennedy as has been routinely reported. Indeed, in the case of Stannard and Rowe, it was the other way round, and shortly after 'Wannabe' reached number one, they were offered a contract with Native/19 Management, which they gladly accepted.

The girls had caused a word-of-mouth sensation in the record industry corridors of power and rejected overtures from some of the most powerful managers in pop. Fuller may have advised, moulded, steered and organised them to take maximum advantage of their talents – just as any good manager would strive to do for any act. But there is no question of him having "invented" or manufactured the Spice Girls. After all, *they* gave *him* the job (and ultimately would take it away again) – not the other way round.

With Fuller now in their corner, the next step was to settle on a record company. The girls did the rounds with their 'Wannabe' tape, dancing on tables in boardrooms all over town, while Fuller orchestrated just enough word-of-mouth hype to ensure that every record company was in the running to sign them up. Only Warners did not put in a bid, making Rob Dickens one of the very few executives who had proved immune to the Spicing up process.

A more typical response was that of Ashley Newton, at that time head of A&R at Virgin.

"You had to be a real dumbo not to get this one. You didn't have to be some A&R visionary *at all*. Because here you had, in Simon Fuller, the stability of experienced, intelligent management – somebody who came from an A&R background with a company which also represented producers, writers, mixers and so forth. You had the girls themselves, who even in the embryonic stage had these very distinct, individual roles, both in look and attitude. And you had three amazing demos – 'Wannabe', 'Say You'll Be There' and '2 Become 1' – which they performed in the office with all this funny, sexy choreography."

The obvious choice of record label for a pop act in 1995 was either London records (home of East 17) or else BMG who had enjoyed striking success with Take That (and had good relations with Fuller thanks to their stewardship of Annie Lennox's recorded output). But Virgin records, the natural home of a rather more hip roster of acts such as Massive Attack and The Verve, were anxious to break into the pop market and mounted a persuasive courtship of the group.

Virgin's previous experience of pop acts consisted primarily of Human League and Culture Club (featuring Boy George), both of which were launched in the early Eighties. Even those groups, successful as they had once been, were a long way removed from the pure, hit-factory pop market that the Spice project was being aimed at. However, Fuller and the girls decided that this could work to their advantage, since Virgin would not only give them their undivided attention, but would also be absolutely determined to ensure the success of the project.

For their part Virgin waged a determined campaign in the face of fierce competition, notably from Sony and London. In order to reassure Fuller (and Geri) of their competence and commitment to breaking the Girls in the USA, Virgin took the unusual step of sending the girls over to America *before* they'd agreed to sign with the company.

Ray Cooper, at that time Head of Marketing at Virgin, took them over.

"I just took them round every office and they just burst in," Cooper said. "Our head of promotion, head of sales, head of marketing, all the key people got to see the routine and meet the girls fresh out of the box."

So too did Ken and Nancy Berry, the husband and wife team who ran Virgin in America. Cooper took the girls up to the Berry household out of office hours, and the executive duo were able to get to know the wannabe pop stars as individuals at close quarters, a luxury which few acts actually signed to the label would have been afforded. Indeed, it is hard to think how Virgin could have done more to reassure the Spice Girls that they would be viewed as a top priority not only in Britain but in America and everywhere else. At no point was there even the vaguest shadow of a doubt about the desire of the record company to sign the group. It was Virgin, the hippest major record label in the world, who were always on trial, never the five young girls.

"I always felt that we could have blown it very easily," Paul Conroy admitted, subsequently. "We might've just said the wrong thing, or someone in America could've said the wrong thing. We were nervous about that. They were our babies and we didn't want to lose them."

The Spice Girls duly signed to Virgin Records on July 13, 1995. The deal was for five albums with a total advance, if all options were picked up, of one million pounds. Although hardly a staggering sum compared to some of the mega-deals that were brokered in the Nineties with acts such as Prince and R.E.M., this was nevertheless a substantial commitment for an untried act launching itself into the choppy waters of the pure pop market.

The day of the signing was memorable for various reasons. London records, who had not given up lobbying the girls to sign with them instead, had invited them to go on a boat trip on the Thames. And even though the girls had made it perfectly clear that they were going to sign with Virgin, the London party on the river nevertheless went ahead as planned. Virgin executives, who knew about this last-minute schmoozing, could have been forgiven for feeling a little uneasy. After all, nothing was settled until the signatures were etched on the dotted line, and who knew what extravagant offers London might make to tempt the girls away at the last minute. Any misgivings which the Virgin suits might have been feeling were not exactly relieved when the limo that had been sent to pick up the girls arrived at Virgin HQ in the Harrow Road, with five inflatable sex dolls in it of corresponding skin tone and hair colour to the Spice Girls. Just a little last-minute prank that the girls had organised.

"If Virgin didn't know yet who they were dealing with, they would now," Victoria remembered with much hilarity.

It was about all she did remember of that night. The girls duly showed up, the contracts were signed, champagne corks were popped and the dolls thrown into the canal behind the Virgin offices. The girls leapt into a taxi, which took them to the Kensington Place restaurant, by which time an extremely drunk Victoria had had her knickers removed and flung out of the window by the rest of the girls. Girl power was nothing if not about having a laugh when the opportunity presented itself.

It was to be exactly a year before the Spice Girls released their first single, which is not an exceptional length of time to set up the launch of a big international pop act, but was nevertheless a bit surprising given the momentum that they had already built up by this point. Obviously there was still work to be done on the writing and recording of the first album. And Virgin wanted their record companies around the world to be fully primed before they let the girls out of the traps.

But there was also a degree of uncertainty about how best to proceed with an all-girl group of this sort. When Take That formally disbanded in February 1996, amid scenes of unprecedented fan hysteria, it was clear that a big gap had opened up in the market. But for most pundits, the idea that an all-girl band, rather than another boy band, would be able to replace Take That as the best-selling teen act, was simply not a credible proposition. The only successful British girl group of recent times had been Eternal, whose appeal was firmly based on the American, R&B model.

"We prefer TLC or Salt 'n' Pepa [to Eternal]," Emma said in one of their earliest interviews. "They're cool and they have an excellent attitude. They're more in your face and sexy – although sometimes too sexy. We're more the cheeky types. Boys love us and that's great, but we're definitely out to appeal more to the girls."

But even within Virgin there were sceptical murmurings, and the MD of Virgin France was by no means untypical when he voiced doubts about the viability of the project.

"I remember this conversation," Paul Conroy said, "where we're saying, 'Girl groups, they might sell singles but are they going to sell albums?' We were scared, but then we just had to remember the effect they had had on us when we met them. I felt almost evangelical about the group. The belief within the company was tremendous but it was a big roll of the dice."

As they subsequently powered their way to global domination, it was easy to see why, in hindsight, the idea that the Spice Girls had been the product of a ruthlessly efficient team of record company image-builders quickly took root. But for all the faith that Virgin had shown in the group, there was nothing obvious about the theoretical appeal of the Spice Girls as far as the industry was concerned. Far from Virgin moulding them to fit into a carefully planned corporate vision, it was more like taking an inspired shot in the dark.

Robert Sandall, who became director of press at Virgin in January 1996, recalled that there was, initially, an element of mystification among some of his colleagues as to whom exactly a group like this might be targeted.

"Because they were a group of girls who weren't conspicuously glamorous," Sandall said, "it was difficult to know who they were supposed to appeal to. There had never been a group of girls who were addressing themselves specifically to a female audience before. This gave a lot of the plans a rather hazy aspect."

Sandall and his colleagues at Virgin were evidently unaware that exactly such a group had, in fact, been launched before, with substantial record company backing and aimed at much the same market. The group, which comprised five lively, girl-next-door types, had even achieved a degree of commercial success, albeit strictly limited to their country of origin: Australia. They were called Girlfriend, and had got together at singing and dance classes while still at school in Sydney in 1991. Within months of signing a management deal and a recording contract with BMG/Arista in 1992, they were heading to the top of the Australian chart with their debut single, 'Take It From Me'. Further hit singles followed and an album, *Make It*

## Girl Power

*Come True*, peaked at number four in the Australian chart in 1993.

Girlfriend initiated all sorts of strategies for tapping into the emergent young and pre-teen pop market. They played shows in shopping malls where, as well as having the opportunity to buy their records, their female fans could find a range of Girlfriend clothing on sale in department stores. They were sufficiently successful in Australia for Arista to fund at least one promotional visit to the UK, where the band was given priority status and a couple of singles and the album were released. But even with the full weight of the Arista marketing machine behind them, Girlfriend never took off in Britain.

"It was hard for any girl band in those days," said Mel Brown, who was press officer at Arista at the time. "There weren't any girl bands around. It was all boys in the pop magazines. They never wanted to write about girls, let alone girl bands."

Perhaps it was because of the untried and untested nature of the all-girl formula. Perhaps it was also because of Virgin's nervousness about getting everything to do with this extremely high-profile new act right, but there was an unusual amount of dithering over the launch of the campaign. In particular, there was a considerable period of time spent wrangling over what was to be the first single.

The Spice Girls were adamant that it should be 'Wannabe', or at least Geri and Melanie B were firmly of that opinion. More than just a song, it served as an introduction to the five personalities and the group's mission statement. "If you want to be my lover, you gotta get with my friends . . ." Girl power in a nutshell.

Victoria, who had missed the session when most of 'Wannabe' was written, did not have such a strong attachment to the song, while Melanie C never really cared for it much, and has since been quite disparaging about it. Be that as it may, once Geri and Melanie B were agreed on a course of action there was little that the others in the group could do to change the situation.

Virgin, however, proved not to be such a pushover. Ashley Newton, who was in charge of A&R, felt just as strongly that 'Wannabe' was not the right song for the first single and wanted to go with 'Say You'll Be There'. There were various meetings about it, when the different tracks were played and discussed. The girls were represented by Geri who was told that 'Say You'll Be There' was a much cooler track and would cast them in a more favourable light.

Part of the problem was that the original recording of 'Wannabe' suffered from a lacklustre mix (it was this version that eventually surfaced in *Spiceworld – The Movie*, as the "tape" that they put into their beatbox to give an impromptu performance to a friend in a cafe). But the girls, and Geri in particular, were implacable in their belief that it was the right choice for the first single.

"Ashley Newton couldn't stop tinkering with the song," Geri said. "He sent 'Wannabe' to an American producer called Dave Way who had a reputation for creating an R&B swing sound. The result was bloody awful."

"I got a little offended when Geri said that," Newton later responded. "'Tinkering' is the wrong word to use. Involved, committed, caring, wanting them to make the best possible pop records they could make – yes. But 'tinkering'? Well maybe I was an irritant sometimes, because I always wanted them to search for perfection."

Eventually Simon Fuller gave the track to Spike Stent to remix. Stent was an engineer who had worked with Depeche Mode and Massive Attack and who later went on to produce Oasis's third album, *Standing On The Shoulder Of Giants*. When Fuller asked him to remix 'Wannabe', Stent was working in Ireland with U2 on their *Pop* album. He remembered thinking that 'Wannabe' was a "weird" pop record that didn't sound like anything else around. He did the remix in six hours, a process which he described as "tightening it up" and "getting the vocals sounding really good". So successful was he in tailoring the sound of the record for pop radio, that Stent was called in to remix all of the subsequent singles from the first album as they came up for release, and eventually to mix the whole of the second album.

The Stent remix solved the impasse between the girls and Virgin over the choice of first single, but there was another clash of opinions over the video for 'Wannabe'.

On Fuller's recommendation, this had been directed by Jhoan Camitz whose visually striking commercials for Volkswagen, Diesel and Nike had been screened all around the world, but who had never made a music video in his life. The girls were very enthusiastic about using him, because he would give their video a different look, which he certainly did. His idea was to do a one-take shoot of the girls arriving at an exotic building in the middle of a park in Barcelona. The decor of the building would be slightly surreal and it would be peopled with mysterious, bohemian Spaniards creating an effect like something out of a Fellini movie. The girls would come tumbling in and take over the place, running riot in much the same way as had long been their practice when invading management and record company offices.

Five days before the shoot in April 1996, Camitz announced that he had been unable to get permission to use the building. With time running out and budgetary constraints in mind, the shoot had been relocated to St Pancras Hotel in London. Suddenly the beautiful Spanish building, the bohemian characters and the warm Mediterranean light were replaced by the sight of the girls tumbling out of a taxi on a dark London night and running through a rather dowdy looking entranceway into an interior that looked like an old gentlemen's club. Once inside, they proceeded not so much to Spice up as terrorise the inhabitants, some of whom looked so ancient that they might have been there since the place was built.

The Virgin suits were horrified.

"The girls were clearly freezing cold, which showed itself in various different ways," Ashley Newton remarked, rather tartly (the video was subsequently banned in parts of Asia because of Melanie B's ostentatiously erect nipples). "They had stuck with the one-take idea, and just about managed it, but even the best of the takes had Geri looking behind her and bumping into a chair. It didn't have this sexy, Spanish light we had been promised. In fact the whole thing had a rather dark, gloomy feel to it."

"It was a big worry," recalled the perennially worried Paul Conroy. "There were *old* people in the video. Would *The Box* find that a bit threatening? And then we were worried about the bit where they jumped up on the table. Was that too threatening? Had Geri gone too far with the sort of circus outfit that she almost had on in it?"

The video may have looked cheap, but it had already had in excess of £100,000 spent on it by this point. High-level discussions were immediately opened about when and where to re-shoot it. But as far as the girls were concerned the 'Wannabe' video, like the song, was more than a promotional gambit; it represented at a fundamental level what they were about.

"It's us, warts and all," Geri insisted. "We're not going to have some slick Elton John/David LaChapelle-type video production. We had a laugh doing it. That's us, and if you don't get that, you don't get us."

Newton argued just as firmly against using the video, but in what was already becoming something of a pattern, it was the girls' wishes which prevailed. Not only that but Newton has since accepted that he was wrong and their instincts were absolutely right.

"We in the record company were trying to overthink in certain situations," Newton said. "The girls were much more impulsive and much more knowledgeable about what a young kid wants from rock and pop stars. They were closer to it than us. They just understood it."

Newton's verdict may seem magnanimous, but in hindsight, he had very little choice but to admit he was wrong. The video turned out to be the trigger for launching the Spice Girls' global success. When it was delivered to *The Box* video channel in Britain, where viewers phone in to vote for the next track they want to see, 'Wannabe' went to number one within two hours of going on air. That meant it was more popular than 500 other videos that the channel was offering at that time and, to begin with, a whopping 10-15 per cent of the 250,000 weekly telephone requests to *The Box* were for 'Wannabe'. The video stayed at number one on the viewers' chart for 13 weeks, until it was replaced by 'Say You'll Be There'.

"The sound of that song, the playground feel of it, worked for them across the world, without exception," Sandall observed. "Whether it was Bangkok, Tokyo, Paris or Buenos Aires, you got the same gaggle of girls, roughly the same age, all absolutely obsessed with that song. They were a sounding board for a change that came over young girls at that time. Girl Power – it sounds like a dumb slogan. But it did actually contain a hard kernel of truth. There was this emergent sense that youngish girls were a newly empowered group. There was a sociopolitical message built into their appeal. And you have to give Geri credit for identifying that."

While the public were quick to make their preferences known once they had seen and heard what the Spice Girls had to offer, Nicki Chapman, who was in charge of promoting the group to radio and TV, remembered an initial resistance to the very idea of an all-girl group, particularly in the press. "They weren't coming on board to begin with," she said.

Kate Thornton who was at that time editor of *Top Of The Pops* magazine was one of several pop pundits who told Chapman that in their opinion an all-girl group of this sort would be too threatening. Girls wouldn't buy into it, and nor would boys, seemed to be the general presumption. "It's not going to happen," Thornton said. (A couple of months later Thornton had been won over. "For me 'Wannabe' is the best pop record of 1996," she declared.)

Another sceptic was Chris Evans, a figure who wielded enormous influence thanks to his breakfast show on Radio One and his popular *TFI Friday* TV show on Channel 4. Chapman took the Girls in to meet his TV producer Suzi Aplin, who was also Evans's girlfriend at the time. Evans was supposed to be somewhere else, and the Girls had just switched on the music really loud, and started their song and dance routine, when Evans unexpectedly came into the office.

"He told us to fuck off back to *Alive And Kicking* where we belonged," Chapman recalled. "He just absolutely hated them. The Girls were mortified. Geri, who was a big fan of his, was saying, 'Let me go and speak to him, let me speak to him,' and I had to hold her back and say, 'No, let it go or else we're going to humiliate ourselves here. He's not the sort of person you want to address it with now.' We had to walk out through the whole office and everybody was looking at us. It was so embarrassing. After that, every day on Radio One he made rude comments and insinuations about the Girls, even though everybody else was supporting them. Then, after they'd been number one for however many weeks, he saw them at a gig in a club called G.A.Y. late at night. He came up afterwards, shook their hands, apologised and said, 'I was wrong. I think you're brilliant.'" It was to be the start of an association with the group which would eventually lead to a much-publicised fling between Evans and Geri, of which more later.

One early piece of press had a profound and lasting effect on the group. Since the start of 1996, when they first attended the Brits as guests on the Virgin table, the girls had noticed people's tendency to refer to them as "those Spice girls". They had also become aware of an American rapper called Spice 1 whose tales of homicidal aggression on albums such as *Amerikkka's Nightmare* and *1990 Sick* suggested that he was not a man who would respond favourably to the idea of sharing his name with five girls from England. So what with one thing and another, they had officially amended their name from Spice to the Spice Girls. Now, in an interview with Peter Lorraine for *Top Of The Pops* magazine they were to receive a selection of unofficial nicknames that were to stay with them for the rest of their lives.

In a quirky, good-natured piece, illustrated by a picture of a spice rack with the girls' heads superimposed on the various bottles, Lorraine gave each of them their own instantly descriptive name: Ginger, Scary, Sporty, Baby and Posh. At a stroke, they acquired an identity that did more to establish the group's presence in the public consciousness than could have been achieved by any formal advertising campaign or marketing strategy that the record company could have devised. Indeed, it was the entirely natural way in which the final piece of the image-building jigsaw had fallen into place that made it so effective, as well as the fact that Lorraine's names for them all were so effortlessly, artlessly *right*. If either the girls or the record company had tried to foist such an idea on the public, let alone the media, it would have seemed cheesy beyond belief. As it was, the girl-next-door image was cemented, and they became, almost overnight, a fondly regarded and instantly recognisable part of British pop's royal family.

Nicki Chapman summed up the impact of the package that Lorraine and *Top Of The Pops* magazine had unwittingly dropped in their laps.

"You know when you get in a taxi and the driver can name *one* of the members of your band that you've hit it big. It wasn't long before taxi drivers could name *every* member of the Spice Girls."

# 5

# Children Of The Revolution

The Spice Girls were in Japan when 'Wannabe' went to number one in Britain. The record had entered the chart at number three on July 15, 1996 (Gary Barlow's 'Forever Love' was at the top) and the Girls had made their first appearance on *Top Of The Pops* by satellite link from Tokyo, where they used a local temple as a backdrop for their mimed performance. This was the second of three promotional visits to Japan that the group undertook in 1996 alone, and later, on September 19, Japan also had the honour of being the first country in which their debut album, *Spice*, was released (two months before it came out in Britain).

From a record company perspective, this made sound business sense, insofar as Japan is a market which is traditionally vulnerable to cheap imports. But it was primarily part and parcel of Simon Fuller's plan to cultivate a perception of the Spice Girls as an international phenomenon right from the start. After Japan, they made brief promotional visits to Germany and Holland. And on their return to the Far East in the autumn they also visited Hong Kong, Thailand and Korea. In August they went to the Mojave desert in California to shoot the video for their second single, 'Say You'll Be There', in which they appeared as a gang of comic book, kung fu super-vixens kitted out in racy PVC and leather catsuits.

But such was the gathering momentum of their popularity at home that demand for them in Britain could never be resisted for long. Unlike the vast majority of records entering the British chart in the Nineties, 'Wannabe' did not peak in its first week, but actually went *up* to number one in its second week, where it stayed for an eventual total of seven weeks. Having deposed Gary Barlow, 'Wannabe' went on to prevent Michael Jackson, George Michael and Robbie Williams among others from reaching the top slot. Talk about a changing of the guard.

Having agonised over the choice of song, Fuller and the executives at Virgin could scarcely believe their good fortune, while even the Girls were slightly taken aback by the instant yet lasting strength of the song's appeal. By the time, the *Spice* album was released in Britain on November 4, 'Wannabe' had sold 2.5 million copies worldwide and been number one in 11 countries – and this was still some two months before it was scheduled to be released in America. The single's eventual worldwide sales tally would be a staggering 4.5 million copies, enough to take it to number one in a total of 31 countries.

With its strutting dance beat and jaunty, question-and-answer lyric, 'Wannabe' caught the ear of an emergent generation of pop fans whose tastes had not been properly catered for previously. There was a gung-ho, tough-but-innocent and quintessentially girlish bravado about the song which seemed to take even those who liked it rather by surprise. Robert Sandall, at that time head of press at Virgin, remembered taking the group early on to do a photo shoot at a girls' school in Camden.

"All these girls came out to look at them and there was this sharp intake of breath, but then silence. They didn't know what to do. They clustered round. But whereas they would have screamed at a boy band, they couldn't seem to scream at a girl group. They hadn't been prompted as to how to respond to them."

Another photo shoot on some waste ground near a tower block prompted a similarly powerful yet uncertain reaction from the kids who came out to see what was going on.

"There was an involuntary attraction which the Spice Girls exerted on teen and pre-teen girls," Sandall said. "The idea of a group of girls going out and making their mark in that rather gang-like configuration was immensely attractive to girls of a certain age, particularly those living on council estates where the gangs were largely run by boys."

More traditional manifestations of teen hysteria soon set in as the Girls became a fixture in the newspapers and a familiar sight on kids' TV. Part of their appeal was their very ordinariness.

"The girls weren't so beautiful that you were threatened by them," said Nicki Chapman, who continued to work closely with the Girls on TV and radio promotions. "They really were 'girl next door' types. And if you look at the early fashion notes, it was very High Street. It wasn't Gucci and Prada. So, you could look like Geri if you went to flea markets and second-hand shops. You could look like Victoria if you went to Morgan or Miss Selfridge. You could look like Melanie C because everyone's got a tracksuit and can scrape their hair back. It was an achievable look. And in the beginning it was very much 'She could be my best friend at school' to the point where, when I took them into *The Big Breakfast*, one of the producers said: 'Crikey! You'll have to scrub them up a bit, Nicki.' One of them had a huge rip on the arm of her top. They weren't polished and sophisticated. They were like five mad girls out for a laugh."

While pop groups have always had an excitable juvenile following, no one had foreseen just how far down the age demographic the Spice Girls' appeal would extend. More by happenstance than design, the larger-than-life personalities coupled with the nicknames they had adopted gave them a cartoon quality which exerted a particular fascination on kids who were not just pre-teen, but often pre-school. Girls (and boys) as young as four and five were attracted to them in much the same way as they were captivated by *The Simpsons*. For the first time a pop group was offering them a window onto the adult world which was sexy and fun without being threatening, and which was not aimed specifically at them as "little kids" with all the patronising connotations which that implied.

In so doing, the Spice Girls cornered a market that had never been exploited to anything like the same degree in the past. Along with girl power, they had discovered kiddie power. My own daughter, Faith, turned seven soon after 'Wannabe' was released, and the effect of the Spice Girls, not just on her, but on every single girl in her class at school, was spectacular. Within the space of a few months, they all became, if not besotted with the group, then at the very least involved with them and by extension with pop music in general. *The Box* and *MTV* and *Top Of The Pops* suddenly became required viewing, and when the faces of the Spice Girls began appearing on the covers of magazines, they too became a treat to be acquired and prized at all costs. When the opportunity to perform a song in front of her school assembly came up, Faith and her friends formed their own group – the Three To One Girls – and worked up a karaoke routine of 'Say You'll Be There'.

For Faith, and her friends, and their friends, the Spice Girls were the first pop heroes in every way. From the autumn of 1996 to the summer of 1998 (when Geri left) they followed the story with keen excitement, somehow got their hands on the records and unconsciously absorbed the girl pride philosophy. In November 1997 I took Faith and her friends Alexandra and Caitlin to see a preview of *Spiceworld – The Movie* at the Empire, Leicester Square, a tremendous outing for all of us. The huge cinema, so often under-subscribed for these sort of occasions (which are primarily for the benefit of the press and broadcasters) was full to bursting with kids, from cool-looking teenagers to children of nursery school age. For every grumpy old critic and hard-bitten media maven, there were half-a-dozen kids in various states of excitement and awe. Every last seat in the cinema was taken and people were sitting on the steps and in the aisles. There was cheering and laughter and a huge round of applause at the end and then an exciting night-time tube journey home. Faith could not believe that anyone could possibly have disliked the movie, although even she caught wind of the hostile tone of the ensuing reviews.

When the Spice Girls played Wembley Arena in April 1998, Caitlin persuaded her dad to organise a trip to the show and five of them, all under the age of ten, trooped off to the first pop concert of their lives. Caitlin's dad had organised stickers for each of them to wear, with name, seat number and his mobile telephone number printed out on them.

Those were occasions which, I would vouch, had an immensely powerful influence on those girls, no matter how vague their memories of them may now be. The kids of a generation whose musical horizons had previously been restricted to Mr Blobby and *Sesame Street* singalongs became sensitised to pop music thanks to the Spice Girls. The scale of the knock-on effect, as the process was duplicated all around the globe is difficult to grasp. Just to give one small example: years later, when Cherie Blair went on a walkabout in Argentina, the questions she was most frequently asked by youngsters were: had she met Princess Diana? and did she know the Spice Girls?

To their credit, the Spice Girls neither took their popularity among children for granted, nor sought to distance themselves from their younger fans. They may have been ruthlessly ambitious, but they were not cynical.

"We are really proud to have an audience of younger children," Emma said, "because they're not corrupted by anything. They don't think, 'Oh hip hop's cool, or soul, so therefore I'm going to like it.' They just hear something and they like it and that's that."

"I love to speak to them, as well, because they're so honest," Melanie B said.

Ashley Newton's daughter was one of the kids who got closer to the Girls than most, thanks to her dad's involvement with the group.

"She used to go to the shows and she was befriended by them," Newton said. "They used to do all girly things. We used to be in a dressing room at some big show somewhere and Mel B and Geri just used to grab her and say, 'Look at all those bloody famous people. Sod 'em. Come on girl.' And they used to take her and sit her on a little basin in the loo and put make-up on her, lock the door and have a chat. She used to be in heaven.

"They completely understood that really the people they were talking to were young kids. And it was something which they did with incredible good grace. It wasn't just with my kid. I've never seen them not be patient and talk to people or be loving around kids. Even now they get kids coming over to them in hotel lobbies. Their patience was just extraordinary, all of them. I never saw them lose it or be aloof. They would always be interested in communicating with kids. They would ask, 'What TV programmes are you watching? Which cartoon do you like best?'"

Having an audience of such tender years looking up to them imposed a burden of care on the Spice Girls which they were always quick to acknowledge.

"We have a responsibility," Emma said. "There's things you just wouldn't do if your fans were there. Obviously you can't let that take over your life. We want to be our own people, and we want to prove to them that we are being ourselves and they can be that as well. You have to get that balance really."

"I think we stand for that, anyway," Melanie B said. "I'm a mixed-race person hanging out with four white people. It proves you don't have to look a set way to be part of a gang. Between the five of us we're so different, but we get on like a house on fire. We go out partying and having a good time together."

And yet you would never see a photograph of the Spice Girls smoking, let alone expect to hear of any dabbling in harder substances.

"None of us takes drugs," Melanie B said. "And I think we wouldn't shout about it, even if we did. It's not a very good thing to do anyway."

"Sometimes I'll make a suggestion about something we might do for a performance," Geri said, "and Emma will say to me, 'I think that's a little bit saucy.' So maybe I'll do it, but Emma won't. You don't want to compromise your art. 'No you can't do it. Think about the kids.' But you do have to think about it."

This lowering of the age of musical consent, which the Spice Girls initiated, opened up a world of largely unforeseen possibilities. These kids did not have much spending power of their own, but they sure had pestering power. They picked up very quickly and unquestioningly on the enthusiasm of their older siblings for the Spice Girls, and not only bought into the music, but also the lifestyle implications and the immediacy of the package as a whole. Whereas boy bands like Take That and Boyzone had been kept on a tight leash by their managements and maintained an unfailingly bland, disciplined public persona, there was something much more spontaneous, passionate and pointed about the Spice Girls which enabled them quickly to reach a deeper emotional understanding with a very young audience.

"We learnt as we went along," Melanie B said. "And most of the time we were left to our own devices, which was brilliant. We decided between us what to reveal in interviews – and no one else had a say in it."

They were remarkably quick to grasp the techniques of media management, far more so than any of their pop predecessors, including Take That.

"We did media training with them," Nicki Chapman said. "Don't talk over each other. Look at the camera. All those basic details, which people hadn't done with pop acts in the past. They weren't star-struck. They brought everyone around them to their level. If you introduced them to someone, they would look them in the eye. And I'd say, 'Don't kiss people until you know them. Don't be overfamiliar.' So they would learn people's names, remember stuff about them, thank the cameraman. They were a joy to be out with."

Whatever their ulterior motives – and the desire for fame and riches beyond belief was never far from the surface – the Spice Girls really *believed* in what they were doing, and managed to communicate an unshakeable sense of confidence in themselves and the power of positive thinking to their fans. It sounds corny – it *was* corny – but the strength of the Spice philosophy, especially to younger kids, resided not only in its unashamedly aspirational designs, but also in its very lack of cool. In sharp contrast to the yobbish air of disaffection that was cultivated by Oasis, Blur and the Britpop crowd, the Spice Girls offered an upbeat, idealised view of life that was infinitely more appealing not only to young kids but also to their doting parents. This latter point was no mere detail, because at the end of the day it was the parents who were required to fork out the cash needed to buy the CDs.

And no matter how sniffy the critics and tastemaking elite were about the group, the plain fact is that the parental generation also grew to like the songs of the Spice Girls, or at least to recognise them as a generally agreeable part of the fabric of popular culture at that time. Indeed, the simple fact is that the dynamic presentation of the Spice Girls image and philosophy would not have triggered anything like the worldwide success story that unfurled throughout the latter part of 1996 and 1997 if their songs had not been as superbly crafted, recorded and produced as they were.

And here we arrive at one of the most intractable and, to my mind, mysterious Spice Girls myths of them all: namely, that their songs were no good. In summaries of their achievements ranging from the most informed biographies to the most aimless of pub conversations it is a generally held and often stated belief that the group which put British music back on the world stage and ushered in a global renaissance in pop, somehow managed to do so without writing or recording any songs of particular note.

A typical example of this prejudice can be found in *The Illustrated Encyclopedia of Music*, a lavish and authoritative volume published in 2003, which claims to be "an essential reference guide for all music fans." In a category on Nineties Pop, the sum total of the Spice Girls' achievements is condensed into one sentence: "Britain's Spice Girls . . . attained a kind of commercial and critical success – based less on their music than on their extraordinary level of celebrity – that no one would have predicted when they emerged."

Compare this, if you will, with the entry on Abba which extends for two full paragraphs under the category of Europop. Here we learn that Abba "went on to conquer the world [although Britain and Europe favoured their innovations more than America] . . . purveying an increasingly perfect and increasingly lovelorn blend of sweeping melody, glistening production and Beach Boys-meets-Mamas & the Papas-influenced harmony pop . . . In seven short years Abba had become the biggest pop group since The Beatles, while simultaneously proving that you did not need a rock attitude – or good dress sense – to create affecting and original pop artistry."

Now, history is subject to the whims of fashion just like any other branch of the arts, and pop history especially so. And one of the more noticeable tendencies when it comes to the use of hindsight in drawing up the critical balance sheet is for acts who were regarded very seriously at the time to be either forgotten or ridiculed in subsequent commentaries, while acts that were dismissed as lightweight pop fads in their day are often reassessed as purveyors of "affecting and original pop artistry". To anyone who came to pop music later than the mid-Seventies, the very idea that Jethro Tull were once revered as one of the most innovative and hip rock groups of the day must seem difficult to believe. But they were. Ditto Emerson Lake & Palmer, Ten Years After, Peter Frampton and any number of other acts with high-blown artistic pretensions and enviable technical ability who have since been relegated to mere footnotes in the historical pageant of pop.

"Pure" pop groups, on the other hand, who pursued a simple, populist agenda that won them little serious acclaim at the time, often find their critical stock rising with the passage of time. The latterday descriptions of Abba are in breathtaking contrast to the critical mauling that they received when they were enjoying their greatest commercial success. Here was a group, from Sweden (itself a bit of a joke), who got their big break by winning the Eurovision Song Contest (an even bigger joke) in 1974 with 'Waterloo' – a song now described as "odd-but-irresistible" by the *Illustrated Encyclopedia of Music*, but more frequently dismissed as "utter crap" by anyone remotely tuned in to what was happening at the time. Their garish costumes, which now seem so lovably kitsch, were regarded as ludicrous, and their songs routinely derided as disposable pap. They were successful, of course. Everybody could see that. But credible? Never.

Now, in hindsight, Abba are universally regarded as pop godheads of the Seventies. So what has changed? Their music has certainly stood the test of time, and songs that seemed instantly disposable when they first became hits, such as 'Dancing Queen', 'Mamma Mia' and 'Money, Money, Money' have – through the agency of the pub karaoke, the West End musical and a succession of cover versions by everyone from Elvis Costello to the once painfully fashionable Danny Wilson – taken on a life of their own and become pop standards.

But there is slightly more to it than that. What seems to happen with pop music that initially relies on a young, chart-watching audience for its core support, is that as that initial generation of fans grows older and takes up positions of influence, particularly in the print and broadcasting media, so their sympathetic memory of the artist starts to take over from the received wisdom of the older, outgoing generation of tastemakers. Thus groups that were once regarded as beyond the pale by "serious" commentators – from the Bay City Rollers to Adam & The Ants – gradually come to earn critical respect in hindsight, once their original fans grow up and start writing their own versions of pop history.

My daughter – who is 14 at the time of writing – and her friends have long since given up on the Spice Girls and currently look back on that period with a mixture of nostalgia and mild embarrassment – what they can remember of it at all. Faith's musical world now revolves around Eminem, Linkin Park, Evanescence, 50 Cent and Nickelback. But just wait another few years until she and her mates get to college and start organising parties where everyone has to go dressed as their favourite Spice Girl. And once we have all had time to get over the overwhelming wall-to-wall presence of the group, and are finally presented with a Greatest Hits album, my guess is that a huge critical reassessment of the Spice Girls' music will get underway.

"I guarantee it's like Abba," said one industry insider, who preferred not to be named. "In ten or twenty years' time there will be the biggest Spice Girls revival you've ever seen in your life and everyone will come out of the closet, saying, 'I bought their records, they were great!' At the moment they're all going, 'Nothing to do with me, guv!'"

But hey, we don't have to wait for that to happen – we can get the ball rolling right here. Far from being puerile rubbish of the sort that "manufactured" groups from Milli Vanilli to Westlife have traditionally produced, it seems to me that the songs on the first two Spice albums are among the finest to have come from a "pure" pop group since, well, Abba if not all the way back to the mother of manufactured groups, The Monkees.

Consider for a moment how many of the songs from *Spice* you can hum, quote or recall with absolute clarity, straight off the bat. 'Wannabe', obviously, 'Say You'll Be There', 'Mama', 'Who Do You Think You Are', '2 Become 1' – all of them absolutely brilliant, unforgettable pop songs. Sure, there is more bounce than beat, and the songs on *Spice* generally have an air of energetic frivolity. But you do not have to be a pre-pubescent girl to appreciate the genuine sense of resolve that runs through all ten of the tracks. The girl power/solidarity theme of 'Wannabe' is echoed in the message of 'Love Thing' – "God help the mister that comes between me and my sisters" – and the album is peppered with slogans – "I'm choosy not a floozy" – that lend it a sassy, assertive ring. One number in particular, 'Naked', hints at a depth of feeling that goes well beyond the superficial concerns of traditional teen-pop. A slow song, full of sexual tension, it features a voice on a telephone insisting that "I'd rather be hated than pitied."

It tends to be forgotten that *Spice* was shortlisted for the Mercury Music Prize in 1997, the annual independent arts award which likes to think of itself as the musical equivalent of the Man Booker Prize for literature. I was one of the ten judges that year, and, believe me, for an album like *Spice* to prise itself onto the shortlist – alongside records by much cooler artists such as the Prodigy, Radiohead, Primal Scream and Roni Size (who eventually won it) – it has to be truly exceptional. Noting that the Spice Girls' songwriting achievements had already been recognised with two Ivor Novello awards, the Mercury Prize judging panel summed up their assessment of *Spice* thus: "At the heart of the Spice Girls' success lies a brilliant collection of well-crafted pop songs, surely the hardest form to get right."

And the Spice Girls worked harder at getting it right than has generally been acknowledged. They instinctively had an ear for a catchy tune without falling back on the formula balladry and bland modulations which the Westlife/Boyzone brigade have traditionally reeled off by the yard. A lot of the magic was in the feisty attitude that the Spice Girls' songs conveyed. It was as if they had hijacked the lad culture that infused Britpop and given it their own female twist, becoming what the editor of *Smash Hits* called "Oasis in a Wonderbra".

But while they poured all that spontaneous, larger-than-life personality into their songs, there was just as much work put into the fine detail of those records. Take, for example, the strings on the outro of the extended version of '2 Become 1'. Arranged by Craig Armstrong – a respected artist in his own right, also known for his work with Massive Attack – and with beats added by Spike Stent, it is a passage that would not sound out of place on a Bjork record.

"There was a musical evolution of the Spice Girls songs," said Ashley Newton, who A&R-ed all the Spice Girls albums. "You started with very pop-driven, young, bubbling-with-attitude stuff, and you captured that in a bottle and then put it through a process of making it sound as good as it possibly could. Great string arrangements and getting Spike to wave his magic wand on that final furlong. And what came out the other end was something that hadn't lost its pop feel, but which had a world-class flavour to it."

It's an extraordinary fact that in all the articles, interviews and overviews that have been written about the Spice Girls, their actual music barely ever gets a mention. Everyone can hum a Spice Girls song, but the undeniable artistry of those recordings has never been recognised.

They did it again with *Spiceworld*, if anything a marginally better, more sophisticated album than *Spice*. Despite the inhumanly hectic schedule that was threatening to overwhelm them by then, they came up with the effervescent, Latinesque shout-out of 'Spice Up Your Life', the cool Motown pastiche of 'Stop' and the evocative, Spanish guitar-driven balladry of 'Viva Forever' with its supremely stylish echoes of Madonna's 'La Isla Bonita'. Peppered with personality, and each conveying a distinctive musical flavour and lyrical theme, these are songs which couldn't sound *less* "manufactured", and which, in several cases, transcend the pop genre altogether. The Spice Girls did not become the biggest British act of the Nineties – comfortably outselling Oasis, the Prodigy and anyone else you care to mention – without having something more substantial than their own celebrity to sell. If Abba's songs were an example of "original and affecting artistry", the Spice Girls repertoire was a blast of immaculate, independently minded, good-time dance-pop wizardry.

One reason why the creative achievements of the Spice Girls have been undervalued is the extraordinary level of celebrity which they acquired so swiftly. They were the first pop phenomenon truly to understand the demands of the modern multi-media age, and to tailor their efforts accordingly. Dance routines and video storyboards were automatically devised at the same time as the songs. Radio producers and television presenters were greeted like long-lost friends, and always left with a suitably upbeat soundbite. But it was the relationship the Spice Girls struck up with the British press that was most unlike anything that had ever gone before.

There is a concrete bunker at Virgin Records in West London where they keep press cuttings relating to their artists. The section devoted to the Spice Girls is about as big as for all the other acts put together. Row upon row of huge, mobile, floor-to-ceiling shelving units are devoted to cataloguing the torrent of newspaper and magazine articles devoted to the group.

Even in their heyday, Elvis Presley and The Beatles attracted only a fraction of the press coverage that the Spice Girls came to regard as routine. This was because pop acts in the Fifties and Sixties were simply not a part of the cultural landscape that held any great interest for the readership of mainstream family newspapers. By the Eighties and Nineties pop had come to be recognised as a core ingredient of tabloid newspapers and a subject to be given due consideration by the broadsheets. But even by those standards, the sheer volume of coverage which the Spice Girls attracted was utterly without precedent.

The fact that they had so quickly achieved such a high level of recognition both as a group and as individuals (the taxi driver test) had a bearing on this, as did the fact that they were five pretty girls. And like all the big media icons they had a natural aptitude for supplying the press with what they wanted.

They beguiled the pop mags with talk about their favourite groups and the innermost secrets of their make-up bags. But confronted for the first time by a journalist from the *Daily Star* they smoothly adjusted their comments to appeal to the paper's male, blue-collar readership.

"None of us fancies celebrities that much," Emma told the *Star*'s reporter. "We all prefer salt-of-the-earth men, like builders, bricklayers, telephone engineers – those kind of guys."

Unlike the majority of pop airheads, let alone the gormless emissaries of Britpop with their impenetrable northern accents and chippy attitude, the Spice Girls were bright, opinionated and shameless in their pursuit of headlines.

They were an obvious choice, for example, to switch on the Oxford Street Christmas lights in November 1996, a commitment which they took conspicuous delight in fulfilling. Melanie B remembered the five of them all "shouting and screaming and falling about the control tower . . . It was an incredible, extraordinary buzz." It was also an occasion which helped to cement their place in the popular consciousness in a way that Noel and Liam Gallagher could not have contemplated.

The previous month, their second single, 'Say You'll Be There', had been another massive hit, entering the British chart at number one, and stoking demand for their album, *Spice*, which finally arrived on British record shop shelves on November 10. The album went straight in at the top where it eventually stayed for nine weeks. It had sold more than 1.8 million copies by Christmas in the UK alone, making it a platinum album six times over.

By the time they came to release '2 Become 1' on December 22, all bets as to what would be the Christmas number one were off.

"One of the greatest regrets of my life," said Robert Sandall, Virgin's

Director of Press, "was that I didn't bet on '2 Become 1' to be the Christmas number one. They were offering odds of 25-1 soon after 'Wannabe' went to number one."

Ray Cooper, Virgin's Head of Marketing, who had put £100 on the song doing just that, was able to finance his Christmas shopping that year from the winnings. The record, meanwhile, held the number one slot for three weeks, stayed in the chart for 19 weeks, and eventually sold a million copies.

The Spice Girls wanted publicity, there was no doubt about that. They also had a highly efficient PR machine working on their behalf. Muff Fitzgerald, their press officer at Virgin from 1996-97, made the point succinctly when he said: "If a story in a market-leading tabloid such as *The Sun* can reach thirty million people, well, there were thirty million reasons why we wanted the Girls to feature there."

But as they quickly discovered, it is a lot easier to get into the gossip columns than it is to get out of them. And to begin with the girls were just as vulnerable as the next celebrity to the guerrilla tactics of the tabloid press. They had to be constantly on their guard against intrusions into every aspect of their lives. As soon as they became successful, former boyfriends started to come out of the woodwork with kiss-and-tell stories. Although Geri had never denied her past exploits as a nude/ "glamour" model, she had glossed over the full extent of the sessions she had done, and it caused acute embarrassment and a palpable tension within the group when nude pictures of her started circulating among the tabloids and elsewhere. The same day that *The Sun* first featured nude shots of Geri, the paper also ran a story on Emma's mother, Pauline, who had been accosted by a journalist and photographer at a church hall where she was running a karate class.

As the Girls' success escalated so did the level of intrusion. When Emma celebrated her 21st birthday at the Atlantic Club in London, a *Daily Star* reporter was dispatched, incognito, to the restaurant. Posing as a member of the public she followed Emma and Melanie C into the ladies toilets and asked if she could have her photograph taken with them to give to her nieces who were big fans of the Spice Girls. The picture showed up the next day in the *Star* above a story proclaiming that it had been the "only paper to be invited to Emma's birthday."

It was at this point, early in 1997, that Simon Fuller took the unprecedented step of hiring a lawyer specifically to oversee the activities of the press vis-à-vis the Spice Girls. Gerrard Tyrrell of the London solicitors Harbottle & Lewis, was a commercial libel and litigation expert whom Fuller had known since the mid-Eighties. An urbane 40-year-old character for whom the adage "Speak softly and carry a big stick" might have been invented, Tyrrell had worked on behalf of all sorts of Hollywood stars, and successfully represented Richard Branson in his battle against British Airways in the so-called "Dirty Tricks" case. Tyrrell's favourite band was The Clash, whose drummer, Topper Headon, he had represented during the break-up of the group. However he quickly adapted to the rather different needs of the Spice Girls.

Tyrrell never spoke to *anyone* on the record. But he had plenty to say off the record. His strategy was to go above the heads of newspaper editors and deal directly with their senior management. Using a mixture of charm, persuasion, threats and coercion he controlled, so far as was possible, not only the flow of stories to the newspapers but the nature of them. Tyrrell let it be known that if the papers printed misleading or offensive stories about the Girls then they would be sued and denied further access to them. But if they co-operated then the Girls would, in effect, be there for them. The idea was to build a long-term relationship with the papers, structured in such a way that their show business editors had a constant flow of stories and photographs of these five attractive women – manna from heaven as far as the tabloids were concerned – while being firmly discouraged from seeking out stories that were unhelpful to the group or damaging to their image.

Tyrrell placed particular emphasis on protecting the Girls' Intellectual Property (IP) rights. IP refers to all aspects of an act's image, including photographs and quoted material, and while Tyrrell could not hope to police the Girls' IP rights on every front, he used those areas that he could control as a lever to influence coverage overall.

As Muff Fitzgerald explained: "Every photographer who took photographs of the group was required to sign a photo-release form which effectively said that the Spice Girls retained copyright and ownership of those images and that aside from the specified and mutually agreed publication date, any further reproduction of those images would require written permission from the Girls or their management."

This did not go down well with the photographers nor the record company who were required to police the arrangement.

"Tyrrell drew up the agreement which *we* had to make all the photographers sign," recalled Robert Sandall. "A lot of them didn't like it and there were all kinds of horrible arguments about this. Well, Virgin is a record company. We're not selling photographs. We use photographs as promotional tools. But we now found ourselves being used to facilitate his [Fuller's] desire to make money out of the photographs of the girls. This was typical of Fuller's approach to the record company. Get the record company to pay for everything, then get them to do everything, and then, if anything goes wrong, you blame them for everything."

But there wasn't much that Sandall or Virgin could do about it. And the arrangement proved so successful that many aspects of Tyrrell's model for maintaining relations between pop stars and the press have since become the industry norm. While Fitzgerald along with Sandall and the rest of the Virgin press office managed day-to-day relations with the press, Tyrrell was quietly dealing with editors and management behind the scenes. The idea was to keep the girls in the news, but without turning out the same rubbishy stories again and again. Loquacious and insistent, Tyrrell took certain ideas to the papers directly, and did his best to guide their thinking towards celebrating the success of a group that was flying the flag for Britain all around the world.

Crucially, the arrangement meant that Tyrrell heard all the Spice rumours *before* they got into the papers and was able to head off most of them before they made it into print. He couldn't do much to stem the tide of kiss-and-tells from former boyfriends: thirteen in all by the middle of 1997. But a lot of malicious gossip and plain untruths were firmly nipped in the bud. It was put to Tyrrell at various times, that the Girls were either dating or having affairs with everyone under the sun. And all the Girls, at one time or another, were said to be pregnant. When issuing his denials of the latter suggestion, Tyrrell would insist that the newspapers should wait for three or four months and then see who was right. Amazingly, they invariably did as they were told, further strengthening Tyrrell's hand when he was eventually proved to be telling the truth.

No pop group had done this before, and the ploy was to prove remarkably successful in regulating not only the quantity but also the quality of press exposure that the Spice Girls subsequently enjoyed. Virtually every day for nearly two years, they received coverage in the newspapers, the vast majority of it upbeat, positive and encouraging in tone.

Typical of a story that didn't get out was the fact that an undisclosed sum of money was paid to a publisher who sued the Girls over an alleged misuse of a sample on 'Who Do You Think You Are'. The deal was quietly concluded behind the scenes, and according to an inside source at Virgin: "It never made the headlines. Gerrard killed it."

Who knows how many other negative or critical stories went the same way. The only catch, so far as the group was concerned, was that Tyrrell was, and would always remain, Fuller's man. This explained why, within five days of them sacking Fuller as their manager in 1998, they would get their first taste of truly bad press. And once the hounds were let off the leash, the anti-Spice floodgates would burst with a spectacular vengeance, of which more later.

But for a while, the popularity of the Spice Girls was such that they became virtually invulnerable. They were also ubiquitous. Every day you would see the Spice-word used in all sorts of contexts – in headlines, picture captions, advertisement copy – anywhere that a sub-editor or writer wanted to grab a reader's attention.

"While the Spice Girls once again wiggle and squeak their way to the top of the charts . . . I chanced to bump into Neneh Cherry, an original Spice woman," was how Pete Clark began his write-up of an interview, not with the Spice Girls, but with Neneh Cherry, who may have been fondly remembered for performing her 1988 hit, 'Buffalo Stance', on *Top Of The Pops* when she was eight months pregnant, but had nothing whatsoever to do with the Spice Girls.

Even *New Musical Express* was forced to bite the bullet. "Yup! That's right. You're not seeing things," blared the strapline to an amazingly positive piece by Paul Moody. "Spice Girls are in *NME*. And too bloody right. So for one week forget your saddo indie band playing down the Arse & Trumpet and prepare to enter the great 'Which one's your favourite?' debate!" True to form, Geri came up with the sort of quote that was so ideally tailored to the *NME* mindset it was almost as if *she* was the one taking the piss out of *them*. Asked what sort of man she was most attracted to, she responded: "I really respect someone like Malcolm X for what he stood for . . . But then on the other hand, someone I wanted to shag might just be any bloke with a six-pack who had a bit of sexuality about him."

Similarly, when it came to an interview with *The Big Issue*, the campaigning magazine sold on the streets of big cities by homeless people, they freighted their usual message with plenty of equal opportunity rhetoric.

"Girl power is giving yourself that little bit of liberation," Melanie B explained. "You decide the kind of life you want to lead. Whether you're black, white, gay, single parent, whatever. Just go for it."

Perhaps viewed in this context, the bombshell that they dropped in December 1996 was not quite so significant as it seemed at the time. Even so, the interview which they gave to Simon Sebag Montefiore in the *Spectator*, remains one of the most enduring and in some ways revealing aspects of Spice mythology.

An upmarket, right-wing, political magazine, the *Spectator* was the last place you would expect to find show business stars of any persuasion being interviewed, let alone an all-girl pop group. But Montefiore, a regular contributor to the magazine who is also a writer for the *Sunday Times*, has something of a track record for eliciting odd or unfashionable opinions from celebrities. During an encounter with Rick Parfitt and Francis Rossi of Status Quo, for example, Montefiore listened sympathetically while the veteran rock'n'rollers embarked on a rant in support of capital punishment ("If you're gonna kill them, hurt them first," Parfitt said). Doubtless, the quotes reflected Parfitt's and Rossi's genuinely held beliefs, but it is hard to think of any other situation in which the pair would have elected to make such opinions so widely known, and with such apparent gusto.

It was Montefiore's editor at the *Spectator*, Frank Johnson, who set the ball rolling vis-à-vis the Spice Girls when he asked Montefiore to interview for the magazine's Christmas edition, "whoever was the most famous British pop singer of our day and question him as if he were a politician: ask him about the single currency, fiscal policy, and so on." Shrewdly realising that the most famous pop act of the day was not a man, but five women, Montefiore duly set up an interview with the Spice Girls. The encounter took place backstage at the *Smash Hits* awards on December 1, where the group carried off the trophies for Best British Group, Best New Act and Best Pop Video (for 'Say You'll Be There').

"I sat them all down," Montefiore revealed in the aftermath of the affair. "It was a bit like a lesson really . . . and I said to them initially: 'I'm not remotely interested in your music, your personal lives or who you're fucking. I just want to know your political manifesto.' They looked alarmed, but I think it was the most calm and low-key interview they had ever given."

The result was a masterful piece of political and social satire, in which Montefiore skilfully interwove the quotes he had obtained from the Girls with his own exaggeratedly highbrow commentary. "Spice Girls Back Sceptics On Europe" was the headline, followed by the deadpan strap: "Opposition to Labour on tax, rejection of single currency. Important interview by Simon Sebag Montefiore".

The overall effect of the article was not only (gently) to caricature the Girls as a bunch of celebrity airheads sounding off on subjects far beyond their area of competence, but also to lampoon the notion of the pretentious journalist over-interpreting his interviewees' opinions to suggest that they contained nuggets of lofty political wisdom.

"The Spice Girls cite Sir Winston Churchill as one of the main influences on their ideology – and music," Montefiore wrote. "I wonder if this refers to Sir John Colville's memories of Churchill singing Harrow School songs in his bath during the war?

" 'Yeah, partly,' said Victoria."

Montefiore assumed the role of the slightly bemused codger, dazzled by the unexpected political "wisdom" displayed by the Girls, but otherwise out of touch with the codes of popular culture – an impression which he bolstered, unwittingly, by misspelling Geri's name (as Gerri) throughout the entire article.

" 'Why shouldn't earls and dukes and marquesses be in parliament?' asked Gerri rhetorically. 'They're a mixed bag. A mixed bag is what you want in parliament.' Even Lord St John of Fawsley never defined the constitution so exquisitely."

The interview would doubtless have attracted little attention in the broader scheme of things but for one startling revelation. The Spice Girls admitted that they were Tories. Not only admitted it, but positively shouted it from the rooftops.

"We Spice Girls are true Thatcherites. Thatcher was the first Spice Girl, the pioneer of our ideology – Girl Power. But for now we're desperately worried about the slide to a single currency."

True to form, Geri had given the magazine what they wanted to hear. But this was one quote that would not be forgotten in a hurry. To begin with, their remarks were seized upon by the tabloids who put their own jolly spin on the development.

"The Spice Girls talk a lot of sense about politics," declared an editorial in *The Sun*. "They say Maggie Thatcher was the first Spice Girl. That's obviously why Maggie was Number One for so long."

Boom Boom!

Then the broadsheet columnists weighed in with a succession of wry, half-mocking commentaries. But jokey as this coverage was, the very fact that the Spice Girls were being written about in connection with such weighty subjects meant that their politics became, de facto, something of a serious concern.

"Before this week, most people over 30 wouldn't have heard of them," noted a *Sunday Telegraph* reporter. "Nevertheless, their views on such important topics as the exchange rate mechanism were thought worthy of prominence in *The Sun*, *The Times*, the *Daily Mail*, the *Daily Telegraph* and, most surprising of all, the *Financial Times*. What has happened? Is it simply an illusion created by editors looking for some good news for the Tories in a pretty brutal week? Or is there something more to it?"

It wasn't long before MPs were queuing up to have their say.

"Perhaps the Spice Girls are the last vestige of Eighties self-interest and self-gratification," suggested Michael Connarty, the Labour Member for Falkirk East, who added for good measure: "Joan Armatrading broke my bloody heart when she came out as a Conservative."

The Christmas 1996 issue was the biggest selling in the 200-year history of the *Spectator*. It shifted 60,000 copies and catapulted the Spice Girls into a different league as far as their public profile was concerned. Whether it was *Blue Peter*, *Newsnight*, the *Today* programme or *Richard and Judy*, the Spice Girls became a subject that demanded attention. Even the most cloistered politician, high court judge or ecclesiastical bigwig could now not fail to be aware of the Spice Girls.

The pop journalist Chris Heath provided an unusually insightful analysis of the Spice phenomenon in the March 1997 edition of *The Face*.

"The Spice Girls' success is of a different order to anything we have had for a very long time," Heath wrote. "With uncomfortable speed, they have become part of the fabric of our world, of our language, and of the way we talk and think about ourselves . . . They are talked about in Parliament. They are fought over by our leaders and our would-be leaders. They are the currently favoured metaphor for any kind of high-spiritedness, or feisty femininity (turn on that radio right now; it's the celebrating female Wrexham supporters returning home on their coach from West Ham, talking on Radio Five Live to David Mellor, being referred to, quite naturally and without explanation, as 'spice girls'), or any kind of trashiness, or any kind of independence, or any kind of wink-wink-guys sexuality, or any kind of gang-flavoured jubilation, or even simply as a metaphor for unfettered popularity itself."

This was all well and good, but the unprecedented celebrity profile which the *Spectator* piece bequeathed on the Spice Girls came at a price. In the pop world there is almost no crime more heinous than being a Tory. No one these days would think anything untoward of a pop star who admitted taking drugs, being an alcoholic or engaging in outré sexual practices with rent boys or prostitutes. Indeed, people are rather disappointed when pop stars do *not* behave like this. And while activities such as drug-dealing, burglary, drunk-driving, pimping, GBH, embezzlement, gangland murders, date-rape and so forth are not encouraged, only a fuddy-duddy would rush to be "judgemental" about the various artists who have become involved in them over the years.

Even voting Conservative in your dim and deluded past can be absolved, providing you subsequently recant vigorously and publicly enough. Paul Weller and Billy Bragg, who both started off as Tory voters in their youth, had put such transgressions well behind them by the time they became poster boys for the Labour party in the Eighties through the agency of the Red Wedge organisation.

But there is nothing that goes more against the grain of the metropolitan pop worldview than Being A Tory. Few pop stars have ever formally come out as supporters of the Conservative party, and even then it is something they are only likely to divulge once everyone is past caring. A tragically unhip superstar such as Phil Collins or a superannuated pop idol like Erroll Brown of Hot Chocolate might be able to admit allegiance to the Tory cause without damaging their credibility. But for a whole group still in the first flush of popularity and enjoying a spectacularly cosy honeymoon with the media to declare themselves to be "true Thatcherites" was an event that sent painful shockwaves coursing through the cultural antennae of the pop community's movers and shakers. Could these girls be serious? What did it all mean?

While the quotes in Montefiore's piece were accepted by the Spice Girls as being accurate, he had spun a story from them that was deliberately simplistic. Although presented as a statement of the whole group's philosophy, the key quotes were those supplied by Victoria and Geri. Emma, who had contributed virtually nothing to the interview, subsequently insisted that she had no intention of voting either way in the forthcoming election. Melanie B, who later described the piece as "twisted beyond belief", was deliberately sidelined by Montefiore. "She didn't know anything about anything," Montefiore recalled, "so I had to tell her to shut up." Meanwhile, Melanie C, who rarely got a word in edgeways during interviews in those days, declared afterwards that she was actually a Labour voter. "I'm from working class Liverpool," she said. "I think Margaret Thatcher's a complete prick after what she's done to my hometown."

The only real Tories in the Spice Girls were Victoria and Geri, a fact which – once the fuss had died down – was rarely mentioned again, but never forgotten.

In some ways it was rather surprising that it had taken so long for the pop world to throw up a group that actively defied the orthodox party line. For despite the almost universal tendency for pop stars to lean politically to the left, they nevertheless operate in one of the most viciously competitive arenas that the capitalist system has ever devised. While espousing egalitarian ideals, even the most politically committed entertainers are part of a rigorously selected elite. And while expressing solidarity with the poor, the weak and the dispossessed in their songs and interviews, even moderately successful pop stars are members of a pampered aristocracy who are engaged, whether they say they like it or not, in a brutal struggle to acquire vast sums of money, amassed inevitably at the expense of their competitors.

The music industry is an example of the economic doctrine of laissez-faire gone mad. You will search in vain in the world of the pop or rock star for examples of collective bargaining, minimum wages, maximum working hours, workers' rights, pension plans or any of the other rules that govern the activities which take place in any "normal" place of work. Every artist who has made it far enough up the greasy pole of pop to matter, will have recruited the services of a lawyer, an agent, a manager, a promoter, an accountant, and sundry business advisers quite apart from the ranks of A&R men, marketing managers and other executives working on their behalf at the record company. The purpose of the operation will be dressed up in all sorts of ways. "I just want my music to be heard by as many people as possible," is a favourite (to which the obvious follow-up question "Why?" is rarely asked). But at the end of the day the collective job of this army of organisers, facilitators, bean-counters and troubleshooters is to maximise the artist's revenue from sales of records, concert tickets and other merchandise while keeping to a minimum such outgoings as wage bills and tax liability. Generally these business people will perform their tasks with ruthless efficiency or else they will be replaced.

Few operators in any other walk of life embrace the spirit of free enterprise with such rapacious zeal as the key representatives of the successful pop artist. Whether it be Chris de Burgh or Bob Marley, Westlife or The Clash, the selling and distribution of pop music takes place in a commercial theatre of war that is red in tooth and claw. In public, artists frequently rail against the machinations of the suits who work so tirelessly on their behalf, but in private they know very well on which side their bread is buttered.

While political philosophies can be separated from business realities with relative ease, there is another sense in which successful pop stars often embody core Conservative values. Whether born and brought up in disadvantaged circumstances or relative affluence, they are usually highly aspirational, self-motivated personalities. They may subscribe to the caring, collective ethos of state socialism, but their actions are those of the self-reliant, risk-taking entrepreneur, the kind of person who will pursue a personal goal or ambition with unswerving dedication, no matter what obstacles (or people) get in his way. Driven by a determination to better themselves and get to the top, successful pop stars are likely to be individualists at heart, with a highly developed sense of rational self-interest to boot. This was certainly the case with Geri, whose faith in self-help manuals and the power of self-belief was matched only by her determination to pull herself up by her bootstraps and improve her lot in this world. Her admiration for Margaret Thatcher was an instinctive response to the example of a woman who had achieved her goals, on her own terms, in a man's world.

"She [Margaret Thatcher] fucked up big-time loads of different things, definitely," Geri said, under pressure to explain herself. "But what I give her credit for is she is the first fucking woman."

The full depth of Geri's political conviction was revealed when she appeared in a TV election broadcast five years later – in support of the Labour Party. Pictured making and pouring tea for a group of pensioners, Geri did not have a speaking role in the commercial, but contributed to the propaganda via a statement released by the Labour Party press office: "A lot of people knock Britain, but I have to say I'm proud of this country and the opportunities it offers people. I genuinely admire and believe in Tony Blair."

Victoria, however, took a more principled view. Despite describing

John Major as "a boring pillock" in the *Spectator* interview, she has never made any bones about her politics. "Personally, I am a Tory," she said afterwards. For her, there were no doubts or conflicts of interest let alone guilt trips involved in belonging to a rich and highly successful pop group. "We want to be as famous as Persil Automatic," she had once declared. Which was probably one reason why it took them so little time to achieve just that.

# 6

# Automatic For The People

On January 1, 1997, 'Wannabe' became the first Spice Girls record to be released in America. It went in to the *Billboard* Hot 100 at number 11, which was the highest first-week entry in the American singles chart since 'I Want To Hold Your Hand' by The Beatles, 32 years previously. By February 14, 'Wannabe' was installed at number one and America was on its way to following a pattern already established in markets as far afield as Southeast Asia, Europe, Australasia, South Africa and Israel.

It was a suitably auspicious start to a year in which the Spice Girls would achieve more than most groups do in their entire careers. More to the point, the five girls actually *did* more in those twelve months than most groups would consider feasible given twice as long. Consider for a moment the sheer volume of work that they produced in that time. Having promoted the *Spice* album from scratch in America, they set about writing and recording their second album, *Spiceworld*, while simultaneously going into production for a feature-length film of the same name. Both album and movie were somehow completed and released in time for Christmas. Meanwhile, in October, they staged their first live concert (at an 8,000-capacity basketball arena in Istanbul). They also cobbled together *Spice – The Official Video, Volume 1* (an entertaining behind-the-scenes "popumentary" which sold half a million copies in the UK alone) and even found time to write a book along the way. This slender volume, entitled *Girl Power*, sold out its initial print run of 200,000 copies within a day, and was eventually translated into more than 20 languages. That's before you begin to factor in continuous promotional visits all around the world, along with sundry other activities such as helping to produce their own quarterly *Spice* magazine ("Written by the Spice Girls just for *you*").

"The amount of work those girls did in an 18-month period was probably greater than I've ever seen any act do that I've worked with in my career," said Virgin A&R man, Ashley Newton. "They did not stop. They were doing promotion in Japan one minute, doing stuff all throughout Europe the next, and trying to keep the UK in play as well. Because the UK, all the time, wants new photographs, new stories, new gossip. They want you on every Saturday morning kids TV show, everything you can think of. And if you just get on a plane and disappear – 'Sorry, I'm not available for three months' – that's no good."

Newton's view was echoed by Simon Fuller's henchman Gerrard Tyrrell.

"Those girls worked harder than anybody else I've ever seen in my life. They were driven – not as in Simon was cracking a whip – they were just determined to go for it. They threw themselves into it in an astonishing way. Too many people get lazy. But they understood. Simon said, 'This is what you have to do to get there,' and they did it. That's why people loved them. Because they put a lot of effort into it."

"The hardest working group in Christendom," said Virgin UK president, Paul Conroy.

Seeing their plans for global domination falling into place with such astonishing speed certainly did not encourage a feeling of complacency among the girls, let alone Fuller.

"As a manager there are two options," he said in 1997. "To steady the ship and steer it through the rough waters ahead, or put the foot down harder and come up with bigger and better things. I'm going for the latter approach. That way you maintain interest."

And maintain interest they certainly did. At the annual Brit Awards staged in the vast Earls Court arena on February 24, they opened the show with a performance of 'Who Do You Think You Are' which was so over the top that it eclipsed everything that followed. Striding down a ramped walkway amid a cacophony of fireworks and exploding cannons, they radiated raw, garish star appeal in a way that no British pop act in recent memory had done.

Geri wore her now infamous Union flag mini-dress, a sexy, skin-tight ensemble which she had designed herself and which her wardrobe assistant had stitched together from a real Union flag. This was a classic Geri touch, reading the Zeitgeist almost by accident and then surfing it as if to the manner born. On the face of it there was nothing very clever or original about using the national flag as a decorative motif for something called the Brit Awards. But in that curious way that she so often did, Geri had hit on an emblem that was perfect both for the moment and for the Spice Girls. In just a few months they had become the most successful exporters of recorded British pop music in the Nineties. In an editorial on the eve of the Brits, *The Times* trumpeted the success of the British music industry, which the newspaper noted "has now grown bigger than shipbuilding, electronic components and water supply, with little help from governments that pour money into more conventional enterprises." The piece was headlined "Sugar And Spice".

The notion of "Cool Britannia", which had been in the air since *Newsweek* ran a cover story in November 1996 declaring London to be "the coolest city on the planet", was about to reach critical mass with a 25-page report in the American celebrity arts and fashion bible *Vanity Fair* which set the official seal on London as the new world capital of pop culture. The cover (in the UK edition, anyway) was graced by a picture of Liam Gallagher and Patsy Kensit lying under a Union Flag duvet. The story inside spoke of the electricity that was supposedly coursing through the cultural veins of London's bars, theatres, restaurants, concert halls and sports arenas. According to the American arbiters of cool there had been an explosion of creativity among the musicians, artists, fashion designers and other vaguely employed celebrities who spent their days shopping, clubbing and partying in the capital's most fashionable, if sometimes less reputable haunts.

The contribution of Oasis, Blur and their various Britpop cronies to this cultural revolution was chewed over in breathless detail. Liam Gallagher was spotted at the *Q* magazine awards. "A few hours later, in authentic Jagger/Richards '67 fashion, he will go on a bender, stay out all night, smash up the snooker room of the Groucho Club in Soho, and get arrested in the street the following morning on suspicion of possessing drugs by a bobby who will mistake him for a tramp." Good old Liam; always ready to go the extra mile when it came to boosting the capital's quotient of cool.

Mention of the Spice Girls, however, was limited to a picture caption dismissing them as: "The Birds – The out-of-nowhere, all-singing, all-dancing, all-Tory-supporting teenybopper pop sensations of 1996."

The writer of the piece was not the last to underestimate their significance as a British cultural phenomenon. But the Girls did not belong with the brawling, Britpop, boys-club crowd. And in any case, the story was out of date.

While Oasis had held court with an air of dour belligerence during the previous year's Brit Awards and likewise Blur the year before that, in 1997 both groups were conspicuous by their absence. Liam Gallagher had earlier let it be known that he wouldn't be attending the event for fear he might be unable to control the impulse to "chin" the Spice Girls. When the Girls went up to the podium later in the show to collect their award for 'Wannabe' winning Best Single of the year, Melanie C offered Liam a typically forthright response: "Come and have a go, if you think you're hard enough," she bellowed in her broadest Scouse accent. The Girls also lifted the Best Video trophy for 'Say You'll Be There'. These, tellingly, were the two awards which were voted for by the public. In what was to become a familiar pattern, the group were passed over in the "more serious" categories (Best Album, Best Group, etc.) which are allocated by the industry tastemakers who comprise the Brits Voting Academy.

While collecting the award for Best Video, Geri thrust her arm into the air causing her dress (not the Union flag one) momentarily to fall off her breasts. "Spice Girls Win Two Big Ones At Pop Supershow" trumpeted the *Daily Star*, which along with every paper – whether tabloid or broadsheet – ran a picture of Geri or the Spice Girls on the front page the next day.

The following month they released the fourth and final single from the *Spice* album, a double A-side comprised of 'Mama' and 'Who Do You Think You Are'. All artist royalties from the single were donated to Comic Relief's Red Nose Day which took place on March 14 and the video for 'Who Do You Think You Are' found the Spice Girls being shadowed by a parody group, the Sugar Lumps, led by Dawn French (in the role of Posh) and Jennifer Saunders (as a rather eerie Ginger Spice lookalike). It was all for a good cause, naturally, but tying the record in to the media juggernaut of Red Nose Day was a marketing coup just the same. What turned the exercise into a stroke of genius was timing it in similarly close proximity to Mothering Sunday. Right on cue, there were the Girls' mothers all proudly displayed in the video for the other A-side, 'Mama'. In marked contrast to the high-energy attitude of 'Who Do You Think You Are' – "The race is on to get out of the bottom" – 'Mama' was as shamelessly sentimental as a greetings card. And yet in some peculiar, artless way – perhaps thanks to the logic of girl power – it was still vaguely cool; not cool like a Blur song, but not mawkish nonsense like Clive Dunn singing 'Grandad' either. Even cooler was the fact that the record's instant ascent to the top of the UK chart made the Spice Girls the first act ever to enjoy four number one hits with their first four singles.

Meanwhile, the *Spice* album was forging ahead in the American chart, where it had reached number two by the time the Girls returned to New York for another promotional push in April. A fully live performance of 'Wannabe' and 'Say You'll Be There' on the top-rated US TV comedy/chat show *Saturday Night Live* was watched by an audience of 20 million viewers, helping sales and bolstering their credibility as a group who, it seemed, could actually sing after all. The following month, *Spice* finally reached the top of the American chart where it stayed for five weeks. With sales of 5.3 million copies, it was eventually declared the best-selling album of 1997 in America by SoundScan (the organisation which monitors sales of records in the US).

Before that, though, back in Britain the Girls fulfilled a television commitment of a different nature when at 6pm on Saturday, March 30, they opened the new terrestrial TV station, Channel 5. Instead of one of their own hits however, they were commissioned to sing an "exclusive" new number, hymning the joys of Channel 5. At the appointed hour, the five girls duly lined up in front of a huge 5 logo and launched into the song which was loosely based on the old Manfred Mann hit '5-4-3-2-1':

> *Welcome to a brand new station (1-2-3-4-5)*
> *Tune in now for a new generation (1-2-3-4-5)*
> *Guaranteed to be the new sensation (1-2-3-4-5)*
> *Take it from us – It's girl power*
> *Take it from us – It's the power of Five*

It was an unbelievably cheesy performance of an unbelievably cheesy song; not even a song when you get right down to it, more an extended jingle. And here was a paradox that went right to the heart of the Spice phenomenon. The biggest-selling pop group in the world at that moment was perfectly happy to come on and sing the kind of advertisement that would cause even a bunch of hard-up "resting" actors or stage-school hopefuls to blanch. Not only that, but they had thrown the full weight of their reputation behind the enterprise, invoking the sacred notion of girl power willy-nilly, like some fairground huckster proclaiming the benefits of the latest tonic that will magically cure all your ailments.

Now, the Spice Girls were doubtless handsomely rewarded for doing the job, not only financially – their fee was reported to be around the £500,000 pounds mark – but in terms of the exposure. And he who pays the piper calls the tune. But was it really necessary to embrace the project with quite such a degree of unabashed enthusiasm? And was no one keeping an eye on the quality control?

They may have made great pop music, but if ever a group regarded their creative endeavours as a means to achieving a commercial end it was the Spice Girls. While pop stars through the decades have generally tried to a greater or lesser extent to protect their artistic integrity by not appearing to endorse unrelated or unsuitable products, the Spice Girls did the exact opposite. They were up for anything.

In Issue 4 of *Spice* magazine, which came out in November 1997 there was a double-page advertisement for a Spice Girls Christmas tie-in with the supermarket chain Asda. A suitably seasonal message was placed above a picture of the girls draped on and around four giant building-block letters spelling out ASDA. "Only at ASDA this Christmas," proclaimed the blurb, "will you find a dedicated Spice Girls Zone, with a whole range of exclusive gifts specially designed by the Spice Girls. From playing cards at just 99p to bean bags at £14.99. There's something to suit every pocket."

Spread around the two pages was a selection of Spice endorsed products: balloons (ordinary and helium), Cadbury's Spice Girl chocolates (carton or collection tray), Christmas crackers (Cracker Power), Kids Meal Box (choice of hot or cold meal), jumbo cushion, Power Rub beach towel (100% cotton), Christmas Cards (from 99p), Celebration sponge cake, a book (*Real Life: Real Spice – The Official Story* by the Spice Girls). And buried somewhere amid this Aladdin's Cave of Spice goodies there was even a copy of the group's new CD, *Spiceworld*, available for just £12.99.

Turn the page and there was a range of streamlined sportswear "for girls of all ages" and also "gifts for men". These included girls' shorts, side-stripe leggings and V-neck sports tops (3-10 yrs), along with men's socks, ties and pyjamas (the latter with "Spice Up Your Life" logo and picture).

When it came to endorsements, it seemed the Spice Girls didn't know the meaning of the word "No". There was apparently no product of consumer interest, however mundane or embarrassing, that it was beyond their ingenuity to adapt to the girl power credo.

In August, they launched an "official" Spice deodorant in conjunction with Impulse. According to the advertising copy the body spray promised to deliver "girl power confidence all day long", with a scent evocative of the fab five themselves. This included a delicate bouquet of lavender and vanilla to represent Baby Spice, warm amber and red pepper for Ginger Spice, jasmine and muguet for Posh Spice, tangerine for Sporty Spice, and rather less flatteringly paduk wood for Scary Spice. God knows what the result of spraying that lot over yourself on a regular basis might have been, but presumably insect repellent, air freshener and incense sticks were all made redundant at a stroke once someone encased in such a fragrance entered the room.

By the middle of 1997, the Spice Girls had signed up for product tie-in deals with Pepsi, Benetton, Fabergé, Sony PlayStations, Polaroid cameras and Walker's crisps. As well as making and marketing their own dolls, their faces were on T-shirts, coffee cups, crash-hats, skates, BT phonecards, watches, bomber jackets, posters, schoolbags, calendars, key-chains and pencil cases. Their name was linked with everything from bed linen to crockery. For a while, Geri's mother tried to keep a collection of all the different items on sale, but eventually she was forced to give up. "It simply wasn't possible to keep track of them all," Geri recalled.

While the girls were enthusiastic and imaginative participants in the whole business, the man behind the strategy was, of course, Simon Fuller. To oversee the operation, Fuller had hired Edward Freedman, the gift-shop guru who had raised Manchester United's merchandising turnover from £5 million in 1993 to £28 million in 1997.

Naturally, the tie-ins netted both Fuller and the Girls a fortune, but that was not the point according to Fuller.

"The sponsorship deals were far more about exposure than the money," Fuller said later. "A lot of money was made, but my thinking was if we can get Pepsi to spend $40 million basically running what was a commercial for my group, then Hallelujah! If Procter & Gamble wanted to launch a new image for one of their body sprays by spending £20 million . . . That was the way I did it. And it happened so fast. Because I thought of it not as a deal in terms of making a million quid. It was about using their money to make my group famous, and then they'd make lots of money anyway."

Fuller's legal sidekick, Gerrard Tyrrell, was responsible for locking in the deals.

"When it comes to getting your name and music across to people, especially outside Britain and America, the record company can only go so far," Tyrrell explained. "If you can do a deal which attaches your name to a popular product in a particular territory then they will do your marketing for you."

Tyrrell cited the example of Chupa Chup lollipops, an especially popular confectionery in Spain, which the Girls were linked with and where, by this time, they were probably the biggest-selling English-language act ever. Similarly, the tie-in with Pepsi gave the Spice Girls massive exposure in Southeast Asia, a vast marketplace, but one in which British record companies had traditionally failed to invest a great deal of effort.

"Endorsement deals and merchandising activities were all part of the strategy," Tyrrell confirmed. "In order to get the Girls known in every part of the world, you've actually got to have something going on in all those territories at any one time. You can't be there, so unless you're on TV you've got no physical presence apart from the record. So to keep the public's attention on the band you do a series of deals with major manufacturers which will bring out products in those territories, which will be a newsworthy item. Simon did it the way he does most things: started small and then got big within a week. It all fell into place very quickly."

Speculation in the media put their earnings from product tie-ins in the millions. How much were these deals worth?

"The earnings from them were not as much as record royalties," Tyrrell said. "It would be roughly equivalent to having an extra territory; like having Germany again. Plus this is cash upfront. Large sums in the bank, not waiting around for royalties to appear months later."

In making these licensing deals the normal practice would be for the artist to get an advance which they would then earn (i.e. pay back) from royalties paid at maybe 6 or 7 per cent of the wholesale price of the merchandise. But with the Spice Girls, Fuller made it his practice to defer the advance and perhaps even contribute to the promotional expenses in exchange for anything up to 50 per cent of the profits at the end. In other words, where most managers would have settled for a comparatively small stake in the profits, Fuller negotiated, wherever possible, a succession of joint partnerships. In the case of Spice Girl cards – little cards with pictures of the Girls on them that kids collected like the cards of footballers – it was estimated by *Forbes* magazine that, by September 1997, Fuller and his venture partner Zone had sold 25 million cards worldwide at about $1 a pack.

"No one has more marketability than the Spice Girls," said John Toone, a lawyer who helped to set up the Spice Girls recording contract with Virgin. "Up to 10 per cent of their income comes from sponsorship, whereas for most artists that figure ranges from zero to one per cent."

The sponsorship by Pepsi was a particularly lucrative and unusually structured arrangement. According to the terms of the deal, which was said to have earned them £1 million, the Girls would release a new single exclusively through a Pepsi promotion, not through record retailers. The song, 'Step To Me', which was co-written by Elliot Kennedy and produced by Absolute, was a leftover from the *Spice* sessions and wouldn't otherwise have seen the light of day. You could tell how much they valued it by the fact that Pepsi gave it away to anyone who could be bothered to send in 20 Pepsi can ring-pulls. But that didn't make the record shops any happier about the situation.

"Music retailers spend a lot of time and effort promoting new acts and then get kicked in the teeth like this," said the chairman of the British Association of Record Dealers.

The practice of getting into bed with commercial sponsors was well established long before the Spice Girls came along, and they were in illustrious company as far as the Pepsi deal was concerned. Previous endorsees of the soft drink included Madonna, Tina Turner, Lionel Richie and Michael Jackson (who famously let it be known that he wouldn't dream of actually drinking the stuff). But the Girls' involvement took them further under the corporate duvet than anyone at this level had ever gone before. As with the Channel 5 launch they donated a specially commissioned performance of the Pepsi theme tune, 'Move Over', which was screened on TV and in cinemas across Europe, Africa, North America, the Far East and Australasia, as part of Pepsi's "Generation Next" campaign. And as well as turning over the new "single" to Pepsi, they also made the tickets for their first concert, in Istanbul, available solely through a Pepsi offer.

"Nothing else could give them this kind of exposure," said Virgin's Deputy MD, Ray Cooper, and you could see what he meant. But was it the right kind of exposure?

Contrary to popular perceptions, a number of deals apparently *were* turned down if the product wasn't right or if it didn't fit into the game plan.

"It would have been very easy to do a lot more deals than we did," Tyrrell said. "And while it may have looked as if they were saturating the markets in Britain and America, if you lived in the Philippines, say, you might only have seen them on the lollipops, and if you were in Japan or South Africa, it might only have been on Pepsi or one of the other products."

In other words, because *all* the products were highly visible in this country, it gave a slightly false impression, according to Tyrrell. Well, maybe so. But the question was soon being asked, did the Spice Girls exist to make music or to market lollipops? Commercial sponsors do not give away this sort of money for fun and while the Girls were getting "exposure" they were also doing a pretty good job of boosting the sales of these products. Walker's crisps reported a 6% increase in the brand's volume share of the crisp market (taking it to 45.5%) within the first eight weeks of the Spice campaign. And Pepsi saw its market share rise from 15.1% on July 12 to 19.6% on August 9, its highest for several years. By this point half a million copies of the 'Step To Me' single had been distributed in return for 20 ring-pulls each – quite a thirst-slaking quantity of cola when you do the maths.

So the sponsors were happy and the group's financial advisers were doubtless cock-a-hoop. But such was the emphasis on the commercial exploitation of the Spice Girls as a brand name that it began to cast their very genuine musical achievements in an unflattering light. On a purely practical level, the sheer amount of time devoted to negotiating and keeping up their end of the bargain – extra video shoots, recording sessions, promotional duties, and so forth – began to eat into the time available for actually making the records. Melanie B was only half-joking when, on being asked by a TV interviewer what the group had been doing this year, she replied, "Commercials and TV ads."

On a deeper level, the sheer volume and nature of the endorsements began to tarnish their image. The anti-corporate ideals of the hippies and the punks had disappeared long before all this came about. If hard-bitten politico-rockers like The Clash were happy to attach their song 'Should I Stay Or Should I Go' to a Levi's advertising campaign, and an iconoclast such as Lou Reed was prepared to recommend that we all go and sign up with MasterCard, there could hardly be too much to complain about if a frivolous pop group aligned themselves with a few everyday products that kids would be interested in. From Take That posing on Kellogg's Corn Pops cereal packets to boy band 911's tour being sponsored by Clearasil spot cream, it had all been done before. And there was certainly nothing duplicitous about what the Spice Girls were doing, no mouthing off to the *NME* about the evils of Western consumerism while quietly signing under-the-table sponsorship deals in Japan.

But there *was* something venal about the Spice Girls' headlong rush to endorse such an unprecedented number of products. Where other artists would at least pay lip service to the notion of retaining artistic independence, and try to avoid making any personal connection between their music and their sponsors' names and products, the Spice Girls displayed no such inhibitions. In for a penny in for a million pounds seemed to be their credo, as they embraced each new corporate suitor with increasingly rapacious enthusiasm.

By June 1997, it was reported that the Spice Girls had applied for more than 100 trademarks. "They are proving ruthlessly determined to exploit the merchandising possibilities of their fame," said the *Daily Express*. "If you thought their confessed admiration for Thatcherism was just a bit of showbiz PR, think again."

So great was the daily bombardment of Spice images and Spice product that it quickly became oppressive even to people who were well disposed towards the group. You could choose to avoid the cinema or the record shops. But even if you took care to avert your gaze from the newspaper stands and magazine racks, no visit to the newsagent or local grocery store could be negotiated without reference to the Spice Girls.

I vividly remember a friend of mine who had been driven to distraction by her daughter's daily pestering of her to buy assorted Spice gear. The breaking point came with the demand for a Polaroid SpiceCam, which my friend reckoned was like any other Polaroid camera except that it came with stickers of the Spice Girls on it and was considerably more expensive. Whether true or not, the idea quickly took root that people were being pressurised by some monstrous, all-pervasive marketing machine into paying over-the-top prices for goods with a very limited shelf life.

By September 1997, the group were estimated to have earned $47 million by *Forbes* magazine, which ranked them at number 32 in their list of highest paid entertainers. This was a staggering achievement considering how little time they had been operating in the marketplace. While noting that the Girls had sold 14 million albums and 10 million singles in under a year, the accompanying commentary drily noted that, "Fuller enlists the most persuasive salespeople imaginable; kids, tugging at Mom and Pop and insisting that they want the Spice Girls product."

Even if you weren't being nagged about them by your kids, the all-encompassing profile of the group alone was enough to rattle the nerves of those of a sensitive disposition. The *Observer* columnist William Leith wrote a typically droll commentary on the ubiquity of the Spice Girls in which he vowed to spend a whole day – Sunday, April 6, to be precise – trying to avoid seeing or hearing any mention of the group. (Attempting not to think about them for such a length of time was plainly out of the question.) After a quiet day spent alone in his garden, and then watching football – but nothing else – on TV, he had almost achieved his goal, when he decided to listen back to the tape of an interview he had conducted a few days previously with a group of poets. Towards the end of the recording one of the poets remarked: "It might sound facetious to say this, but perhaps Byron was, in a way, the Posh Spice of his time."

Aaaaaaaaaaargh!!!

When the first marketing meetings took place for the *Spiceworld* campaign in the summer of 1997, the album had not even been recorded, and many at Virgin harboured doubts that it would be finished in time for a release that year. It would have been a close run thing even without the small matter of the Girls having undertaken to make a feature-length film at the same time. The schedule which they embarked on between the end of May and September that year would have broken many sane people. They got through it in one piece – but only just – emerging from a sleep-deprived tunnel of non-stop work and travel with a film and a new album – but no manager.

After their visit to New York in April, the Spice Girls embarked on three weeks of promotion in the Far East which included visits to Taiwan, South Korea and Bali. On May 29, they attended the Ivor Novello Awards at London's Grosvenor House Hotel where they collected the trophies for International Hit of the Year and Best-selling British Single, both for 'Wannabe'.

Work started in earnest on both new album and film in June. The girls would get a wake-up call at 6.30am to be on the film set by

7.30am. They would generally leave the set at 5pm and then go to the recording studio where they would work on the album until 11pm. Not only was the schedule physically arduous, it was a logistical nightmare. The film, which was directed by Bob Spiers (director of *Absolutely Fabulous*, *Fawlty Towers* and *Are You Being Served?*), was shot at various locations in London and the Home Counties. Meanwhile the Girls' writing and production partners – Matt Rowe, Biff Stannard, the Absolute boys and Spike Stent – were scattered all over the place: sometimes stationed in mobile studios on or near that day's location, or else beavering away in the Abbey Road and Olympia Studios.

The script for the movie had been written by Simon Fuller's older brother Kim, with help from Jamie Curtis. Kim Fuller, who had written scripts with and for Lenny Henry, Tracey Ullman and others, was a canny choice for the job of teasing out a comical narrative from the group's real life adventures. An experienced and professional scriptwriter on the one hand, he was also part of the extended Spice family, so to speak, and was thus able to win the trust of the Girls a lot more quickly than might otherwise have been the case. That didn't mean the job was a soft touch. The Girls had already rejected a film script submitted by Disney, and Fuller was keenly aware that if they hadn't liked the script he produced, they wouldn't have used it.

Given the budgetary constraints, and the likelihood that none of the Girls would prove to be great character actors, Fuller opted for a lighthearted romp, designed to showcase the songs from the new album, with the Spice Girls playing an exaggerated, spoofy version of themselves.

"I talked to them and hung out with them a bit to get a sense of their characters and who they were," Fuller said. "Geri was much more involved in talking about the script than any of the others. She was more ambitious and she was helpful. She would say to me: 'Well actually Victoria wouldn't say that.' And then you'd change it around to make sure the lines were ringing true."

A starry supporting cast included Roger Moore, Richard E. Grant, Stephen Fry, Hugh Laurie and Barry Humphries along with cameo appearances by Meat Loaf, Elvis Costello, Jools Holland, Elton John, Bob Geldof, Jonathan Ross, Michael Barrymore and Gary Glitter.*

---

\* Glitter was hurriedly airbrushed out of the final cut after it was made public that a cache of child pornography had been discovered on the hard drive of one of his computers.

Comparisons with *A Hard Day's Night* were ambitious but apt, not least because Fuller had taken The Beatles' 1964 movie as his blueprint. While The Beatles movie condensed a seemingly random sequence of events into a 36-hour snapshot of the group's hectic life, the more coherent story of *Spiceworld* took place within the time frame of a week leading up to a big concert at the Albert Hall. Scenes of the Girls being chased by hysterical fans mirrored the reality of their daily life – just as it had in The Beatles movie. Before filming had started the girls made a promotional visit to the Cannes Film Festival, where they found themselves mobbed at every turn by fans and paparazzi. On the way to a party at Planet Hollywood, their van got caught in the crowd.

"People were hammering on the side and rocking the van back and forth," Geri recalled. "What if the van tipped over? What if we couldn't get out? A guy filming us for a documentary was punched in the face as he tried to intervene."

Sometimes working on the movie, the Girls would finish a scene where they had been battling their way through mobs of extras, only to find a real mob waiting for them at the studio door. Meanwhile paparazzi would be hanging out of trees and hiding in haystacks. Two of them even went to the lengths of dressing up as a cow, and were apprehended wandering in a meadow close to the set.

In one of the most frequently quoted lines from the movie, their domineering, though not very bright manager, played by Richard E. Grant, rebuffs a request from the Girls for a day off with the words, "You don't have lives, you have a schedule." Fed up with this state of affairs the Girls end up giving both him and his shadowy boss – played by Roger Moore – the slip. You couldn't help wondering whether the prescience of Fuller's script was entirely accidental. Had he and the Girls been using the film to try to tell his brother something? Or had making the film planted the seeds of an idea in their minds?

"It was a sort of comic cynicism rather than clairvoyance," said Kim Fuller. "If you're going to make a film it's got to be dramatic. What can you inject in it? Well, what if the band were thinking of splitting up? Why would they be splitting up? I put in the mad Richard E. Grant manager as someone that they could all kick against, because I rather like subverting reality. But he wasn't supposed to be playing Simon. We did the svengali joke with Roger Moore. He was more the Simon figure."

In the story of *Spiceworld – The Movie*, the Girls had been rehearsing in an old manor house for their first proper concert while plotting to escape the clutches of their tyrannical manager. Almost as soon as they had finished filming, life began imitating art when, on September 17, they moved into a mansion near Cannes in the South of France to prepare for their first *real* proper concert in Istanbul. It was the start of a year which, on Simon Fuller's insistence, they would be spending outside Britain in order to minimise their tax liability. Fuller's logic was difficult to fault. The speed with which they had accumulated so much income left them liable to a monumental tax demand. And when you are travelling through uncharted territory at that kind of velocity, there is always a danger of the wheels flying off the bandwagon at any moment. Besides, a significant chunk of the year was earmarked for touring; not the whistle-stop promotional junkets that they had used to promote the *Spice* album to such extraordinary effect, but a proper, full-on, live, world tour. So they weren't going to be able to spend much time in Britain in any case.

Even so, the fact that they would now be allowed to spend only a limited number of days each month at home in England did not sit well with any of the Girls. They had traded in their lives for a schedule and were becoming rich beyond their wildest dreams. But now their freedom was being curtailed even more than before. What was the point of that?

The rehearsals for the Istanbul show took them back, in some respects, to the days at the house in Boyne Hill Road, Maidenhead. The conditions could not have been more different. Instead of the cold, rattling radiators and peeling paint of Trinity Studios, they were installed in an opulent mansion with nine bedrooms, several drawing rooms and a lounge, set amid acres of grounds with a high wall patrolled by security guards to keep the paparazzi at bay.

But the daily routine harked back to the old days. There was a marquee set up in the garden where Geri and Mel C started the day doing gym workouts and aerobics. Then at 10.30am they drove to a rehearsal venue. From 11am until 1pm they had singing rehearsals supervised by a vocal coach who helped them with their breathing and singing techniques. Some of the harmonies and individual vocal parts, which had been created in the recording studio, had to be rearranged for the purpose of performing live.

From 2pm until 5pm they practised with a full backing band comprising bass, drums, guitar, two keyboards and percussion. Then they

The Spice Girls with an admirer in California in July, 1995. Virgin Records waged a determined campaign to lure the girls and took the unusual step of sending them over to America on a 'meet and greet' tour *before* they'd agreed to sign with the company. *(Courtesy of 45 Management)*

Girlfriend, the Australian all girl band with an almost identical image to the Spice Girls who predated them by three years but split up after fleeting success in their home country. Left to right: Siobahn Heidenrich, Robin Loau, Jacqui Cowell, Melanie Alexander and Lorinda Noble. *(LFI)*

Dressed up for a night on the town, the Spice Girls pose outside Virgin Records' London offices in 1995. It was around this time that they acquired their nicknames: Ginger, Baby, Scary, Posh and Sporty. *(Andy Phillips/SIN)*

The Girls in early 1995 at Kempton racecourse where they first met Robert Sandall, chief pop critic of *The Sunday Times* who later became their press officer at Virgin Records. "They took me into the gents toilets and sang to me," he said. "I can't remember what the song was, but I remember thinking they could certainly sing… It was an unusually bold thing for a group in their position to do." *(Courtesy of 45 Management)*

Filming their first *Top Of The Pops* appearance by satellite link from Tokyo, where they used a local temple as a backdrop for their mimed performance of 'Wannabe'. *(Antony Medley/SIN)*

It wasn't all work in Tokyo – Emma (right) and Melanie B enjoy a champagne fuelled evening in their hotel bar. *(Antony Medley/SIN)*

Emma, Geri, Melanie B, Victoria and Melanie C on the streets of Tokyo during one of three promotional visits to Japan that the group undertook in 1996 alone. *(Courtesy of 45 Management)*

Among the five Spice Girls, it was Melanie B and Geri who competed for the role of 'leader'. "If anything went on it would always be to do with Geri and Mel B," said PR Nicki Chapman. "It was those two who instigated the removal of Simon Fuller." *(Andy Phillips/LFI)*

The Girls on stage at the Capital Radio Summer Music Jam, July 1996. *(David Fisher/LFI)*

The Girls in a rare contemplative mood. *(Harry Borden/IPG)*

Emma with songwriter Matt Rowe.
*(Courtesy of 45 Management)*

Melanie C and Victoria with songwriter Richard 'Biff' Stannard.
*(Courtesy of 45 Management)*

Simon Fuller confronts Victoria at Daphne's Restaurant, London, in early 1997. Writer Adrian Deevoy recalled another encounter in a Cantonese restaurant in Hong Kong, where Victoria, finding the food not to her liking, had pushed away her dish uneaten. "You are not going a whole day on just a bowl of rice," Fuller said, firmly. "Don't be stupid. You've got to eat properly." Victoria reluctantly resumed her meal. *(Nikos/Rex Features)*

did two hours of dancing, again with a coach to help with the choreography. After two weeks of this they transferred to a bigger performing area where they rehearsed with the whole stage setting. In the evening there would be an hour of aerobics in the marquee and sometimes individual tuition in singing, dancing or fitness as deemed necessary. Relieved of many of the outside pressures and once again focused on a clearly defined goal, it was just like the old days again. Or was it?

Both Geri's and Victoria's autobiographies point to this period as being one of mounting uncertainty.

"It was not a happy time," according to Victoria. "None of us were happy. But instead of talking about it like we would have done in the old days we just kept to our rooms."

Geri, who as usual had to work twice as hard as the others to keep up with the programme, called the place Spice Kampf.

But whatever tiny insecurities might have taken root deep inside Spiceworld, the show in Istanbul was a qualified success, sufficient to prove they could do it, whatever anybody said, and enough to lay the groundwork for the forthcoming tour. "Competent and capable . . . but with plenty of room for improvement" was the verdict of *The Sun*.

Meanwhile, the promotional treadmill rolled ever on. Prior to rehearsals in September, they had travelled to New York to shoot the video for 'Spice Up Your Life', which was scheduled to be the first single from the forthcoming *Spiceworld* album, and to attend the MTV Awards where the video for 'Wannabe' – director Jhoan Camitz's "dark", "gloomy", "threatening", one-take sequence that had caused so much wailing and gnashing of teeth among the Virgin executives – was declared the Best Video of the Year.

Sadly, Camitz was destined to die in a freak traffic accident three years later, in August 2000. The black armbands which the girls wore at the 1997 ceremony were in recognition of a much more public tragedy: the death of Diana, Princess of Wales in a road accident in Paris on August 31. As well as sending shock waves reverberating around the world, Diana's death propelled Elton John's hastily adapted homage, 'Candle In The Wind', to the top of the charts virtually everywhere that records were sold. In Britain, it was just about the only event that year which knocked the Spice Girls off the front pages. And John's record, as Fuller shrewdly calculated, was the only thing capable of keeping a new Spice Girls single off the top of the charts. In such circumstances discretion was undoubtedly the better part of valour, and the release of 'Spice Up Your Life' was quietly delayed, ostensibly as a mark of respect to Diana (and presumably Elton John).

There was respect in the air too when, dressed in black, the Spice Girls launched the Royal British Legion's Poppy Appeal on October 29, solemnly reading Laurence Binyon's poem *The Fallen*.

> They shall grow not old, as we that are left grow old:
> Age shall not weary them nor the years condemn.
> At the going down of the sun and in the morning
> We will remember them.

Well, it was certainly a change of gear from "Welcome to a brand new station (1-2-3-4-5)", but there were those who felt that the British Legion was in danger of trivialising its message. An official explained that the legion was hoping that the Spice Girls would help them to "harness the support of the younger generation", which had been ebbing way in recent years.

Here again was a reminder of just how woven into the fabric of mainstream British life the Spice Girls had become. The last singer that anyone could remember doing this kind of thing was the Forces' sweetheart Dame Vera Lynn, who was still there to share the platform with the Girls in 1997. Previous generations of pop stars, no matter how big or popular, tended to steer clear of the event, with its old-fashioned echoes of public service and patriotic endeavour. Nor were many of them ever invited to lend their support in the first place. And yet, when you think about it, what an amazing piece of PR it was. When it came to thinking big, as opposed to being cool, truly the Spice Girls have had few rivals in the history of planet pop.

Sandwiched in between all this was another exhausting round of whirlwind promotional visits. In the weeks either side of playing the show in Istanbul on October 12, they visited Singapore, Bangkok, Delhi, Hong Kong, Tokyo, Granada, Cologne, Paris, London and Johannesburg.

The purpose of the stopovers was to prime each market in turn for the imminent arrival of the new *Spiceworld* album on November 3. I went on a couple of these trips myself, in my capacity as pop critic of *The Times*. In Granada, Spain, where they travelled on October 6, the hoopla surrounding their brief stay was simply unbelievable. The schedule, which lasted barely 24 hours, was typical – a hit-and-run operation that was more like a commando raid and royal visit rolled into one than a promotional stop-off by a pop group.

Travelling separately from the Girls and their entourage was at least one planeload of media and record company folk from London and elsewhere in Europe. The plan had been to hold the album launch in the famous Alhambra Palace, the most visited monument in Europe; "a thousand years of Moorish decadence meets 18 months of girl power," as Adrian Deevoy of Q magazine put it. In the event girl power lost out to local tradition, when Palace officials ruled that to host such a gathering would have been "an inappropriate use of a historical building". The location was hurriedly rearranged and the first sight we got of the Girls was at a press conference in the early evening in the Carmen de los Chapiteles, where they were staying. This white-walled building, with its vine-shaded terraces set amid the network of cobbled alleys that weave through the old Arab quarter known as the Albaicin, had recently been the hotel of choice for the King and Queen of Spain.

Even so, the modest size of the building, not to mention its air of old-fashioned elegance, were quite unsuited to the needs of a media scrum on this scale. The place was absolutely heaving with assorted journalists, photographers, cameramen and record company liggers from all over the world, so much so that only a comparatively small core of guests were allowed access to the actual press conference itself.

Just as they were masters of the art of the "private", one-to-one interview, the Spice Girls were brilliant at conducting that most artificial of media gatherings: the pop press conference. No one ever expects anything of any substance to emerge from these question and answer sessions, which are usually dominated by journalists of indeterminate European origin, enquiring in halting English what message the group has for their fans in Greece or if they have plans to visit Helsinki any time soon.

If due care and attention to detail is not paid, these shallow PR exercises can either become terminally boring or else quickly degenerate into farce. But the Spice Girls put as much energy into their press conferences as they did into every other aspect of projecting themselves as a group. Sitting in a line at a table, they parried a barrage of ridiculous questions with appropriately facetious answers.

"What's the worst rumour you have ever heard about the group?" asked a spectacularly glamorous TV reporter from Ecuador.

"That Victoria's a man in drag," answered Melanie B.

"How do you cope with spots?"

"Everyone gets them," Victoria said. "We're only human."

"Will you marry me?" a man called Frank asked Geri.

"Ooh, you're a bit forward," Geri said. "Have we met?"

In among the banter, they talked up the album and film as best they could, drawing attention to the Latino influences on 'Spice Up Your Life' and focusing in particular on 'Viva Forever', which we discovered was a "tribute to Spain". Then the President of Virgin UK, Paul Conroy presented the Girls with a specially created award – a huge, oblong, framed presentation display – in recognition of worldwide sales of 18 million copies of the *Spice* album. Afterwards, Simon Fuller materialised to be included in a group photograph of the Girls with key members of the Virgin team and the trophy. Fuller then melted away into the corridors of the Carmen again.

At least one million of those *Spice* CDs had been sold right there in Spain, making it the group's third largest market after the USA and the UK. The exceptional interest in "Las Spice Girls", or "Las Chicas Piquantes" as they were known locally, stemmed partly from Geri's connections with the country through her Spanish mother and partly because, as with so many other countries that weren't primary destinations for Anglo-American pop acts, the Spice Girls had taken the trouble to go there and court the market.

After the press conference, the Girls decamped to a secret location in a different part of town where the rearranged album launch party had been organised for the evening. Some secret. It was a huge affair, again with various inner and outer sanctums, to which access was granted strictly according to one's precise level of VIP status. On a raised pavement running outside the building were hundreds of fans, mostly girls, who screamed and waved frantically any time they caught a glimpse of one of their heroes. In the courtyard below, the Spice Girls mingled among the most important of the guests. But here was the strange thing: even the "special" guests behaved like hysterical schoolchildren. Whenever one of the Girls moved across the yard, the crowd would reconfigure itself around her like a shoal of piranhas, knocking over chairs and tables, flattening potted trees, in their eagerness to get into closer proximity to the five stars.

At about nine o'clock the *Spiceworld* album was played in its entirety after which the night sky was lit up by a long and thunderous display of fireworks. So powerful was one of the explosions in the sky that it broke a window in a block of offices nearby. The odds against anyone anywhere in the South of Spain still being unaware that the Spice Girls had come to town were by this point very long indeed.

When the evening seemed to be almost over, the Girls appeared on a balcony overlooking the crowd, as if to wave goodnight. But then somebody had the bright idea of playing the record again. A few bars in, and the Girls were all miming along to themselves as if they were on *Top Of The Pops*. Shrieking and shouting like a gang of over-refreshed revellers at a hen party, they jumped and danced around as if unable to stop themselves. This impromptu performance went on for several more tracks, a preposterously uncool and very public display of their continuing enthusiasm for being in a pop group, which was silly and naff but also, under the circumstances, rather disarming.

The next morning, in a classic piece of Spice chutzpah, they went to the Town Hall to meet the Mayor of Granada. This was typical of the group's brazen approach to these little junkets abroad. They weren't another bunch of pop stars passing through town to sign a few copies of their CD in the nearest HMV store and give themselves a plug on the local radio station. They were visiting dignitaries, the Queens of Spiceworld, here to greet the people. Like any other head of state in a foreign land, the least they expected was a civic reception from whoever was in charge of the city.

By 11am the crowd in front of Granada's Town Hall was a seething mass of overexcited humanity, mostly female and some of it very young indeed. There were several Spice lookalikes, including one troupe of five little girls (aged maybe seven or eight) who were dressed up to resemble each of the five Spice Girls. This involved the exposure of much bare skin and heavy application of lipstick and make-up, producing an unnaturally sexualised effect, which went beyond precocious, and into realms of mini-Lolitadom that many adults might find rather uncomfortable to contemplate. A photograph of these five little darlings which found its way into a magazine was captioned: "Scary Spice, Scary Spice, Scary Spice, Scary Spice & Scary Spice".

"I wouldn't let any daughter of mine dress up like that," said one of Virgin's international promotions staff disapprovingly, as she patrolled the reception area inside the building, clipboard in hand.

Meanwhile, in another corner, Gerrard Tyrrell was holding court (off the record, naturally). He had been out earlier in the morning, purchasing bootleg Spice Girls videos from unofficial salesmen in the street. His manner was jovial as he described the "complete rubbish" that these rogue merchandisers had sold him, and outlined his plans for slapping an injunction on them as soon as he was finished with the business in hand.

The meet and greet with the mayor took place behind closed doors. But then, at last, the Girls emerged on to the balcony of the Town Hall overlooking the square. The mob let out a deafening shriek. The Girls waved. Nothing else was needed to create considerably more excitement than most groups could generate at a gig. Hours later the Girls were on a plane to their next destination leaving behind a corner of Spain which had been well and truly Spiced up.

And this was Granada, remember, not London or LA or Tokyo or the Big Apple where any number of international stars will routinely be passing through town at any given time. For most of the local people who saw them, and the mayor who met them, and the townsfolk who witnessed the fireworks display, this would have been a truly memorable occasion. Imagine the effect of such a day being repeated all around the globe – from Delhi, where the Girls performed at a charity concert wearing saris, bindis and bangles, to Auckland, where they upset Maori Tribal leaders by performing a ritual dance which is traditionally performed only by men.

By uncoupling their promotional activities from all the physical encumbrances entailed in setting up and playing a live show, Fuller and the Girls were able to execute a fast-moving, high-impact campaign that reached the parts of planet pop that other Anglo-American acts didn't even get around to considering. The strategy reached its apogee when the globe-straddling Girls arrived in Johannesburg as all-conquering heroines to be hailed by Nelson Mandela and Prince Charles. At that moment, the Spice Girls were sitting on top of the world.

How different it would all look just one month later.

# 7

# Queens Of The Spice Age

The Spice Girls arrived in Johannesburg on Saturday, November 1, 1997. 'Spice Up Your Life' had just topped the UK chart, their fifth number one out of five attempts. And the *Spiceworld* album was due for release the following Monday, exactly a year after the release of *Spice*. At that moment there was not a single territory in the world where Western pop music is sold in significant quantities in which the Spice Girls were not one of the biggest, if not *the* biggest-selling act. They were well on the way to being the biggest-selling act that Virgin had ever signed (Genesis may have sold similar quantities of records over the course of a much longer career, but not all of them for Virgin). And while a handful of artists from preceding generations including Elvis Presley, The Beatles, Abba and Michael Jackson had achieved a similar global reach, it had taken them much longer to do so. No other act in the history of pop had been remotely as successful as the Spice Girls in such a short space of time.

They were in South Africa ostensibly to perform at a multi-artist event called *Two Nations In Concert* presented by the Nations Trust, a charitable foundation established with the active support of Nelson Mandela at the time of the Queen's visit to South Africa in 1995. As well as raising money to help support young South Africans to set up their own small businesses, the idea of the concert was to celebrate the musical and cultural links between Britain and South Africa, to which end an elaborate line-up of local and international acts with a South African connection – such as easy-listening singer/songwriter Jonathan Butler and guitarist Trevor Rabin (formerly of prog-rock warhorses Yes) – had been booked to appear in fairly quick succession in the 28,000-capacity Johannesburg Stadium. According to the organisers, many tickets had been sold at a "greatly reduced" rate and as many as 10,000 tickets had actually been distributed for free among the poorer people living in the townships.

But as is often the case with these show business galas, the intentions were a lot better than the musical programme itself, and the proceedings were badly in need of a lift by the time the Spice Girls made their fleeting appearance towards the end of a long and frankly rather tedious evening. The crowd responded with genuine enthusiasm as the Girls ripped through just three songs (sung live to backing tapes) – 'Spice Up Your Life', 'Say You'll Be There' and 'Wannabe' - and then disappeared amid a storm of fireworks, leaving the South African star Lucky Dube playing to a markedly depleted audience. Looking down from the departing helicopter at the sea of waving hands and faces below them, Geri remembered that it "felt like a bit of a Michael Jackson moment".

"It couldn't have happened ten years ago because of apartheid," Melanie C breathlessly remarked later. "So it was unbelievable to be on stage with so many different races. Black and white musicians just wouldn't have been able to perform together like that in the past." Indeed, as a mixed-race group themselves, even the Spice Girls performing on their own would presumably not have been a viable proposition only a decade earlier.

As ever, delivering the music was only part of the job. The real coup de théâtre had been engineered earlier in the day when the five girls met for a photo opportunity and press conference with President Mandela and Prince Charles at Mandela's residence in Pretoria. The meeting had been brokered by Gerrard Tyrrell, who had encountered initial resistance to the idea among Mandela's representatives. Wielding an iron fist within the usual elegantly tailored, velvet glove, Tyrrell had insisted from the start of negotiations that the Girls' appearance at the concert (for no fee) would be conditional on a get-together in front of the media with Mandela.

A reception was duly organised at Mandela's house for artists appearing in the concert, including Omar and Billy Ocean, with the Spice Girls as the guests of honour. Owing to the vagaries of travelling by Virgin Airways, the Girls were late, and Mandela and Prince Charles were chatting together when they arrived. Mandela greeted them all and then, rather amusingly, produced a collection of his grandchildren who emerged from a backroom to be presented to the Girls.

Later, the Girls wandered outside, where a red carpet had been rolled out on to the lawn and, in the blazing sunshine, lined up alongside the two world statesmen as if to the manner born. It all seemed remarkably civilised, and even the pack of (mostly British) journalists and photographers on hand to record the event for the next day's front pages, behaved with a sense of decorum not often observed in their line of work. The 79-year-old Mandela, with Geri hanging on one arm, and the other draped around Melanie B's shoulder, smiled benignly. Charles squinted awkwardly into the sun. The resulting photograph has since become one of the iconic pop images of the Nineties.

Mandela may have withstood unimaginable tests of his will during the course of his life. But the man was like putty in their hands.

Someone asked him what he thought about the Spice Girls.

"I think I'm too old for them," he said.

"No you're not," Geri contradicted him, loudly. "You're as young as the girl you feel, and I am 25."

"I will take that up," the President responded, somewhat bemused, but clearly getting into the spirit of the occasion. "These are my heroes."

"He is our hero as well," Melanie B gushed.

"This is one of the greatest moments in my life," Mandela volunteered, a curious comment for a man who in 1990 had emerged from a 28-year spell of incarceration in an apartheid jail cell, and then gone on, just four years later, to become the first President of South Africa to be elected on the basis of universal suffrage.

"Is it your greatest moment?" one of the press pack asked Prince Charles, gallantly trying to draw him in to the performance.

"Second greatest," the Prince responded, pausing to just the right effect. "The first time I met them was the greatest."

It was Charles's first overseas visit since the death of Princess Diana, and he was accompanied by their younger son, Prince Harry, then 13, who popped in to say hello to the Girls at the concert. Charles seemed relieved to have an assignment that took his mind off other worries.

The banter was glib and light-hearted, the mood a million miles away from the combative idealism of the anti-apartheid rock and rap stars who only 12 years before had expressed their support for the continuing cultural boycott of South Africa with a record in which they solemnly pledged never to play in the nearby leisure resort of Sun City. Now the battle against apartheid had been won, but would the so-called Artists United Against Apartheid – an ad hoc group featuring Bono, Peter Gabriel, Bruce Springsteen and many others who recorded a protest song called 'Sun City' in 1985 – have imagined that the result of their efforts would produce a scenario like this?

Here was the ultimate symbol of a pop world that had been turned on its head; a world in which the earnest politics of Eighties protest had been replaced by the frivolous show business gesture of the Nineties. For many observers the very idea of a man of Mandela's gravitas being manoeuvred into a meeting with the Spice Girls was a trivialisation of everything for which he stood. Many of the local press reports adopted a patronising tone, suggesting that Mandela would not have had the faintest idea who the Spice Girls were before he met them. But according to Tyrrell, who had a long conversation with him, Mandela was better informed than people assumed.

"He's a pretty savvy individual," Tyrrell recalled. "He is certainly a man who knows what is going on in the world."

And, although it can be difficult to remember now, the sheer intensity of Spicemania at that time meant that the group's presence registered with people from every walk of life, and on every level. Even a cursory interest in his grandchildren's progress and enthusiasms would have left Mandela in little doubt about the influence of this particular pop group on his own family and by extension the youth of his country.

Whether or not his role was trivialised, as far as Mandela was concerned, there was a very simple reason for him agreeing to meet the Spice Girls. In return for him bestowing his saintly endorsement, they would perform at his concert, thereby helping to raise money for his charity.

"Don't worry, I'm used to being used," he apparently told Tyrrell, with a wry grin.

As far as Emma was concerned there were no doubts about Mandela's sincerity nor about the significance of the meeting.

"Of course it was the greatest moment of his life," she said, later. "He met the Spice Girls!"

Not surprisingly, the publicity generated by this encounter was mind-boggling. In 15 minutes the Spice Girls garnered more worldwide media coverage than U2 or The Rolling Stones achieved during the entire course of their visits to South Africa. And whereas those groups were accompanied by unwieldy stage sets, massive road crews, and full travelling entourages, all the Girls had done was show up with their overnight cases and backing tapes, and voilà! – another majorly Spiced-up territory in the bag.

Having wooed Mandela and completed their turn at the *Two Nations* concert, the Girls arrived for the first night of their stay at Sun City, surely one of the most surreal places on earth. A purpose-built tourist facility situated in an ancient, volcanic crater 110 miles outside Johannesburg, it is an African version of Las Vegas and Disneyland rolled into one. Look up and you will see the overhead sky train which delivers guests to the Welcome Centre, from where it is but a short hop to such diverse delights as the Jungle Casino, the Temple of Creation and Leonardo's Pizza Workshop. Huge, heavy foliage brushes against the plate-glass windows of the Sun City Hotel where the predominantly black staff waits with a quiet, rather unnerving deference on the resort's mostly white and necessarily wealthy clientele. The sun burns down from a cloudless sky, and exotic birds with startlingly bright red and green plumage sit among the branches making raucous conversation.

There was more raucous banter the following morning at yet another press conference, this time in the Eagle Room of the Sun City Entertainment Centre. The Girls were in high spirits after the meeting with Mandela the day before and were excited about plans to go on a wildlife safari when their work was finished.

"What was Prince Harry doing with you backstage?" asked a journalist from Scandinavia.

"Oh he was just very normal, talking about school and hanging around with his little mate Charlie," Melanie B replied. A ripple of nervous laughter went round the room, causing the PR woman who was moderating the questions to interrupt rather sternly.

"Can I just clarify that 'little Charlie' is Prince Harry's young friend," she said, presumably anxious to head off any potential tabloid headlines about Melanie making disparaging remarks about the future King of England.

But Melanie was ready with her own clarification.

"Not the drug Charlie," she said to shrieks of merriment all round.

"We treat everybody the same, whether they're a prince or not," Geri said.

Visiting Mandela's house had apparently been "surprisingly normal".

"There wasn't anything major went on," Melanie B said. "But we wouldn't tell you lot anyway. That's private. I just think that it's really mad that the Spice Girls philosophy, the Spice Girls vibe got us in a position where we are at Nelson Mandela's house. When you think about where our pop life has taken us that is pretty serious stuff. It was really relaxed. We pinched some bog-roll, and I said to him, 'I've just pinched some bog-roll from your toilet.' And he just looked at me."

Emma: "It felt a bit like we were his children, cuddling up. He was very warm, like a father."

After the press conference, there was a meet and greet session with 165 competition winners who had been flown in from 19 different countries to attend the event. The fans, most of them young girls, many too overawed to speak, were ushered in to the Lynx Room in groups of four or five to meet their idols and receive bundles of autographed pictures, CDs and other goodies.

On the surface, it was all pretty much business as usual. But this was an exceptional trip in more ways than one. Simon Fuller had adjusted the schedule to allow the Girls a couple of days off to spend at Sun City, a rare enough occurrence in itself, and the Girls had flown their mothers out to join them for the break. Even more unusually, Fuller was not actually present in South Africa himself, although he had intended to be. Instead, having undergone emergency surgery in New York the week before to remedy a painful back complaint, he was convalescing in hospital in London. The combination of Fuller's absence and a momentary break from the treadmill enabled the Girls to draw breath and think their situation through. It was a moment when an accumulation of low-level but deeply felt dissatisfactions finally came to a head.

Fuller's management style was nothing if not proactive, and by this point, two-and-a-half years after he had signed a contract with the Spice Girls, his dealings with the group had become both dictatorial and at the same time unusually personalised. Where Chris and Bob Herbert had failed to grasp the scope of the Girls' ambition, and set a management tempo which lagged behind their urgent appetite for advancement, Fuller had done the reverse. His vision was Napoleonic; his ambition limitless. It didn't stop with the Spice Girls either, as subsequent events have shown. But he was keenly aware that the Spice Girls were the one act which could give him a big enough platform on which to build an empire that would change the face of pop. His vow to "put the foot down harder" had produced the desired results, but he had misjudged the wear and tear which the policy had inflicted on the vehicle of his good fortune. The relentless schedule, which they had joked about in the movie, was no joke in real life. The Girls were being run ragged.

"At the moment I feel like a headless chicken," Melanie B wrote in her diary on October 21. "I am physically drained," she wrote, two weeks later, during the Sun City break. "I can't stand it any more. And no one gives a shit. No one."

According to Victoria, Fuller's strategy for managing the girls was divide and rule. He travelled everywhere with them and kept tabs on all their activities, insofar as it was possible, both inside and outside the group.

"He made no secret of the fact that he knew exactly what I was eating and not eating," Victoria recalled. "It might have been for my own good, but that's not the point . . . It was very rare that we were all five together without our hands-on manager busying around. No wonder we didn't talk."

And when Geri went to plead with him, for the umpteenth time, for a week off, his reply was like that of a schoolteacher patiently explaining why she couldn't miss classes to go to the fair.

"There are two reasons Geri. One it sets a bad precedent amongst the girls. If you take a week off then everybody will be asking for one. And two, we sold 18 million copies of the first album. That set the benchmark. We want to sell 19 million copies this time."

Fuller, naturally, saw these developments from a different point of view. For him, it was all about maximising potential, while keeping the lid on a headstrong combination of personalities.

"So much had happened so fast, and I was full of ideas," Fuller recalled, years later. "And in the nicest possible way, I dominate. Not in an aggressive way. Just I'm charging away at the front of the pack and these young girls who started off wanting to be famous and rich and have a laugh – it all got to be quite serious. It felt as if the fun had gone out of it, which it does. And that's when the professionalism and the artistic vision and the integrity takes you through that pain barrier. For the most part, they didn't really have that, because that wasn't where they were coming from. If you go back to how it started, it was living a dream. But then it became seriously hard work. Nobody wants to get up at 5am in the morning day after day. But when you're as young as they were, all you need to do is go for it for three or four years and then you can do whatever you want."

Fuller's management style was the subject of much lively debate in and around the offices of Virgin Records. Despite his almost clairvoyant skills at devising strategies and planning ahead to milk the maximum advantage from virtually any situation, his interpersonal skills were curiously undeveloped.

"He had an oddly distracted manner," recalled Virgin's director of press Robert Sandall. "We'd always have these meetings which would drive everyone nuts. We'd sit there and someone would say: 'Simon, we'd like to do this with the Girls, this photoshoot or whatever, or this radio programme,' and Simon would go: 'Yeah.' And then someone from the Press would say, 'Oh yes and so-and-so would like to do this interview for *The Face*,' and Simon would go: 'Yup. OK.' Then it would be: 'Well – when are we going to do it?' And that would be the sticking point. You'd never hear. He'd write all these things down, then he'd just sit there, apparently agreeing with everything, but never actually fixing a date to do it. This week? Next week? And it simply would never get put in the diary. Then, when it didn't happen or something went wrong it was always the record company's fault.

"You always got the sense with Simon that the record company was just one of the people that he was talking to. His ideas for the Spice Girls were much bigger than just records. He was probably sitting there dreaming of sponsorship deals, while we were sitting there discussing how to sell records, which after all was the business in hand."

Fuller's demeanour did not accord with his status as someone who wielded such unquestionable clout. At around the same time as the Spice Girls were enjoying their first flush of success, Nigel Martin-Smith, the former manager of Take That, had set up a company called Nemesis which Virgin had bought into. Smith was thus much in evidence in the Virgin offices at the same time as Fuller, and provided a striking contrast in management style. His acts did exactly what he told them to do, and jumped when he told them to do it. None of them enjoyed anything like the success of the Spice Girls. But while Smith was a figure who commanded attention and exuded authority – typical of the alpha dog types who tend to get drawn towards management – Fuller's style was much more gentle.

In many ways this had been a big advantage, particularly when it came to winning the Girls' confidence in the first place. Terri Hall, who set up 19 Management with Fuller in 1985, and now runs her own PR company, Hall Or Nothing, recalled Fuller's management style as having a uniquely soft touch, which had appealed to artists like Annie Lennox and Cathy Dennis no less than it had to the Girls when they were shopping for a manager.

"He's about as far from that banging-his-fist-on-the-table type manager as you can get," Hall said. "He's very polite, he won't shout and scream, but he gets what he wants by being thoughtful and studied. If there's a problem, he goes away and thinks about it and comes back with a solution. He's also very playful, always joking. There'd be times when you'd think, 'Can't he just be serious for a moment?' That sounds contradictory for someone who has achieved so much, but that's exactly what he's like."

"Critics probably don't like me because I'm so nice," Fuller once said. "I'm incredibly articulate, thoughtful and moral, and I think about what I do. I want to be known for doing something good."

Another industry associate commented of Fuller: "He is a sweet man with a limp handshake, but I would never cross him. He is a very clever marketing man and a very dynamic human being with an eye for the main chance. He is so gentle you are lulled into this sense of great calm, and then you are a pushover."

The girls certainly did not jump at Fuller's command. If you walked into a room and didn't already know he was their manager, you would be unlikely to guess it. And sometimes, when his mild-mannered approach came up against the more loud-mouthed face of Girl Power, he gave the impression of being oddly ineffectual.

An industry insider recalled a record company reception at which Melanie B, after a couple of drinks, was coming on strong to a French A&R man from Virgin called Thomas. She was in mid-conversation when Fuller came up to her and said, "Right Mel, we're going now."

"Ah, shut up Simon, I'm talking to Thomas," came the reply. Thomas maintained a polite neutrality, as you presumably do when someone from your record company's biggest act is sitting, blathering away to you. A minute later Fuller tried again – "Look Mel, we've got to go now" – and was ignored again. Exasperated, Fuller left her to it. The unhappy codicil to this little incident arrived a couple of days later, when Fuller sent a formal letter of complaint to Virgin about Thomas's behaviour in detaining Melanie B at the party when she should have been getting ready to leave. It seemed that Fuller had tried to explain away his lack of control over Melanie – and the resulting loss of face – by blaming it on the record company's employee.

At other times, Fuller's manner was more like that of a father than a manager. The journalist Adrian Deevoy reported an encounter in a Cantonese restaurant in Hong Kong, where Victoria, finding the food not to her liking, had pushed away her dish uneaten.

"You are not going a whole day on just a bowl of rice," Fuller said, firmly. "Don't be stupid. You've got to eat properly." Victoria reluctantly resumed her meal.

"He's not a hard man," Melanie C said before the split. "He doesn't raise his voice. Everything is very, very calculated – but in a nice way. And he never gets wound up, not even with us lot."

"You were never quite sure what he was thinking," Sandall said. "Partly, he had his mind on the bigger picture, no doubt; partly he wanted to keep the record company in the dark as much as possible; but partly it was because he had quite a limited control over the group, and wanted to disguise that by being evasive."

Clearly, Fuller's relationship with the girls was never that of boss and employee. His personal ability to make them do what he wanted was by no means a given, so his solution was to take individuals off into corners, soothe ruffled feathers where possible and manipulate the different personalities in such a way that he kept the upper hand.

"I think what happened in South Africa, when he wasn't there, was that they started to compare notes and started to catch him out," Sandall said. "Because he's a very feline and rather creepy character like that. They realised how he'd been trying to keep them slightly at arm's length from one another and hence locate himself at the hub of the wheel. And they didn't like that."

With Fuller continuing to mastermind deals and organise insane work schedules on their behalf, which he could not possibly have consulted them about in any detail, if at all, ownership of the group had gradually become a big issue.

"It was definitely a control thing," Sandall said. "They had a very strong desire not to be his creatures. They were visibly not at his beck and call and deep down I think they were always slightly embarrassed by the fact that they were this "girl power" group that was managed by a bloke. I don't think the Girls realised the implications of all those sponsorship deals, which were beginning to get them a certain amount of negative publicity. I think Simon had been going off and doing loads of deals that they weren't particularly aware of. And at that stage they were starting to believe the Girl Power hype. They wanted to be running their own affairs."

"They didn't want to be answerable to anybody," said Nicki Chapman, who had been in charge of TV and radio promotion from the first single. "They didn't want management telling them what to do. They wanted to be in charge of their own destiny. And all the time they had Simon behind them it was like having a sixth Spice. They heard the whispers: 'So, actually Girls, you didn't do it all on your own. There's actually a very clever man behind you.' And I think after a while that started to rattle them. Because he did hold the reins."

The media had started referring to Fuller as Svengali Spice, and portraying him as a guru figure who orchestrated their every move. Chapman recalled seeing a photograph in the *Mail On Sunday* of Geri, bending down and sticking her tongue out at the camera, while ten steps behind her in the shadows stood Fuller. It was a picture which symbolised the increasingly widespread perception of Fuller as the hidden manipulator behind their success, an impression which the Girls found irksome, to put it mildly.

"It could just be that Simon overstepped the mark in certain ways," Sandall said. "You know how it gets in groups. They'd been on an incredibly tense treadmill for two years, and small things which now you'd look back on and think, 'Oh, come on!', in that hothouse atmosphere can suddenly blow up into, 'Look what he's done now! Is it his group or is it our group? What do you say, girls?' You can just imagine a conversation like that happening over something very little."

But the imagination is where such conversations must remain, for the time being. The precise details and discussions that took place regarding the decision to sack Fuller remain a closely guarded secret among the five Girls. The atmosphere had obviously become pretty fraught after all they had been through together, but if there is one thing they had learned from their experiences with the media it was the value of keeping their own counsel.

The Girls returned from South Africa on November 4, by which time Fuller had gone to Italy to recuperate from his back operation. The following morning, Geri and Melanie B had a meeting with the group's lawyer, Andrew Thompson of Lee & Thompson, and accountant Charles Bradbrook to establish exactly what their legal status was vis-à-vis Fuller. Thompson could have been forgiven for experiencing a twinge of déjà vu. The Girls had first hired him in 1995, to organise a pay-off for Chris and Bob Herbert.

That evening, November 5, revolution was in the air as the group flew to Rotterdam, where they were booked to appear the following night on the MTV Europe Awards. On arrival, they encountered the final straw that broke the camel's back. Fuller had wanted the Girls to stay in a different hotel from all the other stars on the show, ostensibly to avoid unwanted press attention. The Girls wanted to hang out with the other guests. "No," Fuller said, "you don't hang out with other people, because you're different." Sure enough, the Girls found that they had been booked into a hotel well away from everyone else. It was a petty detail in the broader scheme of things, but typical of everything about the Fuller regime that they resented. Why shouldn't they stay at the hotel they preferred? They were the Spice Girls, goddamn it, not a bunch of kids on a school outing.

That night they stayed up and held a group meeting in which it was formally decided to sack Fuller. In the small hours of the morning they instructed Thompson, by phone, that they wished to terminate their contract with Fuller. Thompson contacted Fuller's lawyers at the start of business the next day and by 9am on November 6, Fuller was informed that his tenure as the Spice Girls' second manager had been terminated.

Rather like Chris and Bob Herbert before him, Fuller couldn't, at first, believe they were serious and issued instructions to keep the story quiet.

"It took Simon's breath away," Chapman recalled. "He had no idea it was coming. None of us did. Not me, not Gerrard Tyrrell who was out with us in South Africa. None of us got even a scent of it."

The Girls spent the day rehearsing for their appearance at the MTV Awards where, that evening, they won the prize for Best Group, beating a list of nominees that included Oasis, U2, Prodigy and Radiohead. The first inkling that something was afoot, came when the Girls pointedly omitted to make any mention of Fuller in their acceptance speech. Geri dedicated the award to Princess Diana – "A true advocate of Girl Power" – and Melanie B, in a curious echo of the Nelson Mandela soundbite, declared that, "Today is the happiest day of my life."

After the show, the Girls went straight to Rotterdam airport where they got a first little taste of what life would be like without Fuller, when they discovered that their security staff and chauffeurs, who were employed by 19 Management, had been taken off the job. A private jet was waiting to take them back to Britain and their security chief, Jerry Judge, a genial Irishman who looked as if he'd been hewn from a block of stone, agreed to escort them back to Luton Airport, after which they were on their own.

The first thing they did on returning to London was to have a meeting with Thompson and Paul Conroy of Virgin Records, where they explained their decision to sack Fuller and their intention to press ahead with all plans as scheduled.

Fuller's abrupt ejection from Spiceworld came like a bolt out of the blue to the record company, just as it did to everyone else. On the day it was announced to the press, Sandall was stuck in a hotel room in Amsterdam where he ran up the largest mobile phone bill of his life – £380 pounds in one day – trying to find out what was going on and responding to the deluge of enquiries.

"We had no idea it was coming," he said. "We had this meeting with them straight afterwards and it seemed pretty clear to me that Melanie B was now running the show. Geri seemed less of a dominant presence in the group. They didn't need Fuller at that point and they realised that. We'd got the tour all in place, the album was out, the film was on its way; and they all had their solo contract options sorted out."

Even so, Conroy urged them to find a new manager to replace Fuller. The Girls agreed to start looking for someone. But, in truth, they had other, more pressing matters to attend to first. Fuller's management extended to every area of their affairs. The drivers, bodyguards, stylists, personal assistants and promotions people that enabled the smooth day-to-day running of the Spice machine were all on Fuller's payroll. And as of November 7 they were off the job. If they wanted to continue working with the Spice Girls they would have to leave 19 Management, an option which few of them chose to exercise.

More importantly, when forced to make a choice, several key players in the Spice regime remained loyal to Fuller. One of these was Nicki Chapman, who together with Nick Godwin co-owned Brilliant! PR. She had worked at close quarters with the Girls on TV and radio promotion since the very start of the 'Wannabe' campaign. Chapman was well aware of the strain that the girls had been under. Apart from all the work she did with them in Britain, she also went on trips abroad with them – 16 in 20 weeks at one point. During one particularly hectic period she found herself in Japan one weekend, back in the office in London during the week, and then back in Japan again the following weekend. It had reached the point where she was wondering if she could physically keep going herself, so much so, that although she was supposed to accompany the Girls on that fateful trip to the MTV Awards in Rotterdam, she was too exhausted, and Godwin went instead.

The first commitment in the Girls' diary after they had sacked Fuller was the rehearsing and recording of *An Audience With The Spice Girls* for London Weekend Television, in front of a nearly all-female audience of celebrities and their children. It was the first chance that Chapman, who had organised their participation in the show, had had to talk with them. The meeting took place in the same rehearsal rooms in Brixton where Chapman would later be a judge in the *Popstars* TV talent show.

"I asked everyone from LWT to leave the room," Chapman said, "which they all did. And there was Geri on the phone, literally booking cars for the band. 'Hello. My name's Geri Halliwell. Can we set up an account with you?' Because everybody had said, 'We work with Simon.' So I asked them, 'Have you really thought this through? I don't think you have. You are at the top of the tree and it would be so easy for you to fall. You've made a quick, kneejerk reaction to something. You're obviously not happy, but why?' They insisted that they wanted to manage themselves. They then offered Nick [Godwin] and me a lot of money to look after them. It was an awful time. They were crying and we were crying. I tried to talk sense into them and they were just adamant. The next night at the show, their lawyers were actually in the dressing room with me, and then Geri came flying through the door waving a document of some sort, saying, 'He signed it! He signed it!' and tripped over a bag and fell flat on her face. She was so happy they'd got Simon to sign it. The deal was tied up within hours. Normally these things take months. And I turned round and said, 'I'm really sorry girls, but I'm resigning too.'

"It was the right decision, but I didn't feel great telling them. It was a question of loyalty, I suppose. I had worked with Simon from Day One on it, and worked with him on other acts. I'm sure the girls had their reasons, but equally I had mine. Because I saw what he put into those girls. I saw everything that he did. If it wasn't for him they would not be what they are. He made them multi-millionaires. I don't think the Girls fully realised this at the time. Like most famous bands, they believed they'd done it themselves. They rewrite history. It happens again and again. They didn't set foot anywhere near Pepsi, but by the time you hear the story, they've done the deal themselves. I thought it was a real pity that they were leaving him.

"So, you have to decide: do you want to go with the fame and the money – and they would have paid me very well to run their office – or do you stand by your principles and work with the people you respect? I didn't actually work for Fuller at that time, I was independent. But I did respect him for what he did, and I thought I cannot go with the band and turn my back on him."

And talking of backs, what about Fuller? Stuck in his hospital bed in Italy, where he was required to stay put if he was to qualify for his tax year out of the country, the once all-powerful sixth Spice was unable to move, let alone get hold of any of the Girls to try to persuade them to change their minds. Perhaps the worst of it was that they had left him in the dark as to what exactly he had done wrong.

"They never actually told him," Chapman said. "They didn't write him a letter explaining their reasons or anything. You know when you hear about people getting divorced and the husband says, 'She didn't ever tell me why. What did I do wrong?' I think it must've killed him at the time. The six of them made an amazing team. It wasn't just the five of them. It was six people who made the band."

"It seemed significant to me that they chose the moment when Simon was at his lowest ebb, physically, to get rid of him," Kim Fuller said. "I always felt that if he had been at the top of his form and been able to drive round and bang a few heads together, I think he would probably . . . And that's what I think they tried to avoid. They didn't speak to him or have any communication at all because they were worried he would persuade them out of it.

"It's hard enough to get anywhere in this business, and to throw it away like that . . . I don't think they thought they were throwing it away. They thought that with their power in the national and international mind, they would be able to carry on. And they did for a while. But I think they really didn't know what Simon did."

"There was no real malice on my part," Simon Fuller recalled, speaking very much in hindsight. "I didn't feel that bad about it. I took a year off, which was brilliant, and I've never said anything publicly bad about them because I quite understood it. Five totally normal girls going through all of that. There were a couple of things which maybe I shouldn't have done. But then I'd go back and probably do it the same ten times out of ten. I sometimes think those one or two things happened because they had to happen. It almost came as a release for me, because I was getting drained. I was ill with my back, which was probably brought on by all the stress. So it all worked out very well for me. All I can say is if ever anyone was looking after me, it was probably then. I'd done everything I could, and if you have to stand back from a project, maybe that was as good a time as ever.

"I've never doubted my abilities. When I had this time off I was absolutely brimming with ideas. I came back with S Club 7 and there I was off to pastures new, which is the great thing about someone in my position. It's much harder for the artist to pick up the pieces after you lose momentum or something goes wrong. I think it's the hardest thing to be an artist in this era. I think it's the most difficult, traumatic, emotional thing to do. I wouldn't wish it on anybody.

"The Spice Girls will always feel unfinished – the one little smudge on my CV. No one ever quite understood what happened. Because, hang on, it was my idea, my project. How can you be sacked from your own thing? Which is my ego probably. I can't talk about it. But they're now beginning to say that actually maybe it was a mistake. That there was no specific reason as to why it all went wrong."

The severance process was very swiftly and bloodlessly executed. There was virtually no sniping in the press, no lawsuit, no lingering bad feeling – from either side – to prevent the wound from healing as quickly as time allowed. Even if it looked a bit shambolic as the Girls initially struggled to regain control of their day-to-day arrangements, there was no hesitation or messing around. Having fired Fuller they simply carried on from where they'd left off – exactly as they had done with Bob and Chris Herbert.

The Spice Girls owed a huge debt to both their managers. Without the Herberts they wouldn't have existed, and Fuller's acumen had set them up for life. Not only that, but he had organised their itinerary for the next year. His reward was an abrupt termination of his contract, without explanation, coupled with a reported £10 million pay-off. Clearly, if you set out to become a global icon, you have to be ruthless, which the Spice Girls were and still are. They always had extraordinary ambition. And they always believed in themselves more than anyone else believed in them.

When the story finally broke, all sorts of explanations were put forward for the sacking of Fuller, ranging from a vague impression that the Girls had simply got too big for their boots, to the specific suggestion that Fuller had been having an affair with Emma of which Geri and the others disapproved (more about this later). Curiously absent from the list of possible reasons was any financial motive. But Fuller's 20 per cent take of the profits meant he earned more than each of the Girls individually (their 80 per cent share was divided by 5, equalling 16 per cent each). "Never earn more than your talent," is an old show business adage.

"They didn't seem to fully appreciate what he'd done for them as a manager," Kim Fuller said. "They seemed to think that deals like the Pepsi commercial just turn up, and all you have to do is say 'Yes' or 'No'. There was no need to have a strategy going on. They probably thought, 'Well, he's getting this percentage. Why?' And also they'd ditched their management before and it had worked out all right. So it was a pattern of behaviour. They got to a certain point, and they thought, 'Well, now we can go.'"

When I met them a few months after the sacking of Fuller, the Girls apparently had no regrets about the decision.

"Right at the beginning, it was quite a big change," Victoria said. "Because even though we've always had the last say, there's lots of paperwork and lots of big decisions that you have to deal with totally on your own. But we enjoy that, because it's like when we write our stuff. We just like to be full-on, all the time."

"The way I describe it," Geri said, "is us five are like the Prime Ministers. And obviously you have to delegate. But all we've done is cut out the middle man. Our managerial position with every manager is different, but at the end of the day they are just a facilitator. They carry out what your vision is, in the best way they know how."

Emma: "Right from the beginning, everything from our merchandising to our singles covers, to starting our own magazine, has come from us. We felt, Why should we give it to somebody else? . . ."

Melanie B: "Who doesn't know what they're talking about."

Emma: ". . . sitting at a desk? At the end of the day we know what our fans want and we can do all that for ourselves."

Melanie B: "We do come across, even today, people who find it very difficult to digest that five girls who are relatively young and are so experienced in so many different areas, that five people can make a decision or control a schedule. Especially for men. I do think they find it subconsciously quite difficult, because they don't sometimes take your word as gospel."

Geri: "We're on the threshold of a new society, like Generation Next, but obviously there is still that kind of . . ."

Melanie B: "Stigma attached to women."

Geri: ". . . old style family where the male is brought up to think that the woman is the submissive one, whether he's the postman or he works down the local supermarket, he will have that self-esteem that he's the dominant one. But times are changing, 'cause he's coming out into the big wide world . . ."

Melanie B: "We're living free!"

Geri: ". . . and finding lots of girls like us lot. And I think the brilliant thing about us lot and all the decisions we make, we are not the same in all of our thinking. But if you've got five people you're always going to come to some sort of rational, sensible decision. There's no hung parliament with us. It's democracy. It's true coalition government, I'm tellin' ya."

Pressed as to whether Fuller had overreached his authority in marketing the group on so many fronts, the Girls were adamant that he had only been following their instructions.

Geri: "The thing about management is you can only give them a vision. It was Victoria who said, 'We want to be as famous as Persil Automatic.' And we said 'We want to do a movie.' Well obviously you get your facilitator to do that. But the point is, we *wanted* to be marketed in such a way. Maybe we were, in certain angles, maybe . . ."

Melanie B: "Overexposed."

Geri: ". . . a little bit. But you learn."

Why did they sack Fuller then?

Melanie B: "We can't go into detail on that. Legally. Do you know what I mean?"

Geri: "I'd love to tell you."

Melanie B: "I would. But at the end of the day, we're five nice people here, so we obviously had a good reason. But doing that has not stopped us in any way from carrying on doing what we want to do. If anything it's given us more belief."

# 8

# Help!

The official announcement that the Spice Girls had parted company with Simon Fuller was made on Saturday, November 8, 1997, exactly one week after the Girls had touched down in South Africa. The next day *Spiceworld* went sailing into the UK album chart at number one. But far from being able to celebrate this latest success and bask in their new-found freedom, the Girls found themselves besieged by negative reactions and tidings of woe from all quarters. On Monday, November 10, shares in EMI, the parent company of Virgin, began falling in response to "fears for the future of the Spice Girls". And the next day Matthew Wright kicked off a campaign in his *Mirror* gossip column, The Wright Stuff, specifically designed to knock the group off its perch or, better still, finish them off altogether. "Has The Bubble Burst?" trumpeted the headline, beneath a mocked-up picture of a *Spiceworld* globe deflating like a punctured balloon, an illustration which the column reprinted when Wright returned to the subject, many times, in subsequent weeks.

"Are you sick of the Spice Girls?" the column began. "Is it now all over for Britain's biggest pop phenomenon since The Beatles? These are the questions everyone's asking as the once Fab Five come to terms with life without their manager Simon Fuller." In order to support his theory that the Girls' star was on the wane, Wright declared that although *Spiceworld* had entered the chart at number one with a whopping first week sale of 191,000 copies, the album had actually been a terrible flop. He explained how he had come to this bizarre conclusion by pointing to the fact that Virgin had shipped out a massive 1.4 million copies to the record shops. Therefore more than one million copies of the album remained sitting in stockrooms, unsold after one week. This Orwellian interpretation of events ignored the blindingly obvious fact that the ship-out had been so huge precisely because the record shops had judged (correctly as it turned out) that these were the sort of quantities of the album which they could expect to sell in the six weeks or so before Christmas. Supermarkets in particular had insisted on buying in the album in unprecedented bulk, presumably fired up by all the other Spice merchandise that was flying off their shelves at the time.

In truth, Wright's perverse interpretation was a politically motivated piece of mischief-making instigated at the behest of his editor, Piers Morgan, who had long resented the fact that when it came to gaining access to the Girls, the *Mirror* tended to lose out to *The Sun*. In dishing out Spice "exclusives" to the tabloids, the Virgin press office, working in tandem with Julian Henry of Lynne Franks's Life PR, had tried to maintain an even-handed approach between the old red-top rivals. But after a while, *The Sun*'s consistently superior coverage, not to mention its much greater circulation, had meant that they got the pick of the stories. Finding his newspaper sidelined, as he saw it, in the battle for Spice news, the vainglorious Morgan had been itching to have a go at the Girls for a long time.

But although it was nonsensical to suggest that an album which had just sold 191,000 copies in seven days could be considered anything other than a resounding success, it was an idea which many people in the media found curiously seductive. If the album wasn't a flop, then it jolly well ought to be, seemed to be the growing concensus of opinion. Never mind that it had topped the charts in six other countries, including Japan, and entered the German chart at number four. The Spice Girls were riding for a fall sooner or later, that much was clear, and a lot of commentators who should have known better simply couldn't contain their impatience to see it happen.

The anti-Spice bandwagon which Wright had set in motion received a significant boost later that week when the Girls travelled to Barcelona to attend the Premios Amigo Music Awards on November 13, where they were to receive an award for their "Contribution To Music". The 1,500-strong audience at this annual shindig were not Spice Girls fans but record industry freeloaders and media types. At the end of a long evening, when the Spanish presenter announced the ceremony's final performance by the Spice Girls, there was no sign of the group. Word was sent that they would not come on until the gaggle of photographers, about 50 of them, mostly Spanish, had left the front of the stage, as previously agreed. Several security staff then attempted to shift the photographers and a bout of mild jostling broke out amid jeers from

*Help!*

the audience. Some of the photographers moved off, but most stood their ground.

When the Spice Girls were eventually cajoled into going on stage and began their mimed performance of 'Spice Up Your Life', they were greeted by a wave of booing and whistling which was loud enough to be heard over the sound of the music. The Girls fronted it out, yelling "This is really great" and "Muchas gracias" as they left the stage, but the look on their faces told a different story.

The official explanation, according to a spokesman for Virgin Espana, was that the organisers had agreed that "the photographers should leave when the Spice Girls came on. Unfortunately they didn't do so. Everything went wrong and the photographers did not play by the rules."

And that, in essence, was exactly what had happened. *Why* it had happened was explained by the fact that, along with Fuller and all their other support staff, the Girls had lost their enforcer, Gerrard Tyrrell. Tyrrell or one of his assistants would have spotted the photographer problem at the event a mile off. The organisers would have been reminded of their contractual obligations well in advance, the photo-release forms would all have been signed before the photographers were allowed into the hall, and security chief Jerry Judge would have been on hand to escort any stragglers away from the stage in his courteous yet unfailingly persuasive manner.

But like Nicki Chapman, Tyrrell had stuck with Fuller. He wasn't around to throw the book at negligent organisers any more, which was bad enough. Far more significant in the coming weeks was the effect of his sudden absence on the media. There could not have been a worse moment, as far as the Girls were concerned, for the British press suddenly to find itself free of the eagle-eyed Tyrrell's restraining influence.

Mark Frith, editor of *Sky* magazine, summed up the feelings of most editors and newspaper bosses when he said: "We have been controlled, manipulated and exploited by [the Spice Girls] in a very intense fashion in the last few months. People don't like that."

"Well they did when it was happening to them," Tyrrell remarked wryly, referring to all the newspapers and pop magazines whose circulations had been boosted – in much the same way as the sales of crisps and cola had been – by the public's interest in the Spice Girls. But that didn't matter now. Not only could the pack smell blood, but without Tyrrell breathing down their necks, they were free at last to make up for lost time.

To read the early reports of the Spanish incident, you would have thought that the Spice Girls' fans had simply shown up in the usual way to cheer them on but then, presumably having all read Matthew Wright's column, decided to boo them off stage instead. But if ever there was a case of the media generating and then reporting its own story the Spanish fiasco was it. No Spice Girls fans had come close to getting into that hall.

That didn't bother Wright, who now had the bit firmly between his teeth. On November 18, he filled another entire page of the *Mirror* with his musings on the end of the Spice phenomenon. There was the exciting news that Wright had not been invited to a preview of (or seen) the *Spiceworld* movie ("Movie Is A Snore Point With Critics") and an equally nail-biting story about the departure of a set designer from the Spice Girls' forthcoming American tour ("Crisis Talks On US Tour"). But the bulk of the page was given over to a succession of unbelievably gormless jokes, which Wright declared were "the funniest things since Baby Spice tripped in her platform shoes." "Why do the Spice Girls work seven days a week? – So you don't have to retrain them on Mondays. What do you call a Spice Girl with two brain cells? – Pregnant. You're on an overloaded, sinking lifeboat with the Spice Girls. Who do you throw overboard? – Yourself."

One imagines that drowning would have been a soft option for Wright if he had found himself stranded in the vicinity of the Spice Girls that week. *The Sun*, guided by the much steadier hand of Showbiz Editor Andy Coulson, remained broadly supportive of the Girls. A report by Coulson on November 17 quoted Victoria as saying, somewhat implausibly, "We thought [the booing] was funny." But it was the *Mirror*'s snide insults and daily predictions of doom which set the media agenda for the next few weeks, and even the supposedly serious papers were soon joining in.

Typical of the reports which followed in the wake of Wright's broadsides was a spectacularly mendacious piece of commentary, dressed up as analysis, by the *Daily Telegraph*'s Media Correspondent. In this piece, the album's debut at number eight in the (much slower) American chart was described as "near-catastrophic", while it was suggested that the decline in UK sales of *Spiceworld* during the second week of release had been so calamitous that it was now selling "barely enough to keep it at number one". The fact that both *Spiceworld* and *Spice* were now simultaneously in the US Top 20 – a feat only ever achieved by a handful of acts – was ignored. Similarly, the sales that were "barely enough" to keep it at number one in the UK were, in fact, sufficient to outsell its nearest rival for the top slot by a ratio of two to one. Meanwhile, the *Telegraph* piece continued, bookmakers had stopped taking bets on Emma being the first Spice Girl to leave the group (although exactly when they had *started* taking them was not made clear). And to cap it all William Hill now had their new single, 'Too Much', as only second favourite for the Christmas number one behind the forthcoming Teletubbies single. How much worse could it get?

Although Tyrrell was now off the case, he naturally kept an interested eye on these shenanigans and was aghast at how inaccurate the majority of the reporting had been in the weeks after Fuller was deposed.

"Most of it is pure conjecture," he said, noting that the broadsheets paid little more attention to detail than the tabloids. A feature in the *Guardian* on November 13, for example, was illustrated by a half-page picture of Geri with a man identified as Fuller, who was in fact one of the Spice Girls' drivers.

A lot of the reporting, even in the "quality" press, had a spiteful ring about it. The *Observer* published a synopsis of the "carefully guarded" plot to the *Spiceworld* movie six weeks before it was due to open. Having revealed the ending (for what it was worth), the writers signed off with a little flourish: "Oh dear. I suppose that means we've spoiled it haven't we?"

With the Spice backlash now in full swing, and independent PR Julian Henry also having stuck with Fuller, it was clear that somebody had to be drafted in to steady the PR ship, and quickly. It was at this point that Alan Edwards came on board. Edwards, an experienced hand who had been press officer for The Rolling Stones and David Bowie among many others, was still smarting from his recent loss of Janet Jackson's account (another Virgin act). "Never mind Janet Jackson, this job will change your life," Virgin's Robert Sandall told him. Years later Edwards bumped into Sandall. "I remember you saying it would change my life," he said. "Because it did!"

Edwards's first morning behind the desk at his new job was the day after the Girls had been booed at the Spanish Awards show.

"I was shocked by the volume and hostility of the calls," Edwards said. "Journalists phoned to tell me the group was finished in the wake of the sacking of Simon Fuller. One national paper went so far as to say that I was a nice enough bloke, but as long as I represented these fucking bimbos they were going to attack me at every opportunity."

It is often remarked that the British press love nothing better than to build someone up only to knock them back down again, a loathsome practice which holds a mirror to the face of an increasingly decadent society. But if ever a group had set themselves up to be knocked down, it was the Spice Girls. They had harnessed the press during their rise to the giddiest of heights. Now they were vulnerable, and suddenly it was payback time. It all seemed utterly predictable in hindsight. But like Edwards, the Girls themselves were severely taken aback by the wave of hostility that had suddenly engulfed them.

"We think it is very sad," said a royally pissed-off Melanie C when I spoke to her on the phone in Paris on November 19. "We think that we've done really well for Britain. Why can't the press be proud of us and support us? And another thing that really confused us was this: We're the band. Why does anyone care about the manager? When I was a kid and I looked up to pop groups, I didn't even know who their manager was. You don't care. You don't even know what a manager is."

This was an interesting point. Why, indeed, had the sacking of Fuller become such an important issue? Blur sacked their manager. Robbie Williams sacked two of his managers. A few months before this all happened, Gary Barlow had parted company with Fuller himself. Pop acts split up with their managers all the time. Why such a rumpus on this occasion?

"We made a really hard decision," Melanie C said. "It was quite frightening to be honest with you. And we thought the media would be behind us. We're not stupid. We had our reasons for doing it. It's more of a legal thing than anything else why we can't discuss what happened. But also we don't want to turn it into a media circus any more than it already is."

Victoria had her own theories about the reasons for the backlash.

"The thing about the media is that it's a very male-dominated industry," she said. "Maybe they don't even realise sometimes what they're doing, but a lot of men, they liked the fact that they thought that a man was behind the Spice Girls. And they don't like the fact that now it's the five girls taking control. We've always been in control anyway, but I think they find the new situation quite hard to accept.

## Help!

"We feel we've done a lot for our country, a lot for our economy, provided jobs and a lot of positive feelings – not just for children, but adults as well, and I think it's a shame that people have to knock you down. The problem hasn't been as bad outside Britain. I don't think a lot of the fans in Spain even know that any of this is going on. Wherever we go abroad they say, 'Well done. We're really proud of you.' The funny thing is we love coming home to England. We love that more than anything. And the one place we get knocked, not by our fans, but by certain people in the media, is our home."

Clearly, it was wishful thinking to imagine that the media would simply accept their decision to sack Fuller on trust and remain supportive of the group. But why was there such a deep wellspring of animosity towards the group?

"What we saw was a bit of blood-letting," Edwards said. "Any rising market is bound to take a dip. It's not that the bubble has burst. There has been a readjustment in their stock as media icons, which was bound to happen sooner or later."

Insiders at Virgin admitted privately that the group had been overzealously marketed and that this had contributed to a cheapening of their image. "They've been presented more as loose-cannon celebrities than a musical group," Sandall remarked.

In the pop industry, where commercial instincts are supposed to be veiled by notions of street credibility and artistic integrity, the Girls' cheerful willingness to endorse products from crisps to deodorant spray was viewed with deep suspicion. Like the highly successful but *déclassé* relative who shows up at family gatherings flashing their newest baubles, the Girls reminded their peers a little too obviously of what their business was all about. And they voted Tory, don't forget.

The only slight difficulty for the tastemakers who had decided that the Spice Girls' time was up was that the facts didn't support the story. While this is not usually a problem when it comes to the British press, on this occasion they had performed their volte-face with such unseemly haste that it did rather expose their so-called news reporting for the heavily slanted personal invective that it actually was. Two weeks before, the Spice Girls had been the biggest success story of the decade, greeting Nelson Mandela as ambassadors of Cool Britannia. Now they couldn't even hold their own against a bunch of Spanish photographers, and their new album was an embarrassing "flop". As Edwards put it: "One minute they were the most cleverly marketed British act for years, and the next they were a PR disaster spiralling out of control." Even the most credulous observer of this spectacle must have wondered quite how such a rapid transformation could have occurred.

The fact was, it hadn't occurred. The "backlash" was all in the collective mind of the commentariat. As Christmas approached, demand for *Spiceworld* steadily *increased* and it ended the year as the fifth best-selling album of 1997 in Britain, where its eventual sales tally was not far short of two million copies, more than justifying that initial ship-out figure of 1.4 million copies which had been used by so many commentators as a stick with which to beat them.

*Spice* (which had been released in November 1996) was the third best-selling record of 1997 in Britain. In America, *Spice* was the number one best-selling record of 1997 with a tally of seven million copies shifted and *Spiceworld* – after that "near catastrophic" start – went on to become the tenth biggest-selling album of 1998.

*An Audience With The Spice Girls*, which was screened on November 29, secured a viewing figure of 11.8 million – one fifth of the UK populuation – despite being pulled to pieces by the critics both before and after it was screened. 'Too Much' was the Christmas number one, confounding Mr Blobby and the bookmakers' predictions. It was their second Christmas number one in a row and their sixth number one in all, another record. And *Spiceworld – The Movie*, which opened on Boxing Day, was a runaway success, becoming the second highest-grossing British film of 1987 (after *Bean*). In America the distributors of *Spiceworld* were presumed to have committed commercial suicide by opening in cinemas on January 23, 1998, the day before Super Bowl Sunday. But lo and behold, the movie set a new Super Bowl weekend opening record, taking $10.5 million, putting it second only in the rankings to *Titanic*, a movie that had cost about 25 times as much to make.

In December 1997, at the height of the Spice backlash, Q magazine conducted an investigation to resolve that old pub closing-time argument of "Who is the biggest band in the world?" Oasis had claimed, with monotonous regularity, that they were the rightful holders of the title, while fans of U2, The Rolling Stones or even veteran heavy rockers Metallica could all point to their sustained worldwide success as either touring leviathans or big-selling album artists or both.

The magazine carefully calibrated a range of achievements by these and other bands in the world throughout the preceding year, including album sales, total income earned, sales of concert tickets, airplay ratings and "media muscle" (number of front covers on national magazines, etc). It was an intriguing attempt to separate hard fact from boastful myth, but rather than trumpet the result of all this rigorous research, the magazine presented its findings in such a strangely muted, diagram format, that it took a moment or two to figure out what the answer actually was. But there right at the very top of the tree – before they had even embarked on their first world concert tour and without taking into account their top-grossing movie – were the Spice Girls! This was an astonishing turn-up for the books, and not, one imagines, what the organisers of the contest, nor anyone else who had been subjected to the barrage of "Spice Girls Finished" headlines over the previous months, would have predicted.

"The backlash, especially in Britain – that happens," Melanie B said in February 1998. "It's the old saying, 'Build 'em up and then knock 'em down.' But at the end of the day, it's not our marketing or our fame that's got us where we are today. It's our music and our attitude and our vibe that has got us there. And it's still there today."

"The media can't make or break us," Geri said. "Only our fans can do that."

"A lot of people want to believe the bubble has burst, but it hasn't," said the editor of *Smash Hits*, Gavin Reeve, one of the very few voices of reason to be heard in the aftermath of the Fuller affair. "It doesn't make a difference to a 10-year-old fan in Spain or the Philippines that they haven't got a manager."

And so it proved to be. You almost felt sorry for Matthew Wright (almost) as the weeks and months went by and support for the Girls among their fans remained rock solid. His rants in the *Mirror*, which had proved so ineffectual in slowing the Spice juggernaut, took on an air of desperation and finally exhaustion. On December 18, 1998, more than a year after he had first posed the question, "Is it all over for the Spice Girls?" Wright could be found lamenting the fact that the Girls were about to enjoy their *third* Christmas number one in a row, a feat only previously achieved by The Beatles.

"As you can imagine, I am not exactly thrilled at the prospect of seeing the Spice Girls singing 'Goodbye' on *Top Of The Pops* next Friday," Wright wrote, before reaching for yet another weary joke. "Frankly, I really wish it were goodbye from this washed out bunch." Surely by this time, it must have been obvious even to Wright, that if anyone in this sorry saga should have been saying their goodbyes, it was him.

While even the most deluded commentators had, by this time, been forced to change tack from the "It's-all-over-now" line, the Spice-baiting continued in the media throughout the rest of their career as a group, and indeed has carried on, with little let-up or deviation, until the present day. For while Wright was wide of the mark on virtually every material point, his puerile insults both echoed and nurtured the prejudices that many people instinctively felt about the group: that they were the manufactured puppets of Simon Fuller; that they couldn't sing, dance, act, think, speak or really do anything very much for themselves; that they hadn't really made any good records and, even if they had, somebody else had done all the work for them; in short, that they were a bunch of greedy, talentless, loudmouthed girls who should have known their place but had somehow lucked into a fortune.

Here's an unsolicited letter I received in 2004 after reviewing a Melanie C concert in *The Times*. It came handwritten on a plain sheet of A4 paper, unsigned, no address:

> MELANIE C
> She has millions in the bank and a meagre talent and yet she still wishes to pursue a pop career which is finished and will only face further humiliation. She is very ordinary – ordinary looking; ordinary voice; no charisma. There are thousands out there who are younger, more talented and prettier. Why does she not just GO AWAY – get married and have a couple of kids. It's over MEL C – nothing lasts forever. You have made a load of money and had your time in the sun. GO AWAY.
>
> VICTORIA BECKHAM
> Another one with millions in the bank and a husband who earns £90,000 A WEEK plus 2 children but who wants to be a pop star. (A kick up the arse is more likely). This one can't even sing and has a little squeaky voice. Anybody who buys her soon to be released single seriously needs their head examined. GO AWAY. JOIN YOUR HUSBAND IN SPAIN AND GET OUT OF OUR ORBIT YOU SILLY, GREEDY BITCH.

There's always something a bit creepy about unsigned letters and this one was no exception. But although it is an extreme example, the

## Help!

mixture of anger, envy and despair that this particular missive conveys seems to me to be typical of a certain sort of knee-jerk response to the Spice Girls. Firstly there is the reference to their extraordinary wealth which is held against them no less than their supposedly "meagre talent". Then there is the very gender-specific critique that, never mind talent, meagre or otherwise, as women of a certain age they should now be thinking about looking after husbands and children rather than trying to forge careers for themselves. Finally, there is the writer's sense of utter frustration and annoyance that we are still forced to accommodate them in "our orbit".

There are dozens of websites devoted to insulting and denigrating the Spice Girls. Most of it is harmless if not especially witty banter, and it seems that having done so much to lower the age at which kids take an active interest in pop, the Spice Girls have had to accept the sort of criticism – in cyberspace at least – that rarely rises above the level of playground name-calling.

But the childish way in which the anti-Spice arguments were frequently framed and the vehemence of their detractors gradually seemed to infect the pop world as a whole. Soon everybody was having a go.

"I should imagine the Spice Girls right now are unmanageable," said Tom Watkins, former manager of Bros and East 17 soon after they had severed their ties with Fuller. "I imagine they think they're all on the level of Princess Di. I certainly wouldn't want to manage five old boilers like that . . . I don't need to prostitute myself that badly."

True, Watkins was not exactly a well-known figure, and was probably still smarting from having been passed over for the job of managing the Spice Girls himself back in 1995, when they signed with Fuller. But you would have thought that someone like George Harrison could have risen above the fray. Not so. In a wide-ranging rant about how pop groups today just weren't as good as they used to be in his day, the ageing former Beatle declared in 1997 that the best thing about the Spice Girls is that "you can watch them with the sound turned off".

Boy George summed it up for a lot of people when he said of the Spice Girls: "They are a cynical corporate creation and proof that a good stylist is more important than a good melody." George, as everyone could see, regarded a good stylist as a much lower priority.

And Phil Spector certainly hit a nerve, when he came to London at the end of 1997 to accept a "Special Award" from Q magazine. "I was just thinking, are the Spice Girls the Antichrist?" his acceptance speech began. "That's the way it feels to me, though there's a big controversy in America right now about them being tantamount to a porno act... Well I disagree with that because there's a big difference between a Spice Girls video and a porno film. Some porno films have pretty good music."

Spector had not shown his face at an affair like this for longer than anyone could remember, and the legendary producer's pearls of comic wisdom were seized on with much enthusiastic chortling by the boozed-up audience of industry insiders and stars. He had caught the mood of the gathering just so, and milked it for all it was worth.

The business of the Spice Girls being a "porno" act was explained by the release in America of a video called *Spice Exposed* which contained numerous nude photos of Geri from her modelling days. Not having had the benefit of the British tabloid press to keep them fully informed on such matters, the Americans were only just getting up to speed on this old story.

But why exactly, I wonder, did Spector feel that the Spice Girls were the Antichrist, and of what relevance was this to the award which he had come all the way to London, so graciously, to accept? Here was a man who had enjoyed some of his most notable early successes by hiring groups of girls – some would say inventing them – taking them into a studio, writing songs for them, recording them and then, once their moment had passed, chucking them on the scrapheap without a second thought. The groups were interchangeable – the Crystals, the Ronettes, Bob B. Sox & The Blue Jeans – their roles more like those of actors than singers, as they went through their lines and lives exactly as scripted by Spector.

No doubt Spector was only castigating the Spice Girls for marketing themselves too enthusiastically and for recording songs that were not quite as brilliant as the ones that he had once supplied his own, much more pliant girl groups with. It surely wasn't anything to do with the fact that he was a lonely old chap on a very rare outing to collect an award for nothing in particular, while the Spice Girls were not only the most successful group in the world, but had made a conscious decision to cut people like him out of the loop?

John Lydon boasted that he was the Antichrist on the Sex Pistols' first single, 'Anarchy In The UK', a song which many years later Melanie C would sing in her first solo shows to howls of indignation from the more self-righteous keepers of the punk flame. But how peculiar that Spector should fix on "the Antichrist" as his epithet of choice for describing five cheerful girls whose selling point was their very lack of anything more diabolical than a tendency to run around shouting "Girl Power" and encouraging other girls to stick up for themselves. Spector, on the other hand, was a man with a history of depression and other psychological ailments. His own reputation for waving guns around, shooting out lights and destroying furniture in recording sessions had been well documented, but never censured, until in February 2003, he was charged with the murder of a 40-year-old woman called Lana Clarkson. She was found slumped in a chair in his hilltop mansion, east of Los Angeles with a bullet hole in her head and her broken teeth scattered around the foyer and stairway. It was later suggested that she had committed suicide and that Spector had fallen foul of some strange twist of circumstance involving his house and his gun, but not him. Stranger things have happened – but not often. Either way, this was murky stuff, even by the standards of the rock'n'roll underworld. But while Spector has been described at various times as an "insane genius" a "tyrannical egomaniac" and a "demented control freak", no one has ever been indelicate enough to label him the Antichrist.

Thom Yorke of Radiohead was one of those who was quick to pick up on Spector's comments.

"I agree with whoever said the Spice Girls are soft porn; they're the Antichrist," Yorke said at the end of 1997. "I don't want any part of it, and if I had kids I wouldn't want them to have any part of it either. I'd go and live on an island where you can't get hold of any Spice Girls stuff."

What is often striking about these remarks, is how similar in their scornful tone and condescending attitude they are to the kind of comments that were routinely applied to the pop music of the Fifties and Sixties by an older generation who felt duty bound to point out what absolute rubbish their kids were listening to and to try to protect them from harmful exposure to it. From George Harrison's "things were better when I was a young man" to Thom Yorke's "I won't have my kids listening to any of that stuff", it all has a depressingly familiar ring. My uncle used to insist that Bob Dylan couldn't sing. And in a bid to set me straight, my English teacher once told me that Jimi Hendrix was not a musician but a circus act who sometimes used Ladies toilets. The Spice Girls are obviously not on a par with Hendrix or Dylan. How could they be? But how quickly the hipsters of yesteryear reach for the patronising language of their parents when their own kids latch on to something different that meets with their disapproval.

It would be stretching a point to describe the Spice Girls as leaders of a new counter-counterculture. But in rejecting both the hippy idealism and punk nihilism which still colours the thinking of the music industry's old guard, in favour of an aspirational, highly commercial, pop star approach, they became genuine "outsiders" in a way that no pop icons of their stature had ever been before.

Looking at the picture of the Spice Girls in the Q magazine spread identifying them as the biggest band in the world, it is almost laughable just how out of place they looked alongside such traditional rock heavyweights as U2, the Stones, Oasis, R.E.M. and Smashing Pumpkins. The Spice Girls were rulers of a universe in which they didn't belong. Not for them the years of slogging round the superbowls with guitars cranked up to 11. Nor was any of the familiar rock'n'roll rhetoric likely to come tripping from their lips: "We just make music we like; if anyone else likes it that's a bonus", "We were so out of our brains on coke/Es/booze it's a wonder the album/tour ever got started let alone finished" or even "How're ya doing, Cleveland?" (that one would come later). The Spice Girls didn't belong with the cool people, and, frankly, they never would. But that is not the same thing as saying they were unpopular.

Even so, did Spector, Yorke and all the others have a point? Were the Spice Girls a group driven by naked ambition and pure commercial greed as opposed to the higher artistic imperatives to which bands like Radiohead and Oasis apparently aspired?

"I don't feel that accusation has legs," said Ray Cooper, who marketed the Spice Girls for Virgin records alongside bands such as The Verve and Massive Attack. "It's just the Spice Girls had a different philosophy, and the kind of people that Thom Yorke talks to as an audience, in the main, are not going to be the sort of people that want to buy a Spice Girls record or live in a world surrounded by Spice Girls products. But Radiohead and their fans do live in a world that is commercial in intent, and they are influenced to buy products, probably on a subliminal level, where they've seen other artists promote the fact that they like the product.

"Maybe the Spice Girls were the realisation of something from the Thatcher years which insisted that commercialism is God. They were of a generation that was brought up by their parents wanting them to succeed. And success in any country is usually measured by how much disposable income you have and how you can live your life. But from a record company perspective it is not that different working on the Spice Girls to working on The Verve. You set out knowing that the ambitions of both groups are different in certain details. Some of them have criteria where they feel they don't want to 'sell out', which is fine. The Spice Girls, on the other hand, were comfortable with it, and grabbed the commercial opportunities that were out there, because they'd realised that the generation that looked up to them was soaked in commercial products. But what ties the Spice Girls and The Verve and any other major group together is an overwhelming desire for global success by making great records.

"And the Spice Girls always wanted to make great records. Mel B had listened to a lot of R&B. Mel C had listened to a lot of music in general. And Geri definitely studied it. They stuck to their guns about the 'Wannabe' single and video when everyone else said it wasn't working. Geri, in particular, used to go through the music with [A&R man] Ashley [Newton] in a very tortured way, with a real attention to detail. At the same time they never lost sight of the fact that their ambition was on a massive scale. With some of the other acts we deal with that's sometimes buried for a while until it reaches fruition. Then it can take on different forms. Thom Yorke may well be just as ambitious in different areas. The Spice Girls just wanted to have a lot of success, they wanted to have an amazing amount of fun doing it and they were just the perfect people to execute it."

They also wanted to make an amazing amount of money, and made no secret of it. They were the wannabes and material girls that Madonna had presaged a decade before, and unlike their indie-rock cousins they had no qualms about maximising their earnings through commercial sponsorship options on a hitherto unimaginable scale.

They did their bit for charity by donating their royalties from 'Mama'/'Who Do You Think You Are' and other activities, but it was remarked by some of those around them that they could be surprisingly ungenerous when it came to disposing of the many more-or-less unwanted gifts that they received on a daily basis. Melanie B was said to be particularly tight-fisted in this regard and items that you might have thought would routinely be donated to a charity were firmly gathered in and kept.

"They probably thought that they didn't want to be one of those stupid groups that got ripped off by people, which was translated in a rather dumb way into them just hanging on to everything they got," said an insider.

Simon Fuller had drummed in to the Girls the idea that they were special – that he was not going to let them be ripped off in the way that pop groups had traditionally been ripped off in the past – and they were certainly determined not to end up as anybody's victims. But their desire to be rich was born more out of classic feelings of working class insecurity than some grand capitalist masterplan.

"We've all come from backgrounds where we didn't expect to become very rich," Emma said. "And I think we all feel, a little bit, well what do we do with it all? When I'm out with Geri we still share our drink. She won't open another one and let it go to waste. We've all got brothers and sisters, and when we used to go out for a meal you used to share your drink. That's just what you do.

"We've raised over a million pounds for Comic Relief. We've sponsored a little boy and I've just bought my mother a house. The thing that all of us has done is that we've treated our families. We've bought houses for our families and holidays and nice cars and things that they couldn't afford. I think our families have been brilliant through everything."

Melanie C: "The things that they could never do for themselves, now we can do for them."

Victoria: "We like going home and doing things like shopping at Marks & Spencer."

Maybe the Spice Girls were too eager to maximise their earning potential. But at least they were open and forthright about their aims and business dealings. They didn't preach the anti-consumerist gospel while selling millions of records and quietly doing under-the-table endorsement deals in the Far East. And they certainly never used the age-old get-out clause of blaming the promotional overkill on management or record company "interference".

"We were involved in every single decision," Victoria said. "It's just the way it's been perceived is wrong. If you look at a racing-car driver, he's sponsored by lots of people. Why should it be any different with a pop act?"

Emma's rationale was even simpler.

"I like Chupa Chups," said the blonde emissary of the Antichrist.

While the Girls put a brave face on the daily pillorying which they had received in the British press, they found it hard to conceal their genuine surprise at the depth of negative feeling which their success had prompted. They weren't cool people who pretended not to read or care about their press. They were still, in some ways, surprisingly naive, and found the picture that had been painted of them to be so far removed from their self-image as to be quite baffling.

"We've had a lot of criticisms," Victoria said. "And I was just thinking, what kind of person, really, wants to sit there and criticise five girls who are giving young children a positive attitude and saying, 'Go for it.' We're nice. We're not promoting drink, drugs and alcohol. We're doing nice things here and we're nice people."

"Yes. But you're wearing a short skirt and you've got a brain," Geri responded.

Victoria: "I just think what kind of person is that? I don't understand it and I don't even like to entertain it because I think it's sad."

"Don't even go there, OK?" Melanie B said, patting Victoria on the knee.

Although exhausted and battered by the unforeseen response to the sacking of Fuller, the Girls were now on a mission to prove their detractors wrong. For a while they went into a kind of euphoric overdrive, but it was a weary group of individuals who hauled themselves towards the end of a year in which they had risen from the foothills of pop stardom to the summit of global celebrity. The effort had taken its toll. Now, as well as fulfilling the packed schedule of international commitments that Fuller had bequeathed them – including trips to Italy, France, America, Australia and Brazil – they had to take charge of all the day-to-day management decisions as well. Meetings with lawyers, accountants, record company and press people had to be factored in to the daily whirlwind of travelling and other promotional activities.

"The greatest irony about sacking Simon," Geri said, "was that it had been triggered by my not being given a week off. Yet since then, we had worked twice as hard to prove that we didn't need him."

The last promotional trip of the year was to Manaus, a port at the mouth of the Amazon in northern Brazil. It turned out to be something of a watershed. The trip was set up in much the same way as previous excursions, such as the one to Johannesburg, where a whole continent was effectively serviced in one quick visit. The Girls were never going to be able to visit Bolivia, Chile, Paraguay or wherever. But in order to Spice up those markets, planeloads of competition winners, journalists and other people that needed access to them from all over the South American continent were flown in to Manaus to meet, or at least catch a glimpse of, the Girls. It was a classic example of the Fuller Method whereby the maximum promotional impact is made in the shortest possible space of time. But it required full cooperation and a tremendous, sustained burst of energy from the Girls to produce the desired result. Until then, their collective work ethic and their ability to bounce ideas and enthusiasm off each other had always carried the day. But Manaus was a bridge too far.

The Girls flew in on a private plane from Las Vegas, where they had collected prizes for Best Album and Best Breakthrough Act at the *Billboard* Awards. Manaus was not the easiest place to get to, and the Girls were already running on empty when they discovered that the hotel they were booked into was well below par. There was no security. Geri complained of reporters and fans "roaming the corridors, knocking on doors", while Victoria discovered "a graveyard of mosquitos" on the walls of her room. The mayor offered them alternative accommodation on his riverboat tied up on the Amazon, which secured them some privacy, but was hardly an improvement in terms of creature comforts. There were problems with the food and Victoria became ill. At which point the biggest group in the world decided that enough was enough.

"We want to go home," they told Bart Cools, the International Marketing Manager at Virgin, who always travelled with the Girls and now greeted them each morning with the day's schedule. For as long as Cools had been doing the job he had never encountered such resistance once they had made a commitment.

"Well, you have to do these things," Cools told them.

"No. Fuck that. We're going home."

Cools had seen this happen with many other artists, in the past. His only real surprise was that it hadn't happened with the Spice Girls sooner. He and the Girls had words – "nothing too major", according to Cools – after which the Girls agreed to do two or three hours work before flying home a day early.

"I think, in retrospect, we worked them too hard," Cools said later. "It was difficult for us [the record company] to say 'No.' We had to keep going and honour the commitments that they had made."

In Britain the Girls attended the *Smash Hits* Poll Winners' Party, which turned out to be something of a bittersweet experience compared to the year before. This time the Spice Girls had not only been voted Best Band but also Worst Band – a quirky result to say the least, but one which underlined just how severely they now polarised opinion, even among their core target audience. Geri was voted Least Fanciable Female and Worst Dressed Person.

Then there was a Royal Command Performance at the Empire Leicester Square as part of a variety bill including stars such as Enya and Celine Dion to be negotiated. On being presented to the Queen, a nervous Geri failed to curtsey with sufficient vigour to satisfy those well-known upholders of royal protocol, the press pack. The Queen, it seemed, had no complaints, but there was still a minor hoo-ha when some of the papers suggested that Ginger had shown a lack of respect for Her Maj.

And finally, there was the world premiere of *Spiceworld – The Movie* held in Leicester Square, which the Girls attended all dressed up in pinstripe suits along with their friends and admirers the Princes Charles, William and Harry. It was a triumphant moment, but one which almost didn't happen thanks to the climate of uncertainty which followed the sacking of Simon Fuller. With the media backlash in full swing, the film's distributors had started to wobble.

"Sony were phoning up and saying, 'We're just going to put it straight through to video,'" Kim Fuller remembered. "They weren't sure if the band were going to promote it or do anything else. It was my first feature film, and for a moment it looked as if it was all going to go down in flames. It could have gone down the pan without a trace."

As it turned out, Sony recovered their nerve, the Girls did promote the movie and it became one of the most profitable films in the history of British cinema. Made on a budget of about £4 million, it grossed a total of £8.5 million in Britain, $30 million in America, and at least the same again in the rest of the world.

But for both Kim and Simon Fuller the success of the project left a slightly sour taste in the mouth. Kim attended the Royal premiere, but for obvious reasons, Simon was not on hand.

"It was the opening of one of the biggest British movies of all time, and the guy who set it all up didn't get to see the film," Kim Fuller said. "I said to him, 'Why don't you come to the premiere?' And he said, 'I can't do it.' So the credits go up on the screen and his name appears about three times at the beginning, and there's a little ripple of applause from some people in the audience – very ironic. The film had raised several tens of thousands of pounds for the Princes' Trust, but Simon wasn't there to shake Prince Charles's hand. Even my mum didn't come."

But while the Spice pantechnicon apparently rolled on regardless of Simon Fuller's absence, behind the scenes the management situation was beginning to drift rather alarmingly. They made approaches to Gail Colson, who had managed Peter Gabriel and others, and to Lisa Anderson, who ran the Brits (and later managed Geri as a solo act), but neither was prepared to accept the job on the terms that were being offered, namely that the successful candidate would be required to work as, effectively, an employee of the group. There was, too, a feeling that the group without Fuller was, somehow, both a loose cannon and a spent force. Colson spoke for many when she confided in one of her friends that she thought the job would be "a nightmare".

"I think that was when the die was cast," Alan Edwards said. "People think it's a myth that they managed themselves after Fuller left. How many times have we heard groups say that they manage themselves and then you find out there's half-a-dozen managers in the background? But I promise you they really did it, and for longer than you would have thought. I remember sitting down in enough meetings with them, and it was very raw. The decision was made there and then, on the spot, which sometimes was great, sometimes a bit too intense. But there was no sanitising process. It didn't go through to the secret person who they discussed everything with. They made the decisions. Which was part of the electricity and excitement of the whole Spice thing. It really was like that."

In December they were put in touch with Nancy Phillips, who used to work in Nicki Chapman's Brilliant! PR company, and who had management experience with indie bands such as the High Llamas, going all the way back to the heyday of The Undertones. Phillips went to meet the group in Paris, where they were doing promotion for *Spiceworld – The Movie.*

"To be honest, I thought it was a bit of a joke," she recalled. "I managed indie bands. I didn't even know which one was which of the Spice Girls. I didn't give a damn. They told me that they were going to manage themselves, but they needed someone to run the office. They didn't really know what they were offering. Melanie B and Emma lasted about five minutes in this meeting, before they got bored and wanted to go. Melanie C didn't say anything. Geri and Victoria were very much asking the questions, trying to be the business people.

"I got the feeling that they didn't want another manager. I don't think it would have worked. It depends how you approach management, of course, but they certainly were not going to have anyone telling them what to do. No one who wanted to come in and control them in any way would have survived. That was absolutely plain."

Phillips, however, had the kind of personality that enabled her to work with them in a more sympathetic, supporting role.

"I'm not an overbearing, forceful person," she said. "I'm quite mumsy and affectionate. I could be caring and nurturing, and artists need that as well as the strong business guidance. For five young girls that was quite important. For them to have someone who could understand their emotional turmoil, plus coax them around to what needed to be done, was probably a good arrangement at the time."

Phillips could also be relied upon to bring the full weight of her organisational skills to bear on the affairs of the group, which by this time were beginning to drift alarmingly. They didn't even have an office, and when Phillips took up her post at the start of 1998, she initially had to work from home. For a while the biggest group in the world was being run from a two-up, two-down in Muswell Hill with a home computer on a dining room table. Phillips's start date was meant to be Monday, January 19, but the Girls felt that where matters of management were concerned 19 was an unlucky number, so her contract was changed to start from January 20.

With Phillips on hand to sort out all the bothersome administrative details and keep an overview of what was going on, the situation in Spiceworld gradually began to stabilise. She located an office in Bell Street, off the Marylebone Road, which had previously been a shop with connections to the rag trade.

"There were lots of rails and mirrors, when we took it over," Phillips said. "It was a bit of sweat shop, I think, which it certainly became again. I mean I lived it, there was no other option."

On the credits of the *Forever* album, there is the legend: "A massive thanks to everyone at Spice HQ . . . especially Nancy Phillips (go home now!)." As with everyone who became intimately involved with the Spice saga, for the next couple of years it would consume her life.

The group's next big hurdle, and really the only area in which they had yet to prove themselves, was the matter of their world tour, scheduled to begin in February 1998. As they had opted to stay out of Britain over Christmas to avoid paying their taxes, and needed a base where they could prepare for the rigours of a proper, full-on stage show, the Girls decamped to Dublin in Ireland. After more promotional trips, to Australia and America in January, it was back to Dublin where rehearsals began in earnest for the live show that would represent the final piece of the Spice jigsaw.

# 9

# Ginger Snaps

"Five girls, that's always going to be a handful," Simon Fuller said, many years after he parted company with the Spice Girls. "I can't think of any other way I could have dealt with it. Because within those five, you had two extremely strong characters – Geri and Mel B – with a love-hate relationship that was not very well balanced. And then you had the other three who were pretty normal, really. Mel C was very devoted to her music – for her the group was a means to an end of doing her own music. And Emma and Victoria, coming from stage school, were just kind of living their dreams really. They were just happy to be along for the ride.

"But the extremism of the other two meant that I got involved in everything. There wasn't a single row that I wasn't in the centre of, basically pulling them off each other or else siding with the one that was about to get pummelled to death or get kicked out of the group. It's one thing being a manager who chooses the songs, guides the image and all the other things. But it's quite another when you're actually brokering the peace on a daily basis. That's kind of full-on.

"My memory of the Spice Girls was just friction all the time. It was battling among themselves. I'm not a battler. I don't like confrontation. I'm completely the opposite. And that's very draining actually. I didn't want to go through that again. I certainly don't know S Club 7 as closely as I did the Spice Girls. Why would I want to? That's probably a bit of a scar I carry with me now, and probably will do forever. I don't think I'll get quite as close to anyone again as I did to the Spice Girls. But I think that's a good thing, because I'm not sure there's any upside to it really."

While the ins and outs of Girl Power have been chewed over *ad nauseam*, a central plank of the philosophy which has held firm throughout the Spice odyssey is the notion of the girl gang that maintains a united front no matter what the internal divisions. "God help the mister/ Who comes between me and my sisters" was more than just a handy rhyme. Even after they parted ways, and certainly when they were together, the Girls never dished the dirt on each other in public, no matter how many times they were prompted by reporters waiting to pounce on the most innocuous remark and somehow frame it as a criticism or insult. In the official version of Spiceworld, the Girls always stood up for one another and never doubted each other. All for one and one for all was the law.

But the Spice Girls did not become a world-famous pop phenomenon without generating a fair amount of creative and personal friction among themselves, and behind the scenes there were tensions and power struggles going on within the group almost from the outset.

The Girls were all intensely competitive in their own ways, a fact borne out by the extraordinary parity of creative input and public attention which they maintained throughout their career together.

Normally in vocal groups, however democratically organised they are at the outset, a leader or lead voice eventually emerges by a process of natural selection. At the very least, certain songs are appropriated as vehicles for individual singers within the group. But in the Spice Girls, this process never occurred. Melanie C was the most technically accomplished singer, and it was often her voice that could be heard rising above the melee in ad lib sections at the end of certain songs. Victoria, on the other hand, probably had the least imposing presence as a vocalist. But the difference in the amount of time Melanie C's and Victoria's voices are featured over the recorded output of the Spice Girls is negligible.

Kim Fuller remembered when they were making the *Spiceworld* movie, how carefully the balance of attention had to be maintained.

"They'd all be in make-up, having their hair done, and I'd go in with the six or seven pages of script for the day. They'd look through their lines and someone would say, 'I've only got four lines.' Then someone else would say 'Why is Geri saying the funny line?' Well, somebody's got to say it. 'So, why can't I say it?' They were always very aware of each other's part in the whole thing."

When it came to decision-making the responsibilities were likewise shared equally – in theory.

"This is coming from us," Melanie B said, after the dismissal of Simon Fuller. "Because there is nobody around saying, 'You have to do it like that, you have got to do this.' We've never had that. If we didn't want to get up the next day and do it we wouldn't have to. But we're doing it, because we like doing it."

"We're very easy on each other," Geri said. "If someone wants to do something, there's no rule. Because we're running our own ship. At the end of the day it's not like . . ."

Melanie B: ". . . being in the army. In some groups you have so many rules. You're not allowed to go out. You're not allowed to do this. And we can't comprehend that. Because if they get famous and they've lived their life like that, how are they going to be able to adjust to a normal environment when they're not so famous one day?"

In practice it was Melanie B and Geri who were the dominant personalities. Both loud, extrovert types with a natural controlling instinct, they enjoyed an intense love-hate relationship that functioned as the emotional heart of the group, pumping blood around the system, and sometimes spilling it in the process. Even when there was nothing specific to peg it to, the relationship between the two of them was like the polarities on a battery. Either they were plugged in and getting on like a house on fire or they weren't talking to each other. There was no neutral position; no middle ground of peaceful coexistence.

Geri was the ideas person, the one with the vision thing. Her talent for setting goals, mapping out strategy, taking care of business and generally making the group's case to the outside world, meant that she tended to be cast in a leadership role, not least in her own mind. But Geri was the least experienced singer and dancer, and it was Melanie B who tended to take control in this department, sorting out the choreography and, with Melanie C, overseeing the arrangements of the vocal parts.

Geri and Melanie B spent a lot of time hanging around together in the early days, egging each other on while simultaneously jostling for pole position in the group. They did most of the talking when the Girls were together. Their banter always had an undercurrent to it. This was Geri trying to explain what it felt like to be a Spice Girl:

"I really wish I could get a thousand people inside my head just to show them what I can see and feel about it," she began.

"Oh God, they'd come out crazy," Melanie B interrupted. "Jee-sus!"

Geri carried on, undeterred: "If I stepped out of here, and I wasn't in the Spice Girls, I'd just think: these girls work so hard and they're really, genuinely nice people."

"Oh, you're gonna make me cry," said Melanie B, "just before I vomit."

Melanie C was quieter but utterly dedicated, and more of a physical presence with her strong, sporty look. Often, if there was an argument, she ended up in the role of mediator. Emma was a more compliant personality, easy-going, a lot of fun, and usually ready to fall in with the general concensus of opinion rather than impose her own views too stridently on the rest of the group. Victoria, although not short of her own opinions, and well able to dig her heels in when the occasion demanded, usually affected a slightly bored and disengaged manner. She was the quietest of the five and perhaps a little unsure of herself. But she was also the most cynical and grounded. If there was a charity lunch or an after-show meet-and-greet to be attended, Victoria would be the most reluctant participant. While the other four would be up and working the room with their usual enthusiasm – "Ooh, that's a smart shirt; where did you get it?" – Victoria would stay put at the table, pushing her food around with a fork. This sense of holding something in reserve contributed to a perception of Victoria in the media as the being the "moody one". But she was actually very witty in her own dry way. She was also highly organised, methodical and business-minded in a way which quietly gave her an edge over the apparently more forceful, yet scatterbrained Melanie B.

The two Mels had the strongest musical interests: Melanie B with her R&B roots and Melanie C with her fondness for indie-rock. While Melanie B was the loudest, both literally and as a personality, Geri was the most alert – always looking to turn every situation to her or the group's advantage. The Virgin suits certainly learned to respect her sharp eye for detail. For example, when the group agreed to contribute their royalties from 'Mama'/'Who Do You Think You Are' to Comic Relief, it was Geri who queried how much the record company was contributing from its share of the profits, and insisted that they pulled their weight as well.

"Geri was very good at manipulating a situation to her advantage, that was evident from Day One," said Nicki Chapman of Brilliant! PR. Chapman remembered meeting Geri for the first time in the offices of RCA soon after the Spice Girls had teamed up with Fuller in 1995.

"I didn't even know her name – she was just the ginger one – but she was very opinionated. She was telling me how to do promotion and my MD, who was in the room, said to her, 'A word of advice: you do what you're good at and we'll do what we're good at. And we're good at promotion.' She was a bit naive but she was certainly flexing her muscles. But there was also a vulnerability about her as well. The thing was that although she was feisty, and they were all feisty, if you said, 'No – you've gone too far,' they always took it on board and took a step back.

"If anything went on it would always be to do with Geri and Mel B. Geri was great at doing a number on people, especially men, really quickly. She's a very clever girl, not academic, but she knew how to get the most out of a situation. Mel B would be straight in there both feet first and she'd say exactly what she thought. Geri was more subtle. It was those two who instigated the removal of Simon Fuller. I could tell as soon as I met them when they came back from the MTV awards. Mel B wouldn't look me in the eye. Meanwhile Geri was sorting everyone out and organising everything. So was Mel B, but you could see that her nose was slightly put out of joint because Geri was doing it all. Victoria, Emma and Melanie C were crying hysterically. They'd been up all night and hadn't had any sleep. Were they convinced or were they cajoled? I think if anyone had had any doubts at that point they would have been too scared to voice them.

"Geri was stopping the others from answering their phones. She was answering all the Girls' mobile phones in case Simon called them and tried to persuade them to change their minds. I looked at Melanie C and I wondered whether she was completely happy about the decision to leave Simon. I don't think the other three [Melanie C, Victoria and Emma] were that happy, but they weren't the leaders. Geri and Mel B were the leaders, definitely."

Whether she wanted to be accepted as the leader or not, Geri came on like she was in charge, and this would often rub the others up the wrong way.

Robert Sandall, Virgin's director of press, remembered one such occasion in the early days when he travelled with them to Bangkok.

"There was some big bust-up between Geri and the rest of them, which is rather bizarrely and beautifully commemorated by a photograph which appeared in *Big* magazine," he said. "The Girls are sitting on a staircase at the top of a tower block, and there are four of them sitting together, all very lovey-dovey, and Geri at the end sitting on her own, looking glum. You can just tell that there was this big friction. It's a very graphic image of the way things were going, even then."

Chapman remembered similar situations.

"There were times when Geri would upset the other girls. I remember once when we were flying to America and Simon just walked up to her and said, 'Congratulations, you've made everybody on this plane cry. You're doing it in front of everybody. If you've got something to say, let's wait until we get to the hotel.' But he would never have a go at them, never."

Chapman, who had travelled extensively with Take That, found life in the Spice bubble a completely different experience.

"Five girls is always going to be difficult. Take That were great fun, loved being on tour, loved to shag, all those things that boys like to do. With girls it is different. There was cattiness and bickering and things, but certainly in the early days they looked out for each other and if there was an issue you never saw it in front of the public. It was always behind the scenes. The girls used to turn on Geri quite a lot. They hated her for organising everything and being the mouthpiece and being the most opinionated. But also there had to be some respect there because she was the one who went off and got things done. And if you wanted a point got across, Geri was the person to do it."

Bart Cools, the International Marketing Manager at Virgin, who travelled with the Girls on every trip they made outside the UK, felt that no one person dominated the group, as such.

"It depended on the day, who was the most dominant," Cools said. "Some people shouted louder than others. But I don't think they had more weight in taking the decisions. It sounds a bit prefabricated and planned this whole thing of the five of them, but it worked that way. Even after ten-hour days when they were tired, pissed off, homesick or whatever, there was always one of the five that could switch it on; either towards the other girls or towards the journalist or TV producer, or whoever. There was always one of them that would say, 'Oh, come on. Let's do it!' or one of them who could establish a rapport with whoever they needed to deal with next. They were a very well-oiled team. Having said that, I think Geri was the best at that. She was also the best at pissing people off."

Geri undoubtedly had great ideas. But her spontaneous, headstrong nature meant that she could be too uncontrolled, sometimes with near-disastrous results. Soon after the booing incident with the Spanish photographers, the Girls travelled to Rome. Anxious to prove that they were still as popular with their fans as ever, and in a bid to counter the negative press that they had suffered in the UK, they had invited Andy Coulson of *The Sun* to accompany them on the trip to write up a story. In order to prompt a public demonstration of just how much their fans loved them, Geri had the bright idea of throwing some roses from a balcony to the fans below. But she seriously misjudged the hysterical reaction of the crowd, and in the ensuing stampede to get hold of the roses it was a miracle that no one was seriously injured, or worse.

Geri was at her most vulnerable when it came to performing live. As the only one of the five who hadn't been to stage school she had received no formal training as a singer or dancer before joining the Spice Girls. Worse, these were not skills that came to her particularly naturally. Working in the studio, she could spend extra time on her parts, and in songwriting sessions, her vivid imagination and command of language was more than a match for the others. When performing in videos and the *Spiceworld* movie, her sheer force of personality meant she was often the most watchable. In public situations she had a natural flair for snatching the headlines, as she did at the Brits when she wore her Union flag dress or when the Girls met Prince Charles and she grabbed the royal buttocks.

But as 1998 began, it was the prospect of the World Tour that loomed largest on the group's horizon. This wasn't going to be another round of whistle-stop promotional junkets of the sort that had helped to establish them in so many far-flung places. This was going to be a different sort of hard graft; two hours on stage in the big arenas and stadiums of Europe and North America, singing live, dancing and generally doing what the biggest group in the world was expected to do, night after night after night. Most groups that become anything like as successful as the Spice Girls would have had this part of the job sewn up long before now. Indeed, for acts such as U2, The Rolling Stones and R.E.M., putting on a live, touring show was regarded as the cornerstone of their success, if not the core reason for their existence. Their prowess as a live act was worn as a badge of pride. It was also a significant source of income, and has become increasingly so in recent years.

So it was important for the Spice Girls to prove that they could cut it as a live, touring attraction. Basing themselves at a big arena and rehearsal complex called The Point, in Dublin, they embarked on a rigorous programme of rehearsals, much as they had done when preparing for the one-off show in Istanbul the year before. First, they assembled a band of top-flight session musicians led by keyboard player

Simon Ellis and featuring Fergus Gerand (percussion), Paul Gindler (guitar), Michael Martin (keyboards), Andy Gangadeen (drums) and Steve Lewinson (bass). Between them these six men had played behind East 17, Belinda Carlisle, Take That, Duran Duran, Level 42, Aswad, Massive Attack, M People and Simply Red. Then they hired some boy dancers, each of whom was supposed to match one of the Girls: a ginger one, a blonde one, one with apparently expensive tastes, one who wore Adidas trackies and one rather scary one, called Jimmy Gulzar, who soon after he arrived, decided for reasons best known to himself, to have his tongue pierced.

The Girls broke off from rehearsals to attend the Brit Awards at the London Arena on February 9. Compared to the triumphant mood of the previous year, their appearance this time had something of a hollow ring about it. Despite having clocked up four number one singles and seen both their albums lodged at number one during the preceding 12 months, the group had been nominated in only one category: Best Video (for 'Spice Up Your Life') which they narrowly lost to All Saints. To make matters worse, All Saints also won Best Single (for 'Never Ever') thus scooping the two accolades which the Spice Girls had won the year before.

The British record industry could hardly have ignored the biggest-selling British band of the decade at the most important corporate awards ceremony of the year, especially not if they wanted the group to come and perform at the event, which they most assuredly did. So the Brits committee – chaired that year, no doubt coincidentally, by the President of Virgin Records, Paul Conroy – created an award to mark the Spice Girls' phenomenal worldwide success. This "Special Award", which was invented two weeks before the show and which has never subsequently been presented to any other act, was inevitably viewed as a consolation prize: "In recognition of their being the biggest band on the planet, really. Oh, and because they didn't win anything else," as one, typical commentary put it. The Girls performed their forthcoming single, 'Stop', and received the Award with a typically upbeat flourish. "1997 was a fantastic year for the Spice Girls and for all females in the industry," Geri said from the podium, unsubtly suggesting that All Saints knew who they could thank for their rapid progress up the charts. "So come on, let's keep it up girls!"

Meanwhile, the boys who had actually won the majority of that year's awards – The Verve, Prodigy and Radiohead – had all declined to show up. Radiohead's guitarist Ed O'Brien summed up the spectacularly jaundiced mood of these reluctant millionaires: "At the end of the day, the Brits is there to sell records, and I'm glad we're in Australia and can't be there." Talk about having their cake and eating it.

At least the Brits had made an effort to include the Girls. At the Grammy Awards in America, which took place on February 25, they were totally blanked. Despite their astonishing success in the US – where they had become the first British act ever to score a US number one with their debut album, and where 'Say You'll Be There' had debuted at number five, the highest entry position by any UK single in the history of the American chart – they were pointedly not included in any of the Grammy nominations.

"We were quite oblivious to it all," Geri insisted at the time.

"In the end it's not important, is it?" Victoria said. "To us, what matters is awards when the fans have actually voted for us. When it comes down to the industry, they're not the people that have made us and put us where we are."

"Although you wouldn't knock it, when you get one," Geri added, rather spoiling the effect. "You think, 'Ooh yeah, very nice.' I noticed at the Brits that all the girls were really excited to get theirs, and all the boys looked really bored."

In truth, the Girls had bigger fish to fry. As the long and laborious Grammy ceremony was unfolding on the other side of the Atlantic, they were starting the European leg of their World Tour with two shows at The Point in Dublin, on February 24 and 25. While reports of the Girls' dwindling popularity continued to circulate in the British press, it was a different story on the ground in Ireland. According to Dublin's local paper, the *Evening Herald*, tickets for the two concerts were changing hands at anything up to £125, five times their face value, after both shows had sold out at the box office within two hours. Naturally, the story was given a negative spin, neatly summed up by a picture of a mum and daughter with the caption: "Definitely Too Much: Margaret Devlin who couldn't afford tout prices for the Spice Girls and a disappointed Emma (5)."

From Dublin, the tour went to Zurich, Frankfurt, Bologna, Rome and all round continental Europe. While the prophets of doom continued to suggest that their live show would be as useless as everything else to do with the Spice Girls, most critics who actually went to one of the gigs were forced to admit that it was actually a thoroughly entertaining affair. The core fans, who were as fresh to the experience of live performance as the group, adored it, and you wonder what the ultimate effect of those shows will be when an entire generation of women right across Europe will have grown up, whose first experience of a pop concert was seeing the Spice Girls.

On April 4, the Girls finally played their first ever live show on British soil at the 9,000-capacity S.E.C.C. in Glasgow. As a live act they had nothing in common with the undemonstrative, anti-star attitude of Britrock heavyweights like Oasis and Blur. Nor did they share much with the pre-teen heroes of previous eras, such as Adam & The Ants or The Bay City Rollers. Instead, their show was a hi-tech song and dance extravaganza of the sort pioneered by American pop-soul acts such as En Vogue and Janet Jackson. The lengthy beginning sequence, during which the Girls "arrived" from Planet Spice in a spaceship, recalled the opening sequence of Michael Jackson's 1996/7 *HIStory* tour.

From there the show was a rollercoaster ride of set-piece routines, bedazzling costume changes and carefully sequenced hits which perfectly showcased the Girls' strengths as a unit while guilefully glossing over individual weaknesses. While none of them could claim to be born singers or dancers, being in the Spice Girls was surely the job that all five of them had been born to do, and by now they knew it.

They applied the same, single-minded vigour to their stage performances that they had to every other aspect of promoting themselves, and their enthusiasm was contagious. Emma sang a solo version of the Supremes hit 'Where Did Our Love Go', usually addressed to some bemused young boy plucked from the crowd, while the two Mels performed a duet of the Aretha Franklin/Annie Lennox hit 'Sisters Are Doing It For Themselves', which was the closest the show got to rock'n'roll. It was past the bedtime of their most dedicated fans by the time the spaceship departed. Mission accomplished.

As with everything else they had done in their short time together, the Girls took the touring experience to the max. They may have cast off Fuller himself four months previously, but they were still marching to the beat of his timetable.

"Sometimes I felt a bit down when I realised I had 90 more shows to do," Melanie B said, "even though it's brilliant and the buzz up there is fantastic. It was just that once you've had a good show, you think, 'I've got to do that 90 times again, and I can't not give it my all, because all these people are paying money to see us.' Once you get up on stage, you do it anyway. But sometimes you felt like you were in prison, ticking off the days."

If Melanie B occasionally felt like that, the strain on Geri was considerably more intense. Being on the road dramatically altered the balance of power within the group. Geri was the group's principal mouthpiece and had always had great ideas, but she was the least able performer, and for the first time she found herself sidelined over a sustained period of time. She had got used to playing a dominant role in the TV studio, the press conference and the planning meeting, but out on the road her ability to project herself as the leader was severely curtailed.

A typical incident was the business of her role as a roller-skating waitress in the song 'Denying'. To begin with, she performed this routine as if starring in her own Broadway musical, despite the fact that she was not even very steady on the skates. Melanie B found it distracting when she was trying to sing her lines to have Geri wobbling past in front of her and an argument ensued which ended with Geri being told by the rest of the group to confine her skating to one small area at the side of the stage.

Quite apart from tensions like this, Geri didn't take well to touring in the first place. She liked the idea of putting on a big spectacle, but she wasn't a performer at heart. Those two hours of gruelling song and dance routines were too much for her. She got overtired and ill. It was tough on everyone, but the others could cope with it.

"Geri couldn't carry it off," Simon Fuller said. "With me gone, she was the leader of the group, but she knew she'd be found out on tour, and the other Girls would probably turn on her. Because I was the one who kept the balance, even though she was probably the strongest. Without me around it was obvious what was going to happen. They probably would have bullied her. She would have said, 'I hate touring. Fuck you. I'm going to do it myself.' It was so predictable. To me it was pretty clear, because I was very involved with that group. I know them all very well. I knew what they wanted out of it. And I knew that if you took me out of the equation and there was no guidance and no calming influence then something like that was bound to happen."

It seemed also as if Geri had turned a corner in her long-term thinking somewhere along the way. The sudden appearance of a new crop of girl groups in the charts, including All Saints, Cleopatra, B★Witched and others seemed to trigger thoughts of a future beyond the Spice Girls.

"At the end of the day, we are realistic," she said just before the start of the tour. "If it all ended tomorrow we have done more than we set out to achieve. We're very proud of what we've done, not just for ourselves but for female bands. When we started we couldn't get our faces on a magazine cover because they said, 'Girls don't sell pop magazines.' That is what we came across. Now they've accepted other girl bands. In a sense, we have done our job. We were on a mission. You've got to be optimistic. We might turn another corner, get another burst of enthusiasm, creativity, and think, 'Yeah, we'll do this.' But at the end of the day, it's not about continuing forever. It's about pleasing ourselves."

Geri was always the most vocal proponent of the Girl Power philosophy, and after she had left the group the other Girls rarely spoke of it again. Her greatest strengths were in motivating and marketing the group, in the initial branding of the product, if you like. Now that their identity was established, perhaps her job with them was indeed done.

There was also the suggestion that perhaps Geri had planned her departure at this juncture in a very calculating, Machiavellian way. Matthew Wright, still banging away in the *Mirror*, was particularly taken with this idea, suggesting that Geri had noted the fact that it was Robbie Williams, the first member to leave Take That, who had gone on to enjoy by far the most successful solo career. Maybe she figured that by leaving at this point she would be one jump ahead of the others in building a career for herself outside Spiceworld.

If Geri "pleased herself" by leaving the Spice Girls, she certainly didn't please the rest of the group. Her sudden departure conformed so closely to the pattern of the group's "departures" from both their former managers, that it rather underlined how closely the instincts of the Spice Girls mirrored those of Geri herself. As with the splits from the managers, no one involved saw it coming. The break was made swiftly, cleanly and with finality, despite cutting straight across the natural rhythm of events. There was no mud-slinging or public recriminations on either side after it was done – just another lingering question mark to add to the Spice mythology.

In truth, Geri had been drifting apart from the other four since the start of the tour, so much so that she had already indicated to them that she was planning to leave when the world tour finished at Wembley Stadium in September. According to Geri, her intentions had been taken seriously enough to warrant a discussion with the group's lawyer, Andrew Thompson, but the Girls had decided to keep the lid on it for the time being — although Victoria has since disputed this version of events. Either way they certainly weren't expecting her to jump ship two days before the end of the European leg of the tour, with the whole of the North American tour still pending.

The issue which ostensibly brought matters to a head was Geri's sudden enthusiasm for promoting awareness of breast cancer. When she was a teenager, Geri had had an operation to remove a lump from her breast. *The Sun* had got hold of the story and Geri had agreed to be interviewed about it so that she could get the "right message" across. The story ran on the front page on May 26, while the Girls were in Helsinki, prompting ITN News to request an interview with Geri on the subject. While Geri was very keen to do the interview, it seems the rest of the Girls vetoed the idea.

The next day, the Girls flew into Britain, where they were due to make an appearance on the midweek National Lottery show that evening. By the middle of the morning the other four Girls had received a call from Andrew Thompson informing them that Geri had left the group.

To begin with the fiction was maintained that Geri was ill. The other four went ahead and made the National Lottery appearance, during which they sent "Get well soon" messages to Geri. They then flew to Oslo for the last two shows of the European tour, which they performed as a quartet, on May 28 and 29. But the reality of the situation was by now clear. Geri was not going to change her mind. She had left the group. Finally, on May 31, two terse press statements were issued simultaneously. Geri's read: "This is a message to the fans. Sadly, I would like to confirm that I have left the Spice Girls. This is because of differences between us. I'm sure the group will continue to be successful and I wish them all the best. I have no immediate plans. I wish to apologise to all the fans and to thank them and everyone who's been there. Lots of love, Geri. p.s. I'll be back."

The remaining Spice Girls responded: "We are upset and saddened by Geri's departure but we are very supportive in whatever she wants to do. The Spice Girls are here to stay — see you at the stadiums! We are sorry to all our fans for having to go through all of this. All our love, Victoria, Emma, Mel C, Mel B. Friendship never ends!"

In the weeks that followed Geri's departure, the other Girls maintained an unfailingly bland, upbeat front. Whatever their true feelings about Geri, they were not going to let the media derive even a grain of satisfaction from anything the Girls had to say about it. In interview after interview they all stuck to the same prepared script.

"There are no hard feelings. We wish her all the luck in the world. We are totally behind her," Victoria said. "We've always said that if anybody was unhappy, they should leave. The most important thing is our friendship."

"We tried to change her mind, but she was set on it," Melanie C said. "And we respected her decision."

"We support her and say, 'Good luck,'" Melanie B said.

However, Victoria was rather more forthright in her autobiography.

"I was . . . in shock. I'd known Geri for four years, we'd shared a room in Windsor, we'd been through the most extraordinary experiences of our lives together. She was one of my best friends. And now she had walked out without a word. What I felt was first anger at the selfishness of it, then betrayal. Total betrayal."

And Emma didn't mince her words a couple of years later when she was asked to pass comment on the video for Geri's first solo single 'Look At Me'.

"I couldn't watch it," she said. "She tried to break up a great group and I just couldn't sit through this."

But when it happened there really wasn't much time to sit around feeling angry or betrayed. Geri's sudden departure forced the other four Girls to pull together with renewed resolve. Only six months after they had parted company with Fuller, they were once again under pressure to prove that they could cope without a pivotal member of the team, indeed the individual who had, as often as not, been assumed to be the leader of the group.

Any doubts about their ability to carry off the live performances without Geri on board had already been dispelled by the two shows in Oslo. If they could successfully rejig the song and dance arrangements in less than a day's rehearsals, they certainly weren't going to have a problem knocking a four-Girl show into shape by the time they got to America for the start of the tour in Miami on June 15. Nor, it seemed, was public demand going to be adversely affected by Geri's absence. In fact, ticket sales *increased* dramatically in North America when the story broke. As for their willingness to carry on without Geri, that was a given, thanks more to pride than expediency.

"Geri leaving has made us stronger, not weaker," Melanie B insisted. And in one sense this may even have been true. As far as the tour was concerned it probably was better to reduce themselves to a lean, motivated gang of four than to find themselves carting an increasingly disaffected Geri around the place. It may even have been the case that if Geri had stayed on, without her heart fully in it, that she would eventually have destabilised the group to such an extent that they would have called it a day before making a third album.

Instead, there was lots of bullish talk about the group carrying on even bigger and better than before, and certainly the North American tour was every bit as successful as the European outing had been. Tickets for their Madison Square Garden gig on July 1 were changing hands for $1,000. They played huge venues to capacity crowds the length and breadth of that vast continent, stamping their distinctly unrock'n'roll mark on an itinerary which had previously been undertaken only by the sturdiest of old-school goliaths.

"They're doing it the rock way," a member of the crew said. "The travelling, the sound checks, the after-show parties, it's just like touring with any of the big groups. Apart from the drugs and the sex, of course."

The *Daily Telegraph*'s reviewer was so impressed by the transformation of the group when he saw them play on the first night of the tour at the 18,000-capacity Coral Sky Amphitheater in West Palm Beach, that he accused the four remaining Spice Girls of engaging in a form of "pop Stalinism".

"Geri Halliwell . . . has been quickly and efficiently expunged from the show," he wrote. "In a concert lasting more than two hours, she was not mentioned once. Her vocal duties (never the most demanding) were fulfilled by the others so effortlessly, you could be forgiven for wondering whether she ever really opened her mouth at all."

In most respects, the four-Girl American shows stuck to the European model. There were numerous costume changes involving lots of sequins and velvet, a few props such as the chairs which they sat on Christine Keeler-style during 'Naked', and the bald, buff Spice Boys, who arrived during 'Do It' to keep the interest level at a high. Even without Geri they put on a raucous 'Wannabe', complete with Melanie C backflipping across the stage, and hammered home the girl power party line with the high-energy fiesta routine of 'Spice Up Your Life' and the kitsch disco stomp of 'Never Give Up On The Good Times', before ending the extravaganza with Sister Sledge's 'We Are Family'.

You had to hand it to the remaining four. They had snatched a clear result from the jaws of disaster. Geri had left them horribly in the lurch. The financial implications of pulling out of a tour of this scope at the very last minute were daunting enough. But the blow to morale could well have been fatal if they hadn't pressed ahead and made a go of it. Some fans, in their haste to cheer on the group for showing such resilience and determination, were inclined to take a swipe at Geri.

"I was really kinda mad that Geri had quit just ten days before our show," a fan from Virginia wrote in her internet diary. "But when they opened with 'If You Can't Dance' and 'Who Do You Think You Are' I didn't even miss her. The other four girls were so in sync with each other. I really didn't miss her constantly screaming, 'Girl Power' every ten seconds."

But in retrospect Geri's departure turned out to be the moment when the Spice Girls magic began inexorably to fade. The practicalities of touring were one thing, the creative implications another. Maybe both of these could be addressed without Geri. But on a more fundamental level, without Geri the chemistry of the group was never the same again. For my daughter – by this time approaching her ninth birthday – and her friends, there was a big philosophical problem about the departure of Ginger Spice. As far as they were concerned she had been forced to leave. Whatever anyone said, no other explanation fitted the bill. And this was not what Girl Power was supposed to be about.

In any case, whatever the precise reason for Geri's departure, it gave the lie to all those declarations of sisterly solidarity which had been part and parcel of the Spice Girls creed. This was no mere detail. Kids of that age take things literally, and for those who had absorbed the cartoonish, one-for-all girl power mantra as an article of faith, the departure of Geri destroyed a lot of the emotional investment which they had made in the group.

Ray Cooper, of Virgin Records, summed up the situation in a marketing man's terms.

"I think it may well have hurt their younger fan base when Geri left, because I don't think they could quite understand why individuals leave groups," he said.

It turned out that friendships did end, after all. And so too did childhood infatuations with pop groups.

# 10

# Back In 15 Mins

In much the same way that the Spice Girls had appeared to ride out the dismissal of Simon Fuller, so the sudden loss of Geri seemed, initially, to have very little effect on their fortunes. Earlier, in March 1998, they had suffered a minor blot on their copybook when their seventh single, 'Stop', failed to reach number one. It had been their misfortune to release this jaunty, Motown-influenced song in the same week that Run-DMC vs Jason Nevins unleashed their hip hop/house battle-chant 'It's Like That', a million-selling phenomenon that stayed at number one for six weeks.

But normal service was resumed with 'Viva Forever', the first single to be released after Geri's departure, although she was still featured both on the record and the eye-catching promotional video. The song went to number one for two weeks in August, and the Girls returned from their marathon trek across North America to perform a final string of shows at Don Valley Stadium, Sheffield on September 11 and 12 and Wembley Stadium on September 19 and 20. It was a triumphant homecoming, and the two Wembley shows – played to a total of 120,000 fans – provided a final, epic flourish to a tour that had exceeded all expectations.

Although Geri had been the first to break ranks, it was actually Melanie B who became the first Spice Girl to release a record independently of the group. 'I Want You Back', was a sleek and sensual duet with the New York hip hop queen Missy "Misdemeanor" Elliott which featured on the soundtrack of the film *Why Do Fools Fall In Love*. Written by Elliott with her producers Gerard Thomas and Donald Holmes, and recorded in New York, it was a track which oozed R&B credibility and was accompanied by an ultra-cool, state-of-the-art video in which Melanie was portrayed in a much more sexually provocative and streetwise way than she ever had been with the Spice Girls. Her subsequent account of making the record gives an impression of the impact working with someone of Elliott's status had on her.

"I coyly introduced myself to Missy, totally in awe, like a fish out of water in her environment. I was really hoping that this was the right move to make in my career, while at the same time I knew that it was a unique opportunity and I had to grasp it." The record sailed to the top of the UK chart the week after the two Wembley shows. This was undoubtedly a defining moment for Melanie, who harboured ambitions of cashing in her chips as a pop star to become a more serious player on the R&B scene. While Elliott and her producers had provided the creative impetus for the track, Melanie had nevertheless acquitted herself well enough to earn some valuable kudos in that world, where credibility is every bit as vital as commercial clout. In return she had given Elliott a hand up on to the big stage in Britain where, for all the respect she commanded, she had never even had a Top 10 hit before.

For Melanie B, doors suddenly opened invitingly. She agreed to be the presenter at the Music Of Black Origin (MOBO) awards at the Royal Albert Hall in London on October 14, where she also performed 'I Want You Back'. Despite getting into a blazing row with Puff Daddy, she took the change of pace in her stride, and the event seemed to pass off smoothly enough.

The genie was now out of the bottle and the next Spice Girl to flex her muscles independently of the group was Melanie C. Her debut was a duet with Bryan Adams on a song co-written by Adams and former Spice collaborator Elliot Kennedy. Adams had tried getting hold of Sheryl Crow and then Janet Jackson to sing 'When You're Gone' with him, before he hit on the idea of approaching one of the Spice Girls. He recorded his part in Vancouver, then sent the master to London with a messenger who sat outside the studio waiting to take it back to be mixed once Melanie had recorded her part. The duet was structured in a simple but unusual way as a two-part harmony, sung at an interval of a third the whole way through. Despite the fact that Adams had had to explain it all to Melanie down a telephone line, their voices blended to perfection to produce one of the jauntiest, catchiest, miss-you love songs in the history of the pop-rock genre.

'When You're Gone' made a low-key entry in the chart a couple of weeks before Christmas. But even with no promotion – bar a dismal video spliced together in a way which did little to disguise the fact that the two had not performed the song in the same continent, let alone the same room – it lodged in the Top 10 for the best part of two months, during which it reached a peak of number three.

Meanwhile, the Spice Girls continued to defy the received wisdom that they were a spent force, when their eighth single, 'Goodbye', made them the only act, apart from The Beatles, to score three consecutive Christmas number one hits.

'Goodbye' was a brand new song which apparently owed nothing to Geri except, it was sometimes suggested, as a source of inspiration. But in actual fact, the chords and lyric of the song had been worked out when Geri was still in the group, at Abbey Road during the sessions for the *Spiceworld* album.

It was written with Biff Stannard and Matt Rowe, who travelled to Nashville to record it during the North American tour in a studio that had been used many years before by Elvis Presley. Stannard and Rowe, who had worked with the Girls since 'Wannabe', were one of the few members of the old team to stick with the group, despite their continuing association with Simon Fuller through Native, a part of the 19 Management group.

"Meeting up with the Girls again was a proper 'God, can you believe we're here?' moment," Stannard said. "It was an amazing, super-posh studio. We finished writing the song and they sang it. Our lives had changed so much in just three years. It was great, but they were absolutely knackered."

What Stannard didn't know at the time was that half the group was by now pregnant.

The story of Posh and Becks has become a modern fable, the celebrity love match that defines our tabloid-driven, soap opera-saturated, reality TV-obsessed times. In some people's minds their still-unfolding tale is the single most enduring legacy of the Spice Girls. Curiously, they were more an invention of Simon Fuller's than the group itself ever was. In earlier, happier days, Fuller had often said to Victoria that what she needed was a famous boyfriend. Victoria would remind him that her heart belonged to Stuart Bilton, a local lad who worked in his family's flower shop business, whom she had started dating in the summer of 1995.

"Don't worry about Stuart," Fuller would say. "I see you with someone famous, somebody like a footballer."

Fuller is a fan of Manchester United – well really, what other football club would you have expected him to support? – and in February 1997 he engineered a meeting between Victoria and David Beckham in the VIP lounge of Chelsea FC, after cajoling her into watching a match between the two teams. The following month, Victoria, who had shown no previous interest in football whatsoever, again found herself with tickets supplied by Fuller to see Manchester United play, this time at their home ground, Old Trafford. Accompanied by Melanie C – a fervent Liverpool supporter – Victoria flew to Manchester. After the match Beckham asked her if she would like to go to dinner. Victoria declined, but left him with her phone number and a suitably romantic proposition of her own to ponder.

"If you don't ring me," she said, "I'm going to kick you in the bollocks next time I see you."

He rang.

Thus was established the template of a relationship that has fascinated, titillated, inspired and appalled the world right up to the present day. Caricatured in the media as the dashing, talented footballer and the trashy, big-mouthed pop star, both of them as rich as Croesus and thick as two short planks, they have battled to maintain their sanity and some semblance of stability, while building a life together in the frequently hostile glare of the international spotlight. Their lives have become public property, as lavishly gilded as the Albert Memorial and yet treated with about as much respect as a municipal rubbish tip.

The comedian Fred Allen described a celebrity as "a person who strives to become well known, then wears dark glasses in order to avoid being recognised." But it is a moot point whether Beckham has strived to do anything other than be the best footballer of his generation and to do his best by the woman he loves. Of course there have been the press conferences, book signings, meet-and-greets and promotional tours, all of which you feel he has gone along with rather than been particularly keen to initiate. Certainly, when he and Victoria met, she was much more famous than him. Now demand for access to both of them is insatiable, so he could certainly put himself about a lot more if he chose to do so.

Victoria conforms more readily to Allen's formula. She had courted fame as part of the Spice Girls and has never been slow to grasp a promotional opportunity when it has been to her advantage. But while her liaison with Beckham brought both of them more media attention than they could possibly have imagined – much of it unwelcome – it seems unlikely that she sought him out for that reason. All the evidence, both visible and anecdotal, tended to support a view of them as a committed pair of soulmates, striving to stick up for each other in circumstances that would very quickly have tested many relationships to destruction.

When Beckham was sent off for fouling an Argentinian player during the World Cup in June 1998, he was vilified in a deeply unpleasant way and to such an extent that he needed police protection when he returned to England. Victoria, meanwhile, was routinely humiliated by the obscene and hurtful chanting of supporters at football matches, whether she attended them or not. Throw in the pressures of constantly being kept apart by work schedules that often placed them at either ends of the planet, and you wonder how anyone could have maintained a healthy and happy relationship, under such conditions. But despite all this, and having chosen to inhabit a show business world not noted for promoting the virtues of loyalty, fidelity or decorum, that is nevertheless what they managed to do, at least on the face of it.

They announced their engagement in January 1998, ten months after they had met, and in August that year, Victoria let it be known that she was pregnant. The baby, a boy named Brooklyn, was born on March 4, 1999, and four months later, on July 4, the couple were married in Luttrellstown Castle, outside Dublin.

Much capital was made of the fact that they sold the rights to photograph and report on the ceremony to *OK!* magazine for £1 million. Indeed, this example of commercial opportunism was used to justify every outlandish invasion of privacy the couple subsequently suffered, on the grounds that by doing so they had put their marriage on the public stage. Of course, if they *hadn't* sold the rights to someone, then the media would have left them in peace to enjoy a quiet, private ceremony while leprechauns frolicked at the bottom of the garden and pigs flew past in formation overhead.

None of the subsequent hoopla which the Beckhams either enjoyed or endured seemed to affect their commitment to one another; or at least, it didn't until several years later when David moved to Real Madrid and apparently began playing away in more senses than one. But back in the spring of 1999, it was plain to see that the overriding concern in Victoria's life was the health, safety and wellbeing of her husband and son. Her involvement with the Spice Girls, let alone the prospect of a solo career, had suddenly become professional commitments of a much lower priority. The wealth and the fame were, by this time, part of who she was, and in her own pragmatic way she got on with making the most of these assets. But it turned out that her core needs were remarkably similar to those of many women who are neither rich nor famous. What Victoria really wanted was her own family to love and be loved by.

If the story of Posh and Becks was a fable, then the parallel relationship of Melanie B and Jimmy Gulzar is more like a morality tale. They met in January 1998, the same month that Victoria and David Beckham got engaged. Melanie was pregnant three months later and she and Gulzar were married on September 13, days before the Spice Girls played the final show of their tour at Wembley Stadium. Their daughter Phoenix Chi was born, one month prematurely, in February 1999. The divorce papers had come through by the summer of 1999.

What a shambles.

While Victoria's and David's romance had an air of shared resolve and inner sanctity about it, Melanie B's romp with Gulzar was a catalogue of inane showbiz clichés. He was exposed as a gold-digging lightweight, and she was revealed as an impulsive and immature woman whose moorings on reality had come seriously adrift. The worst thing about it, from the (momentarily) Melanie G's point of view, was that they ignored Spice Rule number one, and played out the whole sorry saga in public. Reading her autobiography, you get the impression that the only thing Gulzar did right in the relationship was to play hard to get. He was the first man she had met in recent memory, if ever, who didn't either fling himself worshipfully at her feet or run away terrified.

"It just didn't seem to matter to him whether we had sex or not. I couldn't understand it," Melanie said, clearly mystified that anyone could prove so resistant to her charms. "But I was intrigued – and determined to win him over."

But if Gulzar held the emotional strings to begin with, there was no doubting who controlled the purse strings.

"Let's face it, he was lucky to be marrying a woman who was happy to pay for both our outfits and wedding rings, along with his family's flights and hotels," Melanie B recalled of their wedding day, not that this was on her mind at the time, of course.

The vast imbalance of emotional need and financial status which characterised the relationship was compounded by the fact that the two of them were working together at close quarters in an industry where the pecking order is so clearly defined. There could only ever have been one outcome, and really it was a mercy that it all ended so swiftly.

We soon got to hear Gulzar's side of the story thanks to the good offices of *The Sun*. "Mel, Sex And Me," blared the front page headline on September 4, 2000, in which "the sensational truth" about the breakdown of the marriage was revealed in such a way that "it will change for ever the way the world sees the Spice Girls."

Gulzar's revelations were, generally, of a self-serving, sleazy and petty point-scoring nature. But they nevertheless painted an all-too-plausible picture of Melanie as a high-handed control freak, with a habit of pushing her weight around in a graceless fashion.

"She was so rude," Gulzar said. "Snapping her fingers at waiters, never saying please or thank you, snapping at her driver . . . I told her she didn't have any respect for people, that the way she behaved was ignorant and embarrassed me."

While researching this book I soon became aware of how rarely I would hear a bad word said about the Spice Girls by anyone who actually knew or worked with them. I wasn't looking for people to bad-mouth them, but even so, you expect a certain amount of gentle score-settling to get done in the course of interviewing people for such a project. But the collective charm and professionalism of the group was such that even people who might well have had cause to bitch about them have either refrained from doing so, or else genuinely felt no desire to. In sharp contrast to the hostile tone that has become the norm among media commentators, I found their former associates to be forgiving to a fault. The exception to this rule, however, is Melanie B.

There have been various scurrilous accounts of "life behind the scenes" with the Spice Girls that have surfaced over the years. This is hardly surprising given the large cast of ancillary workers who have been involved at close quarters with them at one time or another, and the substantial sums of money which newspapers and sometimes publishers were prepared to pay. Most of these tales are a mixture of inconsequential gossip and informed (but not necessarily reliable) conjecture. But one common thread that emerges throughout is the domineering personality of Melanie B.

"Mel B has a problem with anyone who challenges her power. As well as being a complete bully towards all the girls, she's extremely stubborn," said Paul Attridge, a chauffeur who sold his story to the *News Of The World*. While one would hesitate to place too much emphasis on a version of events relayed from such a source, his is one of many similar stories which suggest that Scary was a more appropriate name for Melanie B than was at first suspected.

"She didn't make a lot of friends," recalled Bart Cools, the International Marketing Manager at Virgin who worked on Melanie B's solo career as well as with the Spice Girls. "She's one of these girls, women, people that believe, 'Hey, I say it as it is, and people just have to deal with that.' Which is fine when you are part of a hugely successful band. But you meet people twice: on the way up and on the way down. Once the balance changes and you need them, they just say, 'Oh, fuck off. You shouted at me . . .' Melanie could be a really loudmouthed, horrible, insensitive person. She could be really sweet as well. But that's not what people remember."

Keeping a grip on things was not Melanie B's strong point. She spent money as if it were going out of fashion, even before she had that much to spend. She could be the life and soul of the party, but she would also scold the musicians and taunt the other Girls for making mistakes on stage. One minute she would be lavishing gifts on family and friends, the next gathering up a pile of freebies with unseemly zeal. She was incapable of self-restraint. No sooner had Melanie identified a want than it was immediately translated into action. Her infatuation with Gulzar would have blown itself out long before she got to the point of marrying him if she had only been able to stop for a minute and take stock of the situation. But that was not Melanie's way.

Her ambition was limitless, and having conquered the world with the Spice Girls she now set her sights on marriage, motherhood *and* carving a solo career outside the group. What Melanie B really wanted was *more* – of everything – and the sooner the better.

With the world tour finished, the Girls had, at last, come to the end of the schedule which Simon Fuller had bequeathed to them. Having rounded off the year with 'Goodbye', and with Victoria and Melanie B both heavily pregnant, they decided to take a six-month break and, as Christmas 1998 arrived, they stepped off the Spice treadmill at last.

It would be nearly two years before another Spice Girls record was released. But there was no danger of anyone forgetting about them in that time. In the 22 months that elapsed between the release of 'Goodbye' in December 1998 and 'Holler'/'Let Love Lead The Way' in November 2000, the individual Spice Girls (including Geri) released a total of 12 hit singles (five of them number ones) and three albums.

The success of the five Girls away from the group was largely ignored or taken for granted at the time. But just take a look at their chart log for 1999, the year in which, as a group, they released no records whatsoever.

1999

| | | |
|---|---|---|
| 22 May | GERI 'Look At Me' | No.2 |
| 19 June | GERI *Schizophonic* | No.4 |
| 10 July | MELANIE B 'Word Up' | No.14 |
| 28 August | GERI 'Mi Chico Latino' | No.1 |
| 9 October | MELANIE C 'Goin' Down' | No.4 |
| 30 October | MELANIE C *Northern Star* | No.4 |
| 13 November | GERI 'Lift Me Up' | No.1 |
| 13 November | Tin Tin Out featuring EMMA 'What I Am' | No.2 |
| 4 December | MELANIE C 'Northern Star' | No.4 |

Only a handful of other acts in the history of pop – solo, group or otherwise – could lay claim to that kind of strike rate in a single calendar year (actually, just over six months). Besides being an astonishing track record, this little snapshot of their individual achievements is also surprisingly revealing. Geri was the most conspicuously successful with Melanie C not far behind. Emma did little more than dip a toe in the water, while Victoria did even less, and was the only one of the five to end the year have released nothing at all.

Perhaps more significantly, Melanie B was the only one to have a single stall outside the Top 10. Indeed, at the time it was released, 'Word Up' was the only record by a Spice Girl not to reach the Top Three, the first time that the Spice magic had ever seriously faltered. So what went wrong?

The song was originally a number three hit for the American R&B trio Cameo in 1986, and had already been successfully covered by the Glaswegian rock group Gun who took it to number eight in 1994. A perennial favourite at office and wedding parties, it looked a sure-fire hit, but was actually a rather lazy choice for the first non-original single to be released by a Spice Girl.

Even so, Melanie recorded 'Word Up' with the highly regarded producer Timbaland, who was known, among other things, for his ground-breaking work with Missy Elliott. But the hip hop guru had evidently left his inspiration in the hood that day, since the production lacked his usual rhythmic inventiveness and left Melanie's rather blustering vocal performance uncomfortably exposed. The song was co-opted for the soundtrack of the second Austin Powers movie, *The Spy Who Shagged Me*, which although a huge box office smash, did little to boost sales of the single.

"I'm really pleased at getting in at 14," Melanie insisted at the time, rather implausibly. "It's not all about number ones."

In retrospect, the failure of the record-buying public to embrace 'Word Up' was a significant warning sign for the future. If the combination of Timbaland, Spice Girl, Austin Powers and tried-and-tested song could not get a record into the Top 10, something was clearly amiss. It was the first sign of popular resistance to the notion of a Spice Girl assuming the mantle of an R&B artist, a sign which both she and the rest of the group would subsequently ignore with dire consequences.

The initial success of Geri's solo career was both predictable and surprising. Predictable insofar as she was always the most imposing presence of the five, and remained the de facto leader of the group in many people's minds, even after she had left. But surprising because to begin with it seemed as if pursuing success as a singer was the last thing on her mind.

Geri's sole concern in the immediate aftermath of her departure from the Spice Girls was to regain control of her life and achieve some semblance of equilibrium. With the world's media in hot pursuit of her for a photograph or quote explaining why she had left the group, this was not as easy as it might have seemed. She initially found refuge with the pop idol of her youth, George Michael, who invited her to stay with him (and his partner Kenny Goss) at his villas in St Tropez and, subsequently, Los Angeles.

She started working on a variety of projects while investigating other options, none of them to do with music. In the days immediately following the split with the Spice Girls, she had begun making a video diary of her life. She then befriended the film-maker Molly Dineen with a view to ramping up this diary into a full-blown fly-on-the-wall documentary of her life, which would be shot over the ensuing six months.

She opened up links with breast cancer charities in America and Britain and offered to help publicise the issue. She auctioned off the trademarked outfits she had worn as Ginger Spice, including the famous cobbled-together Union flag dress from the Brits, raising £150,000 for Sargent Cancer Care for Children. She accepted an offer to become a "goodwill ambassador" for the United Nations Population Fund, her brief being to promote the benefits of birth control in underdeveloped countries in Africa and elsewhere in the third world. She discussed the idea of a TV career with Chris Evans, by this time head of Ginger TV and a media mogul in his own right. She began writing a book. She auditioned (unsuccessfully) for a role in a James Bond movie. Finally, when she had peered down virtually every possible avenue for a route forwards, another thought occurred.

"Although I was afraid to say it out loud, deep down there was an idea that refused to be pushed aside or ignored: I kept thinking about going back into the studio and singing again."

How odd that the key figure in the most successful group of the Nineties should take so long to hit on the idea of making a solo album. Clearly, the desire to make music was not a primary factor in the shaping of Geri's career, a trait she shared with Victoria and Emma. And yet, when all was said and done, it was still by far the strongest card in her pack.

If Geri lacked confidence in her ability to make an album without the Spice Girls, she had no problem persuading Paul Wilson and Andy Watkins of Absolute to work with her again. In doing so they were effectively putting themselves out of the frame for working on the third Spice Girls album, a decision which, for all they knew at the time, could well have cost them a fortune in potential royalties.

"The remaining Spice Girls became aware that we'd made contact with Geri and that we were considering working with her and we were told to choose between the two of them," Watkins recalled. "We were given a weekend to make up our minds. We chose Geri because, one: we didn't want to be put in that position by anybody, and two: Geri for us was the catalyst. We'd made a lot of money from the Spice Girls and we'd reached a point where we could make our choice for artistic reasons, and we just thought it was more exciting to do Geri."

"We were both totally sure that working with Geri was the right thing to do," Wilson said.

"It came from our experiences working on the *Spiceworld* album as much as anything," Watkins said. "We'd written 'Too Much' predominantly with Geri, we'd written 'Stop' predominantly with Geri and 'The Lady Is A Vamp' was totally with Geri. We just thought she had a lot of great ideas. We went with our hearts. We're not great businessmen. For us it was about making the right musical choice, and she was definitely the right choice for us."

"Writing *Schizophonic* was almost like going back to writing the first Spice Girls album," Wilson said. "It was that kind of energy, and that's why we were glad we made the decision."

It also turned out to be a pretty astute business move in light of subsequent events, and certainly when compared to the fate of their songwriting rivals Stannard and Rowe. Having stuck with the remaining Spice Girls after the splits with both Fuller and Geri, Stannard and Rowe did a few studio sessions with them for the third album. But apart from the single 'Goodbye', their contributions were passed over in favour of collaborations which the Girls pursued with various heavyweight American producers.

Meanwhile Geri, with Watkins and Wilson on board, fashioned an album which cleverly established her identity as a solo artist while continuing to tap into the pop/dance musical formula which had proved so successful for the Spice Girls. *Schizophonic* was released in June 1999, a year after Geri had walked out of the group. The album had an impish energy, and while Geri's technical shortcomings were more exposed than in the past, particularly on slower, more conventional songs like 'Sometimes' and 'Someone's Watching Over Me', she made up for it with her strength of personality and sheer force of will.

There were big, brassy fanfares on 'Bag It Up', a song which borrowed inspiration from Heatwave's 'Boogie Nights', and subsequently became one of three number one hits which she spun off the album. On 'Mi Chico Latino' she continued to explore the Riviera-pop theme of the Spice Girls' hit, 'Viva Forever', murmuring sweet nothings in a peculiar brand of estuary Spanish while castanets and timbales clattered alongside a cod-flamenco guitar.

However, the centrepiece of this flawed but feisty collection was undoubtedly 'Look At Me', a song with a lyric that was a bolder and more personal statement of intent than any of the other solo Spice Girls have made, before or since.

Released before the album as her first single, 'Look At Me' was –

rather like 'Wannabe' – as much a manifesto as a song. The video, which according to Watkins was invented in the room on the same day that she and the Absolute boys wrote the number, was a bizarre amalgamation of images, which memorably included that of a hearse taking Ginger to her final resting place. The funeral scene, although slightly macabre, certainly made its point. Geri was not only out of the Spice Girls; she had buried her Ginger persona for good.

'Look At Me' was set to a big beat-style organ riff that echoed the Propellerheads' hit 'History Repeating' featuring Shirley Bassey. Big and brassy, in all senses, it gave an intriguing insight into Geri's inner world. Behind the fast-talking, brass-necked, attention-seeking façade, a broad streak of self-doubt was laid out for inspection: "Sometimes I don't recognise my own face/ I look inside my eyes and find disgrace/ My little white lies tell a story/ I see it all, it has no glory."

More than any other song she has ever performed, with or without the Spice Girls, 'Look At Me' came closest to nailing the peculiar essence of Geraldine Estelle Halliwell. Unlike the other Girls, who were motivated by a mixture of needs and ambitions, Geri was driven by one simple desire: to be the centre of attention. Love would be nice if she got it. Money would always be welcome, and was never wasted. But fame – that was what Geri craved above all else. Whether it brought adulation or humiliation, happiness or misery, what pushed her on, through good times and bad, was the need to be noticed.

"Look at me, you can take it all/ Because this face is free/ Maybe next time use your eyes and/ Look at me, I'm a drama queen if that's your thing, baby/ I can even do reality."

None of the Spice Girls were especially materialistic people, not even Victoria. But Geri was the least materialistic of them all.

"I think if you asked Geri to choose between one million pounds or fame, she'd go for the fame every time," Nicki Chapman said. "She just loves being in the public eye."

'Look At Me' was a much stronger song than most people had expected Geri to come up with left to her own devices, and the video had a huge dramatic impact. But unfortunately for her, the single's release coincided with that of the latest record by Boyzone, 'You Needed Me', another in a long string of ballads featuring a typically insipid performance by Ronan Keating. The nation's pop fans voted with their wallets, and Geri had to be content with an opening position of number two. *Schizophonic*, which came out soon afterwards, peaked at number four. In America, where it was released at the same time, *Schizophonic* peaked at number 42, a disappointing result, at least until you consider the fact that it was the only record – single or album – released by a solo Spice Girl ever to register in the US charts.

Geri's album was not, and was never going to be, a success on the scale of the Spice Girls' albums. But it would remain in the UK chart for 43 weeks, during which time it sold more than 600,000 copies in Britain, enough to earn it double-platinum status. Worldwide sales were well over one million. But if the media could sell the fiction that *Spiceworld* had been a commercial failure, they were hardly likely to report that Geri had managed to make a successful record. Where would be the mileage in a story like that?

Geri's solo career was thus written off before it had even begun. "How sad Ginger lost her spice" was the headline of a piece in the *Daily Mail* by a journalist whose picture by-line bore an eerie resemblance to that of the Polly Filler character in *Private Eye*. Writing in the week that the album was released, the columnist concluded via a quote from "an insider" that: "Unfortunately the die is cast for Geri. It'll be tricky to turn her career around." The journalist even took it upon herself to decide, well in advance of its publication, that Geri's autobiography, *If Only*, was also sure to be a flop. "Who wants a 26-year-old's self-conscious navel-gazing?" she asked. Enough people, as it turned out, to keep the book installed at the top of the bestseller lists for several months, and to make it the UK's biggest-selling autobiography of 1999. Subsequently issued as a paperback, *If Only* went on to record sales just short of half-a-million copies by 2003.

With all eyes on Geri, nobody had been paying much attention to Melanie C, which was pretty much the story of her life as far as being one of the Spice Girls was concerned. The Cinderella of the group, Melanie was widely believed to be the best singer of the five, and yet always seemed to get sidelined while her noisier sisters either squabbled among themselves behind the scenes or vied for attention in front of them. But Melanie was fiercely determined to make her mark, and with group activities on hold while Melanie B and Victoria were having their babies, she set about getting her own career underway with a single-minded determination that not even Geri had been able to muster. There were no acting auditions or video diaries or any other distractions for Melanie. She wanted to make music – her own music.

Above all, what Melanie C really, really wanted was to be taken seriously. In interviews she began to deviate with increasing frequency from the usual sunny, Spice message.

"I've got this pent-up aggression inside and I want to get it out," she said. "It's not personal anger. It's anger at outside things. The world has been fucking good to me but it's not always good to itself. I'm angry about AIDS. I'm angry about cancer. I'm angry about children being abused. I'm angry about racism. I'm just angry about general things that people with morals are angry about."

Melanie took herself off to Los Angeles, not for anger management classes, but to record an album, *Northern Star*, with the help of various producers including Rick Rubin, William Orbit, Marius De Vries, Rick Nowels and Craig Armstrong. Rubin, the producer best known for his work with the Beastie Boys, Red Hot Chili Peppers and latterly with ageing country legend, Johnny Cash, had worked with the Spice Girls in 1998 when they recorded a track intended for the soundtrack of *South Park*, but which never reached fruition. De Vries, Orbit and Nowels (with whom she co-wrote several of the songs) had all collaborated with Madonna among many others. Between them this stellar cast helped Melanie to achieve a modern American, grunge-lite sound, pitched for the most part somewhere between Garbage and, well, Madonna.

While in LA, Melanie stepped out for a while with Anthony Kiedis of Red Hot Chili Peppers, and met Steve Jones, formerly guitarist in the Sex Pistols. Jones was fronting The Neurotic Outsiders, a band featuring John Taylor of Duran Duran, and Matt Sorum and Duff McKagan from Guns N' Roses. They had a residency in a club called The Viper Room, and Jones suggested that Melanie should get up on stage and sing with them there.

"I went to see them and they were fucking brilliant!" Melanie recalled. "They're quite punk, pretty hardcore. So I just got up and did 'Pretty Vacant', 'Anarchy In The UK' and 'White Wedding', and it went down a storm. They were fucking rocking!"

Returning to Britain with her own album in the can, Melanie was invited to perform at the V99 Festival, a two-day event in Chelmsford and Staffordshire. While the V Festival, at this time in its fourth year, was by no means as rough or partisan as comparable events such as the Reading Festival or Scotland's T In The Park, it was still not the kind of place you would expect to find a Spice Girl. The two-day show was held simultaneously on two open-air sites at either ends of the country – in Chelmsford and Staffordshire – with the two line-ups of performers swapping locations overnight.

Melanie's half of the bill was headlined by the Welsh class warriors Manic Street Preachers and featured among other acts, Supergrass, Super Furry Animals and Travis, who were just on the verge of making their breakthrough to the big league. The audiences were of an informed, indie-rock persuasion, and in another life the sort of crowd that Melanie might well have found herself milling around with as a fan.

Playing such an event was a gamble. In much the same way as Robbie Williams had done when he left Take That, Melanie was putting herself forward as an artist who had shed the image of a squeaky-clean pre-teen idol and emerged as a more grown-up, indie-rock performer ready to stomp, shout and swear with the best of them. Indeed, Williams had played this very festival the year before, under similar circumstances, and had converted an initially sceptical audience to his cause. Unfortunately things didn't turn out so well for Melanie.

Her strategy was flawed on two counts. Firstly, whereas Williams had been booted out of Take That for bad behaviour and hit rock bottom in his personal life before his solo career eventually took off, Melanie C was still a proud member of the Spice Girls, a group which was still "the Antichrist" to the indie-rock fraternity.

Secondly, Antichrist or not, she seriously misjudged the effect that a Spice Girl singing 'Anarchy In The UK' would have on an audience of committed British rock fans. Performing that song in the company of Steve Jones (who co-wrote it) may have gone down OK with an American bar-band crowd who wouldn't view it as being a lot different from a number by Billy Idol or, for that matter, Green Day. But to sing such a significant number in front of that most tribal of gatherings – the English festival crowd – was another matter altogether.

Released in 1976, 'Anarchy In The UK' was the first single by The Sex Pistols, and became the battle cry for a generation of music fans who felt alienated from society and excluded from the pop hierarchy. In its original form, the song was both a declaration of opposition to the status quo and a howl of indignation, a three-and-a-half-minute blast of righteous defiance aimed at the heart of the establishment. The punks abhorred any form of cheesy commercialism and despised, among many things, American capitalism and the British monarchy. They had decided to tear it all down and start again. Twenty years later, the Spice Girls had become the biggest group in the world by embracing global capitalism, cheesy commercialism and the British monarchy with a calculated enthusiasm displayed by no other group before or since. Clearly things had not quite worked out the way the architects of punk had expected; indeed, the punk generation had by now picked up kids and mortgages of their own. But while punk as a prescription for action had gone the way of all things, that didn't make the memory any less precious.

The sound and lyric of 'Anarchy In The UK', which Johnny Rotten spat out in a demonic, guttural sneer, rolling his Rs like machine-gun fire, was a call-to-arms which changed the course of British music. For a generation of fans who came of age at the time, 1977 was Year Zero in pop. For them, punk was still an article of faith, and 'Anarchy In The UK' the closest thing to a sacred text.

When Melanie C played it at the end of her set on the first of the V99 shows in Chelmsford, the crowd was more bemused than hostile. But when she repeated her set the next day in Staffordshire, they came prepared, and she was greeted with a hail of missiles – water bottles, oranges, doorstops of bread – as she ploughed through her performance. Leaving the stage she stuck up her middle finger in defiance and thanked the audience for "every present" they had delivered. She hadn't been hit physically, but she had been hurt.

"Being part of the indie crowd as a fan, I never imagined I would not be accepted," she said. "I love Manic Street Preachers. I love Blur. I'm into all the people that play the festivals. I just saw myself as one of them. So I was quite shocked. I'd been a little bit naive probably."

The reaction to this, her debut solo performance, in the music press was one of outrage. Steve Sutherland, the editor of *NME*, was practically frothing at the mouth as he denounced her performance in general, and in particular for appropriating the Sex Pistols song. Sutherland argued that her version of 'Anarchy In The UK' was the Establishment's revenge for the late Sid Vicious singing 'My Way'. While Vicious had ravaged Frank Sinatra's showbiz standard – turning a machine gun on the audience in the accompanying video – Melanie had performed no less of a violation on the Sex Pistols' song, turning a punk classic into pop cabaret. So now Sutherland knew how it felt, and he didn't like it.

For while the *NME* editor and his ilk could just about put up with the Spice Girls as part of an alien culture that didn't really impinge on their world, they never forgave Melanie C for attempting to colonise their turf. When *Northern Star* came out, Sutherland reviewed it in terms which left no doubt that this had become a personal matter.

"Listen, Melanie," he wrote, "What we *do* need right now is a little *belief*, a little *commitment*. Words, of course, from which you and 'your sisters' have wrung all meaning and turned into empty slogans. You may think it's cool to reduce rock to karaoke but you're very much mistaken and, in the sheer unshakeable arrogance of trying to show that our music can be assimilated, mastered, bought and sold by any little stage-school twerp daft enough to get tattooed, what you have actually achieved is the exact opposite. *Northern Soul* [*sic*] is such a pathetic pastiche of the music we're all trying so hard still to love that the more the tabloids puff it up and the more successful it becomes, the more our hate will grow." Rating the album out of a possible ten points, Sutherland gave it minus ten.

"It's all snobbery and a lot of politics," Melanie said, in response. "And I think it's really pathetic. When I was a kid I hated Duran Duran because I was a Wham! fan. Now, when I look back it seems such a childish thing. I don't dislike anything so long as it's good. So why do we have to have all these different little cliques? I think I'm pretty good especially compared to some of the crap that's out there."

But she protested in vain, and in much the same way that Melanie B would always struggle to win acceptance from the serious R&B players, so Melanie C had failed to convince the arbiters of popular taste that she should be taken seriously as a rock chick. That's not to say that she was unable to shift a substantial number of records. She did. But it took her a while to do it. Her first single, 'Goin' Down', a faux-heavy rock song made a reasonable showing at number four in the chart, while her album, released in October 1999, initially only just made the Top 10.

However, Melanie persevered. Evidently not put off by her experiences at V99, she went out on the road and toured relentlessly. Her first outing took her round the world in just over a month: from Liverpool's Royal Court to London's Astoria via New York, Toronto, Los Angeles, Sydney, Tokyo and across Europe. It was the sort of itinerary that she had got used to tackling with the Spice Girls, the difference now being that instead of miming three numbers and showing up for a meet-and-greet with the mayor, she arrived with a backing band and staged "proper" shows.

Geri in her iconic Union Jack dress at the Brit Awards at Earls Court Arena, London, February 24, 1997. She designed it herself and her wardrobe assistant stitched it together from a real Union flag. This was a classic Geri touch, reading the Zeitgeist almost by accident and then surfing it as if to the manner born.
*(Richard Young/Rex Features)*

Merchandise central: as well as making and marketing their own dolls, the Spice Girls' faces were on everything from bed linen to crockery. Their sponsorship by Pepsi was particularly lucrative, earning them £1 million, with the soft drink company having the rights to a single released exclusively through a Pepsi promotion, not through record retailers. *(left: Nils Jorgensen/Rex Features, right: Emma Boam/Rex Features)*

Launching their *Spiceworld* album, in Granada, Spain, October, 1997, and accepting an award in recognition of worldwide sales of 18 million copies of the *Spice* album. The Girls soon became adept at handling press conferences like this. "What's the worst rumour you have ever heard about the group?" asked a TV reporter. "That Victoria's a man in drag," answered Melanie B. *(Courtesy of 45 Management)*

The Girls with Prince Charles and Nelson Mandela, November 1997. "This is one of the greatest moments in my life," said Mandela, evidently without irony. "Is it your greatest moment?" one of the press pack asked Charles. "Second greatest," the Prince responded, pausing to just the right effect. "The first time I met them was the greatest." *(Corbis Sygma)*

The Queen meets at the Girls at the Royal Command Performance, at the Empire Leicester Square, London, December 1997. A nervous Geri failed to curtsey with sufficient vigour to satisfy the press pack. The Queen, it seemed, had no complaints, but there was still a minor hoo-ha when some of the papers suggested that Ginger had shown a lack of respect. *(Graham Tin/Corbis Sygma)*

Victoria confers with Richard E. Grant and Kim Fuller (standing) on the set of *Spiceworld – The Movie*. "She came up to me… and said 'You know my character in this movie, I'm just a laughing stock really, aren't I?'" remembered Fuller. "And I said 'Yes. You are.' And she said, 'OK, that's fine. As long as I know.' And she just went with it. There was no side to her at all." *(Alex Bailey)*

Geri and Emma in *Spiceworld – The Movie*. The premiere was full to bursting with kids, from cool-looking teenagers to children of nursery school age. For every grumpy old critic and hard-bitten media maven, there were half-a-dozen kids in various states of excitement and awe. *(Alex Bailey)*

Spicewatch – the Girls dress as characters from the cheesy US TV series *Baywatch* for a photo shoot in LA. *(Courtesy of 45 Management)*

Nicki Chapman, who would later became famous as one of the *Pop Idol* judges, did radio and TV promotion for the Girls. "We did media training with them," she recalled. "Don't talk over each other. Look at the camera. All those basic details, which people hadn't done with pop acts in the past." *(David Fisher/LFI)*

TV personalities Jonathan Ross, Dale Winton, Richard Madely, Brian Conley and Howard Anthony dress up as the Spice Girls for *An Audience With The Spice Girls* for London Weekend Television, November 1997. *(Ken McKay/Rex Features)*

Geri bends down and sticks her tongue out at the camera, while ten steps behind her in the shadows stands manager Simon Fuller. This picture, published in the *Mail On Sunday*, symbolized the increasingly widespread perception of Fuller as the hidden manipulator behind their success, an impression which the Girls found irksome, to put it mildly. *(David Fisher/LFI)*

"Can I order a car for the Spice Girls please." Geri assumes management responsibility for the Girls after the abrupt departure of Simon Fuller. "It took Simon's breath away," Nicki Chapman recalled. "He had no idea it was coming. None of us did." *(Dean Freeman)*

The car arrives. Emma and Victoria smile sweetly from the rear window of a Rolls-Royce. *(Robert Lewis/SIN)*

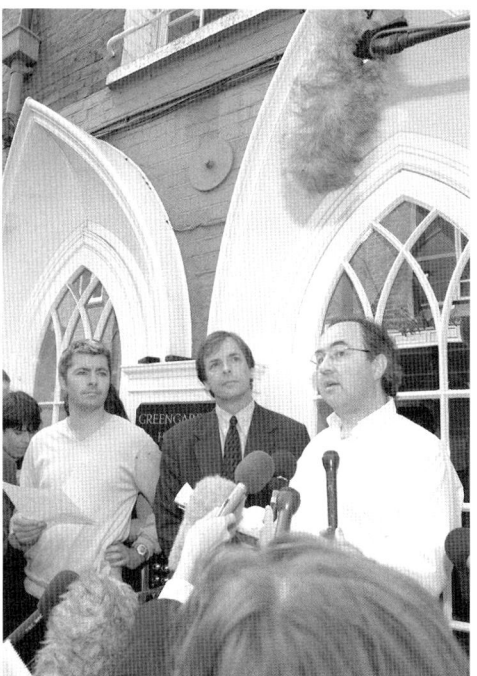

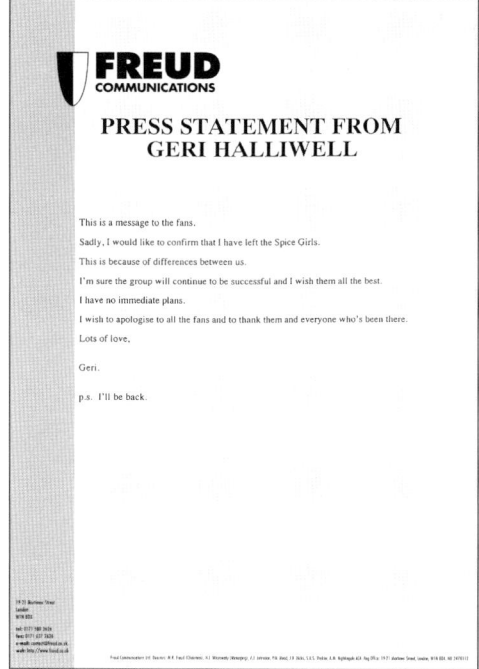

May 1998: the press conference called to confirm that Geri had quit the group. In the centre are, left to right: Spice Girls PR Alan Edwards, Spice Girls lawyer Andrew Thompson and Geri's lawyer Julian Turton. *(Brian Rasic/Rex Features)*

**FREUD**
COMMUNICATIONS

**PRESS STATEMENT FROM GERI HALLIWELL**

This is a message to the fans.

Sadly, I would like to confirm that I have left the Spice Girls.

This is because of differences between us.

I'm sure the group will continue to be successful and I wish them all the best.

I have no immediate plans.

I wish to apologise to all the fans and to thank them and everyone who's been there.

Lots of love,

Geri.

p.s. I'll be back.

Geri's press statement. "She was one of my best friends," wrote Victoria in her book *Learning To Fly*. "And now she had walked out without a word. What I felt was first anger at the selfishness of it, then betrayal. Total betrayal." *(Brian Rasic/Rex Features)*

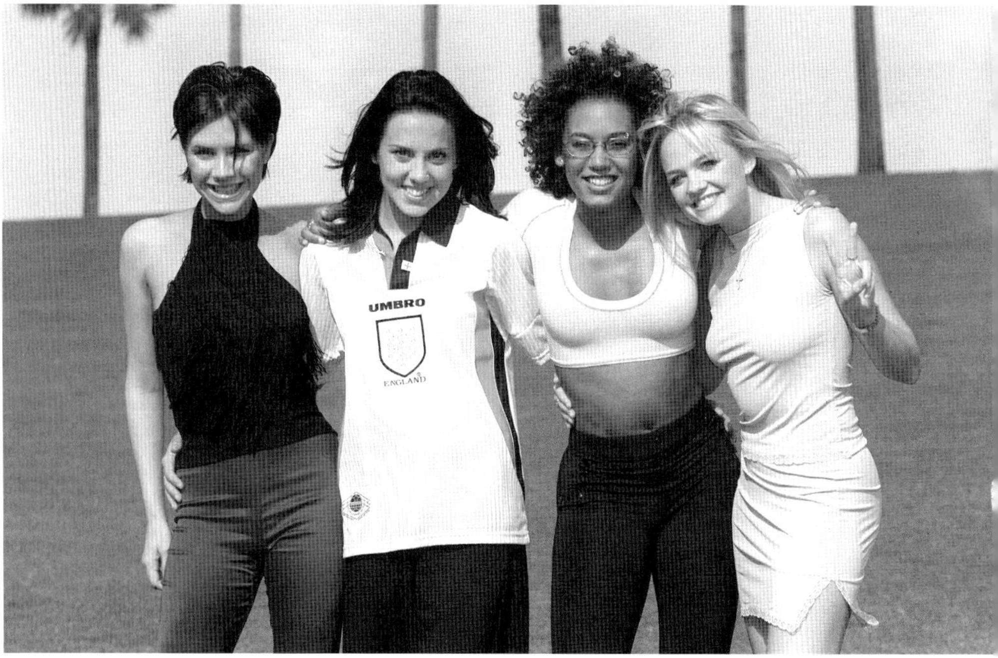

And then there were four. "Geri leaving has made us stronger, not weaker," Melanie B insisted. *(Dave Hogan/Getty Images)*

"For three years with the Spice Girls I have done every single bit of promotion the record company wanted me to do. And now I'm not doing it any more," Melanie said. "The only promotion I'm doing is live gigs."

The title track of *Northern Star* was released as a single just before Christmas and also made a solid chart showing, entering at number four. But it was two, atypical songs that really took off for Melanie C and which, after an uncertain start, turned the album into a serious international best-seller during the course of 2000. 'Never Be The Same Again', released in March, found Melanie teaming up with the late Lisa "Left Eye" Lopes from TLC, who, in this pre-Destiny's Child era, were America's biggest girl group. The song, which was co-written by Melanie and Lopes, together with producer Rhett Lawrence and Paul F. Cruzs, had a distinctive R&B flavour, including a street-smart rap by Lopes, which set it apart from Melanie's other records. It cruised to number one on April 1, 2000, taking over the top slot from Geri's fourth solo single, 'Bag It Up', much to Melanie's satisfaction.

Then in August, 'I Turn To You' became a huge summer hit, particularly among the Ibiza/rave crowd. The production by Rick Nowels, which was remixed for radio by Hex Hector, turned the track into a trance anthem – with a tune. It was not at all the sort of music that Melanie gravitated towards ordinarily, and certainly not indicative of the direction of the album as a whole, but in becoming a big hit all across Europe, it helped to push the album into the arms of a different market.

Meanwhile, Melanie toured, playing the kind of venues which "real" rock acts would regard as their natural habitat, but which the Spice Girls had never ventured into, nor ever wanted to. Melanie's live show underlined just how much of a rock chick she was at heart. Rarely dressing up in anything more elaborate than jeans and a T-shirt, she flung herself about, headbanging vigorously during the heavier numbers. Her punk credentials having been rumbled at V99, she wisely gave up trying to sound like the Sex Pistols or any of the other cool British bands from the post-punk era. Instead, accompanied by a well-drilled five-piece band, she set her sights on a more mainstream rock sound that recalled North American acts like Heart and Joan Jett & The Blackhearts. It was always slightly odd, however, that her two biggest hits, with which she ended the show, were the two songs that bore least resemblance to her core musical values: 'Never Be The Same Again' followed by an encore of 'I Turn To You', during which the stage was transformed into a throbbing, holiday-island nightclub.

The freedom of being released from the Spice mothership affected Melanie C more profoundly than it did any of the other Girls. She virtually underwent a personality change. When she had been with the group she was demure and disciplined – to a fault. Her body was trimmed and toned to an unnatural extent, the product of a strict diet and punishing training regime. And she grew accustomed to keeping her own counsel, not for want of a strong opinion on things, but in order to keep the peace when the more forceful personalities of Geri and Melanie B were asserting themselves in group situations. The famous "Spice Girls vote Tory" interview with Simon Sebag Montefiore was a classic case in point, where Melanie's socialist beliefs had been completely overridden by the more strident opinions of her peers.

Left to her own devices, however, a different Melanie began to emerge: a garrulous rocker, fond of her food, who liked an occasional drink. She put on a bit of weight. However, rumours that she had started taking something harder – the Internet scandal sheet *Pop Bitch* latterly took to calling her Snorty Spice for a while – were well wide of the mark. Melanie admitted in one or two interviews with the music press to having "dabbled" with drugs in her college days, although this may well have been an ill-advised manoeuvre to bolster her "indie-Spice" credentials as much as anything. But she was and is a genuinely health-conscious person. Indeed, Melanie C was the only one of the Spice Girls who never smoked, and her intense dislike of smoky environments was such that it became another source of background tension within the group.

As a solo act she was no longer required to toe the Spice party line, and began letting off steam in interviews. In one particularly hectic piece for Q magazine she declared that the Posh and Becks wedding was "over the top", admitted there were tensions between her and Melanie B ("some days I don't even bother talking to her") and damned Geri's album with the faintest of praise: "She's not a talented musician and she's not a very strong singer." To cap it all, she cheerfully declared that, "The Spice Girls for me is a hobby. My solo stuff is my proper job. This is the real me."

Melanie had to spend quite a bit of time back-pedalling after that interview. But the fact was that almost from the moment she had begun working on her own album she became a semi-detached member of the Spice Girls.

And what of Emma? Cheerful, easy-going, blonde, smiley, in-love-with-her-mum Emma; the straightforward Spice Girl who sneaked in under the emotional radar and found a place in your heart before you even knew she was there. Emma was the Spice Girl that everyone talked about least, and yet loved most (or found the hardest to hate) – once they got around to thinking about it. Stick "Baby Spice" in Google and she comes out with way more results than any of the others, although many of the sites are pornographic or have questionable Lolita-esque connotations.

"Emma was always the most popular Spice Girl, by miles," Simon Fuller said. "She always came top of the polls of fans in magazines. We had a database of about a million, and about 35-40 per cent of them rated her as their favourite. The others were very in your face; it was either love or hate the others – or not notice them. But Emma you loved, especially if you were a little girl. And their fans were the little girls."

It was not just the little girls that were said to be keen on Emma, either. For a while it was widely believed that the real reason the Spice Girls had parted company with Fuller was that Emma and he were having an affair of which the other Girls disapproved. The story was reported as fact in many newspapers and was given a cautious degree of credence among those around the group at the time. Fuller has never commented on the allegation, while Emma has flatly denied it on numerous occasions.

"I did *not* have an affair with Simon Fuller. Really. No," she insisted. "I really don't know where people get these stories from."

Emma was always a very tactile person, with everyone, and she and Fuller obviously shared a special friendship. It seems fair to say that, on a personal level, she was his favourite of the Girls.

According to Bart Cools, "They were always very cuddly and she would say to him, 'Can you please stroke my neck?' and things like that. They were close to each other, but you can't avoid it if you travel that much with each other."

It is absolutely part of Fuller's management (and personal) style to form emotional and in some cases remarkably deep attachments to his predominantly female roster of clients. That isn't to say that he sleeps with all or indeed any of them. He was said to have had an affair with Cathy Dennis, the Norwich-born singer who he steered to success in the early Nineties. But, if so, it certainly did nothing to destabilise their very long-term professional relationship which continues to this day (Fuller now manages her as a songwriter).

No one has suggested that Fuller has had an affair with Annie Lennox, and yet he talks about her in unashamedly emotional terms.

"Annie is probably the perfect example of how I can work with someone as a team," he said. "I met her and I gave her confidence, which is a daily battle for her, strangely, for someone so talented. My relationship with Annie is: if Annie calls then I have to be there. You can't do that with too many artists, because it's quite consuming. She would think it was fake. If I had four or five of them, she would hate that. She tolerates all the other stuff I do, because she knows it's so different and that's my world, not hers. I could maybe do it with one other artist. But I haven't gone there with anyone else."

Maybe not. But did he go somewhere he ought not to have done with Emma? As the years have passed, and not one single piece of hard evidence has emerged from any quarter to lend material support to the story that Fuller and Emma were having an affair, the likelihood of it being true seems to have diminished in the minds of most people who were around them. Even those who were convinced it had happened at the time seem to have their doubts in hindsight.

While Emma displayed no burning desire to start making records away from the Spice Girls, even she started to get itchy feet after a while, and was happy to accept an offer to work with Tin Tin Out, who were also signed to Virgin. The production duo of Lindsay Edwards and Darren Stokes had enjoyed hits as Tin Tin Out with a variety of singers, notably 'Here's Where The Story Ends' featuring Shelley Nelson in 1998, and had also produced Top 10 hits for The Corrs ('Runaway', 'What Can I Do') and Des'ree ('You Gotta Be').

They agreed with Emma to record a version of 'What I Am', a haunting song with a simple, cyclical melody which had been a minor hit for Edie Brickell & The New Bohemians in 1989. Its lyric chimed pleasantly with Emma's down-to-earth personality – "I'm not aware of too many things/ I know what I know, if you know what I mean" – and given a fair wind from the Virgin marketing machine, the single seemed a safe bet to top the chart when it came out in November 1999.

Unfortunately for Emma, it was released on the same day as 'Lift Me Up', the third single from Geri's album, *Schizophonic*.

Both parties claimed to be unaware of this impending clash beforehand – which didn't seem very likely – and once alerted to it, neither of them was prepared to back down and change their release date in order to avoid the confrontation. Geri was now signed to Chrysalis, a subsidiary of EMI, while Emma and the rest of the Girls, both as a group and as solo artists, remained under contract to Virgin, also a part of the EMI group. But regardless of the record company politics this was presumably not what either Geri or Emma would have wanted: a head-to-head battle for the number one slot which could be talked up as some sort of point-scoring vendetta between Geri and one of her old bandmates.

For Geri this was a pivotal stage in her post-Spice career, since her autobiography, *If Only*, had been published by Bantam Press the week before. And it was also, coincidentally (or perhaps not), the same week that the remaining four Spice Girls published their book *Forever Spice*, a slender volume, about 90 per cent of which was given over to the photographs of Dean Freeman. Given the inevitable jockeying for position in the media that all this Spice-related activity would entail, there was considerable cynicism among many observers when it transpired that this should be the week that Geri and her fellow "ginger nut" Chris Evans should let it be known that they were in the grip of an uncontrollably passionate, whirlwind love affair.

Matthew Wright, of all people, was on hand to stir the pot with his account of a "frank and revealing" interview granted by Evans in a heartfelt bid to set the record straight for readers of the *Mirror*.

"I really like her, we're having a great time together," Evans said. "At the moment it's all about having fun, but who knows where it will lead. Hopefully, it will go on forever."

The press went mad, and the couple were plastered over the front pages for two or three days while details of the "story" emerged. It was no doubt a coincidence that Geri and Evans both shared the same PR agent, Matthew Freud of Freud Communications, who found the job of publicising Geri's record and book that week being done for him, several times over.

"All this stuff the other papers are saying about us doing it to publicise Geri's new record just makes us laugh," Evans insisted. "We've been to every restaurant and bar, even feeding the ducks in Hyde

Park," he said, just in case there were still any lingering doubts about the depth of their romantic commitment.

Victoria tells a revealing story about Geri in her autobiography. Four months after Geri had left the Spice Girls, Victoria was on holiday at Elton John's villa in the South of France when Geri called her, out of the blue, and invited her over to dinner at George Michael's villa, where she was staying, in St Tropez. Victoria was up for it, but was also very aware that this would be the first time that the two of them would have met since Geri had quit the group. Still, as long as it was in Michael's villa they should be able to avoid the attention of the press. Only when she got there, Victoria discovered there had been a change of plan, and that Michael had arranged for them to go out to a restaurant, where the paparazzi were lined up outside as if for a staged photo opportunity. Victoria came away from the encounter with the distinct impression that Geri had engineered the meeting not to build bridges with her old friend so much as to get her face back on the front pages of the papers.

Who knows what Geri's feelings for Chris Evans truly were? All relationships have a transactional dimension, and when two egos of such colossal proportions collide (or collude?), it must be hard even for them to disentangle the multiple motives underlining their emotions and actions. Geri, by this time, was keenly aware of the impact that developments in her personal life were likely to have on her public profile, while Evans would no doubt have welcomed the boost that such a high-profile conquest would give to his laddish notoriety. Both had a keen sense of what could be bought with the hard currency of celebrity, but maybe it was even simpler than that. As part of the first generation of stars to regard celebrity as an end in itself, they were simply seizing the moment to stock up on some pleasurable attention.

"I don't think it was plotted out," said Melanie Phillips, the new Spice Girls manager without portfolio. "I don't think you could do that. I think, genuinely, she fell in love with him. That's the impression I got. She'd always had a soft spot for him and, bless her heart, had a rotten time with it. But why did she have to go in to *The Sun* to tell her story? Oh dear. Don't do that. But that's Geri. It's a two-way street. The press manipulate, and some people like being in the press. Melanie C would have probably run a mile rather than go and tell *The Sun* all about it."

Whether it was real or not, their romance was both convenient to Geri's purposes, and curiously short-lived. At a press conference to launch their book, *Forever Spice*, the Spice Girls were bombarded with questions, not about themselves, but about Geri and Evans.

"We are here to talk about our book," Melanie C said, tartly. "It's not for us to comment."

Under ordinary circumstances, Emma's profile in the print and broadcast media that week would have seemed pretty comprehensive. Indeed, the *Guardian* made her the star of its weekly "Hard To Avoid . . ." column, with a selection of quotes from "just about everywhere", including the *Sunday Telegraph Magazine*, *Clive Anderson All Talk* (BBC1), *MTV News*, *The Sun* and *Company* magazine.

But Geri won the PR war hands down – which doesn't always guarantee the success of the record. She had garnered vastly more column inches and TV coverage than Boyzone when her debut single, 'Look At Me', failed to reach the top slot. But on this occasion she prevailed in the chart as well. Emma was typically magnanimous.

"I'm really happy for Geri," she said, through gritted teeth. "She did really well and congratulations are in order. I'm very thrilled to get to number two with my debut single. It's been a lot of fun."

# 11

# That Difficult Solo/Third Album

Although the Spice Girls' third album was not released until November 2000, the group actually began working on it a full two years earlier, in November 1998. Compared to the time they had spent writing and recording *Spiceworld* – barely six months from start to finish, while also making a movie – this was an eternity. Maybe that's why they called it *Forever*.

The world tour was all wrapped up by September 1998, but the Girls continued to work on the promotion of the 'Goodbye' single. The transition from being on the road to back at home may have looked seamless, but already changes were afoot in Spiceworld. With Melanie B and Victoria both in the latter stages of pregnancy, it fell to Emma and Melanie C to undertake those promotional duties which involved any travelling, as for example when they flew to Milan in November to attend the MTV Awards. The band which used to do everything together was now forced to take a more pragmatic approach to its working arrangements.

The first sessions for the album took place in November with their old stalwarts Biff Stannard and Matt Rowe, with whom they had already written and produced 'Goodbye'. Stannard and Rowe, although still on amicable terms, had not been working together as a writing/production partnership, since Stannard had moved his base of operations over to Dublin following the completion of the second Spice Girls album. However, he now returned to London, and they started writing with the Girls again. They worked up four or five new tracks with the Girls, none of which were eventually used on the album. While he remained philosophical about this, Stannard was particularly disappointed that a number called 'W.O.M.A.N.' was passed over.

"I thought that song was really interesting lyrically," he said, "because it was making the progression from girls to women, which was something Matt and I thought it was time for them to do. They needed something to suggest that they were still the same group of friends, but that they were gaining more maturity."

The Girls were obviously taken with the song, which has never been released, since they performed it live during the sequence of shows which they staged in December 1999.

But while the sessions with Stannard and Rowe progressed apace, it gradually became clear that the Girls were nurturing musical ambitions for this album that were somewhat different from the previous outings. One factor was that of Ashley Newton, who had A&Red the first two albums. Newton had moved to Los Angeles, where together with Ray Cooper he had taken over the running of Virgin America and, inevitably, his focus had shifted towards what was happening on the other side of the Atlantic. R&B music had always been his first love, and he was now particularly tuned in to the sounds of radio-friendly American urban artists such as TLC and Destiny's Child.

Newton certainly encouraged the Girls to explore an R&B direction as opposed to sticking with their pop roots. It seemed a natural development, which he believed would extend their appeal to a more mature audience, particularly in America. But Newton also recalled that his involvement with the Girls had, by this stage, diminished significantly.

"I'm somewhat reluctant to take more credit than I should for that album," Newton said. "It was pretty difficult, given all the duties of my new role in the States. I did help with the A&R team in Los Angeles, in hooking the girls up with some American producers."

The Girls, with or without Newton's influence, were thinking along the same lines, especially after their experiences during the American leg of their tour. When they played in Minneapolis they had met producer Jimmy Jam, who together with Terry Lewis, had been responsible for producing and playing on a long history of hits for various acts, most notably Janet Jackson. Jam arrived at a backstage gathering, together with the city's key musical dignitary, Prince, and received a warm Spice greeting.

"They just kind of mentioned that it would be nice to work together," Jam said. "It's always nice when people say that. It's a compliment. But I don't put a lot of stock in it, 'cause it's just something that people say."

While Jam could doubtless afford to be blasé about the idea of working with the Spice Girls, it was a much more flattering proposition to the Girls themselves. They had sold a vast quantity of records, but working with such an experienced and highly regarded production team as Jam and Lewis was a tremendously exciting prospect.

But why stop there? During a break from working with Stannard and Rowe in November, Melanie C and Emma went on a trip to America where they began courting the cream of the R&B producer/songwriter fraternity. In Minneapolis they met up once again with Jam and Lewis, then travelled to New York where they had dinner with Rodney Jerkins, and a breakfast meeting at the Four Seasons with Kenneth "Babyface" Edmonds. Victoria and Melanie B remained at home, which was an ironic division of labour given that it was the two mums-to-be who were far more interested than either Melanie C or Emma in pursuing such a musical direction.

"All we did was sit in a studio," Jimmy Jam recalled of the meeting with Emma and Melanie. "I just sat at a keyboard, I played a bunch of things, just to get a feel for where their voices were, where their range was and things that they liked and things that they didn't like. It was a really nice meeting and we hit it off really well."

The encounter with Jerkins was equally successful, although there was no attempt at a musical evaluation. Instead, Rodney, together with his older brother Fred and their father, the Reverend Fred, met Emma and Melanie in a restaurant. According to Melanie, the Jerkins contingent arrived late, and the boys ate a lot of bread.

Nothing further came of the meeting with Babyface.

Jam and Lewis subsequently travelled to London where they spent a week writing and recording the two tracks of theirs that would go on the *Forever* album: 'If You Wanna Have Some Fun' and 'Oxygen'.

"Our preference back then was to always work in Minneapolis," Jam said. "But under the circumstances, we thought, 'Let's work where the artist is comfortable.' We needed an excuse to visit London, because it's one of the places we don't get to enough. We brought over five tracks that we thought would be good, out of which the Girls picked those two. We had the melodies. And we sat in a room with a CD player and just played the track over and over again, and the Girls would periodically blurt out a line or a chant or something. It was very much collaborative. They had a good hand in writing it. We wanted them to put their personality into it. Their personality was one of the biggest factors in what it was they did. Everyone had a piece of paper, and everyone would say a line, and we'd just kind of hash it out like that.

"We very much want the artist involved in the process. We didn't want it to sound like Jam and Lewis. We wanted it to sound like the Spice Girls. It's the same with Janet [Jackson] or Usher or whoever we're working with. We want them to sound like them, not like us."

Asked how he would compare working with the Spice Girls to working with Janet Jackson, Jam was keen to emphasise the positive.

"The Spice Girls certainly held their own," he said. "Every artist is different. The fun factor was definitely on a par. Janet is a lot of fun to work with. But I can't think of a more fun experience than working with the Spice Girls. I thought it was absolutely tremendous. I thought the Girls were really nice. Really talented."

Owing to her solo commitments, Melanie C was not present for the whole of the London sessions with Jam and Lewis. The tracks were completed with the other three, but Melanie's vocals had to be recorded later in Los Angeles and patched into the final recording. There had been plenty of distractions during the recording of *Spiceworld*, but the demands of solo careers, particularly Melanie's, was a new challenge to the cohesion of the group. Even so, Jam paid tribute to their unflagging work ethic.

"I was surprised at how focused they were," he said. "And I was surprised at how hard they worked and how well they got along. I don't think they are the world's greatest singers from a technical standpoint. But I think they are good stylists and they have a lot of personality. What you have to do is match the singing with the right songs and the right melodies. If you gave that line from 'Wannabe' – 'I'll tell you what I want/ What I really, really want' – to Whitney Houston or Mariah Carey, who are great singers, they couldn't do that and make it sound right. But if you gave 'Vision Of Love' to Mel C, she probably couldn't do that right. It's not so much a matter of whether you can sing or you can't sing, it's what you can do really, really well. And what the Spice Girls did was sing with a lot of personality and they made you want to sing along with them. Not listen to them sing, but sing along with them. And that's a quality that a lot of very popular groups had. I don't think back in the day anybody thought that Diana Ross had the most killer voice in the world. But she did sing songs that made you want to sing along with her. I think Janet Jackson is like that."

The Girls kept their options open, and for a while it was almost as if they were making two parallel albums at the same time. In August 1999, they spent two weeks in Abbey Road with Stannard and Rowe, then a week in Sheffield back with their old chum Elliot Kennedy with whom they wrote and recorded two or three songs, including 'Right Back At Ya', the only non-American-led track to get on the album, apart from 'Goodbye'. Returning to London the same month, they went straight into a string of sessions with Rodney Jerkins.

Jerkins was king of the American super-producers who had followed in the footsteps of Quincy Jones (known for his work with Michael Jackson). Instead of being cast in the role of faceless technicians behind the mixing desk, a new breed of writers and producers such as Timbaland, Max Martin and She'kspere had become almost as well known as the artists whose records they helped to create. But none of them was as big – in all senses – as Rodney Jerkins.

Brought up in Pleasantville, New Jersey, Jerkins was the son of a pentecostal preacher. The Reverend Fred Jerkins, who still preaches in church every Sunday, did everything he could to steer his son away from popular music as a child – then later became his manager. The Jerkins children were not allowed to listen to pop music in the house, and as a youngster, Rodney was immersed in classical music, taking piano lessons from the age of five to 13. But his enthusiasm for R&B was such that when he reached his teens, he persuaded his father to borrow $1,900 against his life insurance to pay for a drum machine and a small keyboard. Soon Jerkins began cutting his own demos. He was already making a name for himself by the age of 15, when he attracted the favourable attention of his hero, the producer Teddy Riley. In 1997, when he was still only 17, Jerkins produced and wrote 'I Can Love You', for Mary J. Blige's album *Share My World*. Lifted as a single, 'I Can Love You' reached number 28 in the *Billboard* Hot 100 and Jerkins was on his way.

By the time the Spice Girls hooked up with him, the man was so hot that you could get singed from standing too close to him. He was already hard at work on Michael Jackson's forthcoming album, *Invincible*, and was lined up to collaborate with Britney Spears in the coming months. His recent songwriting and production credits included US number one hits for Brandy & Monica ('The Boy Is Mine'), Jennifer Lopez ('If You Had My Love') and Destiny's Child ('Say My Name'). While you don't have to be a strong-willed woman to work with Jerkins, it obviously doesn't hurt, and two of his most powerful

## That Difficult Solo/Third Album

productions from this period were 'It's Not Right, But It's OK', Whitney Houston's ingenious essay in the mechanics of emotional betrayal, and 'He Wasn't Man Enough For Me', a breathtaking display of female hauteur by the incomparable Toni Braxton.

"His trademark sound, which mixes irresistible pop choruses, stuttering hip hop beats and orchestral disco, has become the Top 40 template," declared the *New York Times* in May 2000. To have such a man on board the Spice ship was considered a major coup for the Girls, both artistically and commercially.

A tall fellow, dripping in gold, and with a build which betrayed his penchant for fast food, Jerkins was an imposing presence. He had set up his own Darkchild Studios in Pleasantville by the time he was 21, and recruited his older brother Fred Jerkins III and close family friend LaShawn Daniels to his writing and production team, also known as Darkchild. His cousin Ruben would welcome visitors to the reception area of the studios, which were decorated with painted portraits of Jerkins. Elsewhere there were framed signs reminding visitors that there was to be NO SMOKING, NO DRINKING, NO ILLEGAL DRUGS and NO DRUG TRANSACTIONS taking place on the Darkchild premises.

"The main thing you have to know," Jerkins once said, "is that you can't do anything without God. So I try to do everything, but I try to keep God first. He's the executive producer of all my projects, everything I do."

Like Jam and Lewis, Jerkins had foregone the routine of working in his usual studio location, and journeyed instead to London to start work on the Spice Girls album. It was his first visit to this country, and he was accompanied, as always, by his brother Fred and LaShawn Daniels.

"I remember being super-excited," Fred Jerkins said. "We've always liked doing work with people at a high level of success and we were definitely impressed by the history of the Spice Girls."

"Coming to London to work on that album was one of the experiences that would change my life," Daniels said. "Even if I develop Alzheimer's disease, I won't forget that!"

The Darkchild gang were a close-knit family unit. "When we're not working together, we're eating together," Daniels explained. "When we're not eating together, we're praying together. When we're not praying together, we're singing in church together." However, their pious beliefs were tempered by a lively sense of fun. They were about the same age as the Spice Girls, and quickly clicked on a personal level. Arriving at the studios on the first day, Fred tripped on the stairs and, instead of catching himself, turned the movement into a comically exaggerated fall. As he sprawled on the floor, Rodney jumped on his back and a typical piece of brotherly horseplay ensued.

Later on, when Daniels spilled something on his favourite T-shirt, the Girls ripped it off his back and took it away to "fix" the problem. The shirt came back festooned with trinkets, zippers and stickers, and with two holes cut in the nipple area. The Girls had autographed their handiwork. Daniels still has the shirt to this day.

Clearly then, there was to be no standing on ceremony when the Jerkins lads were around. But at the same time, there was no place in their studio regime for either slacking or swearing. "We definitely uphold a certain standard with our productions," Fred Jerkins said. "The people that we're working with definitely appreciate the way we handle our sessions. Our sessions are definitely in order."

While the Spice Girls were renowned for their work ethic and were hardly a group that needed to curb any rock'n'roll excesses in order to fit in with the Darkchild code of abstinence, even they found it hard to observe the "no swearing" rule.

"They used bad language a little bit, here and there," Fred remembered. "But if they did they would usually catch themselves – 'Ooops! We're not supposed to do that because the Jerkins boys are here' – and laugh about it. They'd make mild cracks about it. Nothing bad."

The London recording sessions with the Jerkins team were split between Whitfield Street in central London and the luxurious Hookend Studios, a state of the art facility located in an Elizabethan country manor in Checkendon, deep in the Berkshire countryside, near Reading. An environment less like Pleasantville, New Jersey, it would be hard to imagine.

The Darkchild team had a well-established method of working, almost a production line approach. Rodney would sit down and create the music for a track on a keyboard and drum machine, then turn it over to Fred and LaShawn to work on the melody and lyrics. For the *Forever* sessions, Rodney worked mostly at Hookend, writing and building the basic track, while at the same time Fred and Daniels would be working with the Girls in Whitfield Street, adding melody and lyrics to the tracks Rodney had started the previous day.

With such a well-oiled team at their disposal, and with the sessions compressed into the limited time span that the Jerkins crew could spend in London, the Girls' contributions to the actual writing process were a lot less integral than they had been in the past.

"They basically told us what they wanted to do and what they didn't want to do," Daniels said. "We sat with the Girls and we came up with different concepts for the record."

When it came to recording the vocals, neither Fred Jerkins nor Daniels were under any illusions about the nature of the task.

"When we first agreed, naturally you listen to the previous albums and see what you think about them," Jerkins said. "We knew it was going to be a little work to get it out of them. Basically, a lot of producers will let an artist sing the track and go home, and they don't come out the best they can be. I remember the Girls would be amazed at how good they were sounding. They just appreciated it so much that we took the time to bring out the best in the vocals."

"I'm known as a vocal slave-driver," Daniels said. "I put people under the whip. I used each of the Girls and I really put a lot of time into making them sound like they did."

But how did the Spice Girls match up to the likes of Toni Braxton and Whitney Houston?

"Toni Braxton is on another level as a singer," Fred Jerkins said. "And Whitney Houston, it's only a few that can compare to them as far as vocal skill. Some artists you go in and it's just a breeze. Then there's some artists you might dread going into the studio with, thinking you're gonna be in there killing yourself to make them sound half-decent. But if that was the case with the Spice Girls we wouldn't have went near them. I don't think it was harder work to do them than any other artist we have worked with."

In November 1999 the Girls began rehearsals at Elstree Studios for a string of shows scheduled for the following month: four at the Nynex Arena in Manchester and four at Earls Court in London. The idea of playing live again had been hatched during the studio sessions in the summer and these performances, staged in the round, provided a welcome chance for the Girls to touch base with their fans. Demand for tickets remained sky-high, and on the surface it all seemed like business as usual. But behind the scenes, cracks were beginning to appear.

"The atmosphere was different," Nancy Phillips recalled. "Everyone had different things on their mind. They all had their own dressing rooms with family and partners. It wasn't like a band. The camaraderie was not the same. I think if you'd said to me, 'Can you imagine them doing this again next year?' I would have said, 'Probably not.'"

Melanie B and Victoria both had new husbands and babies to attend to. And although both had declared the need for the group to take a six-month break, Melanie B had started work on her solo album in May and by the end of the year Victoria had begun writing for her album. Emma, meanwhile, was busy promoting her record with Tin Tin Out, with whom she played a couple of gigs in October, and later the same month she had begun writing sessions for her solo album with Matt Rowe.

But the Girl who was most preoccupied with her life and career away from the group was Melanie C. Earlier, in the summer, when the Spice Girls had been in Sheffield, writing and recording with Elliot Kennedy, Melanie C was simultaneously preparing for her shows at V99.

"It was a bit of a balancing act," Kennedy said. "We'd got a rehearsal room underneath our studio with her band in it. We'd be writing in the afternoon, and at some point I'd say to Mel, 'Well, you can go if you want.' And she'd go downstairs and rehearse with her band."

At the end of the week, Melanie played a warm-up gig at the Leadmill in Sheffield.

"David [Beckham] came over," Kennedy said, "and Victoria and David went to the gig, and we all kind of hung out and watched Mel perform. Melanie B had also started on her solo record, but she didn't have anything to play us at that time. There was no animosity or anything. It was just, 'Where's the energy coming from?' There was no Simon [Fuller] watching over things. No Geri. And they were all bound up with other things. I got the feeling that they were going through the motions most of the time."

It was particularly noticeable to those around the group how much Melanie C had drifted apart from the other three at the Earls Court shows in December. By this time, her solo album, *Northern Star*, which had been released in October, was beginning to reach critical mass and she was working ceaselessly to promote it. But while no effort was spared on behalf of her own album, she didn't want to do any press for the Spice Girls. Nor did she hang around with the rest of the group before or after the shows.

## That Difficult Solo / Third Album

According to one insider, "She didn't stay, she didn't meet fans, she just didn't seem to be there. In my mind, she'd already left, mentally, if not physically, by then."

The concerts at Manchester and London had a Christmas feel to them which seemed to reflect the expectations of the generally young crowds who attended, at least half of whom were primary school age children with their parents. The centrally placed stage was linked to a "grotto" area by a long overhead catwalk and for much of the second half of the show the four girls were dressed in Santa outfits, red mini skirts with red tops and white trimmings. No musicians were visible, only the girls. The show even ended with a medley of Christmas songs that included Roy Wood's 'I Wish It Could Be Christmas Every Day' and Slade's evergreen 'Merry Xmas Everybody', the words of which appeared on giant screens above the stage so that everyone could sing along. 'Wannabe' was delivered twice.

At Earls Court the bars were deserted but the merchandise stands were swamped with customers buying all manner of clothing and knick-knacks, three or four deep, thrusting forward their credit cards on behalf of their children. Most of the kids waved fluorescent green lights and wore tinsel-decked headpieces, £2 a throw, and screamed their heads off, producing that eerie sound of which the poet Allan Ginsberg, describing a similar clamour at a Beatles concert, wrote: "A single whistling sound/ of ten thousand children's/ larynxes a singing / pierce the ears . . ."

Although no one knew it, these gigs would be the last time that the group would ever perform together in public, bar one final appearance at the Brits on March 3, 2000. If there had been a vague air of a group treading water at the live shows, their contribution to the Brits had a positively valedictory feel about it. As in 1998, the Brits committee had somehow to devise a way of making sure that the group received an award. Melanie C and Geri were both nominated in the Best Female Solo Artist category, while Geri was also nominated for Best Pop Act. But the Spice Girls as a group were not even eligible for any of the other categories, having not released anything in the preceding year. The solution was to give them the Outstanding Contribution to the British Music Industry Award, a prestigious "lifetime" accolade which traditionally went to the veteran act which closed the show. The fact that the Spice Girls were still engaged in a career which could hardly have been deemed to have lasted a lifetime, or anything like it, was glossed over with vague references to their dominance of the decade which had just passed.* The Girls were presented with the award at the climax of the show, and performed 'Spice Up Your Life', 'Say You'll Be There' and, somewhat defiantly, the brand new 'Holler', which wouldn't be released as a single until the end of the year.

Victoria had received a death threat before the performance, and was understandably on edge. And Melanie B had a blazing backstage row with Robbie Williams (or attempted to; Williams slammed the door on her and instructed his security goons to keep her at bay). So it was pretty much business as usual.

However, there was much speculation beforehand that Geri might be invited to rejoin the group for the occasion. It was known that she would be there, performing her new single, 'Bag It Up', and being a "lifetime" award it was as much in recognition of Geri's achievements as it was those of the remaining four Girls. But emotions were still raw, and it was much too soon for a rapprochement of that kind to happen. Geri, who had also received a death threat before the show, performed her song, having emerged down a pole as if from a giant vagina. This was not a concept that won her much in the way of critical approval, although as she later noted in her memoirs, "It seemed I had got their attention."

There was confident talk about the future of the group as the Girls continued to forge ahead with their recording sessions which had now moved to America. But although work on the third album was moving fast, the splintering process of what was left of the group was moving even faster. Straight after the Brits, Melanie C released 'Never Be The Same Again', which became a huge number one hit, not only in Britain, but right across Europe. In the same month Emma, Melanie B and Victoria could all be found, at various times and places, in America recording tracks separately for their solo albums. The Jerkins mob was usually not far away.

Sessions for the Spice Girls album had to be slotted in around these

---

* It subsequently became known that Paul McCartney had been offered the Outstanding Contribution Award for the year 2000 but as he was unwilling to perform live the Brits Committee had withdrawn the offer. Chairman Paul Conroy was at pains to point out that this did not mean that the Committee deemed the Spice Girls' contribution to music to be of greater merit than that of the former Beatle – but eyebrows were raised nevertheless.

individual sessions, rather than the other way around. Thus it was that in April 2000, Emma, Victoria and Melanie B convened at the Hit Factory in Miami to continue recording the Spice Girls album with the Jerkins posse who were there to work with Britney Spears and Michael Jackson. The three Girls were joined later by an increasingly frazzled Melanie C, who must have been asking herself why — with her own single topping the charts all over Europe — she had journeyed halfway across the world to continue working on material which her heart was not in. The travelling was tiring enough, let alone the emotional tug-of-war between her personal ambitions and her feelings of loyalty towards the group.

There was more drama before the summer was through. In August, while Melanie C was enjoying another pan-European number one with the Ibiza/rave anthem 'I Turn To You', Victoria became the last Spice Girl to release a record away from the group when she teamed up with True Steppers and Dane Bowers to write and record 'Out Of Your Mind'. This was a big step for Victoria, who had been taunted relentlessly by every pundit in the land for her supposed lack of ability as a performer. Like Tin Tin Out, True Steppers was a production/songwriting duo whose working method was to provide skilfully crafted musical backdrops for a succession of guest artists. Comprised of Jonny Linders and Andy Lysandrou, the partnership had already scored a number six hit earlier in the year with 'Buggin', also featuring Bowers.

Bowers had been a singer in the British pop vocal group Another Level, who enjoyed a string of hits at the end of the Nineties, including 'Freak Me', which reached number one in July 1998. Although targeted at a teen audience, Another Level enjoyed credibility which was indeed on another level to that of the Spice Girls, thanks in part to a succession of collaborations which they had pulled off with American hip hop heavyweights including Jay Z (on 'Summertime') and Ghostface Killah of the Wu Tang Clan ('Be Alone No More'). True Steppers, likewise, boasted impeccable credentials as a cutting-edge dancefloor act — "former drum'n'bass whizzkids turned UK garage dons", as *Ministry* magazine put it, in a cover story bearing the legend "Posh and Decks".

"Victoria really knows her stuff," Lysandrou said. "When we first met her she reeled off all the big garage tunes. She really got into our groove."

Victoria's detractors could scoff all they liked, but this was the kind of company that would lend valuable kudos to her as an artist as well as helping her to fashion a track with gilt-edged chart potential.

The song they delivered was indeed a fabulously cool piece of UK garage/pop with a vocoderised effect on the vocal that had become fashionable after Cher used it on her 1998 hit, 'Believe'. It was a neat move by Victoria, not only musically, but tactically, to position herself in a way which kept her within the pop mainstream and yet set her apart from the other Girls stylistically.

August is not normally a difficult month to pitch a record at the top of the singles chart. The music business goes on holiday, the same as politicians and everyone else, and sales are generally down on the rest of the year. However, with the media on the lookout for stories to fill up their pages and schedules during the so-called "silly season", it is a time when a good pop story can blow up out of all ordinary proportions – as when Blur and Oasis released singles simultaneously in August 1995, and found themselves embroiled in a chart battle that got them on the *Six O'Clock News* before the week was out.

As the release date for 'Out Of Your Mind' loomed, there was a slight worry in some quarters that Robbie Williams might prove difficult to dislodge from the top slot with his hit, 'Rock DJ'. In the event Melanie C put paid to him with 'I Turn To You', which was sitting at number one, when 'Out Of Your Mind' was released on Monday, August 14.

What had not been reckoned on was the emergence of a massive, one-off summer hit from the unlikely quarter of a seven-foot-tall Italian DJ called Cristiano Spiller. 'Groovejet (If This Ain't Love)' had spread like a virus through the discotheques of Europe during the preceding months, and with demand having gradually built to a crescendo, the record broke like a tidal wave on the chart when it was finally released in Britain, also on Monday, August 14.

What turned an unfortunate coincidence into the biggest pop story of the summer was the fact that Spiller's record featured an obscure singer called Sophie Ellis-Bextor, who really was "posh". Ellis-Bextor had made a bit of a name for herself with theaudience, an under-achieving indie-pop group whose self-titled album had almost reached the Top 20 a couple of years earlier. The daughter of the former *Blue Peter* presenter Janet Ellis and the TV producer Robin Bextor, she was educated at the top private school Godolphin & Latymer in West London and oozed a certain well-spoken poise. She had dabbled in

## That Difficult Solo / Third Album

acting and modelling while working to establish a career as a singer. What a gift for the subs at the redtops who duly delivered a deluge of "Posh vs Posh" headlines.

Faced with this unexpected challenge, Victoria went into hyperdrive. She had not gone to all this trouble, and stuck her head above the parapet after such a long time, only to be upstaged by some unknown girl five years her junior who was being hailed as the "real" posh. Victoria went on a promotional bender, travelling the length and breadth of the country, showing up at the dodgiest local radio stations, doing signing sessions at record shops, and sometimes combining the two as when she announced on air that she would kiss anyone who bought her single during a signing session later that day in a Cardiff record shop. It was reported that during the first week her single went on sale, Victoria travelled an estimated 8,100 miles and required a sales update to be faxed to her every three hours.

Thanks largely to the saturation coverage which ensued from this "battle of the Poshes", the overall sales of singles increased that week by a whopping 24 per cent across the board. Spiller's disc, which entered the chart at number one sold 202,500 copies, the highest weekly sale by a single up until that point in 2000, while Victoria's first week sale of 181,000 copies made 'Out Of Your Mind' by far the biggest-selling number two record of the year.

Needless to say that was not the way the commentariat saw it. The failure to reach number one was reported as "a catastrophe". Posh was said to be reeling from the "huge blow" to her career, which had underlined once again that she was a singer who couldn't carry a tune in a suitcase. While doubtless a disappointing result for Victoria, it was hardly the end of the world. Both records were massive hits, and while 'Out Of Your Mind' did not reach number one, it went on to log 20 weeks in the chart, eventually selling close to half-a-million copies all told. And there was certainly nothing to be ashamed of compared to the other Spice Girls. Neither Melanie C nor Emma nor even Geri had reached number one with their debut singles, while Melanie B's second single, 'Word Up', had not even reached the Top 10.

However, the new criticism which emerged in the wake of her efforts on the True Steppers campaign trail was that Victoria had been trying too hard. It looked as if she was getting a bit desperate. As genuinely posh people are aware, in these kind of situations much depends on maintaining an aloof façade.

Maybe she had gone a bit over the top. But what the episode really underlined was the unexpected depth of her determination. While her slightly disengaged manner had set her apart at the beginning of the Spice Girls, and her family circumstances had increasingly claimed her attention in more recent times, Victoria was driven by personal ambition every bit as much as the next Spice Girl.

"When Victoria has got the bit between the teeth, there is no stopping her," Nancy Phillips said. "I've never known anything like it. She works hard. She will do anything. She'd be on the train travelling here, there and everywhere; promotion, promotion, promotion. I'd think 'God! Give it a rest.' Really determined. And I think you've got to respect that. But she also had such a laugh. People would say she was this desperate, mad woman, but she had so much fun doing that True Steppers promotion. She's exceptionally funny."

This was a side of Victoria which the public often seemed to miss.

"They always had it in for her at first, because they thought she was po-faced and stuck up and had no sense of humour," said Alan Edwards, who was still doing press for all four of the Girls at this point. "And I always thought she must be a bit miserable or something, but when I got to meet her I found she was a real laugh. I used to think of her as Witty Spice. Very funny one-liners and not at all po-faced. She has put her foot in it a few times. There's been some gaffs. That comment about David wearing her underwear, which might be kind of funny when you're with her, those kind of jokes are open to misinterpretation. But they're gags, mostly funny gags. It's just they didn't all translate in the right way."

Far from being "desperate", Victoria is very organised and methodical, according to Edwards.

"She has a very good grasp of marketing, and a good understanding of visual presentation," he said. "She pays attention to detail. She's very meticulous. Very business-minded. The polar opposite of Mel B, who was all instinct and emotion."

Embarrassing as Victoria's setback with her debut single might have been, it was the merest wobble compared to the bombshell that Melanie B dropped in October. Freed of all moderating influences since the jettisoning of Fuller and the departure of Geri, Melanie had become an increasingly headstrong player within the group, and pretty much beyond the reach of anyone so far as her solo aspirations

## That Difficult Solo/Third Album

were concerned. With the Spice Girls' album scheduled for release in November, it made no strategic sense – from the group's point of view, at any rate – to put out Melanie B's solo record the month before. But if anybody still had the group uppermost in their mind at this point, it was not Melanie B (or Melanie C, who carried on touring right up until the Spice album came out). The increasingly marginalised executives at Virgin, contemplating an autumn schedule crowded with Spice-related singles, albums and touring activities, tried to persuade Melanie B to hold off her solo album until after the release of *Forever*, but to no avail.

"Everyone's always advising Melanie B to delay things," said a friend of the band. "But whether it's putting out a record or getting married, she never pays the slightest attention."

The album, entitled *Hot*, was duly released on October 16. It entered the chart at number 28 and never rose any higher. This would have been an abject failure for a key release by *any* established chart act on a major record label. For a debut album by a Spice Girl it really was – to use a word that had often been bandied around in the past – a catastrophic result.

The album itself was really not as bad as the received wisdom now suggests. The eleven tracks included 'I Want You Back', her chart-topping duet with Missy Elliott, together with a bunch of new songs co-written with Rodney Jerkins, Teddy Riley (of Blackstreet, Jay Z and Michael Jackson fame) and Sisquo (a star in his own right who had also worked with Mary J. Blige and 2 Pac). There was a song co-written with Biff Stannard, and another with the American actor and musician Max Beesley, with whom Melanie was by now romantically linked.

The album's opening song, 'Feels So Good', and closing statement 'Feel Me Now', were both produced and co-written with Jimmy Jam and Terry Lewis who had actually ended up working with Melanie as a solo act before they worked with the group as a whole.

"We were fans of the group," Jimmy Jam said, "and when we first met them backstage in Minneapolis, Mel was very cool, very engaging. And part of our criteria for working with somebody is what Terry calls 'hang factor' – whether we enjoy hanging out with the performer. She had good hang factor. We'd seen the record she'd done with Missy Elliott, and we thought that was quite good. And then there was the inspirational factor. If you mention an artist and a song pops into your mind, then that's usually a good sign. And when she was mentioned there was an immediate idea of what a song should sound like for her.

"Working with Melanie B was a great experience. She had a lot of energy. She didn't really have a whole lot of confidence. The thing we found ourselves doing the most with her was trying to give her confidence. The psychology of it has to be a bit weird. She was in the biggest group in the world at the time, but I know she had some experiences with producers who told her, 'You flat out can't sing. You don't have it. Whatever.' There's a lot of different ways to react to that and her reaction was to work really hard. There was never a day when she was lazy in the studio. She was really willing to try anything. When I work with a vocalist like that, I like them to do all their own backgrounds, and she wasn't used to doing that. But she did it, and it took a couple of days, and it sounded great. I think even she was surprised by how good it sounded. I think it gave her a lot of confidence. And I wish we could have done more songs with her. Because I felt like we were just scratching the surface of what she could potentially do."

Melanie had certainly not been toying with this project. There were plenty of neat tunes, nice hooks, slick beats and no 'Word Up'. But the dismal sales were not an accident. Something had gone drastically wrong. While none of the many theories that have been put forward to explain the drastic underperformance of *Hot* is definitive, put together they paint a picture that gets close to the heart of Melanie B's problem.

Her decision to release 'Tell Me' as the first single, ahead of the album, set an emotional agenda for the campaign which stuck in many people's throats. Taking a leaf out of Geri's book, Melanie had opted to flag up the album with the most personal statement she had yet committed to disc. But instead of a jolly discourse on the nature of the fame game, Melanie's song was a straightforward character assassination of her husband, with a lyric which did not deploy any poetic niceties in putting the hapless Gulzar in his place. After letting him know that he "couldn't be the type of man to meet my needs" and telling him to "get from under my roof – I don't want you", Melanie delivered a punchline that was graceless in every respect: "Now I see you didn't have no self esteem/ And all you loved was Mel B's money."

There have been lots of great kiss-off songs in the history of pop from Bob Dylan's 'Positively Fourth Street' to Jack White's 'There's No Home For You Here'. But 'Tell Me' wasn't one of them. Apart from anything, it was just way too personal. This, after all, wasn't some unidentified schmuck; it was quite clearly and specifically the father of

## That Difficult Solo/Third Album

her daughter she was singing about. The public washing of this heavily soiled laundry was compounded by a succession of interviews designed to talk up the album, in which she took the opportunity to develop the theme of what a cheap, money-grubbing lowlife Gulzar was and how badly he had treated poor Melanie. Her rotten marriage, already a PR disaster, now became a central plank in the marketing of her album. And the selling of the album became a platform from which she could justify her side of the wrangling over the divorce proceedings. What a monumental turn-off.

Gulzar, we learned, was demanding £3 million to dissolve the marriage. Melanie had offered him £750,000.

"It's my hard-earned money, so it's true I'm feeling a bit upset about it," Melanie told the man from the *Mirror*.

"I wouldn't say he broke my heart," she told *Sky* magazine. "He crushed me. Y'know, like an Evian bottle."

Meanwhile the same "crushed" – and indeed still married – Melanie was pictured frolicking in a warm sea somewhere with her new paramour Max Beesley. It was real and it was honest and it was in your face and it was definitely all Melanie; but it really wasn't the way to win the sympathy vote.

Then there was the nature of the music itself. Melanie's love of R&B was absolutely genuine, and the people she had chosen to collaborate with were the best in the business. She had something of a feel for the genre. But for all her galloping self-belief – if not actual confidence – she wasn't Beyoncé Knowles or Aaliyah. She was a member of the most succesful pop group of the last ten years, so naturally people like Rodney Jerkins and Teddy Riley would return her calls. But that did not make her a serious player in that world. Her pop fans didn't buy it and the R&B audience wouldn't touch it with a bargepole.

While producers such as Jimmy Jam and Terry Lewis recalled the Melanie B sessions in unfailingly positive terms, there was a mismatch between their vision of who she was, and the way in which her fans, particularly in Britain, perceived her. Take, for example, the song 'Feel Me Now' co-written by Melanie, Jam and Lewis. This was a meandering, boudoir-sex routine – 'Feel Me Up' would have been nearer the mark – involving a lot of heavy breathing and close miking. "It's all about the different layers of my body, all right?/ Just explore me," Melanie commands, in a sultry whisper, which might have sounded more seductive without the flat Yorkshire vowel sounds. "Please go down/ If you take the lead I won't mind/ 'Cause I'm a woman and a woman needs to feel pleasure/ And the pleasure is all mine," she moans.

Jam recalled that Melanie was initially reluctant to take this route: "She would always say, 'I don't do sexy.' And we were like, 'Watch. You can do sexy.' Because we thought she was sexy."

Well, perhaps Melanie had a point. For while this kind of steamy soul sister rap might have sounded raunchy coming from Janet Jackson or Mary J. Blige, it is hard to take Melanie quite so seriously in such a role. You feel she is about to crack up into a raucous, Sid James-type laugh, halfway through.

The issues of Melanie's personal popularity and musical credibility were compounded by the album's staggeringly bad timing.

"I think that Melanie's focus was not 100 per cent at the crucial moment, sadly," Alan Edwards said. "She was dealing with personal issues. She didn't have a specific manager at that stage, and you know when a project just drifts? That one drifted at the crucial moment. It was only about four weeks. But it was the four weeks just before the album release. And it was a shame. Because actually, a real head of steam had built up for her. I think if they had released 'Feels So Good' [the other Jam and Lewis track] first, history would have been different. Because she had such star appeal. She really could pull it off. People have mixed opinions about her. But she is pretty good fun and pretty lively when you can bottle that energy. She's also a very nice and generous person."

Mixed feelings turned to intimations of disaster as far as Virgin Records was concerned. It seemed as though everything was out of kilter for Melanie B's solo album. Despite the best efforts of Nancy Phillips to keep the diary straight and the schedules manageable, Melanie wasn't actually being managed. She wouldn't let herself be managed. Nor would she take direction from the record company, which meant that she was essentially being allowed to drive the project herself.

The knock-on effect of not having anyone (other than Melanie) in charge meant that the nuts and bolts of the campaign were not being taken care of. Melanie scripted a video of which Virgin did not approve. The decision to release 'Tell Me' as the first single was seen as a fatal mistake. With the Spice Girls album due out the following month, and confidence in Melanie's future as a solo act ebbing away, it appears that Virgin simply pulled the plug. While no one would formally admit to it, it seems the record company switched the money off about a month before the album came out.

## That Difficult Solo/Third Album

"She's such a good star in a genuine sense," Edwards said. "I think if it had been done correctly, she could have really made an impact. But she was a bit uncontrollable. She didn't listen to anybody really, at that juncture in her life. So there was nobody there to fight her corner. The Girls were very much making their own decisions. They got into the habit of managing themselves and they never really got out of the habit. They all called their own shots. So the problem was, who was getting priority at that stage? I don't think anyone was really watching out for her interests."

The media response to this unprecedented change in the fortunes of a Spice Girl was curiously muted. After labelling so many of their projects – from the multi-platinum *Spiceworld* album and top-grossing *Spiceworld* movie to Victoria's huge-selling 'Out Of Your Mind' single – as "flops" or "catastrophic" setbacks of one sort or another, the pundits didn't seem to notice the dire fate that befell Melanie B's solo album. Either that or they didn't feel it was a big enough story to merit their attention. Faced at last with a genuine lack of public interest in a Spice product, the media, by and large, ignored the story. Perhaps they were saving themselves for the big one.

Although in hindsight, the Melanie B disaster was an obvious harbinger of the even greater fall that was about to come, it looked at the time as if the Spice Girls' third album was on course to repeat the success of its predecessors. There was much bullish talk of the transition that the Girls had made from giggling ingénues to sophisticated women of the world. The names of Rodney Jerkins and Jam and Lewis were vigorously bandied around, suggesting an association with a different order of world-class stars: Whitney Houston, Will Smith, Brandy, Janet and Michael Jackson. And when the first single from the album, 'Holler'/'Let Love Lead The Way', went straight in at number one at the start of November, it looked as if the Spice magic was still intact. The group's ninth number one hit – taking their UK tally of number ones above those of Madonna and The Rolling Stones – this double A-side featured two songs co-written with the Jerkins brothers and LaShawn Daniels, which pretty much summed up the sound and direction of the album as a whole. Indeed of the eleven tracks on the album, seven were co-written by the Jerkins posse.

"At the moment, people my age don't care about the Spice Girls," the 21-year-old Jerkins said. "But they will." While the wunderkind producer may have been blessed with many talents, clairvoyance was not one of them.

The reviews of the album were uniformly bad. Nothing new there. What had changed, however, was the way in which critics who had been implacably opposed to the Spice Girls from the outset could now be heard lamenting the loss of the great pop group they had spent so long trying to bury in the first place.

"Victoria, Mel C, Mel B and Emma Bunton have reinvented themselves as a bizarre cross between Jennifer Lopez and Celine Dion in a quest to be taken seriously as the adults they've become," Betty Clarke wrote in the *Guardian*. "But *Forever* ultimately makes you yearn for those heady days when the Spice Girls were pop and proud of it. Come back Baby, Ginger, Sporty, Scary and Posh. I miss you."

Meanwhile, Angus Batey in *The Times* made a canny prediction: "*Forever* is set to alienate the Spices' natural constituency while failing in its attempt to garner a new one."

# 12

# Gone West

The imminent demise of the Spice Girls had been confidently predicted since November 1997 when they had sacked Simon Fuller. And yet, three years later, when the end finally came, it was swifter than anyone had imagined. Despite the Girls' belief that they could manage their long-term affairs by themselves, the group's progress since parting company with Fuller had actually resembled one of those oil tankers that takes about ten miles to change direction. Once set on course, such a vessel can continue to travel for a very great distance, but eventually, without a guiding hand on the tiller, it will either end up hitting the rocks or simply running out of steam.

In some ways, it was a considerable achievement for the Girls even to have completed *Forever* and got it in the shops. They had done so with no proper manager in charge of long-term strategy and no executive producer or A&R person with an overall idea of what the album was supposed to sound like. They no longer had Geri to badger everyone, spark ideas and instil a sense of purpose in the project. They had only just hung on to Melanie C, who frequently missed sessions because of her solo commitments and had to add her vocals after the original recordings had been completed on several occasions. Victoria and Melanie B were coming to terms with marriage (and divorce in Melanie's case), motherhood and solo careers. Only Emma was able to devote herself to the Spice Girls as a group with anything like the commitment of the early days, and even she was working on a solo album.

Much of this situation was of their own making. They hadn't wanted a manager; they had long been in the habit of keeping the record company at arm's length; they didn't see the need for outside guidance, either musically or in a practical sense. Looked at in one way, it was a remarkably gutsy display of independence. But it was also a monumental act of hubris.

Nemesis duly arrived in the shape of the Irish boy band Westlife. Having sniffed a change in the wind, this well-drilled but unutterably dull combo, under the guidance of Eurovision and management svengali Louis Walsh, had decided to challenge the Spice Girls' position as rulers of planet pop by releasing their second album, *Coast To Coast*, on the same day as *Forever*.

Westlife had enjoyed an extraordinary run of chart success, thanks to a musical and business formula which rolled back every advance in pop which the Spice Girls had made. They came from Dublin where they had been not so much manufactured as cloned from the original Irish boy band, Boyzone. Indeed, Boyzone's singer, Ronan Keating, had a stake in the management of Westlife. Having arrived at number one with their first hit, 'Swear It Again', in May 1999, during the Spice Girls' leave of absence, Westlife proceeded to dominate the charts with a stiflingly dreary mixture of ballads, more ballads and covers of other people's ballads. They sat on stools and performed with a sickly professionalism from which every ounce of personality and individuality had been purged.

While people had complained about the contradictions of Girl Power and the cheesy commercialism of the Spice Girls, the hard-nosed careerism of the Westlife philosophy put the Spice Girls in the shade. The five, flaxen-haired boys were so ordinary that no one could tell them apart. But concealed behind their heavily styled image and a manner that was blander than baby food there lurked a bunch of business brains with reflexes as sharp as a mantrap. One of them wrote himself a memo when he was 12 saying, "I am going to be a millionaire before I'm 21." It was no idle boast, and when he was not on stage, he spent his time checking the group's balance sheets and investing in the property market.

These pop automatons had seduced the teen audience and their mums by using every well-rehearsed trick in the book. Their version of the Phil Collins song 'Against All Odds (Take A Look At Me Now)' featuring a guest performance by Mariah Carey, was about as calculating – and unimaginative – a pop record as has ever been made. Having notched up a tally of seven consecutive number one hit singles in just eighteen months they had achieved a momentum which they guessed – correctly, as it turned out – the Spice Girls were no longer capable of stopping.

## Gone West

The Spice Girls trumpeted the release of *Forever* with a fact sheet that made impressive reading. "Sales: *Spice* – 22,000,000; *Spiceworld* – 13,917,020; Total sales of singles – more than 25,000,000." But it was Westlife who actually went out on the stump and promoted their album – in keeping with its title – virtually from coast to coast.

"We're going to do as much as we can to kick their asses," one of the clones said. Starting in Glasgow, where they signed 2,000 autographs at Virgin's megastore, they travelled to Manchester, Carlisle, Birmingham and London, snatching just two hours sleep in 38 hours of travelling. It was the kind of stunt the Spice Girls would have pulled themselves five years previously – but not now.

For their part, the Girls had done a week of promotion when the single came out in October, based on a whistle-stop spin round the usual TV shows: *Top Of The Pops*, *The Lottery*, *CD: UK*, *SM:TV*. It was not a very intensive or imaginative campaign.

As it turned out, the battle for number one was all over before it started. After two days in the shops *Coast To Coast* had sold 60,000 copies, while *Forever* had sold 21,000, less than half the Westlife total, and not that far ahead of the U2 album, *All That You Can't Leave Behind*, which was now in its second week on the chart, and had sold 18,000 copies in the same two days.

Thanks to the swift, computerised collection of chart data, and the vast immediate disparity in sales between *Coast To Coast* and *Forever*, everyone knew the outcome of the chart battle before the official launch parties for the two albums. Both events took place on the day of the albums' release – Monday, November 6 – in two clubs a stone's throw apart in London's West End. At Westlife's gathering in the Asia de Cuba restaurant in St Martin's Lane Hotel, there was a mood of jubilation as the Irish boys were feted by their friends, their record company acolytes and the media. They had cheekily invited a Spice Girls tribute band to join them at the do and, adding insult to insult, Melanie C's ex-boyfriend J from the boy band Five was also spotted among the happy throng.

In sharp contrast, the mood at the Spice Girls party in the Red Cube club in Leicester Square was more like a wake than an album launch. Melanie C, who hadn't wanted to be there in the first place, had finally reached the end of her tether. Cornered by Dominic Mohan of *The Sun*, she was not exactly magnanimous in the face of impending defeat.

"Westlife are a useless bunch of talentless tossers," she said, "and they don't deserve to be in the charts, let alone number one. I think it's fucking disgusting that bands like A1, Steps and Westlife get to number one. It's all crap – marketed rubbish. We don't care if they beat us to number one – they probably will – it sums up how shit music is at the moment. They try to be these smiling, angelic Irish boys and they make me sick. They have no personality. It's all dull, dull, dull."

Meanwhile, Melanie B, always quick to enter into the spirit of these things, acknowledged the arrival of the three show business gossip columnists from the *Mirror*, known as the "3am Girls", by loudly enquiring, "What the fuck are those sluts doing in here?"

"Oh God! It was horrific," Nancy Phillips recalled. "I remember being incredibly depressed. It had been really difficult, because Melanie C had been on tour in Europe since October. She'd played Wembley Arena the night before. So she was knackered. And I remember her saying, 'I don't want to go to a party.' And I said, 'Well you have to.' Discussions had taken place about what would be done in terms of promotion. And Melanie had put her cards on the table and made it clear that it was limited what she was prepared to do. So it was really, really difficult. Melanie was very unhappy, because she was being torn. I was very unhappy. The others were very unhappy. It wasn't a happy camp.

"I remember being inside the club when the Girls were arriving. And I remember there was a bit of a contretemps with Alan Edwards and [his assistant] Caroline McAteer. I had said that it was a party, but the Girls were not going to do interviews. The press were invited but it was not an interview situation. The Girls were arriving at the entrance, which was obviously surrounded by paparazzi, and then as they were coming in to the entrance Alan stopped them to introduce them to the 3am Girls. Melanie had done the fingers to say, 'I don't want to talk to anyone, right now, Alan.' So whatever was said wasn't meant to be personal. It was more just someone lashing out who didn't want to be there and certainly didn't want the tabloid press in her face the moment she walked in the door.

"Emma and Victoria came over and said, 'Melanie, you're so rude. You shouldn't do that to people.' So then the Girls started fighting among themselves. Next thing I know, Alan Edwards comes over to me, absolutely ashen-faced and says, 'You've got to come and calm this down.' I think I was probably already completely off my head and thinking, 'I don't care any more.' Because there was nothing I could do. To be honest, at this point in the whole set-up, I'm powerless. I mean I can take care of the nuts and bolts. But in terms of trying to smooth things over, by this point, there's no one who can do that."

"The night of the album launch was a disaster," Alan Edwards recalled. "It was just appalling. It was a horrible night. Badly handled. Everything. Mel B and Mel C were a bit out of control that night. It wasn't just the 3am Girls they had it in for. In fact, it was more like a Sex Pistols album launch than a Spice Girls reception that night. B was partying, but really partying, while C just didn't want to be there. Her heart wasn't in it. And for once, she couldn't fake it. She didn't care, and everybody could see she didn't care. And I remember the four of them on the stairs. Emma was practically in tears. Victoria was trying to pull the other two Melanies into line. It was all over the place.

"I remember coming out of there very upset and depressed and going for a walk at about 10 o'clock that night and walking for about an hour through the West End just feeling sad. Because it was the end of the whole thing. The night of the album launch was when it ended for me."

In hindsight, there was obviously no turning back for the Spice Girls as a group from this point. But at the time they put a brave face on the situation and soldiered on. After all, the record had only been in the shops for one day. By the end of the week Westlife had indeed trounced them in the race for the number one slot, but who knew how things would pan out in the rest of the world? They certainly wouldn't have Westlife breathing down their necks in America where the whey-faced boy band were unknown.

Putting the launch party behind them, the Spice Girls airily dismissed the Westlife contest as a parochial storm in a teacup and announced that they were more concerned with focusing on the apparently "booming" sales of *Forever* in America and elsewhere. It didn't take long, however, for observers to realise that sales in America, if anything, were turning out to be even more disappointing than in Britain.

After the fuss that had been caused by the ship-out figures of *Spiceworld* back in 1997, Virgin kept information about the precise number of copies of *Forever* that had gone out to the shops close to its chest. But it seems safe to say that there must have been a staggering quantity of unsold Spice Girls CDs clogging up the stores during the weeks before Christmas 2000.

With the full extent of their fall from grace only just beginning to sink in, the Girls travelled to Stockholm for an appearance at the MTV Europe Awards on November 16. They performed 'Holler', but unsurprisingly claimed no prizes. They were not allocated their usual star dressing rooms, and found themselves attracting much less attention backstage than Jennifer Lopez and Eminem. The next day, they were largely ignored by both press and television, an experience which they found infinitely more humiliating than being slagged off by them. They were less than two weeks into the campaign for *Forever*, and the wheels had well and truly come off the wagon.

In the post-mortems that followed, much criticism was inevitably levelled against the album itself. The R&B direction had obviously failed to impress their fans. Indeed it had failed to impress some of the participants, notably Elliot Kennedy, who had co-written 'Right Back At Ya' with the Girls.

"It was one of the funkiest tracks I've ever done," he recalled. "The idea was to get a comeback record that would hit you right in your face. The Girls were buzzing off it, the record company loved it."

However, the song was re-recorded by Fred Jerkins III and Darkchild's mix engineer Ben Garrison before it got on to the album. Kennedy was not impressed with the result.

"I was gutted," he said. "So much so that I really wish it hadn't gone on the album. I wish we'd saved it in its original form and done something else with it. They'd taken all the fun out of the song and reduced it to this plodding, boring, bottom drawer R&B song. This was such a bad call. They were trying to make an American record with four very English girls. I remember saying, initially, 'Why on earth are they doing this?' And the answer came back, 'Oh, we can't get away with another album like the other two in America.' It was nothing to do with music that third album. They wanted to try and max the sales as much as they could by making an American record for America. And they lost all their audience in the process. It was a terrible A&R decision. Their audience didn't understand it. 'Holler' was quite a cool song. And that was all they needed to do – one song like that. One song by Rodney Jerkins who was a very happening producer, perfect. But don't let him do the whole bloody album, for God's sake. That was just a nightmare. I said to the record company, 'Who's made this decision?' And they said, 'Ashley Newton's A&Ring it.' And that said everything I needed to know, really."

Newton, who has since distanced himself from the project, recalled his own feelings of disappointment at the outcome of the liaison between the Girls and the American producers.

"Unfortunately, along the way, some of that character, some of the Girls' flavour seemed to be drained by working with state-of-the-art American producers. Instead of making it bigger and grander and more important, somehow I felt as though some of the life force was lost. Whether or not that is my recollection of it based on just the music or whether it was just symptomatic of everybody around the project and in the general public just having a sort of fatigue of overexposure and exhaustion and everybody moving on with their own agendas . . .

"It was a rickety old project to put together. It didn't have the complete love and energy and commitment and spontaneity and hunger and vibe that the first two records had, when the foot was totally on the gas and they were just full of ideas and points of view. So here they were working with A-list producers like Rodney Jerkins and Jam & Lewis, and actually the track I was most fond of was 'Goodbye', which they'd done on the hoof, in Nashville, with their old sparring partners Matt [Rowe] and Biff [Stannard]. But you know, you have to encourage people to grow and to change and to experiment. Some things work and some things don't. But you don't want to keep them harnessed to something for ever.

"The novelty of the Girls had kind of worn a little thin. And if they were going to be able to come out with an A-list song produced by an A-list American producer and start competing there, it was something that I thought we could probably do some business with. But it was not the case. The bubble had most definitely burst by the time that album came out in America."

Fred Jerkins stood by the music on the album. The problem, as far as he was concerned, was more to do with bad timing and the lack of promotional effort that went into the selling of the album.

"They were such a phenomenon," Jerkins said. "And what goes up comes down. When you're so big, I think it's hard to top it. Of course it was disappointing. We were at our peak and they were at their peak, so coming together you're looking for an explosion! But it's not something we regret doing at all. It was a good album. They put their best foot forward. But I know that when the album came out they weren't trying to get together and do a tour. If they'd gone out and toured, God knows what would have happened. Sometimes artists don't understand how important that tour is."

LaShawn Daniels was equally philosophical about the outcome.

"At the time, I believe they were ridiculed so much about the bubblegum pop type of thing that they wanted to display how much more musically they were inclined. I don't know if the public accepted that they really could sing. I don't think the public accepted that they were really into the music and could really do it, to really get their message across. I don't think the public was ready for what they were doing. But I think they achieved what they wanted to achieve in the studio and they were right for wanting to achieve it."

A besetting problem which the Spice Girls had in America was getting their music played on the radio. Unlike Britain, where other factors, such as press coverage, can have a very direct bearing on record sales, in America radio speaks through a singular megaphone to the record-buying public. Minutely researched, rigidly genre-specific and incredibly powerful, American radio is intimidating to record companies at the best of times, but especially when they are trying to get a record by an English group off the ground, even the Spice Girls.

For various reasons, the Girls had never had a very good relationship with American radio, whose producers and DJs felt that they had been bounced into playing the group's early records by an army of kids who had bought into the Spice phenomenon. The Girls had a better relationship with TV, where they always gave good value when appearing on chat shows or giving a performance. But in America, radio was, and still is, the fast track to getting a record in the charts – not least, because in the case of the singles chart, a record's position is gauged not by how many copies it has sold (as in Britain), but by how many times it has been played on the radio. The irony was that in attempting to woo American radio by working with the likes of Jerkins and Jam & Lewis, the Girls lost the support of the core audience who had forced the radio stations reluctantly to play their records in the first place.

Another part of the problem was that America, no doubt inspired by the Spice Girls, had re-learned how to do pop for themselves. In their absence Britney Spears, N-Sync and the Backstreet Boys had risen up, acts whose appeal was aimed at exactly the same market that the Spice Girls had located, if not created. While the Girls' tour of America had been well received, they had spent little time while they were there courting the media, and the advances they had made were quickly rolled back. It was the start of a period when the barriers went up against outside music in general, and with the advantage of hindsight, the Girls' achievements in America seem all the more remarkable. The insular nature of American society – about 60 per cent of the population does not own a passport – means that it is a country which prefers its own music. And when it comes to pop-flavoured R&B, where the homegrown variety comes in the shape of acts like TLC and Destiny's Child, you can see why.

It had been three years since the last Spice Girls album, and things had moved on. Radio programmers sensing a dip in the Spice Girls stock were only too happy to drop them like a hot potato. However, as Newton pointed out, there were other, more fundamental problems, that were also affecting the group by this time.

"To get the Girls even to want to be working together was difficult," he said. "Everybody by then had made a lot of money, they had their own personal agendas, they had solo things in their head, it was not quite the spirit they had originally. And this happens with a lot of projects, especially when you're going for that pressure cooker environment that they had in those three years. It was unlike anything I've seen before or since. And it just changes people and relationships and work ethic and everything. I think Melanie C, bless her heart, was dragged screaming into those Rodney Jerkins sessions. She'd moved on and was carving a different niche for herself. That generic, urban-leaning pop was something that she wasn't really attached to. Emma and Mel B, on the other hand, felt that was a good direction. And Mel B's album, musically, was a companion piece to *Forever*. Sadly, it met the same fate."

If nothing else, the failure of the third album gives the lie to the frequently aired suggestion that the success of the Spice Girls had nothing to do with their music. The rise of the Spice Girls had everything to do with the giddy exuberance of the music on the first two albums, and their fall was compounded by the lifeless air of professionalism exuded by *Forever*. The sense of friendship, fun and sentimental charm that was the calling card of *Spice* and *Spiceworld* had been replaced by a self-consciously grown-up, soul-by-numbers routine that lacked the sparkle and zip of their previous releases. The absence of Geri's witty ideas and brassy edge was critical. And who knows how differently the album would have ended up sounding if it had been subject to the guiding hand of Simon Fuller?

The Spice Girls ended as a group abruptly and without any fanfare.

There was no announcement, and certainly no scenes of mass hysteria as when Take That split up and "helplines" were set up for distraught fans who felt they needed a sympathetic ear. Shortly before Christmas 2000, the four Girls met in their Bell Street office off the Marylebone Road. While Melanie B and Emma were prepared to carry on promoting *Forever*, Melanie C and Victoria had had enough. It would have taken a superhuman effort to reverse the album's fortunes and, as a group, they no longer had the stomach for a fight from which they could only have emerged as second best. It was decided not to release another single from the album and all further Spice activity was quietly suspended until further notice.

"I think we did pretty well," Nancy Phillips said. "We'd done three years [since the sacking of Fuller]. In that time they'd had Spice Girl number ones, and all the solo careers launched to a greater or lesser degree."

*Forever* eventually sold three million copies worldwide, a resounding success by the standards of virtually any other act, but a terminal disappointment when compared to the tens of millions the Spice Girls had become used to selling.

The decision to suspend activities remained a private matter, with all public statements being hedged around with the usual nothing's-set-in-stone remarks. While doubtless a sad and sobering moment for the Girls, the impact of the group's downfall was masked by the gathering momentum of their careers as individuals. Melanie C's album, *Northern Star*, had by this point sold about as many copies as *Forever*. Work on both Emma's and Victoria's solo albums was well in hand and they could be optimistic about their chances of achieving a similar degree of success to that of Melanie C. Privately, there was a rueful feeling among the Virgin executives that the company had worked *Northern Star* rather too well, and that its success had fatally destabilised the group. If *Northern Star* had gone the same way as Melanie B's album, *Hot*, then maybe Victoria and Emma — not to mention Melanie C herself — would have put a more determined effort into the making and promoting of *Forever*. Perhaps too, their audience would have had a chance to catch their breath before the arrival of the new Spice Girls album.

As it was, *Forever* had got rather lost amid the constant flow of Spice-related releases. Once the decision to suspend group activities had been taken, Victoria and Emma immediately threw themselves with renewed vigour into their solo albums. For Melanie C it was a huge relief to be free of her commitments to the group. So if it was goodbye from the group, it was hardly going to be goodbye from the Spice Girls as individuals.

However, for those with keen ears the sound of a warning bell in the night could be heard. The miserable end to the year was compounded by the release of 'If That Were Me', the last single to be lifted from Melanie C's solo album. A mawkish ballad about the plight of homeless people, it limped in to the chart at number 18, thus wresting away from Melanie B's 'Word Up' the unwelcome accolade of being the lowest charting single ever released by a Spice Girl – so far.

There is an Aesop's Fable which tells the story of a dog carrying a bone, who catches sight of his own reflection in a lake. Attempting to grab the "new" bone from the mouth of the dog he can see in the water, he ends up losing the bone he has already got. The Spice Girls were all so hungry for that second, solo career, which seemed to beckon invitingly, that they simply let go of the group. Compared to their success together as a group, their solo careers turned out to be almost as chimerical as a reflection in the water. But not to begin with.

Here is a log of chart activity for the individual Spice Girls in 2001, the year after the group had unofficially ceased activities:

| 3 March | MELANIE B 'Feels So Good' | No.5 |
| 14 April | EMMA 'What Took You So Long?' | No.1 |
| 28 April | EMMA *A Girl Like Me* | No.4 |
| 12 May | GERI 'It's Raining Men' | No.1 |
| 26 May | GERI *Scream If You Wanna Go Faster* | No.5 |
| 16 June | MELANIE B 'Lullabye' | No.13 |
| 11 August | GERI 'Scream If You Wanna Go Faster' | No.8 |
| 8 September | EMMA 'Take My Breath Away' | No.5 |
| 29 September | VICTORIA 'Not Such An Innocent Girl' | No.6 |
| 13 October | VICTORIA *Victoria Beckham* | No.10 |
| 8 December | GERI 'Calling' | No.7 |
| 22 December | EMMA 'We're Not Gonna Sleep Tonight' | No.20 |

No wonder the demise of the Spice Girls barely registered at the time. If anything, with all five of them on the loose, the flood of Spice-related records *increased* in the months after the group itself had been laid to rest. Put them all together, and this was another staggering succession of chart placings, even if the cracks were now beginning to show.

As the new year began, Melanie B, Melanie C, Emma and Victoria were in the odd position of not being together any longer as a group (whatever they said in public) while still sharing the same office, the same record company, the same press officer and the same manager. Friendship never ends, of course, but given the intensely competitive nature of the four personalities involved, it wasn't long before goodwill was beginning to wear thin. Nancy Phillips, who had been hired three years previously to sort out the group's business affairs in the wake of Simon Fuller's departure now found herself with a four-way brief which stretched her powers of patience and diplomacy to the limit.

As January got under way, Melanie C was touring North America, Melanie B was pulling together a campaign in a vain attempt to resurrect her album *Hot*, Emma was finishing work on her solo album and Victoria was writing her autobiography, while also working on her album.

"I tried to divide my time as best I could," Phillips recalled. "But I was very aware that I was dividing myself. Melanie B already didn't seem very keen on having my advice. Whenever I made a comment, she would say, 'You're very negative.' To which I would reply, 'No, Mel. I'm realistic.' I never went on the road with Melanie C, which I regretted. I tried to keep it London based. But then I did go to Los Angeles with Victoria in February. I remember proof-reading the whole of her book while she was in the studio."

At the beginning of March, as Melanie C's tour progressed onwards to Singapore, Moscow, St Petersburg and Tallinn, Melanie B released 'Feels So Good', the opening track from her album, which she had co-written with Jam and Lewis. Although the song reached number five, and restored a bit of confidence in Melanie's stock, it made no difference to the album whatsoever. At which point Melanie C, whether by accident or design, drove the final nail into the Spice Girls coffin.

Speaking to a Reuters journalist, Dean Goodman, in Los Angeles, she insisted, at some length, that she had outgrown the group.

"I don't intend to do any more work with the Spice Girls," she said. "Really, I've not been comfortable being in the Spice Girls for probably the last two years. It doesn't really feel that natural to me any more.

I've grown up and I just feel that I want to do things my own way and not compromise. We were such a huge phenomenon and there's not really anywhere else to go with that. It was a question of sacrificing our lives and trying to maintain the success, or just being honest with ourselves. We've all been very honest and all wanted to pursue solo careers. We're still linked business-wise and we're still friends, but I don't really consider myself to work as a band now."

The reaction of the media was, not unreasonably, to report this as signifying the end of the group, and it is hard to interpret Melanie's comments as meaning anything else. The old excuse, that she had been misquoted, or quoted out of context, was quickly trundled out. But it did not wash thanks to *The Sun*, who had helpfully made a tape recording of the interview available on the end of a phone line for anyone who wanted to hear Melanie's comments for themselves – at a cost of 60p a minute (58p from the Republic of Ireland).

The reaction of the other Girls was thinly disguised anger, not because the report was inaccurate, but because Melanie had broken ranks and spilled the beans in this way. The democratic decision between the four of them had been to play the No Comment card and keep their option of returning at some point in the not-too-distant future open. But by making such a forthright declaration, Melanie had unilaterally finished the Spice Girls off.

"We all know she has been unhappy and depressed," a source close to the group told *The Sun*, "but she's always shooting her mouth off and doesn't think about what she's saying."

"I don't think Mel C meant to say it," Emma said. "She has been working very hard and was probably very tired."

"As far as I know we haven't split up," Melanie B said.

Maybe not. But the writing was now not so much on the wall as spelt out in capitals on a 10 metre-high billboard. Melanie C no longer considered herself a member of the Spice Girls, in which case the group was effectively finished. And that has remained the position until the time of writing in June 2004.

The immediate consequence of Melanie C's pronouncement was a crisis in what passed as the management of what was left of the group. Emma had just begun promoting her forthcoming single, 'What Took You So Long?', and Nancy Phillips was acutely aware that Emma's campaign was in imminent danger of being buried under an avalanche of speculation about the fate of the Spice Girls. This was hardly fair on

Emma, and on March 10, when Emma was appearing on *CD: UK* Phillips persuaded Mel C to phone in to the programme and retract, on air, what she'd said. "It's not true, it's all fine, the group's still together," Melanie C said, soothingly, if not altogether convincingly.

This dampened down the speculation and solved the immediate problem for Emma, but the situation was getting far too complicated for Phillips.

"I thought, 'I can't do this any more,'" Phillips said. "I just decided that I couldn't cope. I went home from the *CD: UK* studio that day and I decided to quit. Bear in mind, I'm employed by Spice Girls Ltd, and I'm doing all these individual projects. It was ridiculous. So I had to morally, in my head, split myself four ways, but it wasn't what my job was. And it wasn't workable any more."

Phillips handed in her notice through the group's lawyer Andrew Thompson, although her involvement with the group was far from over. She agreed to work out her notice, during which time she set up her own company: 45 Management. Melanie C, with whom she had formed a much closer bond than the other Girls, immediately threw in her lot with Phillips, and asked her to be her manager. Melanie B almost as quickly jumped ship, taking her personal assistant with her, and deleting all diary records relating to her from Phillips's computer before she left, an action which Phillips found baffling and bemusing.

Emma and Victoria opted to stay with Phillips for the time being, only now they were clients of her management company rather than her employers. The fact that they wanted to continue under these circumstances came as rather a surprise to Phillips, and while it didn't exactly solve the problem of her divided loyalties, it did afford her a much greater measure of control over the situation.

It was under this new, halfway house arrangement that Phillips guided Emma and Victoria through the launch of their solo albums. Emma's came first, a cheerful hotchpotch of ballads and pseudo-R&B pop songs that was preceded by the single 'What Took You So Long?' This easygoing, soft rock song, which was illustrated by a classy looking video shot in the Nevada desert, secured her the coveted number one slot the week before the album came out.

In assembling the album, Emma had called on the services of a familiar cast of writing and production names, including Biff Stannard, Spike Stent, Rhett Lawrence and Melanie C's old duetting partner Bryan Adams. A couple of tracks were recorded with Rodney Jerkins, but didn't make the final cut. The result was a collection of pleasant, but disposable tunes, that lacked any clear sense of purpose or direction, let alone adventure.

"*A Girl Like Me* is so safe and derivative it makes Olivia Newton-John sound like Lydia Lunch," Barbara Ellen wrote in *The Times*.

But despite the lukewarm response from the critics, the album, which also included the previous year's hit with Tin Tin Out, 'What I Am', cruised into the chart at number four, equalling the peak positions of both Geri's and Melanie C's albums, and a good way ahead of Melanie B's.

No sooner had Emma's album reached the shops, however, than Geri was back on the promotional merry-go-round with the build-up to her second solo album, *Scream If You Wanna Go Faster*. She had already finished recording the album when she was approached by the film producer Eric Fellner to record a new version of 'It's Raining Men' for the soundtrack of the movie *Bridget Jones's Diary*, starring Hugh Grant and Renee Zellweger. The song had been a number two hit for The Weather Girls in 1984. Geri dashed it off in a day, under the guidance of producer Steve Lipson, and thought no more about it. Then Fellner suggested she put it out as a single. Again, this was not part of the plan, but having been talked into the idea, Geri hurriedly put together a video which was essentially a homage to the Eighties movies *Fame*, *Flashdance* and *Footloose*. Directed by Jake Wynne and James Canty, the video portrayed Geri, supported by a cast of no less than 120 backing performers, as a lithe, vivacious dancer, apparently able to do the splits and even an acrobatic backflip (wasn't that Sporty's trick?).

It had been more than a year since Geri's last hit, 'Bag It Up', since when she had toned up and lost weight. The transformaton in her look was startling enough, but there was also a spontaneity about the song and the video which had a galvanising effect. Released with perfect timing, just as the first of the Eighties revivals was kicking in, 'It's Raining Men' raced to number one, giving Geri her fourth chart-topping single and becoming by far the biggest hit of her solo career.

It was to be the last time that any of the Spice Girls would enjoy a number one record.

With such a massive success to kick things off, and having sold an impressive 1.5 million copies of *Schizophonic*, Geri had high hopes for *Scream If You Wanna Go Faster*, which was duly released in May 2001.

She was the first Spice Girl to put out a second solo album, and in many ways this would be a more rigorous test of her long term prospects for building a solo career than anything that had gone before. While collaborating once again with the tried and tested Absolute team on four of the tracks, Geri had also looked further afield. Producer Steve Lipson, of Eurythmics and Annie Lennox fame, worked with her on five songs, including 'It's Raining Men', while other contributors included Rick Nowels, who had worked with Dido, Texas, Anita Baker and Madonna, and Gregg Alexander of New Radicals fame, who was very much the golden boy of American pop songwriters at that time.

"I am really proud of this album. I have put my whole heart and soul into it over the past year," Geri said.

Unfortunately, *Scream If You Wanna Go Faster* failed to live up to expectations. Geri's appeal as a singer was, by now, beginning to wear a little thin and while there was nothing inherently wrong with the songs, there was something rather too strident about the package as a whole. The cover artwork – featuring Geri on a pair of roller skates, clinging on to the tail fin of a big American car and apparently being dragged along at speed – prompted immediate protests from child safety lobby groups. The back cover picture which featured Geri standing on the front seat of the same open-topped car, bellowing out the song titles through a megaphone, was a joke that seemed to ring a little too true for comfort. Geri's constant clamouring for attention was beginning to yield negative results, even among her core audience, and this was not a reassuring image, however tongue in cheek it was intended to be.

The album entered the chart at number five, a respectable showing, but then quickly started to fall. The release of the title track as the second single did not arrest the decline. The song was something of a departure for Geri. She described it as "by far the most rock'n'roll song I had ever recorded" ascribing its "adrenaline-packed" feel to her newfound enthusiasm for listening to Led Zeppelin. As the other Spice Girls had already discovered, their audience did not respond well to shifts in style that took them too far away from the first principles of pop. The single's arrival in the chart at a meagre number eight in August marked a sea change in Geri's commercial fortunes.

The third and final single from the album, 'Calling', was released at the end of November. Co-written with producer Peter Vettese, the song was a smoochy, string-drenched ballad exploring the nature of "true love". Geri's performance was so soft and knowingly seductive, it was almost as if she was offering the number as some sort of penance for the raucous diversion of *Scream If You Wanna Go Faster*.

"I honestly believe this to be one of the best songs I have ever written," Geri insisted. "Whether the public agrees remains to be seen."

The song peaked at number seven, and Geri had her answer.

While Geri was having to acclimatise to life on the lower rungs of the Top 10, Melanie B was having to make even harsher adjustments to her expectations. 'Lullabye', the third single from Melanie's album peaked at number 13 in June, after which it was announced that she was "parting company" with Virgin Records. In one of her more adroit PR manoeuvres, Melanie seized the initiative with a statement, preceding Virgin's, declaring that: "Melanie, who is still signed to Virgin Records as a Spice Girl, has had an excellent relationship with Virgin Records but feels that it may be more appropriate for her to be at a record company with an urban A&R department. This is the route she is taking musically and she feels that specialist attention here will be of great benefit to her."

Or, to put it another way, she had been dropped by Virgin.

With 'Take My Breath Away', the second single from Emma's album, reaching number five in September, the days of chart battles and the race to notch up another number one already seemed a fading memory by the time Victoria became the last of the Spice Girls to release a solo album in October 2001.

Although Victoria had started off working with Spice stalwarts Elliot Kennedy and Biff Stannard, the songs she ended up recording for *Victoria Beckham* were assembled with the help of numerous producers and writers, most of whom she met and worked with in America. Key among these was an Australian songwriter called Steve Kipner who together with his colleague Andrew Frampton supplied the first single from the album, 'Not Such An Innocent Girl'. Pop with a hint of R&B flavouring was Kipner's speciality, and on tracks such as 'That Kind Of Girl' and 'A Mind Of Its Own', he steered Victoria in an upmarket pop/soul direction that was hardly going to set the town alight, but then again was not going to scare the horses either.

Other contributors to the album included the expatriate Danish duo Soulshock & Karlin (who had worked with Whitney Houston), Rhett Lawrence (who wrote 'Never Be The Same Again' with Melanie C),

Matt Prime, Dane Bowers, Harvey Mason Jr, Damon Thomas and Chris Braide. Musically it was a professional, if rather cautious effort, with Victoria's lyrics tending either to be "intimate" declarations of undying love for David and Brooklyn or romantic fantasies, no doubt starring a certain footballer who played for Manchester United.

Bizarrely, the closest thing to a genius pop song that Victoria had chalked up away from the Spice Girls – 'Out Of Your Mind' – was not included on the album. But whatever the merits of the record, Victoria was up against it in more ways than one. Not only was the perception of her as the least talented member of the group by now firmly entrenched, but *Victoria Beckham* was the *seventh* Spice-related album to be released in less than two-and-a-half years. 'Not Such An Innocent Girl' was the twenty-first Spice-related single over the same period of time. No other act has ever bombarded its audience with so much product in such a short space of time. Talk about audience fatigue. The fans who still had the energy and the money to buy another Spice Girl's record were, by now, getting thin on the ground.

Victoria had the misfortune to release her single, 'Not Such An Innocent Girl' the same week that Kylie Minogue released 'Can't Get You Out Of My Head'. Minogue's song, co-written by Cathy Dennis (still very much a part of Simon Fuller's 19 empire), was one of the biggest hits of the year. There was some half-hearted talk of a "chart battle" between Kylie and Victoria, but in truth, this was never going to be a contest. Kylie crashed in at number one while Victoria had to be content with a number six placing. Under the circumstances, you would have to say that Victoria did well to get her album, released a couple of weeks later, into the Top 10, albeit for just one week, after which it sank like a stone.

One of the more feisty lyrics on the album, which was rather overlooked at the time, was 'Watcha Talkin' Bout', in which an unidentified friend was chastised in no uncertain terms for letting success go to the head: "It started when the fame and fans kept coming in/ And then you changed on us/ Then you told us you were cool and we were wrong." At the time, Geri seemed the obvious target for a dig of this sort, but with the benefit of hindsight, it could equally well have been directed towards Melanie C. "You gotta lot of problems and you need to solve them/ But it's not gonna be with me around, oh no."

A couple of years later, when Victoria released a double A-sided single 'This Groove'/'Let Your Head Go', Melanie C was unusually quick to put the boot in. "I thought it was atrocious," she said in a radio interview on *Heart FM*. "I'm not being horrible, I'm just giving my opinion. I thought it was a terrible song. Lyrically, it was weak. If I was Victoria I would enjoy my husband, enjoy my family, enjoy the money that they've got and give the music a rest. She's got such a great life. I don't know why she doesn't just sit back and enjoy it."

Whether or not Victoria was getting at Melanie or Geri, no one was really interested in the lyrics or the music or anything else to do with her album. For it was already plain by this stage that Victoria's status as an icon far outweighed anything she was likely to accomplish as a singer or songwriter. As one half of the Posh and Becks soap opera, she had turned into something beyond a pop star. She had become a key figure in the daily ebb and flow of British popular culture, a celebrity apparently on a par in many people's minds with the late Diana, Princess of Wales.

This strange state of affairs now applied to a greater or lesser extent to all five of the Spice Girls. And like so much about the group, it was a situation which had no obvious precedent. Their stock as a recording act had never been lower, and indeed their very existence as a collective enterprise was now seriously in doubt. For my own part I suddenly found discussions with book publishers and newspaper editors framed in a completely different way from just a few months before. No one wanted to buy into the Spice Girls any more. They were last year's thing. Finished. I remember coming out of one such meeting with my publishers, in the spring of 2001, where it was decided to shelve the writing of this book for the immediate future. Lack of interest. Walking into the newsagent next door, I glanced at the magazine racks. Geri was on three covers (*New Woman*, *Marie Claire*, *Heat*), while Emma was on the cover of *Sky*, Melanie B was on the cover of *Now* and Victoria (and David) were on the cover of *OK!* The place was more like a Spice shrine than a newsagent. Well, someone must have been interested!

"Today, as you read this, Geri Halliwell is Britain's most famous celebrity," Mark Frith trumpeted in the introduction to his interview in the May 11 edition of *Heat*. "More famous than when she was at number one with 'Wannabe' and the world started going around talking about this newfangled thing called Girl Power. More famous than when she wore that Union Jack dress at the Brits and people reckoned her to be Britain's number one sex symbol. More famous than the day she left the Spice Girls and everyone said they'd be finished without her."

The Spice Girls had become transformed from a pop group into the first of a new breed of über-celebrity. Their success or otherwise as singers had become an incidental part of their lives, which from now on would be lived out almost entirely in the public eye. Geri and Victoria in particular had become objects of intense scrutiny, their bodies, personal relationships, houses, children, pets, diets, shopping habits and fashion accessories all generating a previously unimaginable level of public interest and comment. Thanks to their ubiquitous presence, they became the focus of a continuing love-hate relationship with the public, carefully fostered and orchestrated by the opinion formers and tastemakers of the mass media.

Sometimes the Girls exploited the situation for their own ends. When Victoria found herself appearing on the same bill as not only Geri but also Sophie Ellis-Bextor at an August bank holiday Party In The Park gig in Birmingham, she wore a fake ring through her lip, but told reporters it was real, insisting that it "hurts like hell". She didn't so much upstage Geri and Bextor in the newspapers the next day as annihilate them. *The Sun*, always the most pro-Spice of the redtops, devoted its entire front page to a single, massive, close-up photograph of her face with "more amazing pictures" and commentary on pages 4 and 5.

The Girls undoubtedly benefited from a lot of the publicity. But the tone of the coverage was frequently as mean as its scope was generous. Melanie B's cover story in the May 9 issue of *Now* was accompanied by a big picture of her dress falling off her breasts during a performance at the South Africa Freedom Day concert in Trafalgar Square on April 29, attended by Nelson Mandela. "Hit or bust for Mel B," ran the headline. "Spice Girl Mel B gives crowds an eyeful as industry insiders reckon she's one flop away from being dropped . . ." The story reported Melanie's problems in gleeful detail. She was accused of "crass" vulgarity for the tits-out episode (so prominently illustrated by the magazine), criticised for "using" her daughter on the "cheap and cynical" cover artwork of her forthcoming single 'Lullabye', and warned that her high-spending lifestyle – along with her contract at Virgin Records – could not be expected to last much longer.

If the writers who churned out this stuff weren't taking vindictive sideswipes at the Girls, they were building them up into ever more ridiculous fantasy figures. When Victoria and David paid a brief visit to Venice, the ensuing (unauthorised) report in *OK!* magazine read like a script from *Lifestyles Of The Rich And Famous* adapted to the style of a Mills & Boon romance.

"Since David Beckham and his Spice Girl wife, Victoria, are largely regarded as the most romantic couple in the world, it seems apt that they should be holidaying in Italy's capital of romance. The loving couple made the most of Venice, walking hand in hand through the city's streets and along its canals during a spring break. It was the perfect place to enjoy a second honeymoon and get away from it all." The piece went on to reveal, rather more prosaically, that Victoria had undergone two breast enlargement operations and that David was tired of playing for Manchester United and was planning to relocate to Spain.

Fascinating as all this undoubtedly was to readers of *OK!* magazine, it was unlikely to have anyone queuing up to buy Victoria's records. Her book, however, was another matter. Published the month before her album, and serialised for a ludicrous sum of money by the *Mail On Sunday*, Victoria's autobiography, *Learning To Fly*, was soon lodged at the top of the best-seller lists.

# 13

# Fuller Himself

Slowly but ever more surely, the house of Spice continued to crumble. In October 2001, Melanie C signed a management contract with Nancy Phillips, setting the seal on a professional relationship which has continued up to the time of writing. Perhaps it was no coincidence that in the same month Victoria, with her book soaring and her album floundering, decided to part company with Phillips.

Victoria had always been unstinting in her praise of Phillips. Indeed the dedication to her among the "Thank Yous" on the *Victoria Beckham* CD insert, was as fulsome as any manager could hope to receive from a star client. "My manager, Nancy Phillips, who not only organises my life and keeps me working hard, but her experience in the music business is second to none. She has become a close friend rather than just a working colleague."

The close friendship came under strain, however, when *The Sun* ran a big feature on Victoria and David, using a photograph that had been lifted from a German TV programme which the couple had appeared on together. Victoria was wearing a diamond necklace and David had on a pair of diamond earrings. The commentary accompanying the picture made a big song and dance about the couple putting their considerable wealth on such vulgar display. Already stung by the hostile reaction to her album, Victoria was furious about this latest piece of negative coverage.

"I told you, I didn't want any press," she said to Phillips.

"If you're on TV and they take a picture of that, you can't control it," Phillips replied.

"That's your job, to control it," Victoria said. "You shouldn't have allowed it to get into the press."

It was later reported that Victoria had left Phillips because the manager had allowed her to become "overexposed". Despite this row, Phillips insisted that she and Victoria parted on good terms.

"She was mad over that story," Phillips said. "And I had views on other things, as well, which I'm not discussing. But we did get on well. It was always amicable with all of them. But at certain times I think I was blamed for things which I don't think was fair. But I do think there was too much for any one person to do effectively. Which is why the deal needed restructuring."

So then there were two. With Christmas coming, the next question to be addressed was which song should be the third single from Emma's album. Having followed up 'What Took You So Long?' with the reasonably successful 'Take My Breath Away', a number five hit in September, Emma had once again been quickly eclipsed, this time by Victoria's campaign. So the pressure was on to come up with a sufficiently strong single to remind people that Emma was still around, and hopefully lift her album back into the chart. Unfortunately, it wasn't that straightforward.

"By now the cracks were showing," Phillips said. "There was a lot of wavering. Virgin weren't confident about what that next single should be. I wasn't confident. I don't think anyone was. Emma wanted a strong view. I think she felt that lack of confidence from me, possibly."

The song they eventually settled on was 'We're Not Gonna Sleep Tonight', a breezy, Latin-tinged dance track written by Emma and Rhett Lawrence. With a pleasant but strangely forgettable chorus, it was the sort of song that George Michael might knock out in his lunch break. Launched at exactly the right time to be the Christmas number one, it scraped into the chart at number 20, yet another new low for a single by a Spice Girl.

"Maybe we picked the wrong one," Phillips said. "But to be honest I don't think there was a lot of choice. I remember thinking what a fantastic single 'What Took You So Long?' was. It was a sweet album, but I don't think it had another obvious smash song on there."

Virgin, whose belief in the long term viability of the Spice Girls had gone beyond wobbly and into full-scale meltdown, took this as their cue to inform Emma that they were dropping her from the label. Emma wasn't at all happy about this turn of events, and, as with Melanie B and Victoria before her, she held Phillips accountable to some extent for the downturn in her fortunes.

As 2002 began, the lease on the Bell Street office was coming to an end. In February, as Phillips was clearing out the office prior to moving, Emma let it be known that she would not be going with her. The association was ended with a straightforward phone call to Phillips. No fuss, no tears, no more Baby.

In the same month Victoria released the second and final single from her album, 'A Mind Of Its Own'. Another Steve Kipner and Andrew Frampton composition, this time written in collaboration with Victoria, the song was a familiar sounding slice of pop/R&B-lite with a low, mumbled, spoken-word verse that couldn't have been better designed to fuel the Victoria-can't-sing myth if that's what they had been trying to do. It reached number six in the chart, selling little more than 15,000 copies all told. And that was that. It would be more than a year before another record by a Spice Girl was released.

"It was the end of an incredible phenomenon," Phillips said, looking back on her time with the Spice Girls. "Simon Fuller was obviously involved when it was at its peak and it was exciting and amazing. I was involved when it was past its peak. And I feel, OK, I held it together for a while and did the solo things, but I don't think you can ever recreate that kind of excitement."

Had the Spice Girls paid her well for her work?

"Reasonably."

Considering all the effort that she had put in?

"No. But I have to say they were very appreciative. What I will say is that there is no man in this business who would have done what I did for that salary."

Had they taken advantage of her?

"No. I don't think that they did. I think that they didn't know any better, and I was a fool. But I have absolutely no regrets at all. They all had something amazing. It was an amazing thing to be a part of. It isn't really about money, and I've never really worked for the money. But you still can't help knowing that really for the amount of work that I did, it probably wasn't sufficient. It was fun. It was great. And the main thing now is that I absolutely love working with Melanie C. So ultimately it led me back to a working relationship that I love with an artist that I love. So, what more could you ask for? The end result was perfect for me."

Maybe so. But for all her efforts on behalf of the Spice Girls, the bond between Phillips and Melanie C had magnified the group's underlying problems in the post-Fuller era. The more involved Phillips became in Melanie's solo career, the more compromised she was as a manager.

"She loved and supported Melanie, which was great," one observer said. "But there was a real conflict of interests when it came to promoting the group and other members of the group. It was an underlying fault line in everything that happened."

An unaccustomed lull descended on Spiceworld. But as one era in pop quietly drew to a close, so another was bursting into life with all the rapacious vigour and ugly consequences of the alien bursting out of John Hurt's chest.

Just as Victoria's single, 'A Mind Of It's Own', was completing its gentle descent down the chart, the debut single by Hear'say, 'Pure And Simple', came crashing in at number one. The song remained in the UK singles chart for half a year. Hear'say were the product of *Popstars*, an eight-week talent contest screened on ITV, in which the "ultimate manufactured band" had been assembled from an initial cast of 3,000 applicants. The brutal audition process by which this had been achieved had entertained around 10 million viewers every week, many of whom were not regular record buyers but had nevertheless invested sufficient time and interest in the resulting band to warrant the purchase of their first single.

Music journalists, A&R departments, pluggers, PRs, radio programmers, record companies, in fact all the established power brokers in the hitmaking process had been bypassed, at a stroke, in the making of this phenomenon. Replacing them had been a small panel of "experts", whose job it was to pass comment and weed out the candidates who didn't make the grade. It was like the big bang. A new pop universe had been created and with it a new audience located – an audience that liked a nice tune and a friendly face and a personality that would generate a bit of gossip at the water cooler, but who otherwise really weren't that bothered about music, per se.

Only the manager retained his importance in this new scheme of things. In Hear'say's case that role was taken by the Spice Girls' old mentor and manager-without-contract, Chris Herbert. You wonder whether he felt a sinking sense of déjà-vu as he clocked Simon Fuller popping his head around the reality TV door. For although he was not involved in *Popstars*, Fuller was quick to spot the potential of the idea – rather as he had been quick to spot the potential of the Spice Girls when they came looking for a manager. With the spadework having, once again, been taken care of by someone else, Fuller swung into action with his own TV talent contest. In devising *Pop Idol* he refined the "manufacturing" process so that the quest was for an individual pop star rather than a group and, crucially, the public were invited to cast the deciding vote, a simple device guaranteed to give them a compelling stake in the fortunes of the winning act.

"I've been dubious about A&R people for many years, because I am one of them," Fuller said. "My first thought was always to want to make music for the public. But for the most part A&R guys are making records for themselves and their tastes, and saying to the record-buying public, 'This is what you should be liking.' There's a real arrogance. But you shouldn't be arrogant about music. Music is for everyone. What I do that is different to most of the A&R community is acknowledge that fact and embrace it. People like to paint people such as myself as the ones who create everything, market it and ram it down the public's throat. But that's not the case. I think the public choose a lot more than we like to admit. It would make my life a lot easier if I *could* tell people what to buy."

Fuller went on to realise his grand populist vision on an international scale, duplicating the massive success of *Pop Idol* firstly in America, with *American Idol* – the final of which attracted 30 million television viewers – and then, in 2003, with its global equivalent *World Idol*. By May 2004, it was reported that the total votes cast by *Pop Idol*'s TV audiences in the 29 countries where the show was made had passed 700 million.

The record industry is still struggling to absorb the lessons of this success. The old model of marketing a pop act, whereby you get on the playlist at Radio One, secure a bit of exposure on MTV and blag a few cover stories in the music press, was beginning to look not only out of date but also fatally one-dimensional by the time Will Young was establishing himself as a star with the potential to rival Robbie Williams. In a beleaguered record industry, when even a successful pop act may barely recoup the massive expenses involved in old-style promotion and marketing, Fuller was making profits on pop acts that most record companies could only dream of through his synergetic use of mainstream multi-media outlets and promotional tie-ins. *Pop Idol* generated CD sales in unheard-of quantities: Will Young's 'Evergreen'/'Anything Is Possible' single sold an astonishing 1.1 million copies *in its first week*, while 'Unchained Melody' by Gareth Gates was

## Fuller Himself

the only other single to sell a million copies in Britain in 2002. Not only that, but *Pop Idol* also got ITV its Saturday night audience back.

A key element of the Fuller method was to keep as much of the process as possible in-house. Employing the talents of his team of songwriters and producers at 19 to generate songs and recordings in tandem with the artists he had "created" and managed, Fuller used any routes he could think of to mass-market pop as never before. It was estimated – albeit by the music-biz online gossip site *Popbitch*, hardly the most reliable of sources – that nearly a quarter of all recorded music sales in the UK in the year to September 2002 had some connection with 19. On January 9, 2004, just after the second British *Pop Idol* contest had thrown up Michelle McManus as the winner, there was an edition of *Top Of The Pops* in which four of the eight acts featured were managed by Fuller – and those that weren't all sounded as if they should have been.

Fuller adapted pop to the age of instant communication and its attendant cult of instant celebrity. He made pop simple, accessible, universal and, of course, disposable. Pop was no longer something that was exclusively aimed at kids; after *Pop Idol* it became an integral part of mainstream family entertainment, as cheerful, unthreatening and inconsequential as *The Generation Game* and *Celebrity Squares*.

You could even join up the dots from the *Pop Idol* Big Band album, released in April 2002, to the explosion of interest in smooth jazz and easy listening that overtook the pop world at the start of 2004.

Fuller was not the first to dabble in that strand of music; Robbie Williams had enjoyed huge success with his *Swing When Your Winning* album released in December 2001, and George Michael had done something similar with his *Songs From The Last Century*, released at the very end of 1999. But Fuller claimed to have had the idea before them. Not only that, but in his own mind he believed that *Pop Idol* aspired to an aesthetic that took its cue from the classic era of lounge jazz and quality easy listening that preceded the rock'n'roll revolution of the Fifties.

"What that era represented to me was great songs and great singers," he said in 2002. "And I think that's been overlooked recently. Radiohead and U2 are clearly great bands, but are they conventionally great singers? I'm not saying they need to be. But for me the great voices are Ella Fitzgerald, Billie Holiday, Frank Sinatra. And what I wanted was to create a platform for great singers to do great songs again." Fuller had nothing to do with Norah Jones or Katie Melua, but his activities and influence in mobilising an older mainstream record-buying audience undoubtedly contributed to the climate in which it was possible for those artists to flourish.

The group that had made Fuller's success possible was, of course, the Spice Girls, and his onwards march towards world domination must be accounted, for better or worse, a key element of their legacy. In a practical sense, it was the unprecedented success of the Spice Girls that gave Fuller the platform on which to build his extraordinary empire. He made them into a seven day wonder the like of which had never been seen before. But they, for their part, turned him from a successful pop manager into a global entrepreneur. Like the booster rockets that propel a spaceship free of the Earth's gravity, the Spice Girls provided the initial stupendous burst of momentum that Fuller was looking for. His success since then has been such that by August 2003 he had overseen 96 number one singles and 79 number one albums in Britain and America alone. His personal fortune was estimated in the *Sunday Times* Rich List of 2004 to be £220 million and rising. Astronomical, indeed.

The Spice Girls must also take their share of responsibility in a philosophical sense for the seismic changes that were wrought on the pop landscape in their wake. They were the first group fully to grasp the requirements of the new era. They came up via the audition route, and thanks to the *Raw Spice* documentary, unwittingly provided a prototype for the reality TV bands that followed. They didn't think in terms of the video and the dance routine and the costume change as separate add-ons to the music; they envisaged the package as a whole. Their hunger for fame was so intense that they made preceding icons, like Madonna, seem demure by comparison. They aspired to a level of instantaneous international success that pop groups had previously only dreamt of – and they achieved it. And they played the fame game with shameless enthusiasm, helping to create a new strata of celebrity, where pop stardom bled into a broader continuum of cultural activity that embraced the worlds of sport, the soaps, fashion, film and reality TV.

Much of what followed on from the Spice Girls was pretty awful. On the one hand you had old rock'n'roll rebels suddenly being absorbed into the new pop reality. From Ozzy Osbourne, former Wild Man Of Rock, performing 'Paranoid' at a Royal Command performance in the grounds of Buckingham Palace to Johnny Rotten, former Wild Man Of Punk, disporting himself in the company of Peter Andre and Jordan on *I'm A Celebrity Get Me Out Of Here*, it seemed that no memory was safe. At the other extreme, wave upon wave of manufactured acts came crashing on to the shore: from boy/girl bands such as B★Witched, Atomic Kitten, Girls Aloud and One True Voice to pop idols including Will Young, Gareth Gates, Darius Danesh and Lemar all the way through to a rockier strand of groups like McFly, Busted and V who arrived in 2004 brandishing guitars and spiky haircuts along with their business plans and investment portfolios. The original wannabes – the kids in the Byrds song who just got an electric guitar, and took some time and learnt how to play – would have been horrified to see where it had all ended up.

Still, just as you can't blame Jimi Hendrix for every overblown guitar solo that was inspired by 'Voodoo Chile', it seems a little harsh to pin the rap on the Spice Girls for *all* of this. They were just as taken aback by many of these developments as anyone else.

"We were very lucky," Melanie C said, looking back on things later, "because we, as a group, were very strong and by the time we got to Simon Fuller and Virgin Records we knew what we wanted to do. But we were still in danger of being manipulated. Now these kids [in *Popstars* and other manufactured bands] are going through the same traumas that we went through but they're not writing their own material. It's all masterminded by record companies, managers, writers and publishers; they create everything and therefore get all the money, so these poor kids are going through hell and won't have anything to show for it."

"We started the whole trend, and it worked," Melanie C said in 2001. "But now it's got out of control. Girl Power worked. But it is time to put the genie back in the bottle. We need a musical revolution right now. There's great bands who can't get a look in because record companies are only interested in the safe bet, which means pop bands, young girls, young boys and getting younger.

"What pisses me off is that I think music should be educational. For me, listening to The Beatles is an education. But I can't learn anything from Steps. And the kids can't learn anything from Steps. Only how to be very cheesy and tacky and very ripped off. I haven't got a grudge against Steps. I think they work hard. I just don't like what they're doing, I don't like the people behind it and I don't like the music they come out with. Aren't they ashamed of the shit they're producing?"

You would think from the number of times that the Spice Girls must have heard the very same question posed of themselves, that Melanie might have hesitated before leaping astride this particular hobby horse. But for her the idea that the Spice Girls might have paved the way for the emergence of a band like Steps was bad enough. Any suggestion that the Spice Girls were in some way comparable to Steps was beyond her comprehension. Quite right too.

Fuller on the other hand was a lot more seriously implicated in the creation of this new pop order. His first venture after the split with the Spice Girls was S Club 7, a project which he described as "a new concept in youth culture". The act was a seven-piece boy-girl group who starred as themselves in a BBC TV series called *Miami 7*, about a pop band trying to make it big in America.

"Pop music is about celebrity and not just about music any more, and people haven't quite figured it out yet," Fuller said in March 1999 at the time of the group's launch. "Pop stars should be icons. S Club 7 will take the extreme end of the pop industry that is dominating the charts and make it more acceptable and broaden it out, taking it out of pop music and spreading it across entertainment."

According to Fuller, the members of the group, who were selected at auditions, were chosen because they could "do everything". The Spice Girls, he said, had been "great at some things and poor at others. I didn't just want another pop band."

But what Fuller also didn't want was another band that would answer him back.

"I did the auditions for the best part of a year, and I just thought, 'I want a group that are really quite gentle and pleasant.' I went out of my way to get a nice bunch of kids. I wanted them to be as talented as possible. And I wanted them to work well together as a unit. But the most important thing when I was considering who to choose was, 'Do I like this person?' I didn't want to go through all the battling I had with the Spice Girls. I couldn't go through all that again. S Club 7 were a really nice group. I don't know them as closely as I did the Spice Girls. But I don't want to."

S Club 7 became another global success story. By the time the TV show got to its third series, it was running in 104 countries. And by April 2003, when it was announced that the group were splitting up, they had sold an estimated 12 million albums. But the vast bulk of the fortune they earned ended up in 19 Management's coffers. According to a report in *The Sun*, S Club 7 had generated estimated earnings of £50 million of which the members of the group themselves had actually pocketed a mere £590,000 each (£4.13 million altogether).

Nice work for Fuller then, but there was simply no comparison with what he had achieved with the Spice Girls. Not even close. S Club 7's fame was never more than skin deep. They may briefly have been highly successful entertainers but, although Rachel Stevens subsequently became a familiar face in the gossip mags, none of them would have passed the cabbie recognition test. They sold a lot of records but influenced no one. So maybe they did extend their appeal as an otherwise common or garden pop group to a broader audience in search of general "entertainment", but as a source of interest or significance within the broader scope of planet pop they were utterly irrelevant.

Fuller knew all this, and try as he might, he could never quite hide the sense of regret he felt for being denied the opportunity to finish off what he started with the Spice Girls – what he called, with typical understatement, "the one little smudge on my CV".

"Time rolled on," Fuller said, "and there were moments when I could see what was going on and I would just feel, 'God! if they only did this or that.' When Geri left, for instance, I remember it so vividly. They should have replaced her. They should have turned it into a global search for a girl to replace Geri. I thought to myself, 'This could be the *Gone With The Wind* of auditions.' It would completely have stolen her thunder. I would just have loved to have orchestrated that. But the problem with that was that because they had chosen to be on their own without me, they couldn't acknowledge that any of them were replaceable. They couldn't accept it in their minds. Because if they had been able to replace Geri that would have meant that they were replaceable. And they couldn't make that leap. But it was a huge mistake not to replace her."

Fuller pointed to other parts of his masterplan that had been jettisoned when he had been given the sack, and how history might have been different if he had been allowed to see the job through.

"It went wrong for them at the worst time, because the second album [*Spiceworld*] was about the movie and the first world tour. My plan was to put a massive amount of money into the production of that world tour and turn it into a pop show on a scale that had never been seen before. I would have made it comparable to one of Madonna's shows, maybe even have spent more money than her on it. The profits would have come from the sponsorship and the merchandising, which would have been millions. But when I parted company from them two things happened. They cut back on the production spend – my production would have been about three times what they ended up spending, maybe more. And then a lot of the sponsorship deals didn't happen, because they didn't know how to do them. And they actually ended up losing money on that tour."

Fuller had also planned to make another feature film out of the world tour which he would then have tied in to the third album. The idea was to film the girls during the tour in the style of the movie *Grand Prix*, starring Steve McQueen, in which bits of cinéma vérité were mixed with improvised scenes and scripted sequences in such a way that you could never be quite sure what was real and what was fictional.

"It would have been a mixture of reality and fiction with a comedic edge," Fuller explained. "The album would have been kind of live and kind of greatest hits and while that was being done they could have taken a year out to recover and recharge their batteries, have their babies, whatever they wanted to do. The first movie [*Spiceworld*] made them millions. The next movie could have made more. I couldn't believe it never happened. And it would have helped maintain the momentum. Instead, they had this long gap before the third album and lost momentum. Momentum is everything in pop music. Look at Madonna. One of the things that goes unnoticed with her is the sheer momentum. She's unbelievable. She's like a machine. You never get more than two years without hearing something from Madonna. And that is more the key to her success than working with the great producers and people she finds."

Needless to say, when *Forever* eventually did come out, Fuller was not impressed.

"They decided to make an American-sounding album, which was a huge mistake. It was bad A&Ring. A total fuck up," he said. "They thought they could do it on their own. And because they tended to like black music, which basically people their age do, they made the fatal mistake of thinking they could make an album of that sort of music. Geri was a lot more cunning. She used Absolute, who are one of my producer teams, and she tried to capture the old sound. But then she can't sing, so she was always being restricted by her own lack of talent. She couldn't really carry it off. She can't go to America and sing live on *David Letterman*."

## Fuller Himself

For Fuller, the Spice Girls would always feel like unfinished business, and in hindsight it was not *so* surprising that, in March 2002, only a few weeks after Emma had left Nancy Phillips, Fuller announced he had signed her up to 19 Management as a solo act. At the time, however, this seemed like a baffling turn of events. Why Emma? She had just been dropped by Virgin and had emerged with the poorest prospects of any of the five former Spice Girls. Melanie C had a stronger voice, Geri had a higher profile and both had sold millions of records as solo acts. Victoria was a media phenomenon while even Melanie B seemed to have more presence and star potential as an individual act.

Another surprise. When he signed Emma, Fuller let it be known that four out of the five Spice Girls "including Geri" had approached him "either directly or indirectly" to manage them as solo acts.

The three Girls who had written autobiographies had all tacitly admitted that, whatever the personal issues at the time, firing Fuller had turned out to be a poor business decision.

Geri, whose solo career had been managed with mixed results, first by organiser of the Brits, Lisa Anderson, and then by George Michael's manager, Andy Stephens, looked back ruefully, on her real motives for wanting to oust Fuller.

"I thought I could fix my internal problems by fixing something external, which was why I thought we should part company with Simon Fuller. Looking back, Simon was a wonderful manager and I wouldn't be where I am today without him but, at the time, I believed that we needed a change. For a while it felt great that the girls and I were in control again . . . The downside was that, without Simon, taking on the world was a tiring business."

Melanie B recalled her own moment of truth when, in December 1999, she suggested that the Spice Girls should plan another tour.

"The others just looked at me as if I was mad. Babies, husbands, boyfriends and solo careers had made the prospect of touring again seem very remote. Maybe things would have been different if we hadn't been managing ourselves. I know things would have been different if we'd still been with Simon."

And Victoria also saw things differently in retrospect.

"For years I said how much I hated him – and he did do things that were wrong – but now I have a lot of respect for him. It's taken a long time for me to come to the conclusion that – in some aspects at least – he had to do what he did. It was hard to admit because I had been hurt, we all had, and that made me angry. But the constant promotion that nearly pushed us over the edge with exhaustion helped make us as successful as we were, and the only way you can keep five such strong people together is to rule them with a rod of iron. Now that I can stand back I understand how it happened."

"I knew it would come around," Fuller said in 2002, with only a hint of smugness. "I knew they would come back, either one at a time or as a group. It gives me personal satisfaction that it has gone full circle. They're all in really tough situations. They are an unattractive proposition. I can't imagine why any top flight manager would want to go there. They'll never be as big as they were. The only person that can go there is me. If I ever did something with them as a group, it would be in an obvious way: a ten year anniversary or to launch a *Greatest Hits* album. I'd put together something and come up with a way of making it work."

But why did he choose Emma?

"Because she is the nicest girl. She's really pleasant, she will always listen, she's just the nicest person. And I won't do anything in my life unless I enjoy it. I'm happy to help her. I don't need to manage her. Just the fact that she was humble and cool about things. I went round to her house and her mum was there and we just talked about it. And after about ten minutes, after she'd asked me a couple of questions that had been bugging her and I asked her a couple of things that had been bugging me I could just see it in her face – God! What a fuck up this has been.

"Emma, in her current position, I can help her. I can take her up. I'm not saying I can take her to the stars or anything bigger and better, but it's a good deal. I get the personal satisfaction that I've been acknowledged. And she doesn't want to give up. So it's mutual."

Fuller also confessed a particular fondness for Emma's voice.

"She's not a powerful singer, but she can sing in tune. She's got a very distinctive, pleasant voice. It's melodic and it's sweet, and if you listen back to those Spice Girls records and took Emma's vocal out of the equation, you'd miss a lot of what their sound was. She is absolutely a better singer than Geri."

Fuller was not the only fan of Emma's voice.

LaShawn Daniels remembered that when he and the Jerkins brothers were working on the *Forever* sessions, all three of them agreed that Emma's was the voice best suited to their musical vision.

## Fuller Himself

"Baby Spice was the one more geared towards doing lead vocals as far as the verse and when you first open up the composition of a song," Daniels said. "We always felt that she should start it off because she'd got that particular tone."

Producer Jimmy Jam, who also worked with the Girls on *Forever*, went further.

"The Spice Girl I would most have enjoyed doing a solo album with would have been Emma," he said. "Her voice was just fantastic. Not only her voice but her instincts. If you didn't give her something to sing, she would just kinda sing it on her own. She just had the most intriguing voice to me. When I heard her sing I just wanted to write songs. We [Jam & Lewis] said, 'When you do your solo record, call us.' Because we really wanted to work with her. It never happened. But I think of *all* the people we've worked with she's got one of the purest voices and the best instincts of where to sing. She doesn't have the confidence, or at least she didn't have it then. Still to this day, I'd love to work with her on a record. I think she is fan-tas-tic."

Such votes of confidence were all very well. But in the spring of 2002, when Fuller signed her, you would have got very long odds indeed on Emma being the one most likely to build a successful solo career from the ruins of the Spice Girls. How would Fuller go about it?

"I can help, immediately," he said. "What's coming up? We've got the Jubilee pop concert in Buckingham Palace. Right. I go to the organisers. 'You want Annie [Lennox], S Club 7, Will [Young] and you want Emma, don't you?' 'Oh, we hadn't thought about Emma.' Well, I happen to know that they've approached another Spice Girl, but now it's going to be Emma on the bill. What I want to do is position her as the keeper of the Spice Girls flame. So I will get her on the bill and then I'm hoping they will let her sing '2 Become 1'."

Emma did indeed perform at the show, and was the only Spice Girl to do so, although she didn't get to sing '2 Become 1'.

Victoria was the fourth Spice Girl to leave Virgin. Like Melanie B and Emma before her, she had proved an expensive property for the record company to maintain. Her album had sold 50,000 copies, which would have been a promising start for a newcomer, but represented a disappointing and costly decline from the multi-million sales figures she had notched up as a member of the Spice Girls. However, the timing of Virgin's decision was complicated by the announcement on February 22 that Victoria was expecting her second child.

A statement by John Glover, who managed Victoria's affairs temporarily after she parted company with Phillips, said: "It is wonderful news and we are very pleased for them. Victoria will be continuing with her work and we are currently planning the promotion of her third single."

Virgin, anxious that their decision to sever ties with Victoria did not appear to have been influenced by the fact that she was pregnant, postponed the inevitable announcement – although not for very long. No third single from the album was released, and after months of increasing speculation, it was confirmed in June 2002 that Victoria's recording contract with Virgin had "come to a natural end".

Victoria gave birth to her second son, Romeo, on September 1. The responsibilities of motherhood put the brakes on her musical and other career aspirations for a while, although she was no longer able to retreat from the public eye. Whatever she and David did, whether they wanted it to be reported or not, was now deemed newsworthy. With the dust beginning to settle on the Spice Girls, it became apparent that while Victoria had made the smallest commercial impression as a solo performer, she had emerged from the group as far and away the biggest individual celebrity. She had logged the least sales as a solo act, and remains the only Spice Girl not to have had her own number one hit. But, in a supreme irony which virtually defined the values of the new era, it was she (and David) who inherited the media kingdom the Spice Girls had created.

For a period after she left Nancy Phillips, Victoria's affairs were managed on a de facto basis by the Spice Girls' independent press officer Alan Edwards, who also did David's PR (but not his management, which was taken care of by Tony Stephens of the sports agency SFX). Edwards, who runs his own Outside Organization, delegated a lot of the day-to-day dealings with the Beckhams to his assistant, Caroline McAteer.

There was a grim inevitability to what happened next. In July 2003 it was announced that Victoria had returned to Simon Fuller's 19 Management – and that she was taking David with her. Not only that, but Fuller had engaged the services of McAteer, who along with independent PR Julian Henry was going to set up a new consultancy, within the 19 Entertainment company, with a view to cornering the market in manufacturing the next generation of footballing celebrities.

The Girls on stage without Geri at the Forum in Los Angeles during the US tour in the summer of 1998. "I was really kinda mad that Geri had quit...," a fan from Virginia wrote in her internet diary. "But when they opened with 'If You Can't Dance' and 'Who Do You Think You Are' I didn't even miss her." *(Jen Lowery/LFI)*

Half of the group were pregnant: Melanie B and Victoria on stage for a soundcheck. *(Dean Freeman)*

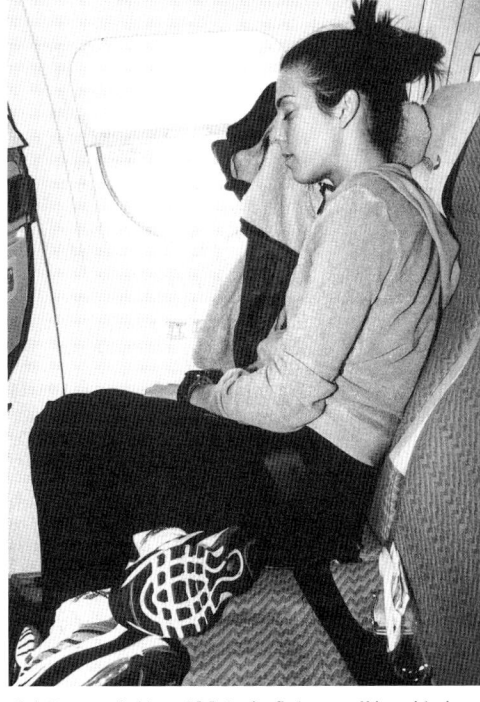

And the other half were knackered: Emma on stage at the LA Forum (left) and Melanie C dozes off in mid-air.
*(left: Jen Lowery/LFI, right: Dean Freeman)*

Melanie B and Jimmy Gulzar together at the London Fashion Week. They met in January 1998, were married on September 13, and the divorce papers had come through by the summer of 1999.
*(Dave Hogan/Getty Images)*

David Beckham and Victoria, soon to be crowned 'Posh'n'Becks' announce their engagement in January 1998. "If you don't ring me," Victoria told him after their second meeting, "I'm going to kick you in the bollocks next time I see you." *(Dave Hogan/Getty Images)*

While Melanie B and Victoria retired from the fray to have babies, Emma and Melanie B took up the slack by travelling around the world to collect the numerous awards heaped upon the Girls. Here they are at the MTV Awards in Milan. *(Grazia Neri/LFI)*

Geri addresses the United Nations in her capacity as a "goodwill ambassador" for the UN Population Fund, her brief being to promote the benefits of birth control in the third world. *(LFI)*

Emma on stage at the Jazz Café, London, with Tin Tin Out, October 1999. *(David Fisher/LFI)*

A spikey haired Melanie C on stage at the Mayan Theatre, Denver, October 1999. *(Jen Lowery/LFI)*

A straight haired Melanie B on stage in Plymouth, August 2000. *(Geoff Swain/LFI)*

Victoria at the 2001 August bank holiday Party In The Park gig in Birmingham, where she wore a fake ring through her lip, thus guaranteeing front page tabloid coverage the next day. *(Dave Hogan/Getty Images)*

Geri camps it up on the Pepsi Chart Show in 2000. As solo artists, Emma, Geri and Victoria often made personal appearances at clubs such as G.A.Y. at the Astoria in London where they were always greeted with wild enthusiasm. *(WJO/Rex Features)*

The four-girl Spice Girls accept their Lifetime Achievement Award at the Brit Awards, March 3, 2000. The fact that the Spice Girls were still engaged in a career which could hardly have been deemed to have lasted a lifetime or anything like it, was glossed over with vague references to their dominance of the decade which had just passed. *(David Fisher/LFI)*

At the same 2000 Brit awards Geri was nominated for Best Pop Act and there was much speculation that she might be invited to rejoin the group for the occasion. In the event she declined and performed her new single 'Bag It Up', emerging down a pole as if from a giant vagina. This was not a concept that won her much critical approval, although as she later noted in her memoirs, "It seemed I had got their attention." *(David Fisher/LFI)*

The Spice Girls quartet pose with their wax models at Madame Tussauds. *(Colin Mason/LFI)*

The Forever album launch party, November 2000. "A disaster," recalled Alan Edwards. "… a horrible night. Mel B was partying, but really partying, while C just didn't want to be there… I remember the four of them on the stairs. Emma was practically in tears. Victoria was trying to pull the two Melanies into line. It was all over the place." *(Richard Young/Rex Features)*

On stage in Stockholm, November 16, 2000 at the MTV Europe Awards – the last time the Spice Girls appeared on stage together. They were not allocated their usual star dressing rooms, and found themselves attracting much less attention backstage than Jennifer Lopez and Eminem. The next day, they were largely ignored by both press and television, an experience which they found infinitely more humiliating than being slagged off by them.
*(Dave Hogan/Getty Images)*

Fuller himself in 2001: "Simon has a good relationship with all of the Spice Girls," says his PR, Julian Henry. "Obviously he speaks to Emma and Victoria the most. But he has spoken to Melanie C, and he enjoys cordial relations with all of them. He is keeping his irons in the fire for when the time is right." *(Richard Young/Rex Features)*

Fuller promised to manage and guide Victoria's career, while overseeing "joint ventures revolving around the Beckham brand".

"I now have the time, energy, vigour and ambition to continue to bring up my family whilst pursuing my career," Victoria said. "Having stayed in touch with Simon over the years, I know there is no one better to help me achieve my dreams and I'm very much looking forward to the future."

"With the Beckham name so renowned the world over for music, fashion and football, there are no boundaries to what we can achieve together," Fuller added, ominously.

While Emma and Victoria set about rebuilding their solo careers under the guidance of Fuller, Melanie C returned to the fray, full of optimism, in the spring of 2003, with the release of her second album *Reason*. If any of the Spice Girls had cause to feel confident about her prospects at this juncture, it was Melanie. Her first album had been a significant success, earning triple-platinum honours in the UK (for sales of 900,000 copies). Not only that, but she had toured her arse off, the only one of the Girls to have done so, thereby building up a solid grass-roots following that was separate from her Spice Girls' fan base. She was widely acknowledged as the most talented singer (even if Jimmy Jam, Simon Fuller and LaShawn Daniels all begged to differ). What could go wrong?

*Reason* is what went wrong. Despite marshalling some initially promising material with the assistance of a vast roll call of writers and producers – including Rick Nowels, Gregg Alexander, Matt Rowe, Phil Thornalley, Guy Chambers, Tore Johansson, David Arnold and Dave Munday, among others – Melanie opted for an upmarket, middle-of-the-road production which rendered the finished album about as exciting as a bowl of rice pudding. Perhaps it was due to Melanie mistakenly thinking that it was time for her to "grow up" and aim her music at a more mature market. Perhaps it was a case of Virgin dictating a safety-first policy at a time when the music industry was experiencing a series of savage contractions, and the company was gripped by a fear of taking risks or making mistakes. Either way, the net result was an album of manicured "adult" pop that had been systematically relieved of all its youthful sparkle and zest.

The reviews, some of which were unbelievably harsh, pointed to the lack of flair and failure of nerve that seemed to beset the album.

"With the cheerful miscellany of *Northern Star* in mind, there is something disappointing, and inevitable, about Chisholm's second album," Alexis Petridis wrote in the *Guardian*. "The eclecticism has been ruthlessly stripped away and replaced with the standard mature-pop blueprint. Its gently strummed acoustic guitars, shuffling trip-hop breakbeats and earnest piano ballads were constructed by a crack writing team . . . but it is somehow empty, and sounds as if it has been focus-grouped into existence."

A Top 10 placing for the first single, 'Here It Comes Again', and for the album itself, which reached number five when it was released in March, briefly fuelled hopes that *Reason*, like *Northern Star*, would prove to be a slow burner. In the event it was more a damp squib.

Clutching at straws, Nancy Phillips, who was by this time managing Melanie full time, put the blame for the ensuing disaster on the choice of 'On The Horizon' as the second single. This bouncy pop/soul song had been co-written by Gregg Alexander who, having built an entire career out of composing endless permutations of his New Radicals hit 'You Get What You Give', had evidently seen no reason to break the habit of a lifetime at this point.

"Melanie was never happy with 'On The Horizon'," Phillips said. "It was the obvious radio smash, but it was the wrong second single. We should have gone with the title track of the album and hooked into the older market. The song 'Reason' was more a reflection of what Melanie's about. 'On The Horizon' wasn't. And I think people can smell that. She came across uncomfortable."

Uncomfortable as Melanie may have felt about that song, it was nothing compared to the discomfort she experienced when she wrenched her cruciate knee ligament while participating in the Channel 4 series *The Games*. The damage required hospital treatment, and with her movement severely impaired for many weeks, her promotional activities had to be curtailed accordingly. With the album campaign unravelling around her ears, Virgin released the third single from the album. Again opting not to release the title track, they went for a double A-side, 'Melt'/'Yeh Yeh Yeh', combining a rather anaemic piano ballad with a remedial disco-rock track. In peaking at number 27 in the chart it became the least successful single ever released by a Spice Girl, and hammered the final nail into the coffin of Melanie's deal with Virgin.

"I've had a shit year," she said, with some feeling, towards the end of her gig at London's Astoria on December 20, 2003. This poorly attended event cruelly underlined how far and how fast Melanie's star had fallen. Whereas she had finished her previous British tour at Wembley Arena (capacity, 11,000) now she could not even sell out the 2,000-capacity Astoria. Indeed, the place was so empty it felt more like a private function than a public gig. Her right leg was still encased in a surgical support brace from calf to thigh, although this didn't prevent her from clumping around the stage in a hefty pair of biker boots and a silver miniskirt, and turning her back every two minutes to hitch up her bra as if she were emerging from the Ladies at a scouse hen party.

The injured leg seemed to symbolise a performance that was lame in more ways than one. Her band was terrible, and when they launched into a cover version of the Darkness's signature hit 'I Believe In A Thing Called Love' followed soon after by Slade's 'Merry Xmas Everybody', it was like seeing the ghost of Christmas future: a middle-aged Melanie, leading a pub-rock covers band, just as her mother had done when Melanie was growing up.

It came as no surprise when it was quietly announced in the first week of 2004 that Virgin had terminated Melanie's record contract. Melanie was said to be furious, in particular because the label had never released the title track of *Reason*, which she believed could have been the key to reviving the album's fortunes.

There was no doubt that the album had underperformed dramatically. It had sold 350,000 copies worldwide, of which 85,000 copies had been shifted in the UK – about one-tenth the sales of *Northern Star*. This was still better than Victoria's album (50,000), but not as good as Emma's (119,000). Virgin would consider these sales figures as pretty good for a new or up-and-coming artist. Indeed, if much more fashionable acts like Auf Der Maur or the Sleepy Jackson had posted a couple of Top 10 singles and sales of 100,000 with their debut albums, Virgin would probably be hanging out the bunting. But for a former Spice Girl, the advances would have been such that much greater volumes of sales were necessary to make it worth the record company's while.

"Melanie was an expensive date," Phillips said. "She was a Spice Girl, so historically, the deal was a heavy one. Then you had all the drama of declining sales of singles that was going on at that time. Record companies were terrified. They were always going to ditch anything that wasn't selling."

And so Melanie became the fifth and final Spice Girl to leave Virgin Records – as a solo act. Interestingly, the Spice Girls, who have never formally split up, are still contracted to Virgin as a group, and according to the terms of the agreement, they still owe the label at least one Greatest Hits record.

# 14

# The Million Dollar Woman

Surprise, surprise. While 2003 was a "shit" year for Melanie C, and a nothing year for Geri, Victoria and Melanie B, it was shaping up to be a pretty good year for Emma. The Spice Girl who, only 12 months before, had been adrift without a manager or recording contract and looking far less likely than Geri or Melanie C to build a solo career of any note, suddenly started to blossom. Not only that. She was in everybody's good books.

The first sign that something new was stirring in the world of Baby came in May with the release of a stand-alone single, 'Free Me'. The song had been co-written by Emma and Mike Peden, one of the 19/Native management in-house team, previously best known for his work as a producer with the Lighthouse Family. A seductive love song with a light orchestral accompaniment, 'Free Me' had a classic, cosmopolitan feel about it that had reviewers reaching for favourable comparisons with the James Bond soundtracks of the Seventies. If the sound was fresh and appealing, then Emma had cultivated the look to go with it. During her time out of the spotlight, she had acquired a personal trainer and embarked on a new fitness regime. Already a green belt in karate (her mother, who taught karate, was a black belt), Emma had turned her attention to toning and sculpting her body, while the stylists had done the rest. Instead of the giggly ingénue of the Spice Girls days, the cover of the new single was graced with the photograph of a slender, elegant, impossibly leggy woman. Could this really be the former Baby Spice?

The accompanying video, which was shot in Rio by director Tim Royes, found this lovely, blonde creature canoodling with Latino star Alexandre Germano against the warm, glamorous backdrop of the Brazilian location. It was a nice enough song. But the really smart thing about 'Free Me' was the way in which it played so precisely to Emma's strengths while subtly repositioning her in the marketplace. Baby had grown up, but not in a boring or brash way. She had distanced herself from the Spice Girls, but not by dismissing or apparently denying the group's legacy (as Geri and Melanie C had sought to do). And while she had undertaken a lot of promotion for the single, it had not been a saturation-level, hard sell.

Like the song itself, her campaign all seemed quite tasteful and soft focus. The album was still some way down the line. Emma was merely touching base, renewing contact with her fans, and generally behaving in the way pop stars used to do, by putting out a single for no more pressing reason than because it was ready.

'Free Me' went to number five in the chart and everyone said "Good for Emma." As she set off on her steady climb back up the greasy pole of pop, she met Melanie C coming in the opposite direction with her new single, 'On The Horizon', which limped in to the chart at number 14 the following week.

It wasn't hard to detect the influence of one Simon Fuller in this spectacular turn of events. I remember taking part as a guest on Steve Wright's afternoon show on Radio Two along with the tabloid pundit Rick Sky, when the discussion turned to which of the Spice Girls had the best prospects of building a long term solo career. This was before Emma had signed with Fuller. I predicted that it would be Geri with her talent for self-promotion and insatiable desire to be in the spotlight who would eventually prevail as the biggest solo star. But, as somebody else pointed out, it could just as easily be Melanie C with her vocal prowess and willingness to build up her reputation the old-fashioned way on the live circuit. Melanie B had star potential, and while Victoria was less obviously talented, people were always going to be interested in whatever she decided to do. I don't recall that Emma was even mentioned.

What a different story by the time she came to release 'Maybe', the follow-up to 'Free Me', in October 2003. The song was co-written by Emma and Yak Bondy, a vocal arranger and keyboard player who had worked with Melanie C and S Club 7. It had a sophisticated, Latin/easy listening feel and was accompanied by another arresting video in which Emma, backed by 20 dancers, performed an energetic routine devised by the choreography team of Nessa and Dean, best known for their work on West End musicals. The mood of the song and the look of the video evoked a golden era of Sixties kitsch, as if Sandie Shaw had wandered into a cocktail party on the set of an Austin Powers movie. But for all its retro stylings, the song actually sounded fresh and original, and quite unlike anything else around at the time. It sailed serenely into the chart at number six, continuing the steady rebuilding of her career, and putting down another marker for the still unscheduled album.

Coinciding with the release of 'Maybe', Emma appeared in a cameo role in the TV comedy show *Absolutely Fabulous*, playing the part of herself as a client of PR boss Edina (Jennifer Saunders). Meanwhile, in real life, she was romantically linked with Justin Timberlake, perhaps the biggest male pop star on the planet (that week).

The commentariat sensed the change in the air, and responded accordingly. There was a steady trickle of light, feel-good pieces in rather unusual places. *Attitude* magazine invited her to take their "How Gay Are You?" questionnaire. Emma scored 49 per cent and was told she "could get gayer if only she'd pull her socks up". She gamely starred in the *NME*'s Peter Robinson "Versus" column, trading double entendres about Spice Girls lyrics and the Darkness. And in a more conventional interview with the *Standard*, she gently parried the usual sniffy questions about Fuller and the other Spice Girls to earn herself the strapline: "Shy about her love life and loyal to friends, Emma Bunton is Nice Spice."

Under the calm but firm guidance of Fuller, Emma's stock had risen to heights that would have seemed most unlikely even a few months before. It wasn't just the music, which was agreeable enough, or the look, which was even more so. People had suddenly started to see what Fuller had spotted long before. After withstanding seven years of scrutiny under the glaring spotlight of fame with hardly a blemish on her CV, Emma had emerged as the shrewdest operator of the five Girls, and the most likeable person.

A new buzz started to be heard echoing around the corridors of the media, faintly at first, but steadily growing as the weeks went by. Emma, it seemed, was All Right after all. I got official confirmation of this when an unexpected call came through from the Arts Desk of *The Times*. Would I write 600 words by Thursday, on Why Emma Bunton Is Cool? They didn't actually go so far as to run the piece mind you, but you could tell something was up. For the first time in a long time, a Spice Girl was almost hip.

It would be a mistake to assume that this was all Fuller's doing.

Emma was by now well known for her hands-on attitude to both her music and her visual presentation.

"My worst fault is that I'm a control freak," she said. "I can't stand it when people organise things for me without asking." Even so, there was no doubt that it helped to have someone as adept as Fuller doing the organising.

A third single, 'I'll Be There', eased into the Top 10 in January 2004, followed a week later by the release of Emma's second solo album, *Free Me*. Described by Emma as a tribute to the music she heard around the house as a little girl, when "my mum was playing Diana Ross & The Supremes, and my dad was playing Marvin Gaye and Barry White," it was an album that played perfectly to the preferences of her fan base, while giving her critics little to object to. Strings, flute and a cool swaying samba beat were the hallmark of songs such as 'Breathing', which she co-wrote with Henry Binns of Zero 7. There were some uncharacteristically soul-searching lyrics on certain numbers, especially 'No Sign Of Life', a story so full of romantic despair that you wondered how she managed to pull through to the next track: "I wake up crying and I think of you/ There's something dying and my world lies broken in two." But pull through she invariably did and always would. One of pop's more dependable troopers had finally found her stride.

By the end of May, when Emma released a fourth single from *Free Me* – a remake of the bustling bossa nova standard, 'Crickets Sing For Anamaria' – the album had sold 110,000 copies. This was on a par with her debut, which had sold 119,000 all told. The difference was all in the presentation. While Emma's first album had been submerged by the backwash from the sinking of the Spice mothership, she had now found some breathing space and carved out an identity of her own. Her sunny blend of latin and easy-listening influences fitted snugly alongside albums by the biggest artists of the day such as Norah Jones and Katie Melua without appearing to be competing with them for attention. With her career on track and her sanity intact, Emma had become the first of the Girls to emerge from the decompression chamber after surfacing from the Spice experience.

Victoria, on the other hand, still had a nasty case of the bends in store. She had not been idle since returning to the 19 Management fold. Indeed, even before she had got back together with Fuller, she had negotiated, with the help of Alan Edwards and her lawyer Andrew Thompson, a new contract with Telstar Records, and begun recording

## The Million Dollar Woman

an album with American hip hop mogul, Damon Dash. Given the Spice Girls lamentable track record with urban American producers, this seemed to be tempting fate. But it was not quite such an odd alliance as it looked at first sight.

Although Dash only came to most people's attention in Britain through his connection with Victoria, in America he had been a producer and businessman of considerable clout and wealth for some years. Born in East Harlem on May 3, 1971, Dash was brought up by his mother, Carol, who worked as a secretary. He won a scholarship to Dwight, a private prep school in downtown Manhattan from which he was expelled, and subsequently attended a South Kent boarding school in Connecticut.

Starting out in the music business as a manager, Dash got his big break when he signed up a young hustler by the name of Shawn Corey Carter, who under the nom de rap of Jay-Z quickly became one of the most successful hip hop stars in the history of the genre. With the income generated from his record sales, Jay-Z together with Dash and his business partner Kareem "Biggs" Burke, bankrolled Roc-A-Fella Records. Within a couple of years they had started up The Roc, a hip hop "lifestyle" brand which as well as music, marketed clothing, shoes, magazines, drinks, watches and anything else that they felt might catch the attention of consumers linked to the urban music fan base.

Sound familiar? People may have thought that the Spice Girls had allowed product tie-ins and commercial sponsorship to overshadow their music, but compared to the Dash method of branding and marketing, the Spice Girls had been positively restrained.

"I'm a lifestyle entrepreneur," Dash said during a typically hectic promotional visit to London in the spring of 2004. "I sell all the time. Whether it's music or sneakers, it's all marketing, marketing, marketing, 24 hours a day. My whole life is a commercial. I can't stop."

Dash maintained a constant one-man drive to boost consumption of his own (and other people's) goods by never wearing the same item of clothing or footwear more than once.

"I like to be fresh to death," he explained. "I gotta pop tags every day. When I wear my sneakers and my clothes I wear them once and then I give them to charity. So somewhere a kid on the street has some good clothes and I remain fresh."

As the figurehead of The Roc, Dash remained, nominally, a producer and manager. But by the time an American survey named him the 15th most powerful man in America under the age of 40, his marketing activities had long since eclipsed his achievements in music.

His business model was inspired by the hip hop entrepreneurs Sean "Puff Daddy" Combs, who created a multi-million dollar industry around his Bad Boy Entertainment, and Russell Simmons, the co-founder of the Def Jam label. These two record producers, both from New York, had exploited the fact that when a hip hop artist name-checked a particular brand name – as when Run DMC recorded a song called 'My Adidas' – sales of the product rocketed. Instead of advertising other people's wares in this way, they started creating and endorsing products of their own. Dash had taken the idea to its logical conclusion and built an empire around goods and services which he and his roster of acts either used, recommended or actually produced.

Dash first heard of Victoria when Naomi Campbell phoned him and told him he should meet up with her.

"When I first met her, she told me she had a little career as a singer," Dash said. "I knew about the Spice Girls and all that, but I hadn't heard her solo album. I didn't even know who she was. So I said, 'Let me hear your stuff.' I listened to it and I reckoned, 'This is some serious bullshit here.' So I said, 'Let me help you out.'

"I had no idea how famous she was until a bunch of photographers started risking their lives to take pictures of her. I liked her because she's not scared. I took her to Harlem and put her with a bunch of people she wouldn't be used to. She was out of her comfort zone, but she handled herself well."

Victoria, who had long been interested in American urban dance music, needed someone to inject fresh enthusiasm into her career and to steer her in a new direction. While Dash was not exactly overwhelmed by her prowess as a singer, he recognised in her a talent for promotion which he reasoned, correctly, would prove helpful in expanding his business interests into new markets in Britain and elsewhere.

In August 2002, the year before she met Dash, Victoria had been voted the world's best-dressed celebrity in a UK survey of more than 1,000 women, an accolade which she would receive again the following year. In April 2003, she landed a £1 million deal to advertise handbags in Japan for the designer Samantha Thavasa. A photo of Victoria sitting beside one of the bags, in white sports gear, had already been unveiled in the brand's flagship Tokyo store, and would soon appear on billboards and in magazines.

## The Million Dollar Woman

Dash offered to help her make a record.

"She's not going to be rapping," Dash said. "All we're going to do with Victoria is give her a hip hop influence. If we can make Victoria hot, we can make anybody hot."

His motives for taking on the project were never in any doubt. As part of the deal, Victoria would wear Dash's Rocawear products.

"She wasn't Mariah Carey," Dash said. "But she did what she had to do. She got the job done in the studio. What she lacked in talent she made up for in effort. The timing was right and I did what I had to do. I took Rocawear to another point of awareness."

This was all very well, but these developments had taken place prior to Victoria's return to the 19 Management fold in July 2003. Everything changed with the return of Simon Fuller to the scene. Dash was anathema to Fuller for two reasons. For one thing, he was not someone that Fuller had any control over. Far from being one of his in-house producer/writers with a clearly designated role lower down the chain of command, Dash was a multi-millionaire manager with a power base of his own and a business portfolio that was almost in the same league as that of Fuller himself. On a gut level, Fuller thus regarded Dash as a rival rather than an ally.

The feeling was mutual.

"That dude, what's his name? Simon Fullershit isn't it?" Dash said. "If you want to talk about marketing I'll talk to him. When she [Victoria] hired him it was so we could go over a gameplan and develop a serious marketing strategy. That's what I'm all about. But I don't think he wanted to sit down and talk to me. Well, sounds like he's a clown. 'Cause if I knew of some hot kid that not only does music but does clothing and so many other things, like a breath of fresh air on the curve of doing innovative and interesting things, then I would want to sit down and pick his brain to see if there was anything I could learn from him – see if he was the hype he was supposed to be. But he didn't even want to sit down with me. I've never even met him."

More to the point, Fuller would not entertain the idea of Victoria pursuing the musical direction that Dash had to offer. Had she learnt nothing from the fate of the third Spice Girls album, not to mention Melanie B's solo album?

"Fuller loathes Dash's music and doesn't think it's right for her," an insider said. "They have very different ideas as to how Victoria should proceed with her career. Victoria likes the kudos she gets through her association with Damon, but if she has any sense she will stick with formulaic pop music."

Although somewhat chastened by her experiences without Fuller as her manager, Victoria was not going to give up on Dash without a fight. Shouldn't they at least put out one of his tracks as a single and see how it fared? Fuller, who was just as adamant that any new single should play to Victoria's pop strengths, arrived at a typically adroit solution. Victoria would release a double A-sided single combining a Dash production, 'This Groove', with a pop dancefloor number more to Fuller's liking, 'Let Your Head Go', written and produced by the Swedish team of Liz Winstanley, Roger Olsson and Klas Baggstrom. The argument as to which was the better track would be decided in the first instance by the viewers of *Top Of The Pops*, who would be given the chance to see the videos to *both* songs on the December 5 edition of the programme. Viewers would vote for their favourite track, and the result would be announced on Radio One's Offical Chart Show on December 7. Victoria would then perform the preferred song on *Top Of The Pops* the following week. All money generated from the phone vote to be donated to BBC Children In Need.

Talk about turning an awkward situation to his advantage. Faced with a potentially damaging difference of opinion with Victoria and a threat to his authority from Dash, Fuller had quietly manufactured a scenario which guaranteed maximum favourable exposure for Victoria and which had a 50-50 chance of solving the problem for him.

As it turned out the vote went in favour of the Dash cut, a cool, somewhat smutty R&B number, in which Victoria tackled the hot topic of phone sex. The video found her writhing around on a bed, by herself, the receiver clutched to her ear, mumbling in the sultry, estuary-English tones of a born footballer's wife: "Hi. It's me. You wouldn't believe what I'm doing. What are you doing?" Well, hopefully he was not fiddling about with any dodgy text messages.

The other song, 'Let Your Head Go', had a much more upbeat Europop feel, and boasted a tune with something of the Kylies about it. "And when it feels so good/ I can almost lose my mind/Ooh, it makes me crazy, every time," Victoria sang. Although a lyric of stunning banality, it was tapped to full comic effect in the accompanying video, in which Victoria played the role of the cracked diva, attacking her clothes with a coat hanger à la Joan Crawford, and having spooky dreams about the OBE which David had received the month before from the Queen for his services to football. If the viewers of *Top Of The Pops* preferred Dash's song, it was 'Let Your Head Go' which gained the greater exposure elsewhere, particularly on MTV. The track also proved a runaway success in the club charts, lending weight to Victoria's credentials as an almost credible pop-dance act.

The humour of the video was a key element in Fuller's strategy for rebuilding Victoria's image. It was a powerful way of countering the perception that she was vain and too full of herself. He knew that audiences, particularly in Britain, warmed to an artist who was prepared to take the mickey out of herself, and Victoria was certainly up for doing that if the situation called for it.

Fuller's brother, Kim, recalled a conversation he had had with Victoria when the Girls were making the *Spiceworld* movie, which he had scripted. Victoria was portrayed throughout the film as the archetypal slightly dim, posh girl who would never muck in with the others if it meant getting her make-up smudged. In one sequence the other four were in combat fatigues being put through an assault course by Michael Barrymore, while Victoria, still in her little dress, simply walked round all the obstacles with her nose in the air, as if they didn't exist.

"She came up to me after we'd done that soldier bit with Barrymore," Fuller remembered, "and she said, 'You know my character in this movie, I'm just a laughing stock really, aren't I?' And I said, 'Yes. You are.' And she said, 'OK, that's fine. As long as I know.' And she just went with it. There was no side to her at all."

Her sense of humour was the first thing that struck Dash too.

"I thought Victoria was very witty," he said. "She's a smart-ass. She likes to take the piss. No one's as smart as me, but she tried. We had a rapport. But I had to show her who was in charge."

'This Groove'/'Let Your Head Go' was released on the strategically chosen date of December 29, 2003. The timing was such that although the record benefited from a big pre-Christmas promotional campaign, Victoria was removed from the race for the Christmas number one, where she would be certain to find herself languishing among a big slate of also-rans. Instead she would be the star that sparkled in the deadest week of the year for new releases.

By a strange twist of circumstance, Sophie Ellis-Bextor's record company had obviously had the same idea, and her single 'I Won't Change You' was also released on the same day. Neither record was ever in contention for the number one slot, but Victoria could take satisfaction from the fact that her single made a highly respectable showing at number three in the first chart of 2004, while her old rival had to make do with a number nine placing.

As with the sudden reversal in Emma's fortunes, it is difficult not to see this unlikely renaissance in Victoria's singing career as a result of the Fuller Effect. Only a few weeks earlier, an AOL internet poll posed the question: "Will Victoria Beckham have another hit?" The great majority of those who responded thought she would not. And yet here she was with the highest chart placing by a Spice Girl since Geri's 'It's Raining Men' in May 2001.

Despite the success of 'This Groove', Victoria would subsequently release no new records for an extended period of time. This was partly due to business reasons. While Dash's relationship with Fuller was non-existent, his dealings with Victoria's record company, Telstar, soon turned actively hostile. Dash had recorded "about twelve" tracks with Victoria, but according to Telstar, his producer's fee alone exceeded the budget for the making of the entire album. They paid him for three of the tracks, including 'This Groove', but baulked at forking out for any of the others. Dash vigorously disputed that his fee was unreasonable.

"My fee was $10,000 per track," Dash said. "See, the record company didn't know too much about music from what I saw. They didn't seem to know who I was. They didn't understand I was doing her a favour. They didn't understand that I'd been selling records for as long as I'd been selling records for, and so consistent, and still strong, and all the other things that I was doing. And I said to them, 'If you guys want to question me, come and sit down and have a conversation and make some sense based on an educated opinion'. When that never happened I'm thinking, 'What kind of record company is this?' I have a record company myself. When they started saying these things about the exorbitant amounts I was charging – being that it was so not true – I thought, 'They must be in some kind of trouble.' 'Cause that was all bullshit."

Dash's continuing inability to persuade anyone to sit down and talk with him was unusual in such an apparently successful businessman. But although he might not have been the easiest person to negotiate with, he may have had a point. Telstar has since gone into liquidation, another reason for the hiatus in Victoria's release schedule.

Heartening as the success of 'This Groove' was, as far as Fuller was concerned, the challenge was about much more than getting Victoria back on *Top Of The Pops* – although that was certainly a start. His eyes were on a bigger picture. He had plans for a fashion line bearing her name, television deals, an international schedule of personal appearances and a host of other ways of promoting her (and David's) lifestyle in such a way as to establish the house of Beckham as a worldwide brand.

"This is not simply about promoting a record," a friend of Fuller's said. "Simon sees Victoria as a huge entertainment proposition. In other words, he views the process of selling her as a whole lifestyle package, not just as a pop musician."

As part of this process, Victoria and David had allowed a team of film-makers to follow them around for a six-month period in 2003 during which David had been making the move from Manchester United to Réal Madrid. The resulting documentary, *The "Réal" Beckhams*, was screened on Christmas Eve, and gave a genial account of the couple and their ridiculously over-funded lifestyle. There was a discreet plug for Victoria's single, but no footage whatsoever of David playing football – a curious omission given the ghastly pun in the title.

Victoria was ubiquitous throughout the season of goodwill. As well as *The "Réal" Beckhams*, she also appeared as a guest on *Christmas Night With The Stars* hosted by Michael Parkinson, and was even rumoured to have been approached to give an "alternative" Christmas Message on Channel 4 at the same time as *The Queen's Christmas Message* was being broadcast on BBC One.

The Christmas message was never on the cards. But the unintended centrepiece of the Beckham charm offensive – and the only Beckham-related programme to earn a place in the Top 10 of the Christmas ratings – turned out to be *Posh And Becks's Big Impression*. A spoof documentary, starring the mimics Alistair McGowan and Ronni Ancona, it bore an uncanny resemblance to *The "Réal" Beckhams* – screened the night before – and seemed only marginally less believable. Of all the characters in the McGowan/Ancona repertoire, none have featured more frequently or prominently over the years than Posh and Becks, and this, surely, was their comic alias's finest hour. As always, the impressionists mercilessly lampooned David's and Victoria's foibles while nevertheless betraying a reluctant fondness for their victims.

A new development in the comedy duo's otherwise familiar routine was the introduction of Simon Fuller as a megalomaniac, Bond-type villain with headquarters located in a cave lit by burning braziers. When

Posh goes to ask for his help in reviving her solo career, Fuller shows scant interest until the idea of including Becks as part of the deal is suggested – at which point Fuller's red eyes light up with a demoniacal glow. Next thing, the manager is seen looming over a board representing the world, pushing figurines of Posh and Becks into position in different locations, like a military commander bent on covering the globe with occupying forces.

The joke may have been on Fuller, and yet against all odds he seemed slowly to be winning the Posh and Becks PR war. But even the best laid plans are subject to unexpected disruption, and Fuller's tactical building of the so-called Brand Beckham was about to suffer a rude interruption at the hands of a woman who, despite her ostensible charms, launched herself into the world of the Beckhams with all the grace and goodwill of a Scud missile.

Rebecca Loos, the daughter of a Dutch diplomat, worked for the sports personality management company SFX which managed the affairs of David Beckham. She became his personal assistant when he moved from Manchester to Madrid in July 2003. With Victoria away for much of the time either in London or New York, where she was working on her album with Dash, the arrangement brought Loos into closer contact with David than was prudent. Loos invited David over to dinner at her parents' home in the Spanish capital. On several occasions, her parents acted as babysitters for Brooklyn and Romeo while David was out training with his new teammates.

Loos lost her job with the Beckhams in December 2003, when David parted company with the SFX group. Three months later, a story ran in the *News Of The World*, brokered by the celebrity publicist Max Clifford, in which she claimed to have had a passionate, though short-lived affair with David. Among the various torrid details which Loos felt compelled to reveal was her and David's habit of allegedly texting sexually explicit messages to each other, a lively selection of which had now conveniently been made available to the newspaper.

David's initial response was to issue a statement which implied, without actually stating, that the allegations were false.

"During the past few months I have become accustomed to reading more and more ludicrous stories about my private life. What appeared this morning is just one further example. The simple truth is that I am very happily married, have a wonderful wife and two very special kids. There is nothing that any third party can do to change these facts."

After which no further comment of any sort on the matter was issued from the Beckham camp. The same could hardly be said of the rest of the world. The story exploded in a way that took even the most seasoned celebrity watchers by surprise. For 10 days or more, the front pages were dominated by lurid details of the affair, while any commentator worth his or her salt – and many who patently weren't – vented their opinions on the matter.

Just about everyone accepted the broad truth of the allegations as a given. Victoria had been away. David, one of the most desirable men in the world, had been left home alone. Loos was too confident and too plausible to be bluffing. The evidence was apparently overwhelming.

Most people found little to fault David on. Of course he'd erred, but what man wouldn't have done the same under such circumstances? Ditto Loos, who although she had systematically betrayed every trust placed in her by Victoria and her employers, was nevertheless absolved by most commentators of all responsibility for what had happened. There were a few "sleazy senorita" jibes, but very little in the way of outright disapproval.

Not so Victoria. The overwhelming consensus was that she had no one to blame for this dismal turn of events but herself. Indeed, such was the tone of undisguised loathing for Victoria displayed by many of her most prominent critics, you would have thought that it was *she* who was supposed to have betrayed *David* rather than the other way around.

Amanda Platell led the charge with a piece of unbridled cattiness in the *Daily Mail*, headlined "Why We Women Hate Posh".

"I don't know a single woman who envies anything about her, except the fact that she sleeps, occasionally, with David Beckham," Platell wrote. "As a female role model, she is past parody; as a model of physical beauty she is past plastic. Victoria is greedy, grafting and graceless. Everything about her is fake – the tan, the breasts, the lips, the nails, the hair . . ." and on and on she went, like a blocked drain given a sudden poke with a plunger.

Not to be outdone, Julie Burchill weighed in with a similarly intemperate slice of invective which, even by her standards, was breathtakingly crude. "Why do I hate Posh? Let's count the ways . . . joyless . . . self-pitying . . . pampered . . . overpaid . . . collagen pouts . . . arrogance . . . financial, rather than physical, prostitute . . . bad, boring, corrupt . . . But most of all I hate Posh because she's about to make me say something that, as a total feminist, I never dreamed I'd say to any woman. Which is: GIVE UP YOUR SO-CALLED WORK, MADAM, AND STAND BY YOUR MAN!"

Only a handful of voices expressed any sympathy whatsoever with Victoria's plight. Victoria Newton wrote a rather touching message of support, tucked away in a sidebar in *The Sun*.

"She is a loyal wife and great mother. She is not the robotic, emotionless cold bitch that everyone thinks she is. She is only human like the rest of us. Prick her and she will bleed. Thousands of women every day hear stories about their partners committing infidelity, but to know that every little detail about those affairs is the talk of every pub and coffee shop up and down the country must cut deep . . . Do we really hate Posh so much that we are happy to revel in the collapse of her family? I, for one, hope that isn't the case."

But Newton was in a minority. To judge from most reactions in the media, the break-up of the Beckham marriage, with Victoria getting her richly deserved comeuppance at last, would have been the perfect end to the story. How did it come to this? When did a girl who dreamed of being a pop star, and did nothing more harmful than make some very popular records, marry a talented footballer and become extremely rich and famous, turn into such a hate figure? Even the most ridiculed pop stars of earlier generations – Cliff Richard, say, or Barry Manilow – had never attracted this level of sustained personal abuse.

The answer seems to have something to do with the 21st century notion of fame as being a commodity in itself. Victoria and David were not really people any more – they had become Brand Beckham. Having accepted the corporate sponsors' money and hired a small army of ad men and PR advisers, the couple had built an image that generated earnings beyond the dreams of most pop stars, let alone ordinary people. This image was an asset when it came to their material wellbeing, but in many people's eyes it had drained them of their humanity. Prick Victoria and she would get the photographer to airbrush the mark out. While previous generations of celebrities had been criticised for what they *did*, Victoria and David were criticised for what they *were*.

Meanwhile, in the course of turning themselves into these so-called lifestyle icons, they had become principal characters among a cast of public figures required to perform in a never-ending "real-life" drama which, although it needs occasional heroes, is far better at creating villains.

With the sole exception of Emma, all the Spice Girls had become cartoon villains in this celebrity burlesque which is played out daily on the airwaves and in the columns of the British mass media. Their wealth and fame was deemed more than sufficient to insulate them from the discomfort of having their lives and their looks and their moments of weakness and unhappiness paraded in close-up in front of the rest of the world. And besides, that is how they had chosen to live. If they didn't like the way the script was written, then hard luck. They couldn't expect the genie to be returned to the bottle now.

Quite what this reveals about us, the audience who have ultimately created the demand for this sadistic spectacle, is not very flattering. Where once we wanted our pop stars to be glamorous and successful and cloaked in a certain starry mystique, now we tend to regard them as targets on a coconut shy. We give them wealth and fame, and in return we demand the right to be as intrusive and nasty about them as we like. In fact, we are quite happy to be nasty about them even *before* they are rich and successful. The spectacle of Simon Cowell tearing a strip off some young hopeful is as much a part of the appeal of the *Pop Idol* formula as witnessing the eventual tears of joy shed by the winner. The process of rejection and humiliation that the majority of candidates suffer is all part of the entertainment, and indeed has become a key part of the fun in the case of many reality TV shows.

We don't want to see the contestants in *I'm A Celebrity – Get Me Out Of Here* or *Big Brother* bonding happily together and making the best of the situation; we want to see them arguing, suffering and hurting each other. Gordon Ramsey, the chef in *Hell's Kitchen*, treats his staff, whether celebrities or otherwise, in a way which would have had him up before an industrial relations tribunal in any other sphere of activity.

The Spice Girls provided the perfect target for this sort of institutionalised unpleasantness. They were more famous than most kings and queens or movie stars or politicians. They were a bit silly and full of themselves, but always eager to please. And they were staggeringly rich. This made them not so much fair game as sitting ducks under the new rules of celebrity engagement. And Victoria (together with David) had become the biggest target of them all. The Loos affair – hardly a news story at all, if truth be told – was an example of the process taken to new extremes.

"As always, the papers were drenched in hypocrisy, revelling in every sordid detail while feigning shock at their exposures," Roy Greenslade, a former editor of the *Mirror*, wrote in the *Guardian*. "What was so noticeable was the amount of speculation presented as fact, innuendo covered by question marks ('Could Victoria be pregnant?') and the widespread reliance on unidentified 'friends' for sensational quotes. None of this is new in the daily diet of celebrity journalism (in other words, the majority of what is published by tabloids) where an assembly line of 'stars' are treated as objects for readers' amusement and what is written about them is often less than true."

As every editor and publicist knows, it is not news which sells newspapers like the *News Of The World*. It is revelations. Celebrities like Victoria and David had thus become targets in another sense, as well. Revelations about their private lives, whether true or false, were now worth unbelievable sums of money to the bounty hunters who roamed the celebrity jungle. Loos was by no means the first or last woman to sell a kiss-and-tell story about David Beckham. But she was the first to become seriously rich from doing so. Indeed such were her earnings from the affair, that it gave new meaning to her claim that, for a while, she was "besotted" by a man who made her feel "like a million dollars".

Loos had been guided in her campaign by the publicist Max Clifford, who was quoted in the *Evening Standard* on April 19 as saying that she had made media deals worth £800,000 out of the story, including £350,000 for her exclusive interview with the *News Of The World*. Clifford was one of the big beasts of this world, a man whose reputation alone would be enough to confer a degree of credibility on a client's story. He first spoke with Loos in January 2004, when he told her to tape all phone calls, keep all texts, photocopy the bills from all the phones and store any other inside information to which she had access. He also told her that if she wanted to sell her story to the news media then she would "never have to work again". He (Clifford) had personally made £160,000 from the deal, based on his standard 20 per cent fee. Whatever else this episode was, it was not an affair of the heart. This was big business.

In the immediate aftermath of her allegations it was reported that a Malaysian woman, Sarah Marbeck, had also claimed to have been Beckham's lover. In an interview broadcast on Australian TV, Marbeck said it had been "love at first sight". This allegation was followed by a rumour that Beckham had also had an affair with a "top" Spanish model Esther Canadas, although a detective hired to look into the matter concluded that, "Their relationship does not go further than having a cup of coffee together."

## The Million Dollar Woman

Then came stories of a romp with an unnamed blonde in a Spanish nightclub toilet. A Madrid "party girl" Nuria Bermudez (nicknamed Muchas Tetas, for obvious reasons) announced that she had exchanged raunchy texts with Beckham and was ready to sell the full story for £12,000.

"There's nine women, including me and Rebecca, that he's slept with since he moved to Madrid," she said. She claimed as her witness Beckham's Cuban-born chauffeur, Delfin Fernandez, who had been dismissed after trying to sell similar "secrets" about Beckham's love life.

"There are people trying to flog kiss-and-tells the whole time with David," said Julian Henry, whose PR company Henry's House has worked for Simon Fuller for many years. "It happened in Manchester, it happens all over the place. They're made-up, opportunistic stories by people he meets in clubs or wherever. Some people think he had an affair with Jordan, because she was making suggestive comments when she was on *I'm A Celebrity – Get Me Out Of Here*."

So why didn't Beckham issue a more categorical denial of the Loos story, especially after she had appeared, again for an astronomical fee, in an hour-long interview telling her side of the story on the Sky One TV channel?

"We had decided by that time we were not going to comment on anything she said," Henry said. "We're not going to give any credence whatsoever."

That approach was all very well and it may have been that Beckham's legal team had good reasons for erecting this wall of silence. As the newspapers grew in confidence so the follow-up stories became increasingly far-fetched. Tales of "tearful confessions" and private conversations between David and Victoria, which were reported as fact, could not possibly have been supported by any evidence whatsoever. Give them enough rope and the British tabloids will certainly find someone to hang.

The difficulty with the "no comment" policy was that Loos had a much more believable story than Jordan or any of the other chancers. For a period of about three months she had exceptional access to David. She helped find a home in Madrid for the Beckhams. She booked apartments and made travel arrangements. She knew the details of David's credit cards. One of her responsibilities was to order and run the seven mobile phones that were used by the family. She ordered the cars. She worked with the family's chauffeur, Delfin

Fernandez, who had tried to sell stories like this to the newspapers before she did.

Just about everyone who watched the tale unfold through the agency of the media equated such a high level of access with Loos having had an affair with David – and maybe she did. But the truth was that only those directly involved actually *knew* what had happened, if anything had happened, because it had happened between two individuals. One of them had told a very entertaining and highly profitable story for herself, and the other one hadn't said anything, except "it's ludicrous".

Whatever the truth of the Loos affair, Victoria had apparently absorbed the barrage of blows to her husband's reputation and her own self-esteem by the time she gave her first interview after the story broke. Speaking to Kate Thornton of *Marie Claire* magazine, she exuded a Zen-like calm.

"It really comes down to knowing the truth yourself," she said. "That's all that matters. I know for a fact David's been faithful to me *and* I know it in my heart. Every single Sunday, you pick up the papers and some footballer or other has allegedly done something with a Page Three girl or a wannabe this or that. It's happened for years. Obviously, there's a market for it."

Was Victoria fighting fire with fire and telling the "just lie" in order to salvage what was left of her pride? Was she deluded? Or was it conceivable that she knew something nobody else was even prepared to consider – that David had indeed "been faithful" to her? It may be worth recalling how it was accepted with absolute certainty that Emma had had an affair with Simon Fuller, and yet how few people, with the benefit of hindsight, subsequently believed that to have been true. Now that Loos had made her fortune out of her association with the Beckhams, who knew what surprises might yet be in store?

# 15

# Never Ends

At about nine o'clock on the evening of February 17, 2003, the Spice Girls sat down for an informal dinner at David and Victoria's mansion in Hertfordshire. It was the first time that all five of them had been in the same room together since Geri's abrupt departure from the group in May 1998. Melanie B had suggested the get-together, Victoria hosted it and Emma had been the most active in making it all happen. Persuading Geri to show up had not been a problem. The most reluctant participant was Melanie C.

The very fact that the original group was meeting again was front page news for *The Sun*, and it was just like old times as the paper's show business reporters Dominic Mohan and Victoria Newton swung into action with a blow-by-blow account of the evening. Their story was a curious mixture of mundane specifics and fly-on-the-wall insight. "First to arrive was Emma at 8pm in a chauffeur-driven silver Mercedes," they wrote, almost as if they had been left standing outside the gate. But elsewhere, there were more intimate details of what had gone on behind the closed doors of "Beckingham Palace".

"Guilt-ridden Ginger broke down as she recalled problems between the girls. She used memory cards to remind herself of specific incidents." The meeting was described afterwards as "emotional, but relaxed and fruitful", by those mysterious "sources" who always seemed to be hovering "close to the group".

"It was great to see them all again," Emma said afterwards. "We talked over old times and there was a lot of laughing. We had a really good time and we caught up."

Any suggestion of the group re-forming was carefully played down. They had got back together on a social footing and rebuilt some bridges, but that was all that had happened. Following the meeting, Melanie B was said to be optimistic about the chances of a Spice Girls reunion at some point in the future. But a stern rebuttal of any such idea was promptly issued by Melanie C's office: "The band is not getting back together with her in it."

In taking this negative position, Melanie could count on the support of *The Sun*. For despite giving the story such prominence, Mohan nevertheless felt duty bound to announce that he was starting a "Stop Right Now" campaign to prevent a Spice Girls reunion from ever getting off the ground. In a distinct echo of the Matthew Wright era, Mohan urged readers of the best-selling redtop in Britain to join him in his bid "to end [the] Spice revival".

"I don't Wannabe rude, but you can have Too Much of a good thing," Mohan quipped. But the Spice Girls were not yet ready to do Too Much of anything as a group in 2003, even if some of the signs now seemed to be pointing in that direction. True, Emma and Victoria had already returned to Simon Fuller and were busy rebuilding their solo careers, while Melanie C was watching her second solo album disappear down the plughole. But, for the two noisiest Spice Girls, Geri and Melanie B, things had gone uncommonly quiet. Both had made approaches to Fuller, and been rebuffed – at least, as solo acts. Now both of them seemed to be cast adrift. It was ironic, given that they had been the driving force within the group, but left to their own devices, Geri and Melanie B were the Spice Girls who most lacked a sense of direction.

Following the failure of her solo album and her marriage, Melanie B began casting around for a way to change her fortunes in various unlikely places. After dispensing with the services of the Spice Girls' manager, Nancy Phillips, in March 2001, she was introduced to Sandie Shaw, the singer best known for singing in bare feet and a string of long-ago hits including '(There's) Always Something There To Remind Me' and 'Puppet On A String', which won the Eurovision Song Contest in 1967. For a few months, Shaw became Melanie's manager, although it was difficult to fathom what exactly her duties entailed, other than encouraging Melanie to explore a recently acquired enthusiasm for Buddhism.

As her musical career languished, Melanie looked for a role in other areas of the media. She hosted a Saturday night talent show on ITV called *This Is My Moment*, which ran for six weeks in the summer of 2001, and presented a Channel 4 travel documentary, *Melanie B Voodoo Princess*, screened at the start of 2002, which took her to the African island of Benin. Neither project led on to a second instalment.

Undeterred, she embarked on a career as an actor.

Her first serious role was a stint in the London stage production of *The Vagina Monologues* at the New Ambassador's theatre, which she joined for a four-week engagement in March 2002. She performed again in *The Vagina Monologues*, for one week, at The Lowry in Salford in September, the same month that her autobiography, *Catch A Fire*, was published.

"I've stopped doing music," Melanie said shortly before playing the role of Claire, a bed-hopping nurse in *Burn It*, a new TV drama which began on the digital channel BBC3 in February, 2003. "I'm doing this now and I love it. It's the first proper job I've had. Walking on set and having to work with different people has been great for me. I don't think I'm an actress yet. I'm just in training."

Her "training" continued in a British horror movie, *Lethal Dose*, the debut for director Simon De Selva, which premiered at the MIFED 2003 film festival in Milan on November 9. Melanie was cast as a member of a group of animal rights activists who were subjected to twisted brain experiments and horrific tortures. But could Scary really do scary?

"Melanie Brown isn't gimmick casting," De Selva said, reacting to the inevitable criticisms. "She can really act. I saw her in the television play *Fish*, and thought she was fantastic. She brings the same credibility factor here."

Any lingering scepticism about Melanie's intentions was largely laid to rest when she took on the part of Mimi in the hit Broadway production of the musical *Rent*. This "controversial" story about "struggling young artists living on the edge and reaching for glory in New York's East Village" had won a Tony Award and a Pulitzer Prize and was the 15th longest-running show in Broadway history by the time Melanie joined the cast on April 16, 2004. Her character was a prostitute and erotic dancer, addicted to heroin and afflicted by Aids, so Melanie could hardly be accused of being yet another pop star simply playing herself. Auditioning for the part held no fear.

"I'm used to rejections," Melanie said. "I've had loads because I've been auditioning for things since I was 12. If something works out, I work hard at it, and if it doesn't, I work hard at something else instead."

While *Rent* provided her with plenty of challenges as a singer, actor and dancer, her career as a solo star had by this point receded into the distance. Returning from a holiday in Mexico to her home in Los

Angeles, she apparently wrote 15 songs in her kitchen, "just jamming out on guitar, and recorded on my friend's computer in ten days." But with no management or recording contract, there were no plans for any of them to be made commercially available in the foreseeable future. Like Victoria, she remained for the time being a one-album act.

Geri's progress after the disappointment of her second album was even more erratic than Melanie B's. She showed up at the Oscars and the BAFTAs and anywhere else there was a high profile party going on. But she didn't really have anything much to do at them. She signed a publishing deal, said to be worth $719,000 to write a second autobiography. She cultivated an interest in yoga and made a demonstration DVD – *Geri Yoga* – which sold 300,000 copies, substantially more than her album, *Scream If You Wanna Go Faster*, which had stalled at around 63,000 copies.

As Melanie B had done, Geri sought to develop a profile as a talking head on TV. She appeared as one of the judges on *Popstars: The Rivals*, and through the agency of Simon Fuller, she co-hosted a TV talent show in America, *All American Girl*, which opened on the ABC network on March 12, 2003. She showed up again at the Oscars that year, commenting for ABC on the dresses the stars were wearing and other red carpet action outside the event.

In July she filmed a scene in *Sex And The City* in which she played the role of Phoebe Kittenworth, an English friend of the character Samantha Jones played by Kim Cattrall. By the time it was actually screened as one of the episodes in the final run of this popular series, Geri's contribution had been hyped out of all proportion – not least, one suspects, by Geri herself. Instead of letting people discover this little feather in her cap for themselves, her appearance was built up into a much bigger deal than was called for. Inevitably, her blink-and-you-missed-it cameo proved a letdown for her fans, never mind the critics, who heaped derision on her performance from a great height.

By the summer of 2003 both Geri and Melanie B had moved to Los Angeles to pursue their acting careers. But despite the friendly get-together at the Beckhams' mansion earlier in the year, relations between the two remained awkward. When they bumped into each other on one occasion in the Sunset Boulevard Coffee Bean Cafe, they all but ignored each other.

In November 2003, Geri's second autobiography, *Just For The Record*, was published. Her first book, *If Only*, had drawn on a wide range of often extraordinary life experiences – from a childhood of abject poverty to the highs of being in the Spice Girls at the peak of their success. But the second book had no such length or breadth of experience to draw on. Instead, concentrating on the few years since she had fled the Spice Girls, it painted a sad picture of a bright but emotionally battered young woman for whom fame and wealth had brought alarmingly little in the way of personal equilibrium, let alone happiness.

The revelations about her eating disorders, while not exactly a surprise, were nevertheless quite shocking in terms of their extent.

"My life became a permanent binge," she wrote, recalling a particularly bleak period at the end of 1999. "I was becoming less of a bulimic and more of an overeater. I wasn't so concerned about expelling the food after eating but was keeping up a constant feeling of being full. Sometimes my back would hurt because my stomach was so full but I would carry on anyway until, eventually, I would pass out. Obviously I started to put on weight and that made me feel even worse."

These descriptions were accompanied by a huge portfolio of photographs by Dean Freeman, in which Geri never looked less than a model of slimline perfection. Talk about sending out a mixed message. While the text spoke in painful detail of how Geri's life had become one long crisis of confidence and self-loathing, fuelled by constant doubts about her body image, the pictures showed a slender, toned, smiling person apparently leading a life full of excitement and variety.

Here was a contradiction that went right to the heart of the new celebrity phenomenon, and which mirrored in many ways the problems that often beset the more enthusiastic upholders of the traditional rock'n'roll lifestyle. Food was Geri's drug.

"I would wake up in the morning and the first thing I would think about was what I was going to eat . . . I'm bored. What shall I do? I'll eat. I feel fat. What shall I do? Eat. I'm feeling sad and lonely. What shall I do? I'll shove something in my mouth. My response to any feeling was to eat because eating seemed to ease the feelings and take the edge off. Pretty soon it was habitual, non-stop eating."

Just like so many of her rock'n'roll cousins, Geri ended up undergoing group therapy. There she confronted her compulsive behaviour and with the help of others in a similar situation embarked on a programme of abstinence (from bingeing) which would have been all too familiar to recovering alcoholics.

Geri was not the only one to emerge from the Spice Girls with a raging psychological disorder. Melanie C also suffered from both eating problems and clinical depression. Her weight shot up during the course of 2001.

"I went to the doctor because I just couldn't cope any more," Melanie said. "I was suffering terribly from this eating disorder. It was such a secret and I felt so ashamed of losing control of my life. I was a dancer all through school, but I was a skinny kid. It wasn't an issue. And then I started growing up and going to a Performing Arts college. I was in a school that was predominantly ballet dancing, so I was scrutinising myself in front of a mirror for eight hours a day. Any insecurity about yourself is magnified already, and then the pressures of how we are supposed to look to be famous adds to the problem. Because when you get to that point of being this thin creature – whether it's natural or not – then it's just trying to maintain it. That can only last for so long.

"I was obsessively exercising. I always ate, but it was a very restricted diet. It became so limited at one point, I was eating no protein, no carbohydrate and God knows how I survived on the schedule that we had with the Spice Girls. Eventually my body was exhausted. I think I was living on adrenaline. And then it just exploded. It was like a catapult that had been stretched as far as it could go and then it was suddenly released. Then came depression, bingeing. I couldn't exercise because I was so ashamed of myself. I went through a period of hating myself. It feels like there's no light at the end of the tunnel – as if you're never going to get better."

Both Geri's and Melanie's problems were compounded by the unwelcome attention of the media and in particular the unsympathetic press coverage. Geri remembered walking through an airport the morning after the news that her romance with Chris Evans had ended and seeing the word "DUMPED" emblazoned across her picture on one of the front covers.

"All I could think was: I am famous, blonde, rich, young and successful and I feel like I've got the word 'dumped' stamped across my forehead," Geri said.

"To begin with the papers mostly left me alone," Melanie C said. "But even in the early days they were quite cruel about my appearance. I was the plain one at the back who didn't do anything. Now I'm a lot more confident, and I've fathomed things out a bit and come to the forefront, so they take more of an interest. When I got ill I went to see lots of therapists and spoke to lots of different people, which is scary when you're a celebrity. Because you're frightened of everybody you talk to just in case it leaks out. Thankfully, by the time everything came out about me in the newspapers, I was well enough to deal with it. But if it had come out at the beginning I think it would've just finished me off. I was so terrified of everyone knowing."

But wasn't there a case for saying that the Spice Girls actually contributed to the pressure on young girls to look thin?

"I think we were victims of it, or some of us were," Melanie said. "I quickly realised that I couldn't be the prettiest Spice Girl or the loudest or whatever, so I thought, 'I'll have to be the thinnest.' I think I was a victim and I think Geri was always a victim. It's not going to affect the other girls. Emma was always a healthy girl and Melanie [B] has a naturally fantastic figure. She eats whatever she wants, the cow. But I was unnaturally thin at the time and Geri's weight kept changing. Maybe I was guilty of putting pressure on little girls who loved Sporty. But if so, I was a victim of previous people and how I thought I had to look to be accepted in the pop world. Perhaps it was a case of the victim becoming the perpetrator, which is a pattern you often find."

Of the five Girls, Melanie C was the one who was most traumatised by the experience of becoming a super-celebrity. She didn't want to present TV shows, or write an autobiography or see pictures of herself shopping in Marks & Spencer splashed on the front pages of the tabloids. Yes, she wanted to be rich and famous, but she wanted to do it by being a musician.

"It's great making a lot of money, and I have made a lot of money," she said, "but I've had to spend a lot of money recovering from the Spice Girls as well."

Melanie's perception of the Spice Girls as something she has had to "recover from" goes a long way towards explaining her refusal to countenance a reunion. According to her manager, Nancy Phillips, Melanie was told by her doctors that it would take as many years to recover from an eating disorder of the sort that she was suffering from as it had done to get to the point of illness that she had reached.

"She's now perfect," Phillips said in March 2004. "She's fit, healthy, emotionally stable. She's back running after her knee injury. And she has a good relationship with her boyfriend Tom [Starr] who she met two-and-a-half years ago."

Perhaps it was no coincidence that at this precise moment of spiritual calm and physical wellbeing, Melanie's career was at its lowest ebb.

With no recording contract she embarked on a tour of UK venues smaller than the backstage area at most Spice Girls concerts. Starting at the 200-capacity Barfly in Glasgow, in June 2004, she played a mixture of new material and her old hits in a setting that could not have been further removed from the gaudy, goldfish-bowl environment which she had inhabited throughout the Spice years. And, what's more, the *Guardian* reviewer awarded her four stars out of five.

From Melanie's perspective, going back to the Spice Girls now would be like a recovering alcoholic deciding to make one last visit to the Munich Beer Festival for old times' sake.

"I wouldn't recommend it for her, emotionally, personally or professionally," Phillips said. "Besides, I don't think you can ever recreate that kind of excitement. It was a phenomenon. They all had a very youthful exuberance. You're not going to be like that in your thirties."

"I love all the things the Spice Girls have done," Melanie C said. "But, I mean, 'Wannabe' . . . it gets to the point where even if I'm just having fun and being a Spice Girl I feel a bit old to be singing 'Zigazig ah'. How long can you sing that? It feels weird. I'm sure I could deliver it. But even just the thought of having to do it exhausts me."

Despite Melanie's implacable opposition to the idea, reports of an impending Spice Girls reunion began to surface with increasing frequency during the early months of 2004.

"We will probably do something together as a group, but not for a while," Melanie B told the *New York Daily News* in April. "I think they are going to release a greatest hits album, and hopefully we will all get together and write a song for it."

Rumours circulated on the Internet that if Melanie C wouldn't agree to be involved then the other four would start looking for a replacement for her. Fergie of the Black Eyed Peas was mooted as a potential candidate and it was said that Danii Minogue had been sounded out on the subject. Whether true or not, here was a development that suggested Simon Fuller was now taking more than a passing interest in the idea. Remember his proposed strategy to stage the "*Gone With The Wind* of auditions" to find a replacement for Geri? Well, if Melanie really wouldn't get on board, perhaps it was time to start thinking along similar lines again. It certainly wouldn't hurt to plant the idea in some people's minds, not least Melanie's as she slogged her way round the lowliest gigs on the British pub circuit.

If it was still too early for the Spice Girls to consider auditioning for a replacement, other acts in the post-*Pop Idol* world were evidently ready to embrace the idea. The Australian group INXS announced that they would be starting a search for a singer to replace the late Michael Hutchence on a TV show to be called *Rock Star*. The American soul sistas TLC were said to be in talks with Fox TV about a series to audition for a singer/rapper to replace the late Lisa "Left Eye" Lopes. Never slow to get in on the act, the Osbournes were planning to find a new band by a TV audition process for the 2005 Ozzfest tour. Meanwhile, in Britain, MTV launched a series called *Breaking Point* which followed the fortunes of several "real" indie-rock bands in their quest to land a recording contract. That kid in the Byrds song with his electric guitar and his hair combed right, would have had to smarten up his act for the cameras if he was still hoping to get a break in the 21st century.

Ultimately, however, it seemed as if the timing was still not quite right for the return of the Spice Girls. "Should the Spice Girls reform?" was the question addressed to users of the AOL internet service provider in one of its daily straw polls in April. Of those who responded, 57 per cent voted No, which was not as bad as it would have been a couple of years earlier, but was still a clear majority against the idea.

Given the continuing stand-off between Melanie C and the other four, it seemed that any tentative plans there might have been to release a greatest hits album in November 2004 were eventually nipped in the bud. According to an unconfirmed report in *The Sun*, Melanie had told the other Girls that she would do some basic promotion – TV interviews and so forth – to publicise a greatest hits album, but the suits at Virgin had insisted that some sort of concert or more general reunion-type event was needed to galvanise the campaign and generate the sort of mega-sales that they would be expecting such an album to achieve.

Simon Fuller was said to be involved in the plans, and had argued in favour of holding off until 2006, by which time it would be the tenth anniversary of the release of 'Wannabe', and Melanie C might have had a change of heart. Perhaps, also, in another couple of years the pendulum of fashion would have begun to swing back in the Spice Girls' favour. When P.J. Harvey performed at Glastonbury 2004 in a ripped Spice Girls T-shirt, it seemed a defiant, almost anti-fashion statement. But could the Spice Girls ever actually be cool again?

One group of fans who would always be rooting for the group, whether they reunited or not, was their gay following. Once again, the parallels between the Spice Girls and Abba were striking. It has often been remarked that the revival of Abba's fortunes was initiated by the gay community. When Erasure recorded the *Abba-esque* EP of Abba cover versions in 1992, it gave the duo fronted by the flamboyant singer Andy Bell their biggest hit and helped to kickstart the reappraisal of Abba among the mainstream audience.

Emma, Geri and Victoria had often made personal appearances at clubs such as G.A.Y. at the Astoria in London where they were always greeted with wild enthusiasm. And it was frequently suggested, mistakenly, that Melanie C actually was gay.

"I was the sporty one with a tomboy image," Melanie said. "Then I was never seen with guys because I never had a fucking boyfriend. And then I got my hair cut short and I got tattoos and I was quite muscular. But I've never had any lesbian tendencies at all."

Biff Stannard, the co-writer of 'Wannabe', 'Spice Up Your Life' and many of the Girls other biggest hits, had no doubts about the significance of this aspect of the group's legacy.

"Being a gay man myself, I can see many 'stereotypical' reasons why the Girls appeal to gay people," Stannard said. "They are strong-minded, empowered women, like Madonna or Sigourney Weaver in *Alien*. There is an air of tragedy about Geri – the single woman with all her problems – and Victoria with her ordeal by media, which equates with female idols such as Judy Garland and Whitney Houston. Victoria has, of course, become a gay icon. And David is the most desirable man in the world!

"All five of them have different, larger-than-life images; the clothes, the music, the whole 'gang' thing. They would make a perfect bunch of drag queens! And on a personal level, the girls are all very liberal. They treated everyone they met the same, whether it was Nelson Mandela or the guys making tea in my studio.

"I remember when we were all exhausted from working really long hours on the first album. It was a few days before Christmas and we were in the studio at three o'clock in the afternoon, and Geri said everyone's got to come upstairs to the dining/social room. So me, Matt [Rowe], the two engineers and all the band walked up there, and Geri tells us all to sit down. And she cleared the room and this male stripper came into the room. And she'd said to him, 'The first thing that comes on MTV, you've got to come in and do an erotic dance to it.' And it was 'Mistletoe And Wine' by Cliff Richard. I'll never forget it. It was the funniest thing. It was broad daylight, and we were sober and it all seemed so surreal. And this is what they were like. Every day there was something like this. I remember thinking, 'This is just the maddest band.'"

It is said that as Abba's core fan base grew into adulthood, a disproportionate number of them turned out to be gay men. Could the same be true for the Spice Girls? A lot of the kids who loved the girls at the beginning are now in their late teens and early twenties and would be able to see a certain irony in still loving them – also just like Abba.

"The gay following is extremely loyal," Stannard said. "The gay fans will be there till the end, especially as pop music has since lost its glamour and throwaway appeal. Being gay, especially when you're young, is all about that moment on a Friday or Saturday night when you forget about everything and lose yourself in the music and express your true self. What better music to do it to than pop?"

And what better pop songs than the feisty, girl-gang anthems of the Spice Girls? It certainly takes more than an image to inspire long term devotion in pop, and there is no doubt in this author's mind that the music of the Spice Girls will eventually stand the test of time. And although they started out as an archetypal act for young kids to adore, there is an "adult" side to the group which, according to Stannard, has yet to be fully revealed.

"Whenever they do get around to doing a greatest hits we've got three or four tracks that are mastered and could go on a bonus disc," Stannard said. "In fact I think there are at least seven or eight songs that have never been heard by anyone other than me, Matt [Rowe] and the Girls."

"There was 'Feed Your Love' which was a kind of downtempo, quite erotic song. It was "feed your love" as in "giving a blow job". That had Geri rapping in it. It was a great song, but too rude and probably a bit downtempo for the first album. Even now, it's one of my favourite records that they've ever done. And I think it was one of the Girls' favourites. There's another one called 'C U Next Tuesday' which is also a bit rude when you look at the initials of the title. That was about dumping a bloke politely, but obviously that one wasn't allowed either."

Viewed in this context, the lyric to 'Wannabe' itself – with its references to Emm as the one who "likes it in your face" – begins to take on shades of ambiguity that one would hope had not occurred to the group's target audience at the time, but which might become part of a new mythology as that audience grows older. And, while we're about it, what exactly was this "zigazig ah" that they all really, really wanted so much?

"That was a phrase that Geri and Mel and all the girls had been saying for ages," Stannard explained. "Basically it was cryptic for 'shagging'. They always used to say it, and then move their hips forward in a fast, suggestive sort of thrusting movement. It was really funny. I remember saying, 'Why don't you put that on the record?' So it ended up on there."

★ ★ ★

On April 19, 2004 Simon Fuller threw an office party for his staff to celebrate the 19th anniversary of 19 Management. Being Fuller, it was no ordinary office party. The Albert Hall, no less, was hired, and the 100 employees of 19 Management were each allowed to bring 19 guests. No press were invited – at least not in a professional capacity – although several editors including Piers Morgan of the *Mirror* and Peter Hill of the *Express* received personal invites and found themselves in a box together. All the bars in the Albert Hall were free and champagne was in plentiful supply.

There were performances and speeches by acts that had been signed to 19 Management over nearly two decades, most of them still very much a part of the "family", including Paul Hardcastle, Cathy Dennis and Annie Lennox. But there was no grandstanding by Fuller, who stayed discreetly in a box throughout the evening with members of his family including his mother Lucy, and brother Kim.

Emma sang 'Maybe' with the full dance routine from the video, and then performed a duet with Will Young. Victoria appeared with David, prompting an ovation that almost lifted the roof off the building. She performed 'Let Your Head Go' in front of a throne – a picture of which found its way into many of the next day's tabloids. David, whose head had been newly shaved, gave a brief speech. "I'm very proud to be part of the 19 party, but I'm even more proud of my beautiful and lovely wife Victoria."

There was a video message from Melanie B and her daughter, Phoenix Chi, now five years old, who seemed to have inherited something of her mother's candour. "Thank you for making my mummy a rich bitch," the little darling announced. And Geri sent video footage of herself on a beach, building a bizarre sandcastle "cake" and putting 19 candles on it while singing 'Happy Birthday'.

There was no message of any kind from Melanie C.

"Simon has a good relationship with all of the Spice Girls," Fuller's PR, Julian Henry, said after the event. "Obviously he speaks to Emma and Victoria the most. But he has spoken to Melanie C, and he enjoys cordial relations with all of them. He is keeping his irons in the fire for when the time is right."

# Discography

## SPICE GIRLS
Chart positions follow release date.

**SINGLES**

'Wannabe'

CD1 'Wannabe' (Single Edit) / 'Bumper To Bumper' / 'Wannabe' (Motiv8 Vocal Slam)
   Virgin VSCDT 1588, July 8, 1996, No 1

CD2 'Wannabe' (Radio Edit) / 'Wannabe' (Dave Way Alternative Mix) / 'Wannabe' (Motiv8 Dub Slam) / 'Wannabe' (Instrumental)
   Virgin VSCDX 1588, July 8, 1996

'Say You'll Be There'

CD1 'Say You'll Be There' (Single Mix) / 'Take Me Home' / 'Say You'll Be There' (Junior's Main Pass) / 'Say You'll Be There' (Instrumental)
   Virgin VSCDT 1601, October 14, 1996, No 1

CD2 'Say You'll Be There' (Single Mix) / 'Say You'll Be There' (Spice Of Life Mix) / 'Say You'll Be There' (Linslee's Extended Mix) / 'Say You'll Be There' (Junior's Dub Girls)
   Virgin VSCDG 1601, October 14, 1996

'2 Become 1'

CD1 '2 Become 1' (Single Version) / '2 Become 1' (Orchestral Version) / 'One Of These Girls' / 'Wannabe' (Junior Vasquez Remix Edit)
   Virgin VSCDT 1607, December 16, 1996, No 1

CD2 '2 Become 1' (Single Version) / '2 Become 1' (Dave Way Remix) / 'Sleigh Ride'
   Virgin VSCDX 1607, December 16, 1996

'Who Do You Think You Are' / 'Mama' (Comic Relief)

CD1 'Mama' (Radio Version) / 'Who Do You Think You Are' (Radio Version) / 'Baby Come Round' / 'Mama' (Biffco Mix)
    Virgin VSCDG 1623, March 3, 1997, No 1

CD2 'Who Do You Think You Are' (Radio Version) / 'Mama' (Radio Version) / 'Who Do You Think You Are' (Morales Club Mix) / 'Who Do You Think You Are' (Morales Dub Mix)
    Virgin VSCDT 1623, March 3, 1997

'Spice Up Your Life'

CD1 'Spice Up Your Life' (Stent Radio Mix) / 'Spice Up Your Life' (Morales Radio Mix) / 'Spice Up Your Life' (Stent Radio Instrumental) / 'Spice Invaders'
    Virgin VSCDT 1660, October 13, 1997, No 1

CD2 'Spice Up Your Life' (Stent Radio Mix) / 'Spice Up Your Life' (Morales Carnival Club Mix) / 'Spice Up Your Life' (Murk Cuba Libre Mix)
    Virgin VSCDG 1660, October 13, 1997

'Too Much'

CD1 'Too Much' (Radio Edit) / 'Outer Space Girls' / 'Too Much' (Soul Shock & Karlin Remix)
    Virgin VSCDR 1669, December 15, 1997, No 1

CD2 'Too Much' (Radio Edit) / 'Too Much' (Orchestral Version) / 'Walk Of Life'
    Virgin VSCDX 1669, December 15, 1997

'Stop'

CD1 'Stop' / 'Something Kinda Funny' (Live In Istanbul) / 'Mama' (Live In Istanbul) / 'Love Thing' (Live In Istanbul)
    Virgin VSCDT 1679, March 9, 1998, No 2

CD2 'Stop' / 'Ain't No Stopping Us Now' (Featuring Luther Vandross) / 'Stop' (Morales Remix) / 'Stop' (Stretch n' Vern's Rock n' Roll Mix)
    Virgin VSCDX 1679, March 9, 1998

'Viva Forever'

CD1 'Viva Forever' / 'Viva Forever' (Tony Rich Remix) / 'Viva Forever' (Tony Rich Instrumental) / Interactive Video
    Virgin VSCDT 1692, July 20, 1998, No 1

*Discography*

CD2 'Viva Forever' / 'Who Do You Think Your Are' (Live) / 'Say You'll Be There' (Live)
    Virgin VSCDX 1692, July 20, 1998

'Goodbye'

CD 1 'Goodbye' (Radio Edit) / 'Christmas Wrapping' / 'Goodbye' (Orchestral Version)
    Virgin VSCDT 1721, December 14, 1998, No 1

CD2 'Goodbye' (Single Version) / 'Sisters (Are Doin' It For Themselves)' (Live) / 'We Are Family' (Live)
    Virgin VSCDX 1721, December 14, 1998

'Holler' / 'Let Love Lead The Way'

CD1 'Holler' (Radio Edit) / 'Let Love Lead The Way' (Radio Edit) / 'Holler' (MAW Remix) / 'Holler' (Video)
    Virgin VSCDT 1788, October 23, 2000, No 1

CD2 'Let Love Lead The Way' (Radio Edit) / 'Holler' (Radio Edit) / 'Holler' (MAW Tribal Vocal) / 'Let Love Lead The Way' (Behind The Scenes) / 'Let Love Lead The Way' (Video)
    Virgin VSCDG 1788, October 23, 2000

## ALBUMS

*Spice*

'Wannabe' / 'Say You'll Be There' / '2 Become 1' / 'Love Thing' / 'Last Time Lover' / 'Mama' / 'Who Do You Think You Are' / 'Something Kinda Funny' / 'Naked' / 'If U Can't Dance'
    Virgin CDV 2812, November 4, 1996, No 1

*Spiceworld*

'Spice Up Your Life' / 'Stop' / 'Too Much' / 'Saturday Night Divas' / 'Never Give Up On The Good Times' / 'Move Over' / 'Do It' / 'Denying' / 'Viva Forever' / 'The Lady Is A Vamp'
    Virgin CDV 2850, November 3, 1997, No 1

*Forever*

'Holler' / 'Tell Me Why' / 'Let Love Lead The Way' / 'Right Back At Ya' / 'Get Down With Me' / 'Wasting My Time' / 'Weekend Love' / 'Time Goes By' / 'If You Wanna Have Some Fun' / 'Oxygen' / 'Goodbye'
    Virgin CDV X2928, November 6, 2000, No 2

## MELANIE B

**SINGLES**

'I Want You Back' (Radio Edit) / 'I Want You Back' (Soundtrack Version) / 'I Want You Back' (MAW Remix)
(Duet with Missy Elliott which featured on the soundtrack of the film *Why Do Fools Fall In Love*.)
    Virgin VSCDT 1716, September 14, 1998, No 1

'Word Up' / 'Sophisticated Lady' / 'Word Up' (Tim's Dance Mix) / 'Interactive Element' (Word Up Video)
    Virgin VSCDT 1735, July 10, 1999, No 14

'Tell Me' (Radio Edit) / 'Tell Me' (Soul Central Remix) / 'Tell Me' (Silk House Workout 7″ Remix) / 'Tell Me' (Enhanced Video)
    Virgin VSCDT 1777, September 25, 2000, No 4

'Feels So Good' (Radio Edit) / 'Feels So Good' (Maurice's Feelin' Good Soul Radio Mix) / 'Feels So Good' (Blacksmith R&B Rub) featuring Know ?uestion / 'Feels So Good' (Video)
    Virgin VSCDT 1787, February 19, 2001, No 5

'Lullaby' / 'Lullaby' (India-I Remix) / 'Feels So Good' (Maurice's On The Fly Dub) / 'Lullaby' (Video)
    Virgin VSCDT 1798, June 4, 2001, No 13

**ALBUM**

*Hot*

'Feels So Good' / 'Tell Me' / 'Hell No' / 'Lullaby' / 'Hotter' / 'ABC 123' / 'I Believe' / 'I Want You Back' / 'Pack Your Shit' / 'Feel Me Now'
    Virgin CDVX 2918, October 9, 2001, No 28

## MELANIE C

**SINGLES**

'When You're Gone' (Duet With Bryan Adams)
CD1 'When You're Gone' / 'Hey Baby' / 'When You're Gone' (Solo)
    Mercury 582821/19-2, November 30, 1998, No 3

## Discography

CD2 'When You're Gone' / 'I Love Ya Too Much' / 'What Does It Do To Your Heart'
    Mercury 582 821-2, November 30, 1998

'Goin' Down' (Radio Version) / 'Ga Ga' / 'Angel On My Shoulder'
    Virgin VSDCT 1744, September 27, 1999, No 4

'Northern Star' (Single Version) / 'Follow Me' / 'Northern Star' (Full Version) / 'Northern Star' (Interactive Video)
    Virgin VSCDT 1748, November 22, 1999, No 4

'Never Be The Same Again' (Single Edit) / 'I Wonder What It Would Be Like' / 'Never Be The Same Again' (Lisa Lopes Remix) / 'Never Be The Same Again' (Video) (With Lisa 'Left Eye' Lopes)
    Virgin VSCDT 1762, March 20, 2000, No 1

'I Turn To You' (Hex Hector Radio Mix) / 'I Turn To You' (Stonebridge R&B Radio Mix) / 'Never Be The Same Again' (Recorded Live At MTV) / 'I Turn To You' (Video)
    Virgin VSCDT 1772, August 7, 2000, No 1

'If That Were Me' / 'If That Were Me' (Acoustic Version) / 'When You're Gone' (Live) Bryan Adams & Melanie C / 'If That Were Me' (Video)
    Virgin VSCDT 1786, November 27, 2000, No 18

'Here It Comes Again'

CD1 'Here It Comes Again' [Radio Edit] / 'Love To You' / 'Like That'
    Virgin VSCDJ 1842, February 24, 2003, No 7

CD2 'Here It Comes Again' [Video] / 'Love To You' / 'Living Without You' / 'Behind The Scenes At Video Shoot'
    Virgin VSCDT 1842, February 24, 2003

'On The Horizon'

CD 'On The Horizon' [Radio Mix] / 'I Love You Without Trying'
    Virgin VSCDT1851, June 2, 2003, No 14

DVD 'On The Horizon' [Video] / 'Never Be The Same Again' [Acoustic] / 'Wonderland' / 'Behind The Scenes At Video Shoot'
    Virgin VSDVD 1851, June 2, 2003

'Melt' / 'Yeh Yeh Yeh'

CD 1 'Melt' [Album Version] / 'Yeh Yeh Yeh' [Radio Mix]
    Virgin VSCDY 1858, November 10, 2003, No 27

CD2 'Melt' [Album Version] / 'Yeh Yeh Yeh' [Radio Mix] / 'Knocked Out' / 'Yeh Yeh Yeh' [Video]
    Virgin VSCDX 1858, November 10, 2003

## ALBUMS

*Northern Star*

'Go!' / 'Northern Star' / 'Goin' Down' / 'I Turn To You' / 'If That Were Me' / 'Never Be The Same Again' / 'Why' / 'Suddenly Monday' / 'Ga Ga' / 'Be The One' / 'Closer' / 'Feel The Sun' / 'Never Be The Same Again' (Single Mix) / 'I Turn To You' (Hex Hector Radio Mix)
    Virgin CDV 2893, October 18, 1999, No 4

*Reason*

'Here It Comes Again' / 'Reason' / 'Lose Myself In You' / 'On The Horizon' / 'Positively Somewhere' / 'Melt' / 'Do I' / 'Soul Boy' / 'Water' / 'Home' / 'Let's Love' / 'Yeh Yeh Yeh'
    Virgin CDV 2969, March 10, 2003, No 5

# GERI

## SINGLES

'Look At Me' / 'Look At Me' (Mark's Big Vocal Mix – Surgery Edit) / 'Look At Me' (Terminalhead Remix)/ 'Look At Me' (Video)
    EMI CDEM 542, May 10, 1999, No 2

'Mi Chico Latino' / 'G.A.Y.' / 'Summertime' / 'Mi Chico Latino' (Video)
    EMI CDEMS 548, August 16, 1999, No 1

'Lift Me Up' (Original Version) / 'Live And Let Die' / 'Very Slowly' / 'Lift Me Up' (Video)
    EMI CDEM 554, November 1, 1999, No 1

'Bag It Up'

CD1 'Bag It Up' / 'These Boots Are Made For Walking' / 'Perhaps, Perhaps, Perhaps' / 'Bag It Up' (Video)
    EMI CDEMS 560, March 13, 2000, No 1

*Discography*

CD2 'Bag It Up' / 'Bag It Up' [D-Bop's Chocolate Vocal Edit] / 'Bag It Up' [Trouser Enthusiasts' Edit] / 'Bag It Up' [Yomanda Edit]
    EMI CDEM 560, March 13, 2000

'It's Raining Men'

CD1 'It's Raining Men' [Album Version] / 'I Was Made That Way' / 'Brave New World' / 'It's Raining Men' [Video]
    EMI CDEMS 584, April 30, 2001, No 1

CD 2 'It's Raining Men' [Album Version] / 'It's Raining Men' [Bold And Beautiful Glamour Mix Edit] / 'It's Raining Men' [Almighty Mix Edit] / 'It's Raining Men' [D-Bop Tall And Blonde Mix Edit]
    EMI CDEM 584, April 30, 2001

'Scream If You Wanna Go Faster'

CD1 'Scream If You Wanna Go Faster' / 'New Religion' / 'Breaking Glass'
    EMI CDEMS 595, July 30, 2001, No 8

CD 2 'Scream If You Wanna Go Faster' / 'Scream If You Wanna Go Faster' [Sleaze Sisters Anthem Edit] / 'Scream If You Wanna Go Faster' [Rob Searle Edit] / 'Scream If You Wanna Go Faster' [Burnt Remix]
    EMI CDEM 595, July 30, 2001

'Calling'

CD1 'Calling' / 'Getting Better' / 'Destiny'/ 'Calling' [Video]
    EMI CDEMS 606, November 26, 2001, No 7

CD 2 'Calling' (Radio Edit) / 'Calling' (Wip 'Coeur De Lion' Edit) / 'Calling' [Metro 7" Mix] / 'Calling' [Mauve's Factor 25 Mix Edit] / 'Calling' [Mareeko Remix Edit]
    EMI CDEMDJ 606, November 26, 2001

**ALBUMS**

*Schizophonic*

'Bag It Up' / 'Goodnight Kiss' / 'Let Me Love You' / 'Lift Me Up' / 'Look At Me' / 'Mi Chico Latino' / 'Someone's Watching Over Me' / 'Sometime' / 'Walkaway' / 'You're In A Bubble'
    EMI 521 0092, June 7, 1999, No 4

*Scream If You Wanna Go Faster*

'Scream If You Wanna Go Faster' / 'Shake Your Bootie Cutie' / 'Calling' / 'Feels Like Sex' / 'Circles Round The Moon' / 'Don't Call Me Baby' / 'Lovey Dovey Stuff' / 'It's Raining Men' / 'Heaven And Hell (Being Geri Halliwell)' / 'I Was Made That Way'
    EMI 533 3692, May 14, 2001, No 5

# EMMA

**SINGLES**

'What I Am' (Radio Edit) / 'What I Am' (Gangstarr Remix) / 'What I Am' (Groove Chronicles Remix) (With Tin Tin Out)
    VC Recordings VCRD 53, November 13, 1999, No 2

'What Took You So Long' / '(Hey You) Free Up Your Mind' / 'Merry-Go-Round' / 'What Took You So Long' (Interactive Video Element)
    Virgin VSCDT 1796, April 2, 2001, No 1

'Take My Breath Away' (Single Mix) / 'Close Encounter' / 'Take My Breath Away' (Tin Tin Out Mix)
    Virgin VSCDT1814, August 27, 2001, No 5

'We're Not Gonna Sleep Tonight' (Radio Mix) / 'We're Not Gonna Sleep Tonight' (3AM Mix) / 'Let Your Baby Show You How To Move'
    Virgin 5461892, December 10, 2001, No 20

'Free Me'

CD1 'Free Me' / 'Who The Hell Are You' / 'Free Me' (Full Intention's Freed Up Mix) / 'Free Me' (Enhanced Video)
    19/Universal 9807472, May 26, 2003, No 5

CD2 'Free Me' / 'Tomorrow' / 'Free Me' (Full Intention's Sultra Mix)
    19/Universal 9807472/73, May 26, 2003

'Maybe' / 'Don't Tell Me You Love Me Anymore' / 'Maybe' (Bini And Martini Club Mix) / 'Maybe' (Enhanced Video)
    19/Universal 9812785, October 13, 2003, No 6

## Discography

'I'll Be There'

CD1 'I'll Be There' / 'Takin' It Easy' / 'I'll Be There' (Europa XL Vocal Mix) / 'I'll Be There' (Bimbo Jones Vocal Mix) / 'I'll Be There' (Enhanced Video)
    19/Universal 9816267/8, January 26, 2004

CD 2 'I'll Be There' / 'So Long'
    19/Universal 9816267, January 26, 2004, No 7

'Crickets Sing For Anamaria'

CD1 'Crickets Sing For Anamaria' (Original Radio Edit – 2:46) / 'Eso Beso' (3:14) / 'So Nice (Summer Samba)' (3:11) / 'Crickets Sing For Anamaria' (Elements' Crickets Dance) / 'On Tequila Booty Mix' (4:15)
    19/Universal 9866826/56, May 31, 2004, No 15

CD2 'Crickets Sing For Anamaria' (Original Radio Edit – 2:46) / 'Maybe' (Latino Version – 3:54)
    19/Universal 9866856, May 31, 2004

## ALBUMS

*A Girl Like Me*

'What Took You So Long?' / 'Take My Breath Away' / 'A World Without You' / 'High On Love' / 'A Girl Like Me' / 'Spell It O.U.T.' / 'Sunshine On A Rainy Day' / 'Been There, Done That' / 'Better Be Careful' / 'We're Not Gonna Sleep Tonight' / 'She Was A Friend Of Mine' / 'What I Am'
    Virgin CDV 2935, April 16, 2001, No 4

*Free Me*

'Free Me' / 'Maybe' / 'I'll Be There' / 'Tomorrow' / 'Breathing' / 'Crickets Sing For Anamaria' / 'No Sign Of Life' / 'Who The Hell Are You' / 'Lay Your Love On Me' / 'Amazing' (With Luis Fonsi) / 'You Are' / 'Something So Beautiful'
    Virgin 9866158, February 9, 2004, No 7

# VICTORIA

### SINGLES

'Out Of Your Mind' (Radio Edit) / 'Out Of Your Mind' (10° Below vs X. Men Vocal Mix) / 'Out Of Your Mind' (10° Below Dub)
(With True Steppers)
    Nu Life, 74321782942, August 14, 2000, No 2

'Not Such An Innocent Girl'

UK CD 'Not Such An Innocent Girl' / 'In Your Dreams' / 'Not Such An Innocent Girl' (Sunship Mix)
    Virgin VSCDT 1816, September 17, 2001, No 6

UK DVD 'Behind The Scenes Footage Of Victoria' (Video) / 'Not Such An Innocent Girl' (Video) / 'Not Such An Innocent Girl' (Robbie Rivera's Main Mix) / 'Not Such An Innocent Girl' (Sunship Dub)
    Virgin VSDVD 1816, September 17, 2001

'A Mind Of Its Own'

UK CD 'A Mind Of Its Own' / 'Always Be My Baby' / 'Feels So Good'
    Virgin VSCDT 1824, February 11, 2002, No 6

UK DVD 'A Mind Of Its Own' / 'Always Be My Baby' / 'Feels So Good' / 'Victoria "Behind The Scenes" At The Video Shoot'
    Virgin VSDVD 1824, February 11, 2002

'This Groove' / 'Let Your Head Go'

CD1 'This Groove' (Radio Edit) / 'Let Your Head Go' (Radio Edit)
    CDVB1, December 29, 2003, No 3

CD2 'Let Your Head Go' [Jakatta Remix] / 'This Groove' [Para Beats Remix] / 'Let Your Head Go' [Radio Edit] / 'This Groove' [Radio Edit]
    CXVB1, December 29, 2003

### ALBUM

*Victoria Beckham*

'A Mind Of Its Own' / 'Every Part Of Me' / 'Girlfriend' / 'I Wish' / 'I.O.U.' / 'Let Your Head Go' / 'Like That' / 'Midnight Fantasy' / 'No Trix' / 'No Games' / 'Not Such An Innocent Girl' / 'That Kind Of Girl' / 'Unconditional Love' / 'Watcha Talkin' Bout'
    Virgin CDV 2942, October 1, 2001, No 10

# Acknowledgements

There are some people who have the knack of falling on their feet. My old friend Robert Sandall is one of them. Having been a successful journalist for many years with the *Sunday Times*, he landed a job, out of the blue, as Director of Press with Virgin Records in January 1996. Having had no prior experience in this line of work whatsoever, as far as I could make out, he was put in charge of a roster of acts which included a new, all-girl pop group called the Spice Girls, which Virgin were preparing to launch in the summer. Within months of taking up his post, Robert was thus overseeing the press for the biggest media phenomenon of the decade, if not in pop history.

I'm glad to say that this sudden elevation didn't go to his head, and as he strode through the Spice mayhem with his usual patrician air, Robert certainly did not forget about his friends. With the full largesse of the Virgin expense account now at his disposal, he generously took me off on trips with the Girls to far-flung locations, like Granada and Johannesburg, and continued to keep me up to date with their various comings and goings, when he doubtless had many other, more pressing matters to attend to.

Enter Chris Charlesworth, editor at Omnibus and my near neighbour in Shepherds Bush, who chanced one day to send me a letter.

"Dear David, On those odd occasions when we bump into one another, I've been meaning to ask whether you ever felt like writing a book. So here goes . . . At our last editorial meeting we discussed an idea for a serious book on the Spice Girls . . . Might you be interested?"

Not long afterwards, I found myself gazing at row upon row of books dedicated to the cobwebbed legends of rock'n'roll in Helter Skelter and wondering why it was that no one had written a proper book about the biggest pop group in the world – as they still were back then.

Robert introduced me to a literary agent, Zoë Waldie of Rogers, Coleridge & White Ltd, and soon she had clinched a deal with Omnibus, which I suspect may have been more generous than Chris had initially intended, but which certainly enabled me to devote the time and effort needed to get the job done. So my very great thanks in the first instance must go to Robert, Chris and Zoë for making the whole thing happen.

Robert subsequently spent hours of his time telling me his side of the story, and putting me in touch with many of the people who could fill in the gaps. I couldn't have written the book without his constant encouragement and practical help. Chris turned out to be the ideal editor; supportive, rigorous, immensely experienced and quietly professional.

Of the people who subsequently talked to me there were those who simply gave me their bit of the story. In nearly every case it was the first time that they had agreed to be interviewed by anyone on the subject of the Spice Girls. Many, many thanks to each and every one of you. This is your story and I hope I have done it justice.

Then there were those who not only contributed to the narrative, but also assisted, encouraged and generally kept me on track through thick and thin. A huge thank you then to Alan Edwards of the Outside Organization and Julian Henry of Henry's House, both of whom maintained a delicate balance between helping me find out what I wanted to know and hanging on to their jobs! Many thanks also to Paul Conroy, Ray Cooper and especially Ashley Newton, all formerly of Virgin Records, who took my calls, talked at length, supplied me with contacts and I'm sure opened many doors.

Pete Evans at Native management put me in touch with all the songwriters and producers with a brisk minimum of fuss. And Martyn Barter, Nancy Phillips and Gerrard Tyrrell all helped in ways that went beyond merely answering my questions. Thanks to you all.

I also wish to thank the following people who contributed time, thought, effort or expertise – and in some cases all of the above – on behalf of this book: Bernard Alexander, Jeff Apter, Keith Badman, Lucy Barnicot, the original Mel Brown, Adrian Deevoy, David Fricke, Sophie Green, Chris Heath, Jules Higgs, Mark Hodkinson, Paul Kinder, Maria Maganto, Tony Michaelides, Debbie Morrison, Caroline McAteer, Shane O'Neill, Rachel Silver, Amanda Silverman, Faith Sinclair, Jack Sinclair, Jill Sinclair, Andrew Smith, John Street, David Thomas, Alexis (Outside).

Finally, there is the help you sometimes get in writing a book that passes all understanding. For this, and so much more, I must thank my darling wife, Pru.

*David Sinclair*
*London, July, 2004*

# Source Notes & References

**1 – So You Want To Be A . . . Popstar**
David Thomas – interview with Bob & Chris Herbert, *Daily Mail*, 1997
Philip Norman – feature *Sunday Times Magazine*, 21.9.97
Yorkshire TV – *Raw Spice*, produced & directed by Neil Davies, 21.3.01
Andy Davis – Spice Invaders! feature, *Record Collector*, May 1997
*Interviews*: Melanie C, Erwin Keiles, Pepe Lemer, Robert Sandall, Nicki Chapman

**2 – The House Of Fun**
Granada – *Raw Spice* (VHS GV0370) produced & directed by Neil Davies
Geoffrey Wansell – The Posh Files, *Daily Mail*, 27.1.01
Sylvia Patterson – Nobby Styles!, *New Musical Express*, 26.8.00
Dylan Jones – *Sunday Times Magazine*, 28.2.99
Bill Dunn & Peter Howarth – *Esquire*, December 98
Tina Jackson – *The Big Issue*, 14.9.98
David Jenkins – *Sunday Telegraph Magazine*, 24.10.99
Jane Moore – *Sunday Times Style*
Neil McCormick – *Telegraph Magazine*, 25.9.99
Stephen Dalton – C99 Go!, *New Musical Express*, 21.8.99
Jan Moir – *Daily Telegraph*, 10.8.98
Doug Kempster – *Sunday Mirror*, 4.3.01
Staff reporter – *Ananova*, 15.9.01
Obituary (Bob Herbert) – *The Times*, 12.8.99
*Interview*: Chris Herbert

**3 – You Hum It, We'll Play It**
Jenny Eliscu – Little Miss Can't Be Wrong, *Rolling Stone*, 20.3.03
*Interviews*: Matt Rowe, Elliot Kennedy, Paul Wilson & Andy Watkins (Absolute), Richard "Biff" Stannard

**4 – Girl Power**
*Telegraph Magazine* circa April 98
Robert Sandall – Bank Your Lucky Stars, *Sunday Times Magazine*, March 03
Profile Simon Fuller – *Sunday Times*, 27.7.03
Lisa Verrico – *The Times*, 10.8.96
*Billboard*, 2.11.96
*New York Daily News*, 11.8.00

*Interviews*: Martin Barter, Paul Wilson & Andy Watkins (Absolute), Robert Sandall, Paul Conroy, Nicki Chapman, Ashley Newton, Ray Cooper, Kim Fuller

## 5 – Children Of The Revolution
Pete Clark – Cherry's aid for Spice Girls, *London Evening Standard*, 22.10.96
Dominic Pride – Virgin's Spice Girls Spread Flavor Globally, *Billboard*, 2.9.96
Paul Gorman – Spice Girls: 12 Months to World Domination, *Music Week*, 5.7.97
Paul Moody – The Rise and Rise of Zigazig-Ah Stardust, *New Musical Express*, 23.11.96
Sheryl Garratt – Spice Grrrls, *Big Issue*, 16.12.96
Simon Sebag-Montefiore – Spice Girls Back Sceptics On Europe, *Spectator*, 14.12.96
Frank Johnson – Spice Girls and their Unwritten Constitution, *Daily Telegraph*, 14.12.96
Chris Heath – Top Of The World, Ma, *The Face*, March 97
Editorial – And Finally . . ., *The Sun*, 14.12.96
Sian Pattenden – Zigga-Zigga-Zeitgeist, *Select*, March 97
Alasdair Palmer – A Popular Singing Group, Your Honour, *Sunday Telegraph*, 15.12.96
John Hind – Naughty But Spice, *Observer*, 15.12.96
Anne Perkins – It's Raining Celebs As Geri Backs Blair, *Guardian*, 14.5.02
Profile Simon Fuller – *Sunday Times*, 27.7.03
Simon Sebag Montefiore – Barnacles On The Rock Of Ages, *Sunday Times*, 21.12.97
*Interviews*: Robert Sandall, Ray Cooper, Gerrard Tyrrell, Ashley Newton, Nicki Chapman, Simon Fuller, Spice Girls

## 6 – Automatic For The People
Paul Gorman – Spice Girls: 12 Months to World Domination, *Music Week*, 5.7.97
Editorial – Sugar And Spice, *The Times*, 17.2.97
Staff Reporter – Smell Of Money, *Plymouth Evening Herald*, 27.8.97
Robert Ashton – Spice Girls Add Fizz To Pepsi, *Music Week*, 10.5.97
William Leith – Play Spot The Spice Girls, *Observer*, 13.4.97
Richard C. Morais with Katherine Bruce – What I Wanna, Wanna, Really Wannabe, *Forbes*, 22.9.97
Natalie Cheary – Over Spiced, *Marketing Week*, 2.10.97
Philip Norman – Spice Lolly, *Sunday Times*, 21.9.97
Alice Rawsthorn – Spicing Up The Supermarkets, *Financial Times*, 11.10.97
Ali Qassim – How The Band Led The Brand To Expand Pepsi's Market Share, *Campaign*, 7.11.97

*Source Notes & References*

Adrian Deevoy – We Have Come For Your Children, *Q*, December 97
David Kamp – London Swings! Again!, *Vanity Fair*, March 97
*Interviews*: Ashley Newton, Gerrard Tyrrell, Simon Fuller, Kim Fuller


## 7 – Queens Of The Spice Age
Adrian Deevoy – The Spice Man Cometh, *Mail On Sunday*, 9.5.97
*Interviews*: Simon Fuller, Robert Sandall, Nicki Chapman, Spice Girls, Kim Fuller


## 8 – Help!
Matthew Wright – Has the Bubble Burst?, *Mirror*, 11.11.97
Alison Boshoff – Booing Ends A Week To Forget In The Life Of Spice, *Daily Telegraph*, 15.11.97
Howell Llewellyn – Virgin Blames Photographers For Fiasco At Spanish Awards, *Music & Media*, 29.11.97
Alex Bellos – Spice Girls Lose Sweet Smell Of Success, *Guardian*, 15.11.97
Paul Gorman – Which Way Next For Spice Girls Following The Big Fuller Fall-Out?, *Music Week*, 22.11.97
Andy Coulson – Booing Was Funny, *The Sun*, 17.11.97
Peter Beaumont & Richard Brooks – Life Imitates The Art Of Spice, *Observer*, 16.10.97
Matthew Wright – Why Do The Spice Girls Work Seven Days A Week?, *Mirror*, 18.11.97
Matthew Wright – Thrice Girls, *Mirror*, 18.12.98
Alan Edwards – Add Sugar To Spice, *Guardian*, 2.2.98
Mat Smith & Jody Thompson – Spice Work, If You Can Get It, *New Musical Eexpress*, 22.11.97
Ben MacIntyre – Beatle Scorns "Boring" Modern Pop Groups, *The Times*, 28.8.97
Boy George – Outside Edge, *Daily Express*, 30.10.96
Transcript of Phil Spector – The Q Special Award, *Q*, January 98
So Who Is The Biggest Band In The World? – *Q*, December 1997
Miranda Sawyer – They Were The Girl Power Rangers, *Observer*, 21.12.97
*Interviews*: Robert Sandall, Melanie C, Victoria, Gerrard Tyrrell, Alan Edwards, Thom Yorke, Ray Cooper, Spice Girls, Nancy Phillips


## 9 – Ginger Snaps
Richard Morrison – And The Winner Is . . . Corporate Spice, *The Times*, 9.2.98
Eugene Moloney – Hot And Sp(r)icey, *Dublin Evening Herald*, 19.2.98
unknown – Divas Forever, *More*, 9.9.98
Dylan Jones – Spice Invaders, *Sunday Times Magazine*, 13.9.98

Neil McCormick – Now Only Four, The Spice Girls Perform Better Than Before, *Daily Telegraph*, 17.6.98
*Interviews*: Simon Fuller, Robert Sandall, Nicki Chapman, Bart Cools, Spice Girls, Ray Cooper

**10 – Back In 15 Mins**
Sue Evison – Mel, Sex And Me, *The Sun*, 4.9.00
Caroline Sullivan – Growl Power, *Guardian*, 9.7.99
Angela Mollard – How Sad Ginger Lost Her Spice, *Daily Mail*, 19.6.99
Tony Marcus – Fit!, *I-D*, January 99
Stephen Dalton – C99 Go!, *New Musical Express*, 21.8.99
Andy Pietrasik – Sublime To Ridiculous, *Guardian*, 24.8.99
Steve Sutherland – Kill A Mock Rocking Bird, *New Musical Express*, 16.10.99
unknown – Emma Spice, *Sky Magazine*, June 98
Matthew Wright – My Love For Geri, *Mirror*, 6.11.99
Hard To Avoid... Emma Bunton, *Guardian*, 5.11.99
Neil Michael – A Pick-me-up For Geri As She Beats Pop Rival Emma To No.1, *Daily Express*, 8.11.99
Sandra Laville & Nicole Martin – Better Red Than Dead, *Daily Telegraph*, 5.11.99
*Interviews*: Elliot Kennedy, Biff Stannard, Bart Cools, Paul Wilson & Andy Watkins (Absolute), Nicki Chapman, Simon Fuller, Nancy Phillips

**11 – That Difficult Solo/Third Album**
Scott Manson – Posh And Decks, *Ministry*, September 00
Betty Clarke – Yearning For The Days Of Old Spice, *Guardian*, 3.11.00
Angus Batey – 'Forever' (review), *The Times*, 4.11.00
Ethan Brown – Production Values, *New York*, 1.5.00
Chairman Mao – The Cut Creator, *Vibe*, 21.5.99
*Interviews*: Biff Stannard, Ashley Newton, Nancy Phillips, Alan Edwards, Jimmy Jam, Fred Jerkins III, LaShawn Daniels

**12 – Gone West**
Dominic Mohan – Sporty Spite! *The Sun*, 8.11.00
3am Girls – Spite Girls v Bestlife, *Mirror*, 8.11.00
Dominic Mohan – End Of The Spice Girls, *The Sun*, 9.3.01
Ben Todd – The End Of Spice Girls, *Daily Star*, 9.3.01
Dominic Mohan – Spice Fury Over Mel C, *The Sun*, 10.3.01
Mark Frith – Geri Tells All!, *Heat*, 5.5.01
Jay Bowers – Hit Or Bust For Mel B, *Now*, 9.5.01
Julia Davis – Victoria And David Beckham, *OK!*, 11.5.01
*Interviews*: Nancy Phillips, Alan Edwards, Elliot Kennedy, Ashley Newton, Fred Jerkins III, LaShawn Daniels

*Source Notes & References*

**13 – Fuller Himself**
Victoria Newton – S Club Get £1/2m While Manager Rakes In £50m, *The Sun*, 23.4.03
Paul Sexton – Technology Creates An Idol World, *Financial Times*, 4.5.04
David Rowan – Devil Woman's Football Game, *London Evening Standard*, 30.7.03
Alexis Petrides – Melanie C – Reason, *Guardian*, 7.3.03
*Interviews*: Nancy Phillips, Melanie C, Simon Fuller, LaShawn Daniels, Jimmy Jam

**14 – The Million Dollar Woman**
Lina Das – I Still Can't Stop Myself Blushing Over My Men, *London Evening Standard*, 9.10.03
How Gay Are You? – Emma Bunton, *Attitude*, Oct 03
Peter Robinson – Versus Emma Bunton, *New Musical Express*, 18.10.03
John Arlidge – Dash For Cash, *Observer*, 9.5.04
Chrissy Iley – Work It Like Beckham, *Sunday Times Style*, 21.12.03
Rick Hewitt – I Spice A Star In Need Of A Hit, *The Scotsman*, 8.12.03
Ben Todd – Me And Beckham, By Rebecca Loos, *Mirror*, 11.4.04
Amanda Platell – Why We Women Hate Posh, *Daily Mail*, 8.4.04
Julie Burchill – Posh, It's Time To Stand By Your Man, *The Times*, 10.4.04
Victoria Newton – Victoria Is A Girl To See It Through, *The Sun*, 12.4.04
Roy Greenslade – The Game Stinks, *Guardian*, 19.4.04
Fiona Cummins, Richard Smith & Pete Samson – Beckham Sex Sensation: Four More Claims, *Mirror*, 8.4.04
Kate Thornton – What Now For Victoria?, *Marie Claire*, July, 04
Lydia Slater – Bye, Bye, Baby, *ES magazine*, 21.5.04
*Interviews*: Julian Henry, Damon Dash, Kim Fuller

**15 – Never Ends**
Dominic Mohan & Victoria Newton – What Really Happened At The Spice Reunion, *The Sun*, 19.2.03
Dominic Mohan – Join Me To End Spice Revival, *The Sun*, 17.2.03
Precious Williams – Scary Goes Straight, *Mail On Sunday*, 30.5.04
Helen Pidd – Melanie C, Barfly, Glasgow, *Guardian*, 14.6.04
Victoria Newton – Scrapped!, *The Sun*, June 04
Gavin Hives – Queries: Melanie C, *Attitude*, February 03
*Interviews*: Melanie C, Nancy Phillips, Biff Stannard, Julian Henry

# Bibliography

B, Melanie, *Catch A Fire* (Headline, 2002)
Beckham, Victoria, *Learning To Fly* (Michael Joseph, 2001)
Brown, Tony, Kutler, Jon & Warwick, Neil, *The Complete Book Of The British Charts* (Omnibus, 2002 & 2004)
Du Noyer, Paul (ed.), *The Illustrated Encyclopedia Of Music* (Flame Tree, 2003)
Fitzgerald, Muff, *Spiced Up!* (Hodder and Stoughton, 1998)
Frith, Simon, Straw, Will & Street, John (eds.), *The Cambridge Companion To Pop And Rock* (Cambridge University Press, 2001)
Halliwell, Geri, *If Only* (Bantam Press, 1999)
Halliwell, Geri, *Just For The Record* (Ebury Press, 2002)
Harris, John, *The Last Party – Britpop, Blair And The Demise Of English Rock* (Fourth Estate, 2003)
Morton, Andrew, *Posh & Becks* (Michael O'Mara Books, 2000)
Palm, Carl Magnus, *Bright Lights Dark Shadows* – The Real Story Of Abba (Omnibus, 2001)
Street, John, *Rebel Rock – The Politics Of Popular Music* (Basil Blackwell, 1986)

**Websites:**

allmusic.com
google.co.uk
lycos.com
popbitch.com
SoloSpiceNews.com

# Index

*A Girl Like Me* (Emma album), 235, 239
*A Hard Day's Night* (Beatles film), 115
'A Mind Of Its Own' (Victoria), 241
Aaliyah, 221
Abba, 85–87, 89, 123, 291–293
'Absolute' (Paul Wilson & Andy Watkins), 40, 46, 49, 55, 61, 66, 68, 110, 114, 189, 240, 256
*Absolutely Fabulous* (TV show), 114, 267
Adam & The Ants, 87, 172
Adams, Bryan, 56, 180, 238
Adams, Christian (brother of Victoria), 20
Adams, Jacqueline (mother of Victoria), 20
Adams, Louise (sister of Victoria), 20
Adams, Tony (father of Victoria), 20
Adams, Victoria, *see* Beckham, Victoria
'Against All Odds' (Westlife), 226
Alexander, Gregg, 240, 261, 262
*Alive And Kicking* (TV show), 77
*All American Girl* (TV show), 286
All Saints, 4, 16, 23, 170, 173
*All That You Can't Leave Behind* (U2 album), 227
*American Idol* (US TV show), 250
*An Audience With The Spice Girls* (TV show), 136, 148
'Anarchy In The UK' (Sex Pistols), 152, 193, 194–195
Ancona, Ronni, 275
Anderson, Lisa, 160, 257
Andre, Peter, 253
Another Level, 215
Aplin, Suzi, 77
Appleton, Natalie, 23
Appleton, Nicole, 23
Armstrong, Craig, 88, 193
Arnold, David, 261
'Around The World' (East 17), 42
Ash, 12, 13
Astley, Rick, 51
Aswad, 170
Atomic Kitten, 253
*Attitude* (magazine), 267
Attridge, Paul, 186

B*Witched, 173, 253
Bacharach, Burt, 51

Backstreet Boys, The, 17, 37, 232
'Bag It Up' (Geri), 190, 197, 214, 239
Baggstrom, Klas, 272
Bananarama, 3
Barlow, Gary, 45, 51, 68, 79, 146
Barrett, Richard, 8
Barrymore, Michael, 114
Barter, Martyn, 59, 62
Bassey, Shirley, 191
Batey, Angus, 224
Bay City Rollers, 87, 172
Baylis, Cary, 51
Beastie Boys, 193
Beatles, The, 38, 50, 64, 89, 102, 115, 123, 149, 151, 181, 253
Beckham, David, 181–183, 212, 245, 246, 260, 272–273, 275, 276–278, 280, 292, 294
Beckham, Victoria, 5, 31, 36, 100, 131, 144, 146–147, 150, 156–157, 171, 176, 202, 212, 244–245, 257–258, 275, 294
  background/family, 20
  pre-Spice Girls career, 21
  as singer, 11
  meets David Beckham, 182
  marriage to David, 183
  birth of son Brooklyn, 183
  birth of son Romeo, 260
  image of 'Posh 'n' Becks', 181–182, 278–279
  media coverage/press intrusion, 182–183, 246–247, 276–278, 280–282
  personality of, 166, 184
  sense of humour, 218, 273
  solo career, 57, 215–218, 235, 241–243, 248–249, 259–261, 268–275
  fondness for 'urban' music, 270
  and Damon Dash, 269–274
Beesley, Max, 219, 221
Bermudez, Nuria, 281
Berry, Ken & Nancy, 70
*Big Breakfast, The* (TV show), 14, 81
*Big Brother* (TV show), 279
*Big Issue, The* (magazine), 94
Bilton, Stuart, 181
Binns, Henry, 268
Bjork, 88

Black, Cilla, 11
Blair, Cherie, 82
Blair, Tony, 100
Blatt, Melanie, 23
Blaxill, Ric, 32
Blige, Mary J., 208, 219, 222
Blur, 84, 104, 105, 172, 195, 216
BMG Records, 69, 72
Bondy, Yak, 266
Bono, 125
'Boogie Nights' (Geri), 190
Bowers, Dane, 215, 242
Bowers, Matthew, 37
Bowie, David, 145
Boy George, 69, 151
Boyz II Men, 12
Boyzone, 17, 84, 88, 191, 203, 226
Bradbrook, Charles, 133
Bragg, Billy, 98
Braide, Chris, 242
Brandy & Monica, 208
Branson, Richard, 92
Braxton, Toni, 211
'Breathing' (Emma), 268
Breen, Richard (aka Abs), 38
*Bridget Jones's Diary* (film), 239
Brilliant! (PR company), 14, 135, 160
Bristol Bass Line, 47
Brit Awards, 103, 105, 170–171, 213–214
Britten, Terry, 51
Bros, 2, 3, 16, 36, 41, 151
Brown, Danielle (sister of Mel B), 21
Brown, Ian, 13
Brown, Martin (father of Mel B), 21
Brown, Mel (Arista PR), 73
Brown, Melanie (aka Mel B), 5, 6, 29, 36, 63–64, 75, 82–83, 90, 95, 111, 131, 149, 155, 164–165, 172–173, 206, 244, 257, 294
  background/family, 21
  pre-Spice Girls career, 22
  role within Spice Girls, 165, 167
  as singer, 11
  extrovert nature, 165
  fondness for R&B/urban music, 155, 166, 221, 241
  marriage to/divorce from Jimmy Gulzar, 184–185, 221
  birth of daughter Phoenix Chi, 184
  personality of, 167, 185–186, 218–220, 222
  solo career, 179–180, 187–188, 218–223, 235, 241, 283–286
  star quality of, 5, 223
  as actress, 285
  as TV presenter, 284

'Buffalo Stance' (Neneh Cherry), 94
Bunton, Emma, 82–83, 90, 91, 145, 156, 203, 294
  background/family, 22
  pre-Spice Girls career, 22–23
  musical influences, 268
  joins group 'late', 31
  as singer, 164, 258–259
  relationship with Simon Fuller, 138, 199–200, 257–258, 282
  solo career, 57, 199–201, 235, 238–239, 247–248, 259, 265–268
  personality of, 199
Bunton, Paul (brother of Emma), 22
Bunton, Pauline (mother of Emma), 22, 31
Bunton, Trevor (father of Emma), 22
Burchill, Julie, 277–278
Burke, Kareem "Biggs", 269
*Burn It* (TV show), 285
Busted, 253
Butler, Jonathan, 123
Byrds, The, 1, 10, 14, 253

'C U Next Tuesday' (Spice Girls), 293
Calettos, The, 20
'Calling' (Geri), 235, 240
Cameo, 187
Camitz, Jhoan, 74–75, 117
Campbell, Naomi, 270
'Can't Get You Out Of My Head' (Kylie Minogue), 67, 242
Canty, James, 239
Carey, Mariah, 12, 207, 226, 271
Carlisle, Belinda, 170
Carroll, Dina, 65
Cash, Johnny, 193
*Catch A Fire* (Mel B book), 285
Catherall, Joanne, 4
Cattrall, Kim, 286
Chambers, Guy, 261
Chapman, Nicki, 14, 76–77, 78, 80–81, 84, 132–133, 134, 135–137, 143, 160, 166–168, 191
Cher, 216
Cherry, Neneh, 94
Chisholm, Alan (father of Mel C), 24
Chisholm, Declan (half-brother of Mel C), 24
Chisholm, Liam (half-brother of Mel C), 24
Chisholm, Melanie (aka Mel C), 5, 6, 60, 105, 124, 146, 150, 182, 206, 227–228, 242–243, 253, 291
  background/family, 23–24
  pre-Spice Girls career, 25
  as singer, 11, 164
  role within group, 166

## Index

fondness for 'indie' rock, 166, 194–196
interest in personal fitness, 116, 198
relationship with Anthony Keidis, 193
solo career, 180, 192–199, 212, 214–215, 235–236, 261–264
reluctance to join re-formed group, 290
weight problems/eating disorders, 288–289
disillusionment with fame, 289–290
Christy, Lauren, 58
Clarke, Pete, 94
Clarkson, Lana, 153
Clash, The, 46, 92, 100, 111
Cleopatra, 173
Clifford, Ian, 44
Clifford, Max, 276, 280
*Coast To Coast* (Westlife album), 226, 227
Collins, Phil, 226
Colson, Gail, 160
Combs, Sean "Puff Daddy", 180, 270
'Complicated' (Avril Lavigne), 58
Connarty, Michael, 97
Conroy, Paul, 62, 70, 72, 75, 103, 120, 135, 170, 214n.
Cools, Bart, 158, 168, 186, 199
Cooper, Ray, 70, 91, 110, 154, 178, 205
*Coronation Street* (TV show), 22
Costello, Elvis, 58, 86, 114
Coulson, Andy, 144, 169
Cowell, Simon, 279
'Crickets Sing For Anamaria' (Emma), 268
Crow, Sheryl, 180
Cruzs, Paul F., 197
Culture Club, 65, 69
Curtis, Jamie, 114

*Daily Express*, 111
*Daily Mail*, 192, 245, 277
*Daily Star*, 90, 91, 105
*Daily Telegraph*, 144, 177
Damned, The, 62
'Dancing Queen' (Abba), 86
Danesh, Darius, 253
Daniels, LaShawn, 209–211, 223, 232, 258–259, 261
Dash, Damon, 269–274
Davies, Neil, 37
De Burgh, Chris, 100
De Selva, Simon, 285
De Vries, Marius, 193
Deevoy, Adrian, 119, 131
Def Jam Records, 270
Dennis, Cathy, 66, 67, 130, 200, 242, 294
'Denying' (Spice Girls), 173
Depeche Mode, 74
Destiny's Child, 205, 208, 233

Diana, Princess of Wales, 9, 82, 117–118, 134
Dickens, Rob, 65, 69
Dineen, Molly, 188
Dion, Celine, 12, 56, 159
Dixon, Andrea (mother of Mel B), 21
'Do It' (Spice Girls), 177
'Don't You Want Me' (Human League), 4
Donovan, Jason, 40, 51
Doyle, Sean, 43
Dube, Lucky, 124
Duffy, Keith, 17
Duran Duran, 170, 193, 196
Dylan, Bob, 13, 153, 220

East 17, 40, 42, 51, 69, 151, 170
*EastEnders* (TV show), 23
Edmunds, Kenneth, 206
Edwards, Alan, 145–147, 160, 218, 223, 228–229, 260, 268
Edwards, Lyndsay, 200
Ellen, Barbara, 239
Elliott, Missy, 179–180, 188, 219
Ellis, Simon, 170
Ellis-Bextor, Sophie, 216–217, 244, 273
Emerson, Lake & Palmer, 86
EMI Records, 201
Eminem, 87, 230
*Emmerdale* (TV show), 21
En Vogue, 172
Enya, 159
Erasure, 292
Eternal, 3, 65, 71
Evanescence, 87
Evans, Chris, 77, 189, 201–203, 288
Evans, Pete, 47, 66
'Evergreen'/'Anything Is Possible' (Will Young), 250
*Everybody* (Hear'say album), 38
'Everything Changes' (Take That), 40, 45, 51

50 Cent, 86
*Face, The*, 97
Faithfull, Marianne, 11
'Feed Your Love' (Spice Girls), 42, 48, 48n., 293
'Feel Me Now' (Mel B), 219, 221–222
'Feels So Good' (Mel B), 219, 235
Fellner, Eric, 239
'Fergie' (Black Eyed Peas), 290
Fernandez, Delfin, 281
Fitzgerald, Muff, 91, 92, 93
Five, 17, 28, 36–38, 227
Flint, Keith, 18
*Forever* (album), 161, 204, 210, 224, 225, 226–227, 229–230, 233–234, 256

'Forever Love' (Gary Barlow), 79
*Forever Spice* (book), 201, 203
Fox, Mark, 47–48, 59
Frampton, Andrew, 241, 248
Frampton, Peter, 86
Franks, Lynne, 142
'Free Me' (Emma), 265, 266
*Free Me* (Emma album), 268
Freedman, Edward, 108
Freeman, Dean, 201, 287
French, Dawn, 105
Freud, Matthew, 201
Frith, Mark, 143, 243
Fry, Stephen, 114
Fuller, Kim, 67, 114–115, 137, 139, 159–160, 164, 273, 294
Fuller, Mark, 67
Fuller, Simon, 35, 36, 47, 66, 69, 74, 91, 115, 117, 120, 143, 145, 150, 151, 156, 157, 159–160, 163, 168, 172, 173, 179, 181–182, 186, 199, 212, 225, 233, 242, 249, 253–255, 259, 261, 266, 267, 268, 271, 272–273, 275–276, 286, 291, 294–295
   background/family, 66–67
   pre-Spice Girls career, 67
   becomes manager of Spice Girls, 67–69
   'fired' by Spice Girls, 94, 133–140, 141, 146
   management/business strategy, 79, 103, 113, 116, 128–133, 199–200, 250–252, 254–255, 273
   merchandising/sponsorship deals by, 108–111
   wealth of, 252
   and S Club 7, 163, 254
   regret at 'losing' Spice Girls, 255–257
   reassumes management of individual Spice Girls, 257–258, 260–261

Gabriel, Peter, 125, 160
Gabrielle, 57
Gallagher, Liam 90, 104, 105
Gallagher, Noel, 53, 90
Gangadeen, Andy, 170
Garbage, 193
Garland, Judy, 292
Garrison, Ben, 230
Gates, Gareth, 250–251, 252
Gaye, Marvin, 268
Geldof, Bob, 114
Gerand, Fergus, 170
*Geri Yoga* (DVD), 286
Germano, Alexandre, 265
Gillespie, Bobby, 18
Gindler, Paul, 170

'Girl From Mars' (Ash), 13
'Girl Power' (Shampoo), 60
Girlfriend, 72–73
Girls Aloud, 253
Glitter, Gary, 114, 114n.
Gloss, *see* Bros
Glover, John, 260
Godwin, Nick, 135, 136
'Goin' Down' (Mel C), 187, 196
Goldfinger (Ash), 13
Goldsmith, Hugh, 14
'Goodbye' (Spice Girls), 149, 181, 187, 190, 204, 208, 231
Goodman, Dean, 236
Gordon, Tony, 65
Goss, Luke, 2
Goss, Matt, 2
Grant, Richard E., 63, 114–115
Green Day, 194
Greenslade, Roy, 279–280
*Guardian, The*, 145, 203, 224, 262, 279, 290
Gulzar, Jimmy, 170, 184–185, 220–221
Gun, 187
Guns N' Roses, 193

Haircut 100, 47
Hall, Terri, 130
Halliwell, Geri, 5, 29, 62, 74, 75, 91, 96, 100, 103–104, 108, 115, 145, 149, 152, 157, 159, 165, 171, 178, 243–244, 294
   background/family, 25
   pre-Spice Girls career, 26
   self-belief/boldness of, 5/6
   inexperience as performer, 10, 169
   as singer, 11/12
   as promoter of 'girl power', 60, 76, 174
   extrovert/headstrong personality of, 61, 168–169
   as 'leader'/'motivator' of Spice Girls, 28, 62, 167–168
   craving for 'fame', 26, 33, 191, 202
   role within group, 62, 165–167
   relationship with Matt Rowe, 42–43
   leaves Spice Girls, 174–177
   attitude towards live work, 173
   solo career, 188–192, 201–203, 214, 235, 239–241, 256–257, 286–288
   relationship with Chris Evans, 77, 201–203, 288
   charity/humanitarian work, 189
   weight problems/eating disorders, 287
   as TV presenter, 286
   as author, 189, 192, 286–287
Halliwell, Karen (half-sister of Geri), 25
Halliwell, Lawrence (father of Geri), 25

*Index*

Halliwell, Max (brother of Geri), 25
Halliwell, Natalie (sister of Geri), 25
Halliwell, Paul (half-brother of Geri), 25
Hardcastle, Paul, 67, 294
Harrison, George, 151, 153
Harvey, P.J., 291
Headon, Topper, 92
Hear'say, 6, 7, 37–38, 248, 249
Heart Management, 8, 28, 65
*Heat* (magazine), 143
Heath, Chris, 97
Hector, Hex, 197
*Hell's Kitchen* (TV show), 279
Hendrix, Jimi, 2, 153, 253
Henry, Julian, 142, 145, 260, 281, 295
Herbert, Bob, 2–5, 8, 10, 15, 20, 32, 33–36, 44, 45, 128, 133–134, 138
Herbert, Chris, 2–6, 8, 10, 15, 19, 20, 26, 28, 30–38, 41, 44, 45, 68, 128, 133–134, 138, 249
Herbert, Nicola, 3
'Here It Comes Again' (Mel C), 262
Hidalgo, Ana Maria (mother of Geri), 25
High Llamas, The, 160
Hill, Peter, 294
'Hold My Body Tight' (East 17), 42
Holland, Jools, 114
Holland/Dozier/Holland, 50
'Holler' (Spice Girls), 187, 223, 230
Holly, Buddy, 50
Holmes, Donald, 179
*Hot* (Mel B album), 219–220, 234
Houston, Whitney, 12, 207, 209, 211, 223, 292
Howard, Adina, 48
Howlett, Liam, 18
Human League, 4, 15, 69
Humphries, Barry, 114
Hutchence, Michael, 291

'I Turn To You' (Mel C), 197, 198, 215, 216
'I Want You Back' (Mel B with Missy Elliott), 179–180, 219
'I Won't Change You' (Sophie Ellis-Bextor), 273
'I'll Be There' (Emma), 268
*I'm A Celebrity Get Me Out Of Here* (TV show), 253, 279, 281
Idol, Billy, 194
*If Only* (Geri book), 192, 201, 286–287
'If Six Was Nine' (Jimi Hendrix), 2
'If That Were Me' (Mel C), 235
'If You Can't Dance' (Spice Girls), 178
'If You Wanna Have Some Fun' (Spice Girls), 206

Iglesias, Julio, 30
'In Your Eyes' (Kylie Minogue), 57
'Independence' (Lulu), 45
Ingoldsby, Oliver, 65
*Invincible* (Michael Jackson album), 208
INXS, 291
'It's Like That' (Run DMC), 179
'It's Raining Men' (Geri), 239, 240, 274

Jackson, Janet, 145, 172, 180, 205, 207, 222, 223
Jackson, Michael, 79, 110, 123, 172, 208, 215, 223
Jagger, Mick, 50
Jam, Jimmy, 205–207, 209, 219–220, 221–223, 231–232, 259, 261
Janus, Samantha, 23
Jay-Z (Shawn Corey Carter), 215, 269
Jerkins, Fred, 206
Jerkins, Rodney, 206, 208–211, 214–215, 219, 221, 223–224, 230, 231–233, 238
Jerkins, Ruben, 209
Jerkins III, the Rev Fred, 206, 208
Jethro Tull, 86
Johannson, Tore, 261
John, Elton, 75, 114, 117–118
Johnson, Frank, 95
Jones, Norah, 268
Jones, Steve, 193, 194
Jordan, 253, 281
Judge, Jerry, 134, 143
*Just For The Record* (book), 286

Kas, Abigail, 31
Keating, Ronan, 191, 226
'Keep On Movin'' (Five), 36
Keiles, Erwin, 3, 9, 11, 14, 16
Kennedy, Elliot, 40, 44–46, 49, 51, 53, 56–57, 59, 68, 110, 180, 208, 212, 230, 241
Kensit, Patsy, 104
Kiedis, Anthony, 193
Kipner, Steve, 241, 248
'Knockout' (Triple Eight), 39
Knowles, Beyoncé, 221

'La Isla Bonita' (Madonna), 89
'Lady Is A Vamp, The' (Spice Girls), 190
'Last Time Lover' (Spice Girls), 49
Laurie, Hugh, 114
Lavigne, Avril, 58
Lawrence, Rhett, 197, 238, 241, 247
*Learning To Fly* (Victoria book), 31, 245
Led Zeppelin, 240
Lee, Ian, 10–11

Leith, William, 113
Lemar, 253
Lemer, Pepe, 11, 12, 16, 23, 31
Lennon, John, 50
Lennox, Annie, 66, 67, 69, 130, 172, 200, 240, 294
*Let Go* (Avril Lavigne album), 58
'Let Love Lead The Way' (Spice Girls), 223
'Let Your Head Go' (Victoria), 272–273
*Lethal Dose* (film), 285
Level 42, 170
Lewinson, Steve, 64, 170
Lewis, Terry, 205, 209, 220, 221, 223, 231–232
Liberty X, 6
'Lift Me Up' (Geri), 187, 201
Linders, Johnny, 215
Linkin Park, 87
Lipson, Steve, 239, 240
London Records, 69, 70
'Look At Me' (Geri), 187, 190–191, 203
Loos, Rebecca, 276, 280, 281–282
Lopes, Lisa "Left Eye", 197, 291
Lopez, Jennifer, 208, 230
Lorraine, Peter, 77
'Love At First Sight' (Kylie Minogue), 57
'Love Thing' (Spice Girls), 45, 49, 87
'Lullabye' (Mel B), 225, 241
Lulu, 11, 45
Lydon, John, *see* Rotten, Johnny
Lynn, Dame Vera, 118
Lysandrou, Andy, 215

M People, 14, 170
MacGowan, Shane, 13
Madonna, 1, 17, 89, 110, 155, 193, 223, 252, 256, 292
Major, John, 100
*Make It Come True* (Girlfriend album), 72
'Mama' (Spice Girls), 17, 52, 87, 105, 155, 166
'Mamma Mia' (Abba), 86
Mandela, Nelson, 122, 123, 124–127, 134, 147, 244, 292
Manic Street Preachers, 194, 195
Manilow, Barry, 278
Marbeck, Sarah, 280
*Marie Claire* (magazine), 243, 282
Marley, Bob, 100
Marsh, Kym, 38
Martin, George, 50
Martin, Max, 208
Martin, Michael, 170
Martin, Ricky, 30
Martin-Smith, Nigel, 45, 130
Mason, Harvey Jr, 242

Massive Attack, 69, 74, 88, 154, 170
'Maybe' (Emma), 266, 294
McAteer, Caroline, 228, 260
McCartney, Paul, 50, 64, 214n.
McFly, 253
McGowan, Alistair, 275
McKagan, Duff, 193
McManus, Michelle, 251
McMurray, Rick 'Rock', 12
Meat Loaf, 114
*Medusa* (Annie Lennox album), 67
*Melanie B Voodoo Princess* (TV show), 284
'Melt'/'Yeh Yeh Yeh' (Mel C), 262
Melua, Katie, 268
Metallica, 148
Mi Chico Latino (Geri), 187, 190
Michael, George, 79, 188, 202, 247, 251
Milli Vanilli, 7, 87
Minogue, Danii, 290
Minogue, Kylie, 14, 51, 57, 58, 67, 242
*Mirror* (newspaper), 141–142, 144, 149, 174, 201, 221, 228, 294
Mohan, Dominic, 64, 227, 283, 284
Money Money Money (Abba), 86
Monkees, The, 39
Montefiore, Simon Sebag, 95, 96, 98, 198
Moody, Paul, 94
Moore, Roger, 114–115
Morgan, Piers, 142, 294
Mortimer, Tony, 51
MTV, 81, 230, 291
Munday, Dave, 261
Murphy, Chic, 8, 9, 10, 19, 20, 35–36

'Naked' (Spice Girls), 49, 88, 177
Native Management, 47, 66, 68, 181
Neurotic Outsiders, The, 193
'Never Be The Same Again' (Mel C), 197, 198, 214
'Never Ever' (All Saints), 170
'Never Give Up On The Good Times' (Spice Girls), 177
New Kids On The Block, 4
*New Musical Express*, 94, 111, 195–196, 267
*New Woman* (magazine), 243
*News Of The World* (newspaper), 186, 276, 280
Newton, Ashley, 69, 73, 74–76, 83, 88, 103, 155, 205, 230–231, 233
Newton, Victoria, 64, 278, 283
Nickelback, 86
911, 111
19 Management, 47, 66, 68, 130, 134, 181, 257, 271, 294
'Nineteen' (Paul Hardcastle), 67
'No Sign Of Life' (Emma), 268

# Index

*Northern Star* (Mel C album), 187, 193, 196–197, 212, 234, 262, 263
'Northern Star' (Mel C), 187
'Not Such An Innocent Girl' (Victoria), 235, 241, 242
*Now* (magazine), 143, 244
Nowels, Rick, 193, 197, 240, 261
N-Sync, 232

O'Brien, Ed, 171
O'Neill, Dennis (stepfather of Mel C), 24
O'Neill, Jarrod (stepbrother of Mel C), 24
O'Neill, Joan (mother of Mel C), 24
O'Neill, Paul (half-brother of Mel C), 24
O'Neill, Stuart (stepbrother of Mel C), 24
Oakey, Phil, 4
Oasis, 7, 53, 74, 84, 88, 89, 104, 105, 134, 148, 154, 172, 216
*Observer, The* (newspaper), 113, 145
Ocean, Billy, 124
*OK!* (magazine), 243, 245
Olsson, Roger, 272
Omar, 48, 124
'On The Horizon' (Mel C), 262, 266
*1* (Beatles album), 38
One True Voice, 253
Optimistic, 3
Orbit, William, 193
Osbourne, Ozzy, 252–253
'Out Of Your Mind' (Victoria), 215–217, 223, 242
Outen, Denise Van, 23
'Overload' (Sugababes), 57
'Oxygen' (Spice Girls), 206

Parfitt, Rick, 95
Paris, Mica, 48
Parkinson, Michael, 275
Peden, Mike, 265
Persuasion, 21
Pet Shop Boys, The, 3
Petridis, Alexis, 262
Phillips, Melanie, 202
Phillips, Nancy, 160–161, 211, 218, 222, 228–229, 234, 236, 237–238, 246–249, 257, 260, 262, 263, 284, 289–290
Platell, Amanda, 277
Police, The, 53
*Pop* (U2 album), 74
*Pop Idol* (TV show), 14, 250–251, 279
*Popstars* (Hear'say album), 38
*Popstars* (TV show), 6, 37, 38, 136, 248, 253
*Popstars – The Rivals* (TV show), 37, 286

*Posh And Becks's Big Impression* (TV show), 275–276
Presley, Elvis, 50, 89, 123, 181
'Pretty Vacant' (Sex Pistols), 193
Primal Scream, 18, 88
Prime, Matt, 242
Prince, 70, 205
Prince Charles, 9, 62–63, 122, 124–125, 159, 169
Prince Harry, 125, 127, 159
Prince William, 159
*Private Dancer* (Tina Turner), 51
Prodigy, 18, 88, 89, 134, 170
'Pure And Simple' (Hear'say), 38, 248

*Q* (magazine), 104, 119, 148, 151, 154, 198
Queen, 51
Queen, HRH The, 159

R.E.M., 70, 154, 169
Rabin, Trevor, 123
Radiohead, 88, 153, 154, 170–171
Ramone, Joey, 13
Ramsey, Gordon, 279
*Raw Spice* (album), 37, 252
'Reason' (Mel C), 262
*Reason* (Mel C album), 261, 262–263
Red Hot Chili Peppers, 193
Reed, Lou, 111
Reeve, Gavin, 149
*Rent* (stage show), 285
Richard, Cliff, 278, 292
Richards, Keith, 50
Richie, Lionel, 110
'Right Back At Ya' (Spice Girls), 208, 230
Riley, Teddy, 208, 219, 221
Robinson, Peter, 267
Robson & Jerome, 14
Rolling Stones, The, 50, 126, 145, 148, 154, 169, 223
Ross, Diana, 207, 268
Ross, Jonathan, 114
Rossi, Francis, 95
Rotten, Johnny (aka Lydon, John), 13, 152, 195, 253
Rowe, Maria, 41, 45
Rowe, Matt, 33–35, 40–45, 48n., 51–52, 54–55, 57, 68, 114, 181, 204–205, 208, 212, 231, 261, 292
Rubin, Rick, 193
Run DMC, 179, 270

S Club 7, 138, 163, 254–255, 266
Salt'n'Pepa, 71
Sandall, Robert, 14, 72, 76, 80, 90–91, 92–93, 130, 132, 135, 145, 147, 167

*Saturday Night Live* (US TV show), 106
Saunders, Jennifer, 17, 105, 267
'Say You'll Be There' (Spice Girls), 17, 49, 69, 73, 79, 81, 87, 90, 95, 106, 171
*Schizophonic* (Geri album), 187, 190–192, 201, 239
'Scream If You Wanna Go Faster' (Geri), 235
*Scream If You Wanna Go Faster* (Geri album), 235, 239–241, 286
Screentime, 38
*Sex And The City* (TV show), 286
Sex Pistols, The, 46, 51, 194–195, 197, 229
'Sexual' (Maria Rowe), 41, 45
Shampoo, 60
Shaw, Sandie, 11, 284
She'kspere, 208
'Shining Light' (Ash), 13
'Should I Stay Or Should I Go' (The Clash), 111
Simmons, Russell, 270
Simply Red, 64, 170
Sisquo, 219
'Sisters Are Doing It For Themselves' (Aretha Franklin/Annie Lennox), 172
Size, Roni, 88
*Sky* (magazine), 143, 243
Sky, Rick, 266
Smallman, Oliver, 65
*Smash Hits*, 88, 149, 158
Smashing Pumpkins, 154
'So You Want To Be A Rock'n'Roll Star' (The Byrds), 1
'Someone's Watching Over Me' (Geri), 190
'Something Kinda Funny' (Spice Girls), 49, 66
'Sometimes' (Geri), 190
Soniks, The, 20
Sony Records, 70
Sorum, Matt, 193
Soulshock & Karlin, 241
Spears, Britney, 208, 215, 232
*Spectator, The*, 95, 97, 98
Spector, Phil, 51, 151–154
*Spice* (album), 45, 49, 56, 79, 80, 87, 88, 89, 90, 102, 105, 106, 116, 120, 123, 148, 233
*Spice* (magazine), 102, 107
Spice 1 (US rap performer), 77
*Spice Exposed* (video), 152
Spice Girls, The
   auditions for, 5
   formation of, 5–7
   early rehearsals, 10–12
   dance & singing training, 17–18
   as singers/vocal style of, 12, 15, 17, 30
   as songwriters, 40, 42, 45–46, 48–49, 51–56, 58, 89
   impromptu performances by, 14, 121
   miming/enhanced vocals by, 16
   contractual dealings of, 19, 30, 32, 34, 36
   communal house at Maidenhead, 19, 27–28
   residences of, 59, 116
   work ethic of, 29, 33, 102–103, 114, 116, 172–173, 207
   videos made by, 74–76
   origin of name, 77
   origin of nicknames, 77–78
   image of, 80–81, 83, 84–85, 154–155
   leave Heart Management, 34–36, 44–45
   relationship with Simon Fuller/19 Management, 68
   leave 19 Management, 133–135, 141, 167
   share of royalty payments, 52–53
   and 'Girl Power', 60, 73, 76, 163–164
   extrovert behaviour/flirtatiousness of, 59, 61–64
   merchandising/sponsorship deals, 107–113, 147
   sign with Virgin Records, 70–71
   promotional tours, 79, 113, 118–122, 157–158
   live appearances/concert tours, 117, 124, 162, 169–170, 171–172, 176–177, 179, 211–213
   attraction of pre-teen fans, 80–84
   media coverage/press intrusion, 89–90, 91, 92–94, 243–245
   press backlash, 94, 141–151, 171, 217, 279–280
   record/video sales, 80, 90, 102, 106, 113, 141–142, 148, 227, 263
   political views of, 95–101, 147
   earnings/financial affairs of/attitude to money, 107, 112, 138, 156, 159, 248
   adverse critical reaction/condescending attitude of critics and fellow musicians, 85, 104, 151–154, 157, 224
   implications of Geri's departure, 177–178, 179
   awards won by, 88, 95, 105, 113, 117, 120, 134, 142, 158–159, 170, 213–214
   making of *Spiceworld* movie, 114–115
   dissatisfaction within group, 117, 129, 134–140, 158, 163
   Geri leaves group, 174–177
   US careers, 171, 232–233
   decline of, 225–226, 228–230, 233–234, 246

*Index*

disbandment, 234–235, 236–237
reunion rumours/denials, 283–284, 290–291, 295
gay following, 291–293
unreleased recordings by, 293
'Spice Invaders' (Spice Girls), 56
*Spice – The Official Video Vol 1*, 102
'Spice Up Your Life' (Spice Girls), 55, 89, 117, 123, 124, 142, 170, 177, 214, 292
*Spiceworld* (album), 55, 56, 89, 102, 113, 117, 118, 120, 123, 141, 144, 148, 192, 204, 207, 223, 233
*Spiceworld – The Movie*, 63, 74, 82, 114–115, 145, 148, 159, 160, 169, 223, 256, 273

Spiers, Bob, 114
Spiller, Christiano, 216
Springsteen, Bruce, 125
*Spy Who Shagged Me, The* (film), 188
*Stage, The* (newspaper), 21, 27
*Standing On The Shoulder Of Giants* (Oasis album), 74
Stannard, Richard 'Biff', 33–35, 40–45, 48n., 51, 54, 57–58, 68, 114, 181, 190, 204–205, 208, 219, 231, 238, 241, 292, 293–294
Status Quo, 95
*Steam* (East 17 album), 42, 51
Stent, Spike, 74, 88, 238
'Step To Me' (Mantronix), 110, 111
Stephens, Andy, 257
Stephens, Tony, 260
Stephenson, George (father of Michelle), 27
Stephenson, Michelle, 5, 27, 29–31, 37
Stephenson, Penny (mother of Michelle), 27
Stephenson, Simon (brother of Michelle), 27
Steps, 16, 253
Stevens, Rachel, 255
Sting, 53
Stock, Aitkin & Waterman, 51
Stokes, Darren, 200
'Stop' (Spice Girls), 89, 170, 179, 190
Strummer, Joe, 13
Sugababes, 57
Sulley, Suzanne, 4
*Sun, The* (newspaper), 64, 91, 96, 117, 142, 144, 169, 175, 185, 202, 227, 237, 278, 283, 284, 291
*Sunday Times, The* (newspaper), 14, 68, 95
Super Furry Animals, 194
Supergrass, 194
Supremes, The, 39, 172, 268
Sutherland, Steve, 195–196
'Swear It Again' (Westlife), 226

'Take It From Me' (Girlfriend), 72
'Take My Breath Away' (Emma), 235, 241, 247
Take That, 4, 14, 16, 40, 45, 51, 69, 71, 84, 112, 130, 168, 170, 174, 194
Taylor, John, 193
'Tell Me' (Mel B), 220, 222
Telstar Records, 268, 274
Ten Years After, 86
'That Kind Of Girl' (Victoria), 241
Thatcher, Margaret, 96, 99, 100
*The Box* (TV show), 75, 76, 81
*The Matrix*, 5
*The "Réal" Beckhams* (TV show), 275
Thirkell, John, 11
'This Groove'/'Let Your Head Go' (Victoria), 242, 272, 273
*This Is My Moment* (TV show), 284
Thomas, Damon, 242
Thomas, Gerard, 179
Thompson, Andrew, 133, 135, 174–175, 268
Thornally, Phil, 261
Thornton, Kate, 76, 282
Three Degrees, The, 8, 9
Timbaland, 188, 208
Timberlake, Justin, 267
*Times, The* (newspaper), 104, 118, 150, 239, 267
Tin Tin Out, 200, 212, 239
TLC, 71, 197, 205, 233
'Too Much' (Spice Girls), 56, 145, 148, 190
Toone, John, 110
*Top Of The Pops* (magazine), 76, 77–78
*Top Of The Pops* (TV show), 13, 16, 32, 79, 81, 94, 121, 272, 275
'Touch Me (All Night Long)' (Cathy Dennis), 66
*Touch Of Frost, A* (TV show), 22
Townshend, Pete, 53
Travis, 194
Triple Eight, 38–39
True Steppers, 215
Turner, Tina, 51, 110
'2 Become 1' (Spice Girls), 42, 43, 68, 69, 87, 88, 90, 91
2wo Third3, 41–42
Tyrrell, Gerrard, 91–92, 93, 94, 103, 108–109, 111, 121–122, 124, 126, 134, 143, 145

U2, 74, 126, 134, 148, 154, 169, 227
'Unchained Melody' (Gareth Gates), 250–251
Undertones, The, 160
Usher, 207

V, 253
*Vagina Monologues, The* (stage show), 285
*Vanity Fair*, 104
Verve, The, 7, 69, 154–155, 170
Vettese, Peter, 240
Vicious, Sid, 195
*Victoria Beckham* (album), 235, 241–242, 246
Virgin Records, 69–72, 89, 93, 113, 123, 129, 170, 178, 219, 241, 247, 253, 259, 263, 264
'Viva Forever' (Spice Girls), 52, 89, 179, 190

'W.O.M.A.N.' (Spice Girls), 204
Walsh, Louis, 226
'Wannabe' (Spice Girls), 17, 34, 42, 44, 54, 66, 68, 69, 73–74, 76, 79–80, 81, 87, 91, 102, 106, 117, 124, 135, 155, 177, 181, 191, 207, 290, 291, 292, 293–294
Ward, Mike, 51
Warner Music, 65, 69
'Watcha Talkin' Bout' (Victoria), 242
'Waterloo' (Abba), 86
Watkins, Andy, 40, 46–50, 53, 55–56, 61–62, 66, 189–191
Watkins, Tom, 3, 41, 44, 151
Way, Dave, 74
'We Are Family' (Sister Sledge), 177
'We Will Rock You' (Queen/Five), 36
'We're Gonna Make It Happen' (Spice Girls), 29
'We're Not Gonna Sleep Tonight' (Emma), 235, 247
Weller, Paul, 58, 98
Westlife, 7, 12, 13, 87, 88, 100, 226–227, 229
Wham!, 196
'What I Am' (Emma with Tin Tin Out), 187, 200, 239
'What Took You So Long' (Emma), 235, 237, 247
Wheeler, Tim, 13
'When The Lights Go Out' (Five), 36
'When You're Gone' (Mel C with Bryan Adams), 180–181
'Where Did Our Love Go' (Supremes), 172
White, Barry, 268
'White Wedding' (Billy Idol), 193
'Who Do You Think You Are' (Spice Girls), 49, 68, 87, 94, 103, 105, 155, 166, 178
Who, The, 53
*Wild Weekends* (TV show), 30
Williams, Emma (half-sister of Melanie Chisholm), 24
Williams, Robbie, 79, 146, 174, 194, 214, 216, 250, 251
Wilson, Danny, 86
Wilson, Paul, 40, 46–53, 55–56, 61–62, 66, 189–190
Winstanley, Liz, 272
*Wired* (TV show), 30
'Word Up' (Mel B), 187–188, 217, 220, 235
*World Idol* (TV show), 250
Worlds Apart, 3
Wright, Matthew, 141–142, 144, 149–150, 174, 201, 284
Wright, Steve, 266
Wu Tang Clan, 205
Wynne, Jake, 239

Yorke, Thom, 153–155
'You Needed Me' (Boyzone), 191
Young, Paul, 57
Young, Will, 57, 250, 253, 294

Zero 7, 268